Working Papers of the
MIT Commission on Industrial Productivity

Working Papers of the
MIT Commission on Industrial Productivity

Volume 2

MIT Commission on Industrial Productivity

The MIT Press
Cambridge, Massachusetts
London, England

Second printing, 1990

The material in these working papers is summarized and analyzed in *Made in America: Regaining the Productive Edge* by Michael L. Dertouzos, Richard K. Lester, Robert M. Solow, and the MIT Commission on Industrial Productivity (Cambridge: MIT Press, 1989). These papers may be freely reproduced for personal, research, or classroom use without obtaining permission from The MIT Press. However, no working paper or any significant portion thereof may be reprinted in another publication without permission of The MIT Press. For permission to reprint for publication, please contact the Permissions Department, The MIT Press, 55 Hayward Street, Cambridge, Massachusetts 02142.

This book was printed and bound in the United States of America.

Library of Congress Cataloging-in-Publication Data

The Working papers of the MIT Commission on Industrial Productivity.

    1. Industrial productivity—United States. I. MIT Commission on Industrial Productivity.
HC110.I52W66 1989   338'.06'0973   89-8007
ISBN 0-262-63128-8 (set)
ISBN 0-262-63126-1 (v. 1)
ISBN 0-262-63127-X (v. 2)

Contents

The Working Papers of the
MIT Commission on Industrial Productivity

Preface

This two-volume set contains nine working papers prepared for the MIT Commission on Industrial Productivity. The Commission was established by MIT President Paul Gray in late 1986. It was charged with identifying the main causes of recent weaknesses in US industrial performance and with recommending actions to overcome these problems. It was asked to give special consideration to measures that might be taken by MIT and other research universities towards this end. The Commission's findings are presented in *Made In America: Regaining the Productive Edge* (Cambridge: The MIT Press, 1989).

The Commission consisted of 16 members of the MIT faculty drawn from 11 departments in the Schools of Engineering, Science, Management, and Humanities and Social Science. A sizeable research staff also participated in the Commission's work. The result was a highly stimulating interdisciplinary collaboration. As Commission chairman Michael Dertouzos noted, "the early dissonance caused by the different views inherent in our diverse professional specialties yielded to a shared vision of a new industrial America, potentially more productive and a leader in tomorrow's world economy."

A distinctive characteristic of the Commission's work was its determination to approach the study of US industrial performance from the bottom up. To that end, eight sectors of the economy were chosen for detailed study: automobiles; chemicals; commercial aircraft; the closely related industries of semiconductors, computers and copiers; consumer electronics; machine tools; steel; and textiles. These industries vary widely in scale, maturity, and technological sophistication. The sample includes both winners and losers in international competition. Some of the industries are highly fragmented, while others are dominated by a few large firms. There are both process industries and discrete-product industries. Altogether, the eight industry clusters account for nearly 30 percent of total value added in US manufacturing. The volume of trade in the products of these industries (i.e., the combined value of US exports and imports) amounts to almost 50 percent of total two-way trade in manufactured goods for the US.

To conduct the industry studies, eight teams were formed from members of the MIT community. Each team, headed by a Commissioner, was asked to evaluate its assigned industry with respect to efficiency, product quality, innovativeness, adaptability, and other aspects of performance. The findings of the study teams are contained in the working papers in these two volumes. The teams compared American practices with those abroad and contrasted successful firms with less successful ones. Altogether, the teams visited more than 200 companies -- including over 150 visits to plant sites -- in North America, Europe, and Japan, and interviewed almost 550 knowledgeable practitioners and analysts in industry, government, organized labor, and universities. An additional study team was formed to study education and vocational training patterns in various countries, and to compare the ways in which governments and companies in different countries develop their human resources.

The Commission's study teams returned with a large mass of detailed evidence. This was reviewed and discussed at length by the Commission. Eventually, several interrelated organizational patterns and attitudes emerged that best seemed to characterize the evidence. Six pervasive weaknesses in the productive performance of American industry were identified; and several broad similarities among successful "best practice" firms were also identified. Based on these findings, the Commission made a series of recommendations to industry, labor, government, and the educational community aimed at laying the foundation for a high productivity growth economy. These results are presented in the Commission's final report, *Made in America.*

The work of the study teams was largely completed during the winter of 1987-88. Though the Commission as a whole does not necessarily endorse all of the many specific findings and recommendations made by each study team, we are publishing the individual working papers in association with our main report both because of their intrinsic interest and also because we believe that they will serve as a useful record of the Commission's deliberations.

Many people made valuable contributions to the work of the Commission's study groups. Our thanks go to the 30 members of the MIT faculty who participated along with the Commission in the nine groups, and also to the many experts in industry, government, and academia who willingly gave of their time and insights. The staff played a central role in the preparation of the working papers, and deserve much credit for their extensive contributions. Special thanks go to Deputy Staff Director Kirk Bozdogan for his diligent and valuable analytical support of the study teams.

Finally, our thanks go to the Alfred P. Sloan and William and Flora Hewlett Foundations for their generosity in providing the funds for the Commission's work.

Richard K. Lester
Executive Director, MIT Commission on Industrial Productivity
Cambridge, Massachusetts
March 1989

MIT Commission on Industrial Productivity

Members
Professor Michael L. Dertouzos, *Chairman*
Director, Laboratory for Computer Science
Department of Electrical Engineering and Computer Science

Professor Robert M. Solow, *Vice-chairman*
Institute Professor
Department of Economics

Professor Richard K. Lester, *Executive Director*
Department of Nuclear Engineering

Professor Suzanne Berger
Head, Department of Political Science

Professor David Botstein
Department of Biology
(left MIT in January 1989)

Professor H. Kent Bowen
Co-Director, Leaders for Manufacturing Program
Department of Materials Science and Engineering

Professor Don P. Clausing
Department of Electrical Engineering and Computer Science

Professor Eugene E. Covert
Head, Department of Aeronautics and Astronautics

Professor John M. Deutch
Provost

Professor Merton C. Flemings
Head, Department of Materials Science and Engineering

Professor Howard W. Johnson
Former President
Honorary Chairman of the MIT Corporation

Professor Thomas A. Kochan
Sloan School of Management

Professor Daniel Roos
Director, Center for Technology, Policy and Industrial Development
Department of Civil Engineering

Professor David H. Staelin
Department of Electrical Engineering and Computer Science

Professor Lester C. Thurow
Dean, Sloan School of Management

Professor James Wei
Head, Department of Chemical Engineering

Professor Gerald L. Wilson
Dean of Engineering

Commission Staff
Deputy Director
Kirkor Bozdogan

Administrative Coordinator
Virginia L. Sherbs

Research Staff
Charles H. Ferguson
Richard F. Kazis
Artemis March
Cathie Jo Martin
James Womack

Rapporteur
Teresa L. Hill

Staff Writer
Robert C. Haavind

Research Assistants
John S. Berg
Thomas Berger
Hans-Georg Betz
Elizabeth A. Downie
Christopher L. Erickson
Stephen F. Filippone
Laura Hastings
Steven Kamin
Louisa Koch
John F. Krafcik
John S. Lin
Aileen Liu
Richard M. Locke
Barbara A. Masi
Michael J. Massimino
Mark J. McCabe
Yiorgos L. Mylonadis
Wayne Nelson
James J. Pastoriza, Jr.
Subramanian Rangan
Brian Thomas Turner

Working Papers of the
MIT Commission on Industrial Productivity

MIT Commission on Industrial Productivity
Working Paper

The US Semiconductor, Computer, and Copier Industries

Prepared by
**Commission Working Group on the
Semiconductor, Computer, and Copier Industries**

**Don P. Clausing, Chair
Jonathan Allen
John A. Berg
Michael Dertouzos
Charles H. Ferguson
Robert Haavind
Joel Moses
Paul L. Penfield, Jr.**

Table of Contents

List of Figures

Executive Summary

This report on the semiconductor, computer, and copier industries, which together comprise a major portion of what can be characterized as the information industries, was prepared as one of eight industrial studies by the MIT Commission on Industrial Productivity. The objective was to increase understanding of the history and major proximate causes of the recent erosion of the industrial economy in the United States.

This study was particularly enlightening for a number of reasons. It was concerned with the progress of high technology growth industries in contrast to most of the other Commission studies which examined more mature U.S. industries. The three market sectors chosen within the information industries also revealed quite different characteristics. Semiconductors give signs of being a declining industry in the U.S., with a steady erosion of global market share over the past decade. Because of this industry's strategic importance—military and economically—this weakening has been the cause of serious concern, and steps are being taken by both the U.S. government and private sector to help stem the decline. The computer sector remains robust, particularly in the younger market segments, although there are signs of stagnation in the older mainframe and minicomputer areas. Originally, the Commission planned to make office automation the third sector within the information industries, but this is a somewhat vague classification and within it the copier segment proved to be a large, well-defined market with an interesting history. A few years ago, Japanese imports became a serious challenge in the U.S. copier market, but Xerox Corp., the major U.S. manufacturer, finally mounted a vigorous defense and thus managed to regain market share.So even though this study deals broadly with the U.S. information industries, within that scope it probes a declining sector, a relatively healthy sector, and a sector that was declining until a strong response by a U.S. manufacturer reversed the trend.

The relative sizes of these information industries is indicated by 1987 factory shipments: $48 billion for computers, $18 billion for semiconductors, and $6 billion for copiers. Overshadowing all of these in size is software, which is estimated to generate some $150 billion to $200 billion annually in the U.S. alone, primarily due to the cost of software generated internally by computer-using organizations. Packaged software sales are estimated to have been $30 billion globally in 1987. Although software was not part of this study, it does have a strong effect on the computer industry and this impact will be discused. The computer hardware segment can also be broken into two segments which recently have been roughly equal in size: peripherals and processing units (historically peripherals has been considerably larger).

IBM is the dominant company in the global information industry, holding close to half of the world computer market. IBM is also the largest producer of semiconductors, with production estimated at over $30 billion in 1987, slightly ahead of Japan's NEC. IBM does not sell semiconductors, however, and the open-market semiconductor industry is now led by three Japanese firms, Toshiba, NEC, and Hitachi. Xerox is the dominant copier company, with world-wide shipments of over $7 billion in 1987.

In the mid-70s U.S. companies had dominant positions in the information industries in both the U.S. market (over 80 percent) and world market (over 50 percent). The U.S. semiconductor industry held over 95 percent of its domestic market and 60 percent of the world market. Since that time there has been a sharp decline in market shares for semiconductors, computer peripherals, and copiers. In semiconductors, Japanese companies now have 48 percent of the world market while the U.S. share has declined to 39 percent. In copiers, the U.S. market share for Xerox in small and medium categories has declined to 10-15 percent, with Japanese companies holding most of the remainder. By contrast, in large, high-speed copiers, U.S. companies (Xerox and Kodak) still have most of the market, with little competition from the Japanese as yet. In computer peripherals the U.S. market share is declining rapidly, with imports (mostly Japanese) now having more than 30 percent of the U.S. market, and over 70 percent of the market for microcomputer peripherals.

Import penetration of the U.S. market has been far less for computer processing units, due primarily to the cumulative investment of computer users in software and peripherals tailored to a particular system. Converting software to another vendor's non-compatible system would be a costly, time-consuming, and risky procedure. As computer systems are increasingly being networked together, however, there is mounting user pressure for standardization of interfaces, communication methods, and system software. As standardization progresses, import pressure on processors. and possibly software as well, may increase in the future.

Although each of the markets studied has unique characteristics, there are some general observations that can be made about the competitive environment. U.S. companies have been the innovators in the information industries, frequently launching whole new market segments based on their inventions. As markets have grown, however, the Japanese have proven superior in production technology, particularly for large-volume products. U.S. firms have had strong shortcomings in product realization: design optimization, production methods, and quality control. The best Japanese companies have had advantages in cost, quality, and product development time that have enabled them to strongly penetrate growing markets.

Often new product categories and market segments have been launched by U.S. start-up companies, which were able to advance strongly when they had little competition. As they continued to innovate, these smaller, often single-product firms frequently licensed their existing technology to large Japanese firms even though they recognized that these firms might become competitors. Their hope was to remain ahead of the Japanese competition by means of a steady stream of new innovations (recently technology licensing has also increased to South Korea and Taiwanese companies). Since Asian markets were usually essentially closed to American high technology products, licensing was the only way these firms could get revenue from them, and these venture-backed companies often had a great need for new capital. In the early phases of a market this strategy frequently worked. But as markets matured and volume grew, production skills and the availability of low-cost capital to upgrade and expand manufacturing facilities became key factors. This enabled larger and stronger competitors (often Japanese) to gain increasing market shares, both globally and in the relatively open U.S. marketplace.

Other factors beyond industry structure have contributed to the weaknesses of the U.S. firms in growth markets such as semiconductors and computer peripherals. High turnover rates (20 percent annually in semiconductors) discouraged training efforts and meant that critical skills were frequently lost, often to newer start-up companies. Management often favored short-term strategies, preferring to manufacture overseas rather than investing in domestic facilities, and to license technology to foreign companies. Corporate emphasis was often on developing new products rather that improving production methods, productivity, and quality. Cooperation was generally poor between system firms, component suppliers, and makers of fabrication equipment.

In the 1980s, U.S. companies have become increasingly aware of the need to strengthen capabilities in product realization, rather than focusing so heavily on innovation. Some firms, such as Xerox in copiers, have taken strong actions to improve. But continuous improvement will be needed to meet the challenge of increasingly sophisticated global competition.

Introduction

This report focuses on the competitive issues surrounding the U.S. semiconductor, computer, and copier industries. It was prepared with knowledge derived from six types of sources. The aggregate industry economic data and productivity data were provided by the MIT Commission staff using primary data furnished by the U.S. government. Various literature sources were consulted and utilized. Personal interviews were conducted in the U.S. and Japan. Another source of valuable insight is the Xerox case study, prepared by Don Clausing, a former principal engineer for Xerox. Finally, these sources were supplemented by the knowledge and insights of the members of the subcommittee who have been active in the semiconductor, computer, and copier fields for many years.

The Semiconductor Industry

Structure and Performance

The transistor invented at AT&Ts Bell Telephone Laboratories in the 1940s launched the semiconductor industry. Semiconductors have been likened to the crude oil of the Information Age. They are the basic building blocks for an expanding array of growth industries in computers, automation, telecommunications, instrumentation, consumer equipment, and military systems. Performance of systems or equipment in any of these fields depends on the capabilities of the semiconductors used to build them. Recognition of this has led not just companies, but whole nations (and in the case of Europe, multi-national consortia) to push for an edge in semiconductor capabilities.

From its beginnings in the 1950s through most of the 1970s, the U.S. semiconductor industry dominated world markets. In the mid-70s, at the height of its success, the U.S. industry held 95 percent of the domestic market and 60 percent of the world market, including half the European market though only a quarter of Japan's.

Since then the U.S. industry has been declining. By 1987 the world market had grown to about $30 billion, but the American share had shrunk to 40 percent while the Japanese had captured over 50 percent, soaring from only 28 percent ten years earlier. Europe's share of the world market had shrunk from about 15 percent to ten percent over this decade. In the same period, Japan's share of the world semiconductor capital equipment market also rose dramatically, from about ten to 35 percent.

In 1987 Japanese semiconductor manufacturers supplied over 90 percent of their domestic demand while simultaneously taking over 25 percent of the American market. The semiconductor market is now bigger in Japan than in the United States, and the U.S. had become a net importer of semiconductors. Five of the ten largest world merchant semiconductor producers are Japanese.

The semiconductor industry developed quite differently in the U.S. and in Japan. In the United States semiconductor manufacturing was divided between the "captives," which produced devices only for their own use, and "merchants," which sold devices on the open market. Merchant production accounts for about 65 percent of the world market for semiconductors. The two largest captive producers are IBM and AT&T, which together account for some 80 percent of production by captive facilities in the United States. IBM is especially notable as the world's largest semiconductor producer, with internal production estimated by Dataquest at $3.35 billion in 1987. The U.S. merchant industry has evolved into five major players (Motorola, Texas Instruments, Intel, National/Fairchild, and Advanced Micro Devices/Monolithic Memories or AMD/MMI) and a large number of smaller entrepreneurial firms. Figure 1 illustrates the size of these companies' semiconductor revenue or production in 1987 along with that of their major competitors.

The emergence of the Japanese semiconductor industry came through the diversification efforts of large industrial complexes (such as Sony, Hitachi, and NEC) rather than through the creation of entrepreneurial start-ups devoted solely to semiconductor production. Semiconductor production in Japan has thus been dominated by the same large, stable, diversified firms that have dominated the computer, consumer electronics, telecommunications, and other electronic equipment industries. Semiconductors represent a small portion of their total business, ranging from about ten to 25 percent, and they use roughly a quarter of their own production internally. For example, Hitachi's semiconductor business in 1981 represented only five percent of its total revenues (then $15.5 billion), NEC's semiconductor share was 19.8 percent, and Toshiba's share was 8.9 percent. In contrast, most U.S. merchant producers (except for Motorola and Texas Instruments) depend almost solely on semiconductor production and services for revenue.

An analogous contrast can be found between the U.S. and Japanese semiconductor capital equipment industries. In the U.S., a few stable, relatively large, established equipment firms (such as Teradyne in test equipment and Perkin-Elmer in photolithography systems) co-exist and compete with many venture-backed start-ups, such as Trillium, Zycad, Master Images, and hundreds of others. As of 1986, 55 percent of U.S. equipment and service vendors had annual sales of less than $5 million. The established firms have seen rough times as well, because, like their semiconductor manufacturing clientele, this U.S. industry has been in serious decline, although a recent market upturn has helped to save some firms.

The Japanese semiconductor fabrication industry is again dominated by large, diversified firms, either affiliated with the large semiconductor producers themselves, or linked to major firms with experience in the relevant optical, chemical, mechanical, or construction technologies. For example, Fujitsu owns 22 percent of Advantest (test equipment), NEC owns 50 percent of Ando (testers), Hitachi owns Hitachi Electronic Engineering (various support products), and all of the largest producers design and manufacture some of their own automated assembly equipment.

The productivity performance of the U.S. semiconductor industry has been exemplary in comparison to most other U.S. industries. As Figure 2 shows, total factor productivity rose at rates above ten percent per year for the period from 1967-1979, and has risen four percent a year since then, compared to about one percent a year for the total U.S. economy. (This measure calculates productivity using labor, capital, and materials—including energy—as the primary factors of production, and using real gross industry output as the resulting output.) Shipments similarly have risen steadily for the most part (see Figure 3). But world trade figures tell a different story. The U.S. maintained well over half the world market through the 1970s, but the decline in global market share beginning in about 1980 has been sudden and rapid. Using one Dataquest time series (semiconductor market statistics are somewhat imprecise), the world merchant market shares for the leading semiconductor producing regions evolved as follows between 1970 and 1979:

	U.S.A.	Europe	Japan
1970	56.5	16.1	27.1
1974	62.3	16.3	20.7
1977	60.0	14.2	25.6
1979	60.9	13.2	25.6

When the Japanese semiconductor industry entered international competition, its rise (and the concomitant U.S. decline) was far more rapid than the competitive reversals suffered by other declining U.S. industries, such as textiles, automobiles, or steel. The Japanese share of the world merchant market rose from roughly 26 percent in 1979 to a little over a third by 1982, about 40 percent by 1985, and about half in 1987. The world share for American producers shrunk from over 60 percent in 1978 to about 40 percent in 1987. The Europeans fared even worse, with their world market share dropping from over 15 percent in the mid-70s to less than ten percent by 1987. Over this same period Japan's share of the world semiconductor capital equipment market similarly rose from about ten percent to 35 percent.

Furthermore, the erosion of the U.S. position is even worse than these figures suggest, because both the American decline and Japanese progress are steepest in some of the most advanced and important semiconductor markets and technologies. Japanese firms now hold 40 percent of world markets for microprocessors, 65 percent for microcontrollers, and 40 percent for ASICs, or application-specific integrated circuits. The slippage is also severe in R&D for future technology generations, and the U.S. capital equipment industry is fighting for survival while Japanese competitors are expanding.

Bilateral semiconductor trade between the U.S. and Japan was even early in the 1980s, but by 1983 the U.S. deficit reached $355 million and rose to over $900 million in 1984. After a decline in 1985 due to a slowdown in the market, rapid growth in the deficit resumed, in part because of fast-rising sales of Japanese supplied memory chips. (Japanese vendors were forced to raise prices for dynamic random-access memories, or D-RAMs in late 1986 as a result of dumping charges, but market shortages pushed prices well above prescribed levels in less than a year anyway).

Examining compound annual growth rates (CAGRs) for Japanese versus U.S. merchant production in various technology categories reveals that the Japanese market share growth is greatest in some of the newer, highest growth technology families:

Comparative CAGR, Shipments by Region, 1974-1984, in percent

Category	N.America	Japan
All semiconductors	14.3	21.0
Integrated circuits	18.9	30.9
MOS integrated circuits	24.0	37.5
CMOS integrated circuits	31.6	62.5

Source: Dataquest Corp. (1985)

Even beyond the push of the Japanese vendors into the higher growth technology sectors, U.S. vendors have lost important ground in product quality. By the late 1970s, U.S. semiconductor buyers were finding that Japanese memory chips were far more reliable than devices produced by U.S. merchant firms. Although there has been improvement in the quality of U.S. chips, major semiconductor users still find that devices bought from the Japanese are less likely to be defective than those from U.S. producers.

Japan has won over 80 percent of the world merchant market for the most widely used integrated circuit in digital equipment, the dynamic random-access memory (DRAM). Invented by Intel in the U.S., DRAMs are now offered domestically only by Micron Technologies, a small Idaho firm, and Texas Instruments, which makes most of its devices in Japanese factories. (IBM and AT&T also make these chips for their own use.) DRAMs have the densest circuitry of any integrated circuits, with simple cells that are replicated hundreds of thousands or millions of times. Thus, advances in fabricating these chips are at the leading edge of IC production technology. Manufacturers who successfully move to the next level of density in DRAMs can then apply similar fabrication techniques to other devices.

Less widely appreciated but probably equally as important, the Japanese have equalled or surpassed all world competition in many types of capital equipment, materials, and services. These areas include packaging, automated assembly equipment, various ultrapure materials, some categories of fabrication equipment, and specialized procedures such as mask-making. For example, IBM's new Fishkill facility was built with Shimizu as a construction consultant. Japanese firms supply nearly half of Intel's masks.

Relative R&D performance has also changed dramatically, with the U.S. still leading in many areas of theoretical research but trailing in applied R&D. With the help of national collaborative programs, the Japanese have moved ahead in a number of key technologies. These include: X-ray lithography, which may dominate very large-scale and ultra-large scale integrated circuit (VLSI and ULSI) production in the mid-90s; gallium arsenide, a more complex material structure than silicon but with an intrinsic speed advantage (five times the carrier mobility); superconducting devices, which also have the potential to boost circuit speed, particularly in large computers; three-dimensional integrated circuits, which may become important for boosting circuit density and also have the potential for unique circuit functions; and integrated optoelectronics and solid-state lasers, which are increasingly used in advanced telecommunications and consumer electronics.

A recent Defense Science Board Task Force study (1987) concluded that the U.S. continues to maintain a lead in only three of more than a dozen critical semiconductor technologies studied. The differing responses of Japan and the U.S. to an important emerging fabrication technology illustrates the problem. The potential for X-ray lithography for chips with line-widths under 0.5-microns was known in the early 1970s (using soft X-rays close to the ultraviolet rather than the hard X-rays used in medical scanning). Synchrotron radiation, a normally undesirable side-effect in particle accelerators built for physics experiments, provided a possible source for soft X-rays. But they are huge, take years to build, and cost in the tens of millions or even hundreds of millions of dollars. The Japanese set up a collaborative program to develop more compact, cheaper accelerators designed to serve as X-ray sources for chip production, and they have made steady progress, while American firms experimented with radiation from existing scientific machines. Only IBM among American semiconductor makers built its own synchrotron, reportedly at a cost of $16.5 million, and IBM is now trying to bring in other American partners to share costs. It is estimated that building a semiconductor production facility using synchrotron radiation in the mid-to-late 1990s might cost a half a billion dollars, which has discouraged individual American semiconductor firms.

History of the Semiconductor Industry

How the U.S. Industry Developed. Until the late 1970s, the U.S. and Japanese semiconductor industries evolved quasi-independently. The U.S. industry dominated the American and European markets, but Japanese industrial structure and government protectionism minimized U.S. penetration of the Japanese market (keeping it below 25%). The Japanese industry imported U.S. technology and capital equipment, restricted both import penetration and direct foreign investment by U.S. semiconductor firms, and produced mainly for its domestic market (particularly the consumer electronics industry, which takes about half of Japanese semiconductor production). During this period the Japanese firms refrained from export drives directed at the United States. The U.S. industry sold technology to Japan, generally acquiesced to closure of the Japanese market, but also controlled the rest of the world market.

The pattern for the American industry began to take shape in the 1950s, when, as part of an antitrust settlement, AT&T, which had been the strongest force in the early semiconductor business, agreed to license its patents and to refrain from open market competition. Dozens of small firms sprang up, many headed by defectors from large, established firms, such as GE and AT&T, to fill the market void left by AT&T's departure. One of these early firms was formed in northern California by William Shockley, a co-inventor of the transistor at Bell Laboratories. Shockley Semiconductor concentrated on a device known as the Shockley diode despite the opposition of bright young scientists, including Robert Noyce, who later invented the integrated circuit (at about the same time as the IC was also invented by Jack Kilby of Texas Instruments). This led the younger men to leave and start Fairchild Semiconductor, which, over the years, similarly spawned dozens of other start-up companies in the region south of San Fransisco that came to be known as Silicon Valley. (Noyce eventually left Fairchild to help found Intel, and numerous firms were later spawned by defectors from Intel).

The merchant sector of the U.S. semiconductor industry evolved into a structurally unstable, fragmented, highly entrepreneurial arena. Most U.S. merchant producers were young, relatively small firms whose semiconductor sales were most or often all of their revenues. Market leadership, employee loyalties, and supplier relationships were transitory; many semiconductor and capital equipment producers rose and fell rapidly, and employee turnover averaged 20 percent annually across the industry. Two producers that were part of larger, diversified manufacturing companies, Texas Instruments and Motorola, were able to grow steadily and remain consistently innovative, and they became the market leaders.

There has been a characteristic life cycle for new U.S. merchant semiconductor firms. The cycle begins generally with creation of a new company focused on a single emerging technology or market opportunity: 1K memories for Intel, 8-bit microprocessors for Zilog, MOS integrated circuits for American Microsystems, electrically erasable memories for Seeq Technology, gate arrays for LSI Logic. Executives defected from an established firm to create a new one, often bringing key personnel such as digital circuit designers or production specialists with them. One to three rounds of venture capital, sometimes totaling up to $50 million or more, were obtained while the new firm raided larger and more established firms, including the founders' former employer(s), to obtain the technical talent needed. Occasionally whole teams working on new technology within a large firm defected as a group, such as the RISC chip group that recently left Motorola to set up a venture in collaboration with Cypress Semiconductor. Within one to three years the firm's products generally were successful enough to generate operating profits. Around this time or shortly thereafter, the firm would issue an initial public offering (IPO) of its stock, usually generating $25 million to $75 million in cash, and making the founders multi-millionaires. (LSI Logic's IPO, the most successful in the industry's history, generated $160 million).

Typically, however, after several years of rapid growth, these firms encountered trouble. The reason was often a shift to a new generation in the technology, making earlier products obsolete. Since they were dependent on current revenues to finance themselves, they seldom invested in the R&D and new production equipment needed to shift to a newer technology. As troubles mounted, employees who were fully vested in stock option and/or profit sharing plans frequently left for new start-ups.

The emergence of many start-up companies in the early phases of an industry is not unusual; it is analogous to what occurred in the early days of the automobile industry, for example. What is strikingly different about semiconductors is that as the industry moved toward maturity the industry leaders in the merchant sector were predominantly giant, diversified Japanese firms, while the major American firms in the business (IBM, AT&T, GM's Delco) were captive suppliers. There is a natural tendency to compare the U.S. merchants with NEC, Hitachi, and other Japanese giants, but from the standpoint of production scale a more apt comparison might be between these Japanese firms and IBM. It is notable that while the Japanese companies chose to sell on the open market as well as making devices for their own use, IBM took the opposite course. It may turn out to be a strategic failure, because in other industries in the past such a failure to compete strongly in the open components market has eventually led to a lack of competitiveness.

While the entrepreneurial merchant sector of the U.S. semiconductor industry has remained innovative, it has not done well against the Japanese competition in design optimization, production capabilities, and quality. This is not so surprising: advanced development specialists are rarely as good at the subsequent phases because they require a far different style. Inventive success followed by subsequent failure is characteristic of start-up companies that fail to flourish in any major new industry. During adolescence there are a plethora of small, innovative companies with great dynamism, excitement, and famous names. During maturation most of these fade away, remembered only by a nostalgic few (Stanley Steamer, where art thou?). The large successors that emerge during maturation are superior in designing for manufacturability, optimization, and production, and they almost always have a longer and more strategic view with more solid financial and marketing arrangements. In the automobile industry most of the dazzling adolescents were in Europe, but when maturation occurred the successful adults were General Motors, Ford, and Chrysler. The movement of the semiconductor industry toward maturation has coincided with the emergence of Japan as a manufacturing power, just as the United States emerged in an earlier era. Thus it should not be too surprising that most of the successful mature merchant semiconductor companies appear to be concentrated in Japan.

The smaller American merchant firms have in the main neither consolidated nor joined with other large equipment or systems firms to form vertically integrated giants on a par with their Japanese competitors. Motorola does make communications equipment, but it sold its TV operations to Matsushita in the 1960s. Texas Instruments has expanded downstream into computers and consumer products, but with limited success. IBM did make an investment in Intel, but more to ensure chip supply than to vertically integrate, and then divested part of its stake during an industry slump.

Factors Leading to the Weak U.S. Industry Structure. Why did the U.S. industry develop as it did, without rationalizing to more closely match the strengths of the formidable Japanese competition? A closer look at the history of the industry helps provide some insight.

Growth of the early industry was spurred by U.S. defense needs. The limited thrust of American rockets compared to Russian boosters in the 1960s limited the weight that could be lofted, so the Department of Defense (DoD) pushed the development of semiconductor and then integrated circuit technology to cut the weight of U.S. missiles and satellites. Defense procurement demanded technology more advanced than that for commercial uses and was not sensitive to costs. The military often paid for R&D as well as early production experience, and more frequently demanded second-sourcing of new devices. This DoD support helped launch the semiconductor industry by reducing risks and by supporting important generic R&D, but it also favored new firms over established ones. This encouraged frequent start-ups of new firms that could offer a better product to the military. It may also have contributed to the industry's emphasis on product R&D rather than manufacturing efficiency, and the willingness of innovative firms to license their technology to second-source producers.

By the mid-70s. the military had ceased to provide substantial, commercially useful industrial support via its R&D and procurement spending. Military demand declined from about 50 percent of U.S. semiconductor production in 1965 to about 15 percent a decade later, and the technology sought by DoD began to lag rather than lead commercial uses. Also, due to Congressional action (particularly the Mansfield Amendment to a procurement bill), defense procurement policies shifted away from generic R&D toward strictly military technology, reducing commercial spin-offs while remaining insensitive to manufacturing costs. This greatly reduced potential technology transfer from military projects to the commercial sector.

Other government policies also probably contributed to the fragmentation of this industry. Anti-trust policy discouraged industry-wide collaboration. Capital gains treatment and other tax policies lowered capital costs for smaller firms compared to larger ones (particularly in the tax treatment of losses), and allowed start-ups to offer higher effective compensation for key personnel (especially through stock options).

The instability and high turnover in the industry contributed to the short-term strategies of the American companies. Technology leakage was seen as inevitable, both because of defections and also because it was easy to "reverse engineer" innovative products by etching away mask patterns layer by layer and photographically copying them. This was a technique used with great success particularly by Asian imitators. Personnel raiding was rampant, with some companies offering a $1000 finder's fee to any employee bringing in a new hire with needed skills. Therefore every effort was made to cash in quickly on any new technological advantage, including manufacturing off-shore in low-wage regions rather than making capital investments, licensing technology to both domestic and overseas companies, cutting basic long-term R&D, and avoiding long-term commitments to suppliers and customers. There was little training, and the learning so important to being competitive in such a sophisticated, highly technological business was often lost through defections and layoffs. Since Asian markets were effectively closed to American devices, selling technology was seen as the only way to generate revenue there.

The U.S. merchant industry tended to be parochial. Executives felt that they could rapidly develop new technology while Japanese competitors tried to catch up using technology previously licensed to them. They failed to monitor Japanese progress and had excessive confidence in the collective dominance of the American industry. A strong venture capital community, particularly in the San Fransisco region, helped to sustain the unstable, fragmented structure of the American industry.

In fact, for decades this pattern of instability, high mobility, and new venture formation was considered to be not only desirable but essential for success in the industry. Although a few small firms were acquired by giant companies looking to diversify (such as Mostek by United Technologies, or Zilog by Exxon) the results were usually disappointing. The common sentiment of those in the field was that this type of highly creative, fast-paced industry required the intense fervor and quick on-the-spot decision-making of a start-up operation. The careful planning, orderly structure, financial and policy controls typical of large corporations were considered to be the route to failure.

One early example of a disastrous failure was the acquisition of Philco Corp. by Ford Motor Co. (circa 1960). Philco made television sets and appliances, had just entered the computer business, and had started a semiconductor operation, all in the Philadelphia area. A nearby laboratory was developing new technology, including innovative devices (such as some of the earliest metal-oxide-semiconductor or MOS structures) as well as large-scale computers and other electronic systems, including optical readers for the postal system. This vertically integrated structure, along with Ford's financial strength, provided a close parallel in American industry to the Japanese model that emerged later. Ford concentrated much of the decision-making for these enterprises at its Detroit headquarters, where the emphasis was on strong financial controls. Under Ford's stewardship all these businesses rapidly declined and were eventually sold off or abandoned while Ford shifted its high technology efforts to the steadier, more lucrative military/aerospace sector (an option not available to Japanese companies).

General Electric similarly had strong capabilities in semiconductors in the early 1960s, recognizing their growing importance for its appliances, controls, electrical equipment, factory systems, and computers. At that time GE's laboratories rivaled the capabilities of such world leaders as AT&T's Bell Laboratories and IBM in developing new semiconductor technology. Under its strong profit-center concept, GE eventually abandoned most of its semiconductor business (retaining power devices) as well as computers (except for process control systems). More recently, GE reentered the integrated circuits business with the acquisition of Intersil. Later, however, after GE acquired RCA, RCA's semiconductor operations were sold and its innovative Princeton research laboratories were given to Stanford Research Institute (SRI), a contract research firm. In late 1968 most of the remnants of GE's revived integrated circuits business were sold to Harris Corp.

The early semiconductor market was a boom-bust business. Periods of shortages and escalating prices were followed, often in only a couple of months, by dramatic downturns. When supplies were tight, buyers overordered, often from multiple suppliers, and then, when the systems business slowed down, device inventories would swell and major orders would be cancelled. This led to wild swings in the fledgling industry. Massive layoffs were common, undercutting feelings of loyalties to employers, and firms without the financing to tide them over the rough periods frequently went bankrupt (not unlike the early automobile business). Semiconductor producers building up capacity as orders soared sometimes suddenly had to stop construction and cancel orders for new fabrication and support equipment as their business plummeted. This intensified the instability of the U.S. semiconductor capital equipment business.

By the standards of mature industries, the merchants' instability was extraordinary. Transitron, second among merchants in 1960, sank to ninth by 1965 and then disappeared altogether. Mostek's revenues rose from $220 million in 1982 to $467 million in 1984, only to decline to $110 million in 1985. The general manager of Intel's EPROM division was one of the co-founders of Seeq, which made similar products and was sued by Intel. Seeq's revenues rose from $9 million in 1983 to $53 million in 1984, and then dropped to $31 million in 1986. The Seeq co-founded Campbell then departed to form Chips and Technologies, which specialized in reverse engineering circuits produced by established firms (particularly for Asian manufacturers of IBM-compatible personal computers). Chips and Technologies' revenues reached $60 million a year by mid-1987. Micron Technologies, which specializes in memory chips, a particularly volatile market, has gone through especially dramatic rises and falls, with revenues going from $5 million in 1982 to $117 million in 1984 (the year of the firm's IPO), and then collapsing to $36 million the following year. Its fortunes rose again in 1987-88 as a shortage of memory chips developed, and an investment by Intel helped the firm expand facilities to meet burgeoning demand.

Because of this roller-coaster performance in the industry, large firms that did acquire semiconductor manufacturers sometimes shuttled aside the engineers who managed them and installed management with financial expertise but typically with little knowledge of the technology or the business. This was very different from the Japanese approach, in which top management generally came up through the technical ranks in the electronics business. By the late 70s and early 80s, caution in pursuing expansion plans began to pervade the industry. Mostek, for example, had become a leader in dynamic random-access memory (DRAM) chips, but under United Technologies' guidance, was careful in expanding DRAM facilities when the time came to shift from the 16K to 64K generation of the devices. Other U.S. merchant vendors were similarly cautious in expanding capacity while they pursued improved DRAM designs for the next generation. Japanese competitors moved quickly to gain market share, simply scaling down the older Mostek design to achieve the required circuit density, and they made the investments in facilities to meet mushrooming demand when the market suddenly picked up again. This gave the Japanese competitors the start they needed so that they could eventually virtually take over this market. Within five years of the Japanese entry, only Texas Instruments and tiny Micron Technologies among U.S. merchant vendors remained in the DRAM business.

Because of shortages of capital, start-up companies frequently shared their unique technologies with Japanese companies, either to get devices manufactured off-shore or through technology licenses. The largest U.S. gate array vendor, for example, is LSI Logic, a spin-off from Fairchild operating in a single market with revenues of $190 million in 1986. In its early days in 1981, LSI Logic licensed its design technology to Toshiba, which now holds a larger share of the world market than LSI Logic does. Japan's share of the gate array market grew from zero in 1980 to 40 percent by 1987. Similarly, MIPS Computers, a semiconductor start-up that was the first merchant vendor of reduced instruction set (RISC) microprocessors, contracts for its production with Matsushita and is 20 percent owned by Kubota, a large Japanese machinery manufacturer diversifying into the semiconductor and computer business. Kubota obtained rights to the RISC technology as part of its $25 million investment.

While IBM remains the world leader in semiconductor production, it has chosen to produce devices only for its own use, a decision that remains controversial within the company. IBM's failure to participate in the open market robbed it of an opportunity to amortize capital equipment and R&D over a larger volume. It also kept it from sharpening its skills in the commercial marketplace. IBM also failed to enter the semiconductor fabrication equipment industry. Although this equipment was simple in the early days of integrated circuits, it has become increasingly complex. Concern about the health of this industry in the U.S. has led IBM to take a very strong part in the recent formation of Sematech, a joint government/industry effort to upgrade U.S. semiconductor manufacturing capabilities.

How Japan's Semiconductor Industry Developed. Initially the United States provided the creative new device and fabrication technologies that drove the semiconductor industry's progress in both Japan and the U.S. Until the late 1970s, the Japanese firms imported U.S. technology and capital equipment to serve the domestic market while restricting both import penetration and foreign investment. A few investments were permitted, but in the form of joint ventures in which Japanese companies would obtain rights to U.S. technology. One exception was Texas Instruments, which was permitted to set up a wholly owned subsidiary in return for access to critical patents. Japanese companies for the most part refrained from exporting during this period. The Japanese technology generally lagged the most advanced U.S. and European device capabilities by a year or two. This added to the comfort level of U.S. firms, both large and small, that licensed technology to Japanese companies while acquiescing to market restrictions. Until the early 1980s the U.S. industry had the dominant share of the world market in spite of their lack of success in selling devices to the Japanese.

The earliest producers of Japanese semiconductor devices, such as Sony, aimed primarily at the consumer electronics market, which Japanese vendors grew to dominate globally. By the late 1970s, however, recognizing that Japan could not be strongly competitive in computers and other electronic systems while their integrated circuit technology lagged behind that of world leaders, the government's Ministry of International Trade and Industry (MITI) organized a national VLSI (very-large-scale-integration) project to raise the integrated circuit capabilities of Japanese industry. With funding of about $280 million from MITI and $80 million more from Nippon Telegraph & Telephone (NTT), the domestic telephone company, five semiconductor and computer firms developed advanced integrated circuit technology, including state-of-the-art DRAM chips, the most widely used of all digital integrated circuit devices.

Numerous national programs coordinated by MITI ensure not only that Japanese industry keeps up with world competition, but in a number of cases help it move far ahead. This is the case for synchrotron radiation for sub-0.5-micron devices, laser-based lithography, and three-dimensional circuit technology. High speed device programs have been devoted to superconducting and HEMT (high-electron-mobility transistor) technology as well as to more conventional bipolar and MOS/CMOS devices. A quick look at a very successful MITI-directed program in optoelectronics indicates how such projects are structured to maximize industry-wide progress while minimizing duplication of effort and potential wasteful market conflict.

The optoelectronics project was the R&D portion of a six-year Optical Measurement and Control System Project launched by MITI in 1979. A national laboratory was set up in Kawasaki near Fujitsu's optoelectronics operations to coordinate the R&D effort and to provide basic research support for the collaborating companies. Initially, a large "system of the future" was envisioned, consisting of interlinked optical subsystems. Although the major uses for such systems were expected to be in factories, they also might be used in large buildings or building complexes, laboratories, or even in residential areas. Fifteen Japanese companies were assigned to develop different components needed for such systems. The Japanese approach concentrated on what are called OEICs, or optoelectronic integrated circuits, which would combine optical and electronic functions on the same chips. At this time American laboratories, such as those at Bell Labs and Hughes, were concentrating on developing all-optical guided wave devices, but the Japanese researchers felt that light beams were so weakly interactive compared with electrons that combined optical-electronic devices would be needed for such operations as switching. Fujitsu, for example, would develop integrated multichannel optoelectronic switches, receiving optical transmissions from fibers, turning them into electronic signals for switching, and feeding them to driver circuits containing laser diodes for retransmission. Mitsubishi would work on process data collection systems, picking up signals from many sensors on an optical loop. Toshiba would work on devices for emitting several wavelengths of light from a single laser diode and devices for demultiplexing the multiple signals at the receiving end.

While the individual companies worked on device technology, the central laboratory did generic research, such as devising methods to reduce defects in gallium arsenide crystals, and developing automated methods for fabricating OEICs. This technology was shared among the participants, which each built crude prototypes of the devices assigned to them and then made requests to the central lab for further research to help improve device performance. As such programs move toward commercialization, the participants tend to keep more of their own work proprietary, and the structure of the program tends to give the companies strengths in different device categories, thus reducing potential market conflict (although major companies like Fujitsu, Hitachi, and NEC all tend to make the most widely used devices, such as laser emitters and optical detectors).

Since the participants were also producers of integrated circuits, the optoelectronics work gave them an opportunity to make gains in gallium arsenide technology for conventional semiconductors as well. With the help of this program, by the mid-80s the Japanese semiconductor industry had moved far ahead of U.S. capabilities in both integrated optoelectronics and gallium arsenide integrated circuits. In the U.S., a military-sponsored gallium arsenide research program at Rockwell International's laboratory north of Los Angeles eventually led to a few venture-backed firms in that area, such as Gigabit Logic and Vitesse. But as gallium arsenide technology moves into the commercial digital semiconductor market, such start-ups must again compete with giant, well-funded Japanese conglomerates with a rich technology base resulting from a successful national collaborative program.

It is not so surprising that Japan's rapid rise in world semi-conductor markets has coincided with the shift of the technology to VLSI. This technology enables the integration of entire subsystems, such as 32-bit central processing units, on single chips. The shift to VLSI greatly increased the levels of investment, systems expertise, and vertical inter-industry cooperation required for success in the semiconductor industry. The structure and strategic behavior of the Japanese industry naturally lent itself to this technology, while that of the United States did not (except, perhaps, in the case of a vertically integrated producer like IBM). VLSI changed the industry's economics in a direction that favored the more concentrated, vertically integrated Japanese industry, but it also brought major changes to downstream industries dependent on electronics and information, such as computers, telecommunications, and office systems. All of these downstream industries are becoming more dependent on advanced digital microelectronics and systems architectures. Since in Japan the same companies dominate both these downstream industries and semiconductor development, they can operate under coordinated, long-term, integrated strategies. The systems branches can push device-makers for the performance they will require in future designs, and they can support the investments needed to insure that these advanced devices will be available regardless of the vicissitudes of the merchant market.

Conversely, in the United States, these sectors are dominated by different firms (except for the captive producers). The systems and semiconductor device industries have often behaved adversarially rather than cooperatively. American semiconductor firms, for the most part, have been generally too small to undertake the large, long-term investments required as circuit integration levels rise. Tax savings might help new ventures for their first few years, but the levels of investment have risen so high that many merchant firms cannot afford afford efficient-scale, state-of-the-art fabrication facilities. It is estimated that the R&D for each new generation of process technology requires at least $100 million, that design of 32-bit chip sets costs $50 million or more, and that efficient-scale factories for the 0.5-micron or less circuit capabilities needed in the early- to mid-90s will cost $400 million to $500 million to build. One result has been the rise of silicon "foundries," which produce chips for outside companies that provide the required mask sets. Recently Texas Instruments agreed to exchange technology with Hitachi in developing 16-megabit DRAMs, and earlier, in preparation to re-enter the DRAM business, Motorola agreed to swap some chip technology with Toshiba. These partnership arrangements even among major semiconductor competitors are likely to increase as the costs to move to new levels of technology continues to escalate, just as they have grown in the commercial aircraft business.

Although American firms continue to license technology to Japan, an increasing portion of advances there are due to indigenous development rather than imitation. Most major Japanese semiconductor firms, including NEC, Hitachi, Fujitsu, and Mitsubishi, have independently designed, and in some cases are already producing 32-bit microprocessors that rival U.S. designs. Fujitsu is now the largest vendor of application-specific integrated circuits (ASICs), an important new category of devices requiring advanced design, software, and services capabilities.

Aggregate R&D indicators yield similar conclusions. Between 1975 and 1982, the U.S. share of world integrated circuit patent activity declined from 43 to 27 percent, while Japan's share rose from 18 to 48 percent. By the mid-80s, over 40 percent of the papers accepted for the prestigious IEEE International Solid State Circuits Conference were of Japanese authorship (versus zero in the early 1960s). By the early 1980s the Japanese industry was spending 28 percent of its revenues on capital investment versus only 20 percent for the U.S. industry. Japanese companies also were spending 12 percent of revenues on R&D versus nine percent for the United States. R&D spending by the Japanese industry now exceeds U.S. merchant industry spending not just as a percent of revenues but in absolute figures, and at the present trend will exceed all U.S. semiconductor R&D spending, including that by the government and captive producers, by the mid-90s.

Strengths of the Japanese Industry. Aside from the national R&D programs, Japan continues to have important advantages over the United States with respect to the relative openness of national markets and in the structure of Japanese industry. Asset markets that are widely open in the United States (such as for experienced professionals, corporate control, capital, and university graduates) are either closed in Japan, or accessible only through persistent, long-term efforts, often supplemented by transferring of technology. The Japanese manufacturers are generally affiliated with one of six major keiretsu, which include strong financial institutions that invest for long-term capital appreciation (untaxed) rather than short-term dividends (taxed at a high rate). These financial institutions provide most of the equity capital as well as low-cost loans, and the equity holdings seldom change hands. For example, the largest shareholders of NEC, a member of the Sumitomo group, ranked as follows in 1986:

Shareholder	percent ownership
Sumitomo Life Insurance	7.1
Sumitomo Bank	5.0
Sumitomo Trust	4.1
Nippon Life Insurance	3.1
Dai-Ichi Mutual Life Insurance	2.9
Sumitomo Marine and Fire Insurance	2.8
Sumitomo Electric	2.4
Sumitomo Corp.	2.3

Moreover, patterns of ownership highly uncommon or even illegal in the United States help facilitate industry-wide cooperation and cohesion. A number of the largest Japanese financial institutions (now by far the largest in the world) hold substantial equity positions not just in one, but in several of the major electronics producers. In 1986, for example, Sumitomo Life Insurance held not only 7.1 percent of NEC (the major electronics producer in the Sumitomo keiretsu), but also 3.7 percent of Sharp and 4.6 percent of Matsushita. Sumitomo Bank not only holds five percent of NEC, but also 4.6 percent of Matsushita. Dai-Ichi Mutual Life, a member of the DKB industrial group which includes Fujitsu, held 2.9 percent of NEC, 2.8 percent of Hitachi, 4.7 percent of Toshiba, 2 percent of Mitsubishi, and 6 percent of Oki. The Industrial Bank of Japan held 2.5 percent of Hitachi and 2.6 percent of Fujitsu. In addition to such direct equity positions, financial institutions also generally have large loans outstanding to the major producers. Japanese industrial firms are far more highly leveraged than their U.S. competitors.

Moreover, these same financial institutions, together with the major producers themselves, also hold large equity positions in the principal firms in the support industry. This holds true not only for the major producers of semiconductor capital equipment, such as those cited earlier, but also for a wide array of materials and services providers. An example is Toshiba Ceramics, which in 1986 was Japan's fifth largest silicon wafer producer, and also was a producer of other semiconductor materials, such as quartz and ceramics. In 1986, Toshiba Ceramics' principal shareholders were:

Shareholder	percent ownership
Toshiba Corp.	50.2
Sumitomo Trust Business Dept.	2.6
Mitsui Trust	2.6
Yamagata Bank	2.5
Toyo Trust	1.6
Nippon Life	1.1
Daiwa Bank Annuity	1.1

These examples are not exceptional; each of the major producers has several dozen consolidated and unconsolidated affiliates in which it owns a substantial interest. Often a firm's competitors, or members of a competitor's larger groups, hold a minority interest in the same affiliates. This insures that capital is available for investments that fit into long-term strategic plans, and helps engender a high degree of cooperation. Such relationships would make it exceedingly difficult for American firms to sell competitive products to companies within such networks. Japanese buyers also depend on long-term relationships to build up trust with suppliers, and most products are sold through labyrinthine distribution networks that are difficult to set up and greatly increase costs for imported goods in the Japanese market. This would make the Japanese market extremely difficult for smaller American firms to penetrate even if they understood the market complexities and had personnel who could speak Japanese, which most of them do not.

Another set of norms and structures inhibit personnel mobility within Japanese industry. Japanese lifetime employment policies as practiced by the major electronics firms (although not by their subcontractors) implied that the choice of an employer by new graduates was essentially a one-time, lifetime decision. Consequently the established strength and long-run prospects of prospective employers were far more important than in the United States, and university recruiting often depended on long-standing relationships between firms and senior faculty members who exercised considerable influence over the decisions of graduates. This system assured that training investments would accrue to the employer and prevented U.S. firms from effective recruiting. It also prevented the formation of independent start-up companies.

The Outlook for the Semiconductor Industry

The remarkable progress of semiconductor technology promises to lead to an expanding array of information and other industries over the next few decades. The world semiconductor market is projected to grow from about $30 billion currently to perhaps $200 billion by the year 2000. This alone would be enough to make its decline in the U.S. of great concern. But semiconductors also play a vital and growing role in many other important existing industries, including computers, instruments, communications, automobiles, machinery, and factory systems. Loss of the semiconductor business could also contribute to the decline of the U.S. in other critical industries dependent on the performance of these devices for their competitive advantage.

The outlook for the American merchant industry versus the Japanese is not bright. The U.S. has belatedly tried to deal with part of the problem, through import penalties and the creation of Sematech, a joint industry/DoD effort to help the U.S. maintain or regain leadership in fabrication technology, production techniques, quality control, and test equipment. In the case of DRAMs, the trade restrictions forced American computer and peripheral producers to pay millions of dollars more to Japanese suppliers for devices, and the hoped-for resurgence of U.S. DRAM production has been slow in coming because of the huge investment required. To match the Japanese competition, the U.S. merchant suppliers must continue to consolidate and to form alliances that can strengthen their competitive positions and share the costs and risk of major new investments in fabrication facilities. They must also boost their skills in production, design optimization, and quality control while keeping pace with advances in fabrication techniques.

From a national strategic perspective, the traditional structure and institutions of the U.S. industry appear to be inappropriate for meeting the challenge of the much stronger, better organized Japanese competition. The merchant industry remains too fragmented and the biggest producer, IBM, has not chosen to sell on the open market.

The technical edge that once enabled innovative U.S. companies to excel, despite their lack of financial and market clout, has disappeared, with the Japanese gaining the lead. One promising development is the possible opening up of the big captive producers, with IBM and AT&T giving signs that they may be more willing to sell to other U.S. firms, even competitors.

But without some dramatic realignment of the American merchant industry, its decline is likely not only to continue but to accelerate. The conventional economic prescriptions, such as tax credits, guaranteed procurement, import quotas, or industry-wide R&D funding, are unlikely to have much success, and, in fact, might impede structural rationalization while propping up the existing inefficient system. To be effective, policies must be aimed at correcting the industry's weaknesses, otherwise any resources offered to help bring changes are likely to be wasted. Incentives need to be shifted, to encourage longer time horizons (including long-term relationships with suppliers and customers), to allow increased profitability for productive investment relative to off-shore manufacturing or to shifting assets to other non-productive activities, and to help ensure that developers can gain long-term benefits from proprietary technology. Policies should encourage structural rationalization, less personnel turnover, and more training. R&D grants, for example, might be dispersed over long time periods to firms with pension plans that encourage long-term employment and with provisos that ensure that employees that remain with the firm will benefit from results of the research (perhaps through an employee stock plan). Imaginative new policy initiatives will be essential if the United States is to stem the decline of the highly strategic merchant semiconductor industry.

The Computer Industry

In its early days the United States computer industry accounted for a very large proportion of all the computers installed worldwide. Exports grew steadily, reaching $3.2 billion by 1977, while the U.S, imported no computers at all. During this period IBM was responsible for over 40 percent of the industry's shipments, and its revenues were eight times larger than those of its nearest competitor. Mainframe computers, by far the largest segment of the market, were made predominantly by IBM and the so-called BUNCH companies (Burroughs, Univac, NCR, Control Data, and Honeywell).

In the past decade or so the structure of the U.S. industry has changed significantly, driven primarily by the steadily increasing capabilities of the microchips from which computers are built. The minicomputer enjoyed increasing popularity, fueling a large expansion of Digital Equipment Corp. (DEC), and vaulting it into the number two spot behind IBM (until the recent merger of Burroughs and Univac into Unisys Corp.). The relative sales of major U.S. and other computer vendors for 1986 are shown in Figure 4. Personal computer and microcomputer peripherals sectors sprang up and grew rapidly, followed by powerful desk-top workstations. The small but important supercomputer sector also has grown rapidly, led by Cray, and supermicrocomputers have begun to move into the low end of this sector. IBM's steady growth has continued, but its mainframe competitors have not kept pace as this sector matured, and there are growing signs of weakness in the minicomputer sector as well.

Computers is one of the few remaining industries in which the U.S. continues to have a positive trade balance, but the trend is downward. The U.S. surplus in global computer trade peaked at $7 billion in 1981, fell to less than $3 billion in 1987, and is projected to be close to zero in 1988 (these figures exclude computers manufactured and sold abroad by U.S. manufacturers such as IBM and DEC; IBM World Trade alone has sales of some $25 billion and much of this is produced abroad). A major reason for the decline in the domestic U.S. trade balance is the rapid rise of Japanese imports.

Japan reached parity with the U.S. in bilateral computer trade in 1982, and achieved a surplus of over $4 billion by 1987. Meanwhile, the U.S. share of the Japanese market has steadily declined. IBM's market share there peaked at about 40 percent in the 1960s, but has shrunk to less than 15 percent now. DEC holds only 1.6 percent of the Japanese market, compared to six percent of the world market.

Japanese penetration of the U.S. computer market has been less dramatic than for other industries, such as automobiles or consumer electronics. A factor that has stabilized the market, particularly for U.S. mainframe vendors, has been the difficulty of switching from one vendor's proprietary system to competing equipment. Cumulative investment by users in applications software, training, and vendor-specific peripherals have made switching to a competing system costly, time-consuming, and risky. Buyers also choose computers on the basis of the applications software available, and the U.S. has been much stronger than Japan in software. Once a mainframe firm builds a customer base, it is difficult for other vendors with different architectures and/or operating systems, even with superior performance or lower prices, to penetrate it.

Using IBM as an example, it is estimated that the cumulative cost of software still in use for the IBM line of mainframes starting with the 360 generation exceeds $1 trillion. This creates both pluses and minuses for a computer company like IBM. It helps by creating a continuous flow of orders from customers who cannot afford to change systems using different architectures and operating systems. But it also hinders by forcing the vendor to maintain an architecture that may become outmoded. In IBM's case, it has been locked into the architecture of the 360 and its follow-ons for 25 years. In 1973, IBM wanted to build an entirely new and advanced machine, called the FS, but management chose not to because they felt that even IBM could not force a new architecture onto its customers. IBM did not extend 360-compatibility to its mid-range (System 36 and 38) and smaller computers, and it was not able to dominate these markets as it has the mainframe sector.

In its early days IBM's move to embrace the 360 architecture was a "bet the company" type of decision. All its other architectures were scrapped at one fell swoop. This was feasible only because of the use of microcoding, thus enabling software emulation of previous architectures so its new computers could still run existing customer programs. A similar decision, albeit not as drastic, was made by DEC in 1978 when it introduced the VAX architecture. The DECSYSTEM 20 line was essentially killed, and the PDP-11 line was drastically deemphasized as a result. The effect of creating a single architecture was almost as dramatic for DEC as the 360 move was for IBM. The software developed for the VAX/VMS line has kept the orders flowing to DEC for many years.

In spite of such barriers, Japan's excellence in manufacturing has enabled it to obtain contracts to build systems that are relabeled and sold by an expanding number of U.S. and European computer vendors. Peripherals, mostly electromechanical devices that roughly split the hardware market with central processors, are much more interchangeable, particularly below the mainframe level. Not too surprisingly, Japanese penetration of the U.S. market has been much greater in peripherals than in processors, capturing perhaps 30 percent overall and over 70 percent of the market for microcomputer peripherals (see Figure 5). Even American-built peripherals frequently are built with Japanese parts, often for critical functions, such as Hewlett-Packard laser printers which are built around a Canon printing engine. Along with semiconductor devices, Japanese vendors have sold circuit boards, such as disc controllers, for incorporation in American microcomputers. Recently Japanese firms have also been investing in U.S. disc drive companies, and they appear to be moving rapidly into this microperipheral segment as well. Because microcomputers use standard operating systems and readily available microprocessors, off-shore competitors, particularly from Japan and other Asian nations, have been able to clone them (especially the IBM PC "standard"), and sell fully compatible machines in the U.S. market. In addition, American computer makers now obtain over half their semiconductors from Japan, buying most of them from the same diversified companies that are their competitors in the computer market.

Software exceeds both processors and peripherals in market size. The packaged software industry sold about $30 billion worldwide in 1987, but this is dwarfed by the value of software developed within organizations. Estimates vary widely, but in the U.S. alone the cost probably is in the area of $150 billion to $200 billion annually (including salaries and other costs for programming groups). American packaged software remains strong globally, and has remained fairly invulnerable to import competition in the United States. The software industry was not included in the Commission's study, but it has important influences on the computer marketplace, so this aspect was considered.

In summary, the U.S. computer industry is thriving. IBM continues to grow even though the mainframe market is maturing worldwide, and companies such as DEC, Apple, Sun, and Compaq are riding the wave of popularity for minicomputers, workstations, and personal computers. Some of the younger sectors, however, may be more vulnerable in the future because they are predominantly made up of smaller, venture-capital-backed firms dependent on narrow product lines that are sold mostly in the United States. Peripheral-makers already face strong import pressure and most of them now manufacture off-shore. Japanese competitors tend to be large, diversified, financially strong conglomerates that market globally. These include companies like NEC in microcomputers, Canon and Toshiba in peripherals, and recently Matsushita and Sony in workstations. Matsushita has entered the U.S. market through a $50 million investment in start-up Solbourne Computer, Inc. of Longmont, Colorado, a company which is already challenging the popular Sun workstation line.

How the Computer Industry Developed in the U.S.

The computer industry began in the United States only a little over 35 years ago. IBM rather quickly became so dominant that in the 1960s the industry was known as "IBM and the seven dwarfs." The competition included RCA and GE as well as the BUNCH companies. RCA tried to sell computers equivalent to IBM's at lower prices. But software and service were vital to buyers, and IBM invested far more than RCA in these areas. RCA finally abandoned the market in about 1970, writing off losses of some $300 million. GE had already abandoned all but its process control computer operations, similarly taking large losses, when computer sales failed to reach financial objectives under its strong profit-center concept.

The U.S. government attempted through legal action to keep the early industry competitive. Although it might seem strange from today's international competitiveness perspective, the Justice Department brought suit against IBM under anti-monopoly statutes with the prospect of breaking the company into pieces (a prospect that some competitors feared might create a set of "little" IBMs that could exercise even greater market domination). The suit cost many millions of dollars and lasted over ten years, only to be finally dropped in 1982 after the industry had gone through significant changes.

Even though the case was never resolved, government pressure did have some effect on the marketplace. For example, IBM modified its practice of pre-announcing computers, which, it was alleged, had discouraged users from buying competitive systems already on the market. IBM was also forced to provide competitors with technical details of its new systems, because they so often set de facto standards in the marketplace. But probably the most important impact was the requirement that IBM unbundle software, selling it separately rather than making it part of the total cost of the system. This helped foster a competitive packaged software industry in the United States, which later grew dramatically with the rise of the personal computer.

The government also provided R&D support for the industry, mainly through the Defense Department. An early program to build the world's fastest computers (in the late 1950s) led to Univac's LARC and IBM's Stretch computers. Although IBM's entry was considered less successful, the project provided a test bed for many design concepts used in its highly successful commercial systems of the 360/370 generation. After Congress pressed DoD to fund only R&D aimed at strictly military needs, there was less opportunity for commercial spin-offs. Even so, the Defense Advanced Research Projects Agency played a big role in the evolution of advances such as time-sharing, computer networks, and artificial intelligence, and continues to support advanced computer research mainly at university laboratories.

As the mainframe sector matured, competitors in the U.S. and Europe, in attempts to cut costs, initially turned to Japan to manufacture their systems, but more recently have increasingly marketed Japanese-designed and -built computers. In the U.S. these firms include: Unisys (formed by the merger of Sperry-Univac and Burroughs), which buys mainframe components from Hitachi; Honeywell, which originally only had NEC manufacture its systems but now sells primarily NEC-designed computers; Amdahl, which markets IBM-compatible computers built by Fujitsu; and National Advanced Systems, which sells Hitachi computers (this is a division of National Semiconductor which the company is trying to sell—possibly to Hitachi). Japanese companies also build computers for such major European vendors as Siemens, BASF, and ICL.

In the past few years remarkable advances in VLSI (very-large-scale integration) brought rapid changes to the computer industry. Following the rise of minicomputers came the explosive growth of microprocessors and personal computers based on them. Powerful desk-top workstations emerged for computation-intensive tasks such as computer-aided design. Rapid performance gains in supercomputers expanded their use in aerospace, scientific research, and weather forecasting. In R&D laboratories and venture-backed companies multiprocessor computers are being readied to extend performance through architectural advances rather than simply by use of faster circuits.

The industry is also moving toward a distributed-computer phase with clusters of personal computers linked to each other and to nearby mainframes as well as to remote systems. This is increasing pressures by computer users for more standard interfaces and operating systems, so that large companies could exchange data (invoices, engineering plans, etc.) with customers, suppliers, and banks, for example. Even though there is discord in the industry, as different powerful groups try to establish a standard version of UNIX, for instance, the market pressures for uniformity are intensifying. One result may be the eventual "cloning" of popular software much as hardware is now imitated. Japan's Sigma network already taking shape will link thousands of powerful software-development workstations (built by several companies but all based on a standard UNIX-based operating system) that are capable of developing software for a wide range of machines (including IBM, DEC, VAX, UNIX, MSDOS, etc.). These systems are designed so that software can be developed for this broad array of American computers without the need to have a target machine. Powerful development tools will be available over the network to increase the efficiency of software development, and programmers will be encouraged to make use of available program fragments or subroutines. It remains to be seen if such efforts will make Japan more competitive in the software arena.

The mainframe sector appears to have passed maturity and is now slowing down. Most of the newer fast-growth market sectors have been launched by start-ups, which later were joined by the major computer companies. The advanced workstation market was pioneered by Apollo and Sun, and personal computers by Apple, with IBM and DEC making later entries. Tandem pioneered transaction-oriented, fault-tolerant computers, with IBM eventually selling systems by Stratus, a Tandem competitor. Convex launched the supermicrocomputer sector. And a number of start-up companies, such as Sequent, Encore, and Thinking Machines, are now offering systems based on the new multiprocessor architectures.

The first generation of these start-up ventures in the minicomputer field—such as Prime, Data General, and Wang—are now beginning to display behavior similar to the stagnation in the mainframe arena: slow growth, occasional serious downturns with layoffs, defections of talented employees, increasing dependence on external suppliers, and low shares of newer markets.

Progress of the Japanese Computer Industry

Japan's early computer industry struggled into existence with the help of the government and Nippon Telegraph & Telephone (NTT), the domestic telephone monopoly (recently privatized). In the 1960s, NTT's supplier "club" (or dendenkosha) included giant firms such as Fujitsu, NEC, and Hitachi, as well as a few others such as Oki, making specialized machines for NTT's needs using devices based on technologies a couple of years behind the Western state-of-the-art.

A government-coordinated effort was started in 1965 for a system to supercede IBM's 360 line, and Japanese firms were urged by the Ministry of International Trade and Industry (MITI) to buy computers from domestic suppliers. A 1970 MITI Vision of the Future envisioned a shift to low-energy industries because Japan was so vulnerable to cut-offs in energy supplies (prophetically, as it turned out). Eventually this led to the very successful VLSI (very-large-scale integrated) circuit program of the late-70s and early 80s, with the major objective of enabling Japanese computer makers to become world leaders. As a result, several major Japanese companies are now strong in both semiconductor and computers. The four largest computer producers, Fujitsu, NEC, Hitachi, and Toshiba, are also the largest semiconductor vendors.

The Japanese government also sponsored a supercomputer program, which has resulted in very high performance systems from Fujitsu, Hitachi, and NEC. These have had little success in penetrating the U.S. market, both because of software compatibility problems and the influence of the U.S. government. Currently Fujitsu and NEC are working on supercomputer designs tailored to UNIX. That means that in the future users of these machines would be able to run popular software written for this operating system, which users of Cray machines could not run due to Cray's proprietary design. It remains to be seen what effect this will have on the marketplace.

In microcomputers, Japanese firms trying to market in the U.S. ran into software-compatibility problems similar to those that slowed their penetration of mainframe processor markets. NEC, however, has had much greater success in Japan (where it has gained over 70 percent of the personal computer market) and the rest of Asia. Its approach was quite different than that typically taken by American firms in launching a new product line. Before entering the market, it is reported that Koji Kobayashi, NEC's chairman of the board, spent a year making personal contacts with software developers, retailers, resellers, and users, and learning the marketplace. The strategy based on this first-hand knowledge was aimed at stimulating market growth, primarily through large demonstration centers featuring a wide range of NEC equipment. The Tokyo center at Hibiya City alone cost $5 million, covers 30,000-40,000 square feet, and employs 44 people. Yet it sells no computers. Such centers allow potential customers to learn about NEC products, and then buy them at low cost from discount stores, such as in Tokyo's Akihabara district. This approach enables NEC to sell about half of its major PC product (about 1.4 million units a year) through simple retail stores rather than higher level outlets with computer-knowledgeable salespeople. Recently (1986-88) NEC made a strong move into the Australian personal computer market, which it typically does in preparation for an assault on the U.S. marketplace. There are signs the company has already begun a strong new campaign to win American personal computer buyers with IBM-PC compatible systems.

The Japanese computer companies have the advantages typical of other industries there. Their strategies are focused on growth rather than short-term profits, and they pay out little in dividends. This is because most of their stock is held by financial institutions and other large firms that are interested in untaxed capital gains rather than taxable dividends. Unlike American companies which must finance growth primarily through retained earnings, the Japanese companies try to minimize profits because of high corporate tax rates. They finance growth primarily through tax deductions (particularly depreciation) and secondarily through loans and equity funds (generally from large financial institutions or other firms in their corporate family, or keiretsu). Over a five-year period, for example, Fujitsu, the largest Japanese computer vendor, financed growth only 17 percent from profits and 17 percent from loans compared to 34 percent from depreciation allowances. Depreciation was accumulated through large expenditures on productivity-enhancing equipment, which is quite common in Japanese corporations. Moreover, in 1986 Fujitsu paid 4.5 percent interest on loans, about half the rate paid by large American companies. Labor costs were also about half those for American computer companies, mainly due to lower salaries for professional and factory workers and dependence on a much younger labor force, particularly low-paid young women, than is typical in the United States. This cost advantage has been reduced somewhat, of course, by the decline of the dollar.

By 1986, Fujitsu, Hitachi, and NEC were together spending more than double what IBM spent on R&D. Their investments in plant and equipment were also higher, with about 20 percent going for such productivity-enhancing equipment as factory automation, robotics, and materials-handling systems. At the same time they had been shifting more of their production to outside suppliers, for sub-assemblies, peripherals, and the like. Combined sales of the Japanese computer companies reached $53.6 billion in 1987 (at 138 yen per $1 U.S.), compared to worldwide revenues of $54.2 billion for IBM, and Japanese computer sales are growing at an increasing rate while IBM's are leveling off.

Japan's fifth generation program, started in the early 1980s, was another concerted effort to increase capabilities in advanced computer research, particularly artificial intelligence. Slated to cost some $500 million over seven years, this research program set an ambitious goal: to develop technology for intelligent machines that could solve complex problems, including automatic language translation, speech recognition, and tasks such as pattern recognition that are difficult for conventional computers. Although the program has fallen short of its technical goals, it has succeeded in what may have been its prime objective: to increase the number of advanced computer R&D leaders in Japan from a handful to probably several hundred. These were drawn from and returned to Japan's computer companies, which should become even more formidable competitors in tomorrow's market as a result.

According to a MITI 2000 Vision, the information industry will rise from 6.4 percent of Japan's GNP in 1984 to 21 percent by the turn of the century (this includes semiconductors, consumer electronics, data processing, and information and telecommunications equipment and services). To accomplish this will mean the information industries must grow at 13.3 percent a year until the year 2000 while the overall economy grows at a five percent nominal rate. This plan envisions 2000 new businesses with the creation of 2.5 million new jobs (44 percent of all new jobs in Japan over that period), with half of these jobs in the computer industry. In the past, the Japanese have been quite successful in meeting the targets developed for such plans. The desire to achieve economic primacy in the worldwide information industry seems logical and strategically sound for a country like Japan, as it requires little in the way of raw materials and depends primarily on a good supply of intelligent, well-educated people.

Outlook for the U.S. Computer Industry

Although the U.S. computer industry remains strong, the outlook will not continue to be bright without strong new initiatives. Japan and other Asian nations, such as South Korea and Taiwan, are gaining the R&D, market research services, and technical skills that their nations need to be strong international competitors. Innovative start-up companies in the U.S. frequently sell their technology and provide market knowledge and often direct assistance to these Asian competitors, help that would be very difficult to get from larger American firms, which tend to be much more careful with proprietary information. Many industry standards that evolve in the U.S. serve as virtual product specifications for imitative competitors with lower manufacturing costs and shorter development times. American universities conduct non-secret R&D and are educating a growing cadre of Asian engineers. All this openness, of course, is one of the costs of leadership and the free enterprise system and the study team does not advocate that we should "shut the door" at the basic research level. But some greater protection of American advances as they get closer to real products may be in order.

In the long run, the U.S. computer industry must take steps to ensure that it remains competitive as challengers gain new strength. Production capabilities need to be retained and upgraded, particularly in view of Japan's growing investments in productivity-enhancing equipment and its reputation for high-quality production of both electromechanical and electronic equipment. The recent decision of Matsushita to have Tandy produce its Panasonic microcomputers in its Fort Worth plant may be the first sign of a reversal of the trend toward off-shore manufacturing. U.S. computer-makers must also work cooperatively with domestic chip suppliers to ensure that they will continue to have access to the latest microcircuit technologies, which are critical to the performance of their systems. Software leadership is another important requirement, especially as Japan develops "software factories," and improves the programming tools that can make software development faster and more efficient.

Proximate Causes of Weakness in the U.S. Industry

Technological Practice. There is some evidence that much of the U.S. computer industry has neglected manufacturing. While detailed public-domain studies of the quality that are available in some other industries (e.g. the automobile industry) are not currently available, the available evidence suggests that aside from IBM, the U.S. computer industry lags Japan's in manufacturing practice, coordination between design and manufacturing, and coordination of product and process development. Visits by team members to both Japanese and U.S. computer assembly plants and to U.S. computer cabinet fabrication and printed circuit board factories, supplemented by the results of a questionnaire suggest that a significant fraction of U.S. manufacturing is well below world standards. While some U.S. companies and plants, including some of the largest, manufacture quite well, some others do rather poorly.

In one major U.S. firm, there appeared to exist both poor manufacturing practice (high costs, high inventory levels, low quality) and poor coordination between high performance CPU design, semiconductor processing, CPU assembly, and printed circuit board process development. As a consequence CPUs were designed in such a way that if individual semiconductor devices departed from strict tolerances, they caused CPU defects detectable only after final assembly. Prior testing of the semiconductor components did not seem capable of resolving this problem, which in several cases required incremental but significant redesigns of the CPU. The same family of CPUs was also designed to require high density printed circuit boards (22 layers). The company's internal technology proved inadequate beyond approximately a dozen layers, and relied upon extensive post-production testing to eliminate its high defect rate. Consequently the company was forced to buy 22 layer boards from one of its Japanese competitors. This Japanese firm sells 22 layer boards (of extremely high quality) to the U.S. company, but already produces and uses 40-layer boards in its own products.

The same U.S. company's high performance CPU assembly operations appeared significantly less efficient than its Japanese competitor's CPU assembly operations. The U.S. company's largest high performance CPU factory maintained an inventory area three times larger than the assembly facility itself; the Japanese competitor maintained an inventory area one-fifth as large as the assembly area, and received parts deliveries daily from its subcontractors. In the Japanese company's factory, high performance CPUs were assembled by teams of two to four people, the leaders of which all possessed at least five years experience specific to such assembly. Furthermore, the Japanese company's factory was collocated with major design and software activities in a complex employing several thousand engineers, while the U.S. company's facility was physically and logistically isolated from related engineering functions, a condition which appeared to cause substantial supply and communications problems.

While these cases may not be fully representative, impressionistic evidence suggests that they are not entirely anomalous, and the two companies are both among the market leaders in their national industries.

A product's design can dictate the success and the productivity of the manufacturing effort. In fact, it has been said that 80 percent of the cost of a product is built in at the design stage. Nowhere can the importance of the design be more clearly illustrated than through the example of the IBM Proprinter, which is produced at IBM's Information Product's Division, Charlotte, North Carolina. IBM officials have highlighted the Proprinter experience as a major recent event in IBM's history.

Professors Dewhurst and Boothroyd of the University of Rhode Island conducted "design for assembly" analysis of the IBM Proprinter and the Epson MX80 dot matrix printer. Their method of design for assembly analysis consists of examining each component, subassembly, and fastener that is required to build the unit. Times are assigned from a data base depending on the operation required such as inserting a screw or reorienting the assembly. These times are summed and a total assembly time calculated. Applying this type of consistent analysis to these two printers demonstrates a surprising gulf in the total assembly time required to build each unit.

The Epson printer required 1866 seconds manual assembly time. In contrast, the Proprinter required only 170 seconds. The difference is in the manufacturing intent of the design. The Proprinter was designed from the beginning with ease of assembly in mind. This ten fold difference in assembly time translates directly into a huge difference in manufacturing productivity. It is important to recognize that this difference cannot be compensated for later in the manufacturing process through added employee incentives or through automation. In fact, Dewhurst and Boothroyd show that manual bench assembly is more cost effective than automation for this application. (But even if automation was less expensive than human labor, automating the assembly of a product at ten-fold disadvantage would be addressing the wrong problem, resulting in what Clausing describes as the "automation of waste.")

At the same time that the Proprinter was being designed for assembly, extensive automation was included in the new Proprinter factory. IBM officials have now concluded that design for assembly provided major benefits, but the automation had essentially zero payoff (except for the experience).

Another design issue which directly translates into manufacturing productivity is the design of computers for testability. During one of the plant visits it was suggested that this is an extremely important issue which tends not to be sufficiently addressed until machine architectures are fixed—when it is too late. The importance of testability is crucial if one considers that ten percent to 50 percent of computer systems produced need to be reworked. This need for rework, while a problem in itself, points to the value of being able to identify a problem quickly and hence demonstrates the significance of testability.

Throughout interviews with engineering managers during the plant visits two themes repeatedly surfaced. One is an inability of American engineers to get to the root of the problems. They were said to solve problems in the same way that aspirin cures the common cold; by addressing only the symptoms. One plant manager felt that this was not always the case, that 20 years ago engineers were thorough. At another plant, however, this inability to get to the root of problems had been convincingly addressed.

This latter plant was taking part in a quality improvement drive with a company plant in Japan. The story was told that the Japanese engineers would ask their American counterparts why a component or process failed. The American engineers would give them "the" answer and feel they had fulfilled their obligation. The Japanese engineers would respond with a new series of "why" questions about the answer which had been provided. A new answer would be given followed by a new series of questions. This loop would continue much like the proverbial Japanese "five whys" until the real problem was found and solved.

What became evident to the engineers at this plant was that problems solved in this fashion stayed solved. Also, it was very clear that this was not the manner in which they had been addressing problems in the past. In response to this lesson, the plant instituted the use of the Deming circle in a drive for total quality control and self-improvement. Only through applying the thoroughness taught by its Japanese counterpart has this plant now been able to move successfully into a Just-In-Time manufacturing environment. Note that in the JIT environment, solving problems is critical as there is not the same inventory available to hide or forgive problems.

Responsiveness and mutual cooperation is a requirement for the transition that is taking place as many manufacturers attempt to move into a Just-In-Time environment. The goal and purpose of JIT is much more than just the timely delivery of materials to production and the elimination of inventory. JIT simplifies materials flow through the factory often exposing problems. The absence of inventory and reduction of work in progress caused by JIT provide pressure, accountability, and visibility such that exposed problems are fixed and stay fixed. This approach stands in contrast to the MRP (Materials Requirements Planning) system adopted by many American manufacturers, where problems are concealed by inventory and the complexity of the system. As Hayes and Clark write:

> The American mentality has kept us from exploring the impact of changing the
> basic structure of problems. If one is confronted with a highly complex factory
> environment—lots of production stages, lots of flow patterns, lots of inventory
> locations...one can deal with it in one of two ways. One can attempt to develop a highly
> sophisticated (and usually computerized) information and control system to manage all
> this complexity, or one can set about reducing the complexity.... As a result, we have
> spent over a decade and millions of dollars developing elegant MRP systems, while the
> Japanese were spending their time simplifying their factories to the point where materials
> control can be managed manually with a handful of Kanban cards.

Hewlett-Packard is one firm which has achieved notable success through the implementation of JIT. Some of their results include:

Hewlett-Packard JIT Plants

Category	percent reduction
Inventory	60 - 80
Floor Space	30 - 50
Lead-time	> 50
Labor Costs	20 - 50

Labor costs for JIT divisions were also said to account for three percent of total production costs, versus nine percent for the company average.

The plants that were visited all indicated that they were moving towards JIT. One of the plants, however, was far closer than the other plants to JIT. It contained similar equipment to two of the other plants, while occupying far less floor space. Also important to note is that this plant, which was far more logically and less confusingly organized, had no complex material handling system. The other two plants both had carousels and automatic conveyors which moved kits to the appropriate location. The leading plant, meanwhile, had originally installed the same material handling equipment, but later had removed it. Plant staff had found that through simplification of the material flow this equipment was no longer needed. Furthermore, the kitting system was seen as inefficient. The staff felt that materials should be handled once, not collected and placed into a kit to be later removed and then assembled.

Probably the most striking revelation that emerged from these plant visits was the amount of rework that is common throughout the computer industry. As mentioned previously, ten to 50 percent of all computer products require rework. This is an extraordinarily wasteful effort when one considers that no value is added to the product through rework.

A similarly wasteful, but necessary, practice is burn-in. Through thermal and electrical cycling, components are aged to initiate any early failures which may otherwise occur in the field (i.e. infant mortality). Burn-in occurs at every stage of manufacturing; the chip level, the board or module level, and the system level. The rationale is that the earlier a defective part is caught, the less expensive it is to fix or discard. (At each successive stage of manufacture repair or rework costs increase by an order of magnitude.) However, one of the U.S. plants stated that its sister plant in Japan does no burn-in on the module level, choosing burn-in only at the system level. Another indicated, meanwhile, that its non RISC machines are currently being burned-in only at the module level. Burn-in was observed to range in the different plants from six hours to four days.

Strategic Failures. In some cases, U.S. firms developed major, extremely innovative technologies which they failed to commercialize effectively. For example, in the late 1970s and early 1980s Xerox developed laser printing technology and marketed the high speed Dover printer, but the mass market for laser printers has been dominated by Canon and Ricoh. Similarly, Xerox was the original developer of the user-friendly workstation technology now successfully commercialized by Apple in its Macintosh systems, and of Ethernet local area networks now produced primarily by DEC and by specialized networking start-ups such as Bridge, 3Com, and Ungermann-Bass.

Perhaps equally important, however, was the internal strategic behavior of the Japanese industry. Once again in contrast to the American case, Japanese firms both cooperated extensively with each other in technology development and were willing to forego short-term profits for long-term advantage. Although the Japanese industry lost money for nearly the entire decade of the 1960s, it continued to invest. Moreover, other firms in producers' keiretsu showed considerable favoritism towards their family firm in computer purchases, despite the short-term penalties associated with using what until the late 1970s was clearly inferior domestic equipment. Even competitors from different industrial groups cooperated, often through MITI projects, until they grew sufficiently that their competition with each other equalled their common interest in displacing IBM. For example, Hitachi and Fujitsu cooperated in developing IBM compatible mainframe technologies until they achieved significant success, whereupon they became relatively less cooperative.

All of the major Japanese producers invested heavily, and over long time periods, in the semiconductor technologies critical to mainframe systems. They are now world leaders in those technologies, for example ECL gate arrays and memories used in mainframe CPUs, and indeed Fujitsu sells only its low-end ECL products on the open market, reserving its most advanced devices exclusively for internal consumption. The same is said to be true of NEC. As with the semiconductor industry, the Japanese computer industry arose principally through the further diversification of large, integrated electronics firms; personnel turnover is low; domestic market rank is relatively stable; U.S. firms have difficulty enlarging their Japanese operations; and venture capital funded entrepreneurialism is absent.

Failures in Human Resource Management. Communication of manufacturing concerns to design, and communication of design plans to manufacturing, is now recognized as extremely important by the management at the plants that were visited. A growing emphasis on early involvement of manufacturing with design has developed. Despite this trend there are still significant problems.

In one firm, an intermediate transition team takes the product from product design and brings it into the manufacturing plant. This may be the worst type of "handoff." The problem according to one source is that these individuals are not up to speed on either the product or the process. The result is that they are of little help to the manufacturing group that they are intended to assist.

While there seems to be nearly universal agreement on the value of the design-manufacturing communication and integration, there are huge logistical difficulties. The greatest seems to be distance. Of the five U.S. manufacturing plants that were visited, only one was collocated with its product design group. The others were all isolated from fifteen to hundreds of miles.

Some of the needed "communication" could be facilitated by the rotation of engineers through research, design, and manufacturing. One plant manager was at odds with this statement. He seemed to feel that there was a distinction between research, design, and manufacturing engineers. "A manufacturing engineer," as he put it, "knows how to really squeeze the nickel." He felt that research and design engineers did not have, nor did they need that talent. "Each is best in his own function." He further stated that he would not tend to be in favor of his manufacturing engineers moving into any type of research assignment.

During one discussion at this plant, it was reported that several manufacturing engineers were not accepted into a newly started company manufacturing research program. These engineers believe that management felt that they were not good enough for this research. This belief appears to be the source of some resentment of both management and the group conducting the manufacturing research on the part of the manufacturing engineers. This policy could represent a lost opportunity to transfer knowledge to these manufacturing engineers, as well as promote difficulty in relations and communications between the manufacturing and manufacturing research groups.

Following a less than completely successful attempt to implement JIT at one of the plants, management was forced to examine what went wrong. They came to the realization that through all the changes they were making, they had forgotten the most important element in implementing JIT: the worker. As they prepared for their second phase of implementation the decision was made that the workers had to be pulled into the decision process. They would design their assembly stations and some of the manufacturing equipment for the production floor.

This proposal was met with stiff resistance from some members of the plant's engineering community. The engineers would now be charged with teaching whatever knowledge was necessary so that these individuals could make their own informed decisions. The production workers would then contact and meet with the vendors of the equipment and make recommendations of the equipment to be purchased.

All recommended equipment was ordered. Astonishingly, only two days after the equipment arrived, the line was in operation. This was far less set-up and training time than had been achieved in the past when engineering assumed total responsibility (in which case an estimated two months would have been required).

Today, at this plant, workers spend 75 percent of their time working on production and 25 percent in training and working on quality issues. In fact, the production workers maintain their own quality records and are actually responsible for quality. During the past three years this plant has experienced a labor productivity gain of 45 percent. Through individual participation, management leadership, and the continuous feedback initiated by JIT, this plant's employees all seemed to have a clear sense of purpose.

The importance of the value of good human resource management or more specifically, a clear sense of purpose and leadership, was illustrated by the experience of another plant where a dramatic turnaround in performance had been achieved in a space of only four months. This plant's initial MRP II rating was a D-. New management observed that individuals and departments were working to their own requirements, not those of customer. Improvements were mainly focussed on making life easier, not doing a better job. The new management identified the objective as turning the plant completely around and doing so quickly. Those who felt that this was impossible were asked to leave.

The task required people's whole way of thinking to be changed. They were told that all the work which did not contribute to the final product or core objective should be stopped. This statement generated great concern within the plant. People were forced to focus on how their job impacted the total effort. Unnecessary work (not jobs) was eliminated. At the end of one year this clear management direction brought about a change from a D- to an A+ MRP manufacturing environment.

The success of these two plants can be explained by the same set of reasons. The changes at each plant helped the individuals define and recognize for themselves a clear sense of overall purpose. Furthermore, each was empowered to contribute to deciding on the manner in which his work was done. Both cases had systems where feedback was consistently supplied. In the first case, JIT helped facilitate feedback through the immediate impact that any action in the production process caused. In the second case, performance metrics were kept and displayed while personal feedback was also given. The clear sense of purpose and feedback were vital elements in job satisfaction as a motivator.

The gains in productivity at various U.S. plants have been impressive. However, when one considers a plant such as NEC's plant in Ibaraki, Japan, they are not. Despite the strong yen and weak dollar NEC maintained constant the price of its product. This exerted extreme pressure on this plant to drastically improve its productivity in a short period of time. The plant responded with a 100 percent increase in productivity in one year. This was accomplished through a variety of measures. It is important to note that these measures were not derived from either management or engineering alone, but came from a unified team working to a single objective. The Ibaraki plant's employees submitted 24,000 productivity suggestions of which over 1,000 were implemented. Also, automation in the plant was increased from a 50 percent level to a 70 percent level. This plant intends to double its productivity again within the next two years.

Copiers

History

1959-1970. The period from 1959 to 1970 was a halcyon interlude for the Xerox Corporation. With the advent of the 914 copier at the end of 1959, Xerox (at that time still the Haloid Corporation) revolutionized the business of reproducing documents. Prior to 1959. equipment to make copies of documents was very slow, very large, very messy, and made poor copies. The 914 copier was the first xerographic copier. It was based on the patents of Chester Carlson, Batelle Memorial Institute, and Xerox. Chester Carlson graduated from the California Institute of Technology with a BS degree in physics at the beginning of the great depression. He could not find an appropriate technical job and finally became a clerk in the office of a patent attorney. As such he had much need for copies. This led him to understand that there was a great latent demand on the part of potential customers for an improved copying technology.

Working alone in his kitchen, to the disgust of his wife who finally divorced him, Carlson finally invented the new technology in 1938. He had begun by correctly identifying the customers needs for new reprographic technology. The two overriding customer requirements that Carlson identified were:

1) The process had to be dry (the existing processes were wet photography and very messy), and
2) The process had to be automatic.

Working from these two basic customer needs and utilizing his basic knowledge of physics, Carlson invented xerography (Greek for dry copying) in 1938. It was still a very long haul from 1938 until 1959. There was no interest in Chester Carlson's invention. Finally, with help from Battelle, Carlson was able to interest a tiny company in Rochester, New York. This company, led by its CEO Joe Wilson, bet its existence on the new technology, almost went bankrupt before the introduction of the 914 in 1959, and then rode the new technology to one of the larger successes in twentieth century business.

When the 914 was introduced it not only swept the market, but created a new market that was even beyond the fondest hopes of Joe Wilson and his crew at Xerox. By today's standards the 914 was a relatively crude copier. It only copied at seven copies per minute, it was a large machine that stood on the floor, and it was expensive, but this was ameliorated considerably by the creative Xerox plan of leasing machines rather than selling them. The machine could not copy photographs, or any other grey-scale originals. However, when it was working well it made beautiful copies of typewritten documents. As a result it quickly replaced all existing means of making copies and led to a tremendous expansion in the number of copies that were made. Prior to the introduction of the 914, copies of correspondence meant using messy carbon papers to make copies that were often barely legible. Library research was very laborious because all references had to be written out by hand. The 914 copier led people to indulge in their latent desire to more completely communicate.

The 914 was relatively crude in its design and production. It had been a long time in development. The Xerographic process is relatively complex and seemed to most engineers to be black magic. Simply getting it to work at all in a commercial machine seemed at the time to be a huge accomplishment. There had been very little emphasis upon rationalized design with the objective of maximizing quality and reducing manufacturing cost. It had been enough simply to get all of this complex new technology to function in a commercial machine. The tremendous commercial success of the 914 and its successors absorbed all of the Xerox talent in simply expanding the line. There was no competition and therefore little motivation to do much to improve quality and reduce manufacturing cost. The entire emphasis was upon expanding into larger and faster copiers.

In the remainder of the period from 1959 to 1970 Xerox concentrated on moving up to higher speed copiers. After the initial success it was perceived that the real money was to be made at higher speeds where much larger volumes of copies were made. By 1970 Xerox had extended the speed range up to 60 copies per minute.

Based on the early success of the 914, Xerox had established a subsidiary company in Europe, Rank Xerox Inc., and an affiliated company in Japan, the Fuji Xerox Company. Rank Xerox was slightly more than half owned by Xerox and was controlled by it. However, Fuji Xerox was half owned by Fuji Photo Film Co. and half owned by Rank Xerox. Therefore, Fuji Xerox was not directly controlled by either of its owners and always had a considerable amount of operational independence. In this time period both Rank Xerox and Fuji Xerox simply took Xerox designs and modified them slightly for local conditions such as electrical voltage and paper size.

Throughout the 1960s Xerox was a darling of America. Their copiers were awe-inspiring ("The copy is even better than the original," was often said.) The stock market loved Xerox, and its stock seemed to have no upward bound. Even the television commercials for Xerox attracted much favorable attention. By 1970 Xerox was on top of the world and could seem to do no wrong. It still had no competition within the United States. However, there was competition in Europe and increasingly so in Japan. The situation was about to change, but Xerox seemed to be paying little attention.

1970-1975. In 1970 Xerox got its first competition in the United States. IBM came out with the Copier I and shortly afterwards with the Copier II. These were noteworthy primarily because they were the first U.S. competition for Xerox. They were not a major threat that caused Xerox to change course in any way. Xerox at this time was busy coming out with a second generation of copiers and extending their speed range up to 120 copies per minute. The 120 copy per minute market was seen to be extremely lucrative. It was the province of offset printing, and Xerox perceived that its superiority in products that were somewhat more consumer oriented would give it an advantage. Therefore, one of the major thrusts in this time period was the development of the 9200 which was introduced in 1974. This and the other second generation copiers were faster, had more features, and were more streamlined in appearance. However, they were still very big, very expensive, had a tremendous number of parts, and were not noteworthy for good quality.

At the beginning of this time period Fuji Xerox was still very successful with its Xerox-designed copier line. However, by the end of this period Fuji Xerox had been overtaken by a host of Japanese competitors. These were led by camera companies such as Canon, Minolta, and Ricoh. By 1975 this onslaught had greatly reduced the market share in Japan for Fuji Xerox. Fuji Xerox profits had shrunk to essentially nothing. At this time Fuji Xerox recognized that they could no longer depend on Xerox products to be winners in the Japanese marketplace. Two major strategic decisions were made: 1) Fuji Xerox would develop its own product line, and 2) a company-wide quality control (CWQC) program would be launched. Both of these strategies proved to be a huge success. The New Xerox Movement, which was the CWQC program for Fuji Xerox, helped Fuji Xerox to win the prestigious Deming prize in 1980. The combination of the New Xerox Movement and the new products that were developed in Fuji Xerox led to a resurgence of profit. The main significance of the developments during this time period, in retrospect, was the clear signal that came from Japan to Xerox that the Xerox products were unable to compete with the best Japanese competition. Thus, Xerox had ample warning that their products were not in good shape vis-a-vis the major Japanese copier companies such as Canon, Minolta, and Ricoh with respect to cost and quality.

1975-1979. In 1975, Kodak came out with the Ektaprint copier. This copier was in the upper middle part of the speed range and attacked a very profitable part of Xerox business. Therefore, Xerox saw it as major threat. Much effort during this time period went into counter attacking against the Kodak threat. Kodak had used its technical superiority in chemistry to have a very good photoreceptor and the copy quality was excellent. In addition they had for the first time introduced a completely automatic recirculating document handler (RDH). Xerox had been planning to develop a RDH for some time, but were caught to some extent by surprise when Kodak introduced a good version of a RDH on the first Ektaprint copier. Xerox spent much of their development resources in this time period in developing both a tactical and a longer-term response to Kodak, with RDH units that would be at least as good as the one that had been introduced by Kodak. This led to the 8200 as a tactical response in 1979, and to the ten75 as the first of the third-generation copiers in 1982.

What Xerox did not do in this time period was respond to the clear evidence from Japan by 1975 that Xerox copiers were not competitive with Canon, Minolta, Ricoh, and several other Japanese copiers. In this time period Japanese copiers started to invade the low volume (30 copies per minute and less) copier market in the United States. Xerox seemed to be uncertain as to whether to make a major effort to resist this invasion. To a considerable extent it was decided to concentrate efforts in the higher volume (higher volume in the copier industry means more copies per month) market that was much more profitable. The decision essentially was to leave the low volume market to the Japanese because there was little profit there. Also in this time period Xerox was somewhat ambivalent about the role of the entire company. Should it be primarily a copier company or should it expand strongly into other fields, particularly computers. There was a strategic desire on the part of top management to expand into the computer and office information systems business. It appeared that the copier business might be used as a cash cow to finance this expansion. However, this thrust into business beyond copiers was never very successful. In 1969 Xerox paid $900 million for SDS to get into the mainframe computer business. In 1974 this was written off. Meanwhile the Palo Alto Research Center (PARC) of Xerox came up with much innovative computer technology. However, in this time frame from 1975-1979 Xerox was unsuccessful in implementing any of this technology in commercially successful products.

Diverted by opportunities in business beyond copiers, and focusing the copier business on the high copy volume, low production volume end of the market where profits were high, Xerox essentially offered no response to the invasion of the Japanese in the low end market. As a result the low end market share for Xerox went from approximately 80 percent in 1975 to a low of 8.6 percent in 1984. By 1979 Xerox had awakened to the fact that the Japanese threat was real and that something would have to be done. The low end business itself was not very profitable, but by 1979 it was recognized that the Japanese were stronger than had been anticipated, and that the low end market would simply provide a beachhead from which the Japanese could expand into the more profitable realms of business. Also, the great resurgence of Fuji Xerox led Xerox to further comprehend that the Japanese were doing many good things. This led to the sending of study missions to Japan and the beginnings of clear understanding on the part of Xerox as to their exact position relative to the Japanese copier companies. This period ended in 1979 with an awakening of reality within Xerox which has led to a steady resurgence from 1979 to the present. However, hindsight as usual being better than foresight, it seems that Xerox could have reached this same level of understanding and begun the resurgence as early as 1975.

1979-1987. 1979 began the resurgence of Xerox. This began when study missions went to study Fuji Xerox and other Japanese companies. The story that they brought back was deemed by many at Xerox to be almost incredible. The Japanese had one half of Xerox's manufacturing cost, their development schedule was one half as long, and it was being done with one half of the people on the product development teams. The Japanese quality was also much superior. By the measure of defective parts found on the assembly line the Japanese quality was ten to 30 times better than that of Xerox.

Armed with this new understanding Xerox has during the time period from 1979 to 1987 taken strong actions to improve their operations. These include the following:

- Reorganized copier development and production. New management was brought in at the top and production, development, and product planning were much more closely integrated
- Increased emphasis on competitive benchmarking
- Great increase in employee involvement
- Use of statistical process control in the factory and with suppliers
- Much earlier supplier involvement in the design process
- Great emphasis on customer satisfaction
- Reduction in the total number of suppliers and in inventories
- Increased emphasis on having a well defined and improved product delivery process for the development of new products
- Introduction in 1984 of a company-wide quality control (CWQC) movement that is known as Leadership Through Quality. This has been a huge implementation activity with 70,000 of the ten0,000 world-wide Xerox employees now trained.

This has been a huge undertaking on the part of Xerox with the intent of beating back the Japanese challenge. Xerox is one of the clear leaders in the United States making such a huge effort with considerable success.

This has been a successful period of resurgence for Xerox. The Xerox market share at the low end has increased from 8.6 percent in 1984 to 11.2 percent in 1986. Xerox likes to boast that it is the only company in the United States that has reversed the trend in market share relative to the Japanese without receiving government assistance. It should be noted that the low end copiers that Xerox now markets in the United States are mostly Fuji Xerox copiers. Xerox has made big improvements in manufacturing cost and quality, and has at least slowed down the Japanese intrusion into the more profitable segments of the copier business. Xerox reduced production costs by a factor of two, reduced the number of people in manufacturing by a factor of two, and improved quality in terms of defective parts on the assembly line by a factor of ten to 30. The ten-series copiers, which began with the ten75 in 1982, have been a considerable success.

With the major improvements that Xerox has made and with the reduction in value of the dollar from 260 yen to its value as this is written of 127 yen, Xerox appears to have staved off major inroads by the Japanese challenge. However, Xerox realizes that further and combined improvements will be required.

Summary. Xerox is an excellent example to study. In many ways it is a protypical U.S. company. It succeeded dramatically in the 1960s on the basis of patented technology. It then proceeded to lose much of its advantage because of the usual American problems of costs that were too high, quality that was too low, and a lack of focus upon customer satisfaction. It seems that Xerox made a strategic error about 1975 in not more clearly focusing upon beating back the Japanese threat. Since 1979 Xerox has been a leader in its resurgence from the typical American problems as they existed in 1979. Thus, Xerox is a good company to study for technological leadership, failures in design and production, and a present resurgence to greatly improve product development and production.

Proximate Causes

The MIT Commission on Productivity has identified several proximate causes of the difficulties that the manufacturing industries in the United States have encountered. In the following sections some of these proximate causes are discussed in terms of the copier industry. The copier industry in the United States has been dominated by Xerox, so this discussion will actually consist of an assessment of Xerox's performances.

Failures in Technological Practice. Xerox's failures in technological practice have been substantial. The pervasive spread of these failures in American manufacturing industries was probably accentuated in the case of Xerox by their easy success based upon the patented xerographic technology. There had been little motivation and therefore little emphasis within Xerox in its days of great success upon achieving low manufacturing cost, high quality, and strong responsiveness to the customers.

Manufacturing costs were excessive when Xerox first started on the path to improvement in 1979. The picture is dramatically described by the following excerpt from *Electronic Business* (October 1, 1987, p. 52):

> David T. Kearns, chairman and chief executive of Xerox Corp., still remembers the initial shock. Sure, he and his fellow executives knew that the Japanese had targeted their copier business. But it was not until they had actually completed their competitive analysis of their new rivals that they realized just how formidable a threat the Japanese would be.
>
> "We tracked them over a long period of time very carefully," the craggily handsome, energetic Kearns recalls. "We knew they were coming. But what really started us was when we really peeled apart their cost structure and found that they were basically selling machines for what it cost us to make them."
>
> Hundreds of American companies have faced the same nauseating moment of truth in discovering that their Japanese rivals have a more competitive cost structure. Like the others, Xerox would have to pay a price: a giant chunk of the copier business it has pioneered.

The excesses of Xerox manufacturing cost compared to the Japanese was due to both excessive production costs and poor design for low cost manufacturability.

In quality Xerox was also significantly inferior to the Japanese. As noted earlier, when measured by percent defective parts on the assembly line Xerox was worse than the Japanese by factors of ten to 30. In terms of more consumer oriented perceptions of quality the ratio was not so bad, but the Japanese were still clearly superior. In the caviar days of Xerox there had been little need to emphasize quality. The copiers were leased and the service cost was included in the lease price. There was no competition and therefore lack of quality was not considered to be a serious problem. In fact, there was even some thought that a large service business was a profitable thing.

What are the detailed causes of the excessive manufacturing cost and inadequate quality that existed in 1979? They are the same as in other major American manufacturing industries. Xerox was not in any way unique. Besides an excessive dependence on the superiority of new technological concepts, there were many detailed failures in design, optimization, and production operations.

Optimization. The process for optimizing new product designs and in bringing about improvement before the design actually entered production, was to a considerable extent chaotic and strongly contributed to extending the development time with only inadequate gains in quality and often with increases in manufacturing cost. Xerox had in the 1970s been a leader within the United States in developing a process of stress testing and operating windows to increase the operating latitude of the designs. This did in some cases bring dramatic improvements. However, it was not universally applied. Often the all too common approach of poke and hope was used until some important subassembly or module was seen to be in dire straits. Then, in some cases, specialists in the use of the method of stress testing and operating windows were called in, often with fairly quick and dramatic improvement. However, although this approach of operating windows and stress testing was dramatically successful in many applications, it was by 1983 recognized to be far surpassed by the developments of similar methods in Japan that had started as early as 1949.

The excessive reliance on trial and error, which in its best form became a rigorous process of problem reaction, led to large numbers of prototype iterations. While four iterations of prototypes may be a reasonable number for a product as complex as a copier, when this number did not bring success because of the inadequacies of a problem reaction approach, larger numbers of iterations were tried. This led to the necessity to shorten the duration planned for each iteration. The net result of this attempt to save the problem reaction approach by increasing the number of the iterations was to create swamps of prototype hardware in the development labs. The swamps often became so bad that for a significant period of time there would be little ability to do any systematic experimentation on the prototypes with the objective of actually improving the design. Similar failures to optimize also occurred with production process.

It should be emphasized that Xerox was not in any way pathological relative to other American companies in having these problems. In fact, as already noted, Xerox was to a considerable extent a leader in the development of stress testing and operating windows. However, the results of the average Xerox practice were inadequate, and clearly inferior to best Japanese practice.

Design. The Xerox designs were clearly excessive in manufacturing cost. They tended to have a large number of parts. They were not well designed for manufacturability. The beginning of the design in terms of the product specifications was usually not adequately responsive to requirements that would produce customer satisfaction. The initial concepts upon which the detailed designs were based were often quickly selected without adequate evaluation of the alternatives. Often much design work was done that was not production-intent design. There was great emphasis upon having a new design without adequate consideration as to whether it was a superior design. There was inadequate involvement of suppliers early in the design process. The product design and development activities were inadequately integrated with production operations. There was a liaison organization known as Advanced Manufacturing Engineering. Although good in intent, it served primarily as another layer of people between the people actually doing the design and the people actually doing the production.

Production Operations. There was excessive dependence upon inspection in the factory, on having large inventories, and upon having a large supplier base with multiple sources for most parts. Corporation between management and the union, although relatively good by American standards, had opportunities for improvement by comparison with the Japanese.

Beginning in 1979 these technological failures have been strongly attacked within Xerox. Much improvement has been made as noted above. As a small example, Design For Assembly (DFA) is now emphasized. Improvements have been made in all areas of technological weakness. Xerox clearly recognizes the need for further improvement.

Strategic Failures. It is probably correct to view the failure of Xerox to strongly defend the low end copier market in the period from 1975 to 1979 as a strategic failure. The decision seems to have been based primarily on the observation that profits were small in the low end of the copier business. To some extent it was a failure to take the Japanese competition with sufficient seriousness. By 1979, it was recognized that the Japanese were a major threat and that not combating them in the low end was leaving them free to establish a strong beachhead which they would then use to expand into the more profitable segments of the business. Failure to protect a market segment that is not very profitable, which will nevertheless serve as an entry beachhead for the Japanese, has been common to many American companies and industries. In the case of Xerox this apparently natural American tendency was reinforced by the tremendous success, and to a considerable extent the ease of that success, which Xerox had enjoyed throughout the 1960s and up until the Japanese onslaught on the low end copier business began in earnest around 1975.

Xerox is still ambivalent about personal copiers, which have emerged as the bottom of the low end copier market. Witness this excerpt from the previously mentioned interview with David Kearns, CEO of Xerox (*Electronics Business*, October 1, 1987, pp. 52-58):

One of the hottest new developments in copiers in recent years has been the personal copier, a business dominated by Canon and one in which Xerox does not even have a strong offering. Kearns was asked why Xerox does not market a personal copier.

Kearns: The reason is that we have not felt that we could figure out how to make much money in it. It's as simple as that. It's not clear to me—and I could be wrong on this—that the people who do that are making a whole lot of money in that area...I wouldn't say that we would never have one. But we're not going to do one just to say we've got one unless we can make money on it. Do you lose out on something by not participating in that market sector? Yes, there are losses. But the part of having a quality company is having quality profits...Do you lose something in the marketplace and in your image and so forth? The answer is absolutely yes. And we've had a lot of debates about that here.

Short Time Horizons. Short time horizons do not seem to have been a problem at Xerox. After all, the company in its modern and highly successful form was based on having a long time horizon and betting the company on the new xerographic technology. It took many, many years of investing every dollar that the company could find to bring this technology to commercial success.

The following quotation from Peter McColough, recently retired as CEO of Xerox, gives a clear picture of the emphasis upon foresight that has been a hallmark of Xerox. (*Xerox World*, Fall 1987)

Joe Wilson (McColough's predecessor as CEO and founder of modern-day Xerox) had tremendous foresight. He was always looking ahead. Joe emphasized to me over and over again that people—in their personal lives or in their business life—tended to grossly overestimate what they could do in the short-term. In Joe's judgement, there wasn't a great deal we could accomplish in the short-term. In the short-term about all you can do is to cut costs. But you can't do anything really fundamental. That goes for your personal as well as your business life.

On the other hand, Joe said, we grossly underestimate what we can accomplish in the long-term. If you really set your mind and your heart to accomplish something, either as an individual or in terms of your business development, you could do enormous things if you keep at it over the long-term.

This is the reason long-term goals are so important. The following excerpt from the recent article in *Electronic Business* (October 1, 1987, p. 58) provides added insight:

Background: This raises the basic question of long-term versus short-term focus. Are American companies, under pressure from investors, analysts, and profit-conscious directors, too concerned with quarterly earnings? It also raises the related issue of dividends. The Asia Advisory Service, Tokyo-based consultants, has compared the cost structure of U.S. and Japanese electronics giants (*Electronics Business*, November 1, 1986) and concluded that the single biggest competitive difference is dividend payout. IBM, for example, paid out 43 percent of its 1985 earnings in shareholder dividends, money that could otherwise be invested internally for competitive benefit or applied to subsidize pricing advantages. Xerox pays out even more of its earnings. With a common stock dividend of $3, Xerox paid put just under $300 million last year, an amount equal to nearly 65 percent of 1986 net income.

Kearns: Our dividend is high versus our current earnings. And we have kept it there because we believe we have a profit growth track that will grow us back into that as an appropriate dividend level....There are some financial structural differences that give the Japanese a competitive edge. I agree with that. But for the moment there is so much that we can do and need to do before you get, in my opinion, to that place. I do not see that as an excuse for our shortcomings yet.

...the problem is not convincing the board, not convincing the shareholders. It's convincing the people inside the company to change it. What I'm really telling you is that our pressures are not from the outside. Now, I agree that there is probably a little more short-term pressure frankly than I would like. But I will tell you that it's not the primary barrier...Excluding the economy, our destiny is in our hands, not someone else's.

Xerox also illustrated a commitment to long range thinking in its implementation of the company-wide quality control activity that is known as Leadership Through Quality. A large, high-level corporate committee developed this program in 1983, and its implementation started in 1984. At this time 70,000 of the ten0,000 world-wide Xerox employees have been trained. This is obviously a huge investment for which the payoff will primarily be in the future.

Xerox has not always been right. However, its mistakes do not seem to have been the result of excessive concentration on the short-term horizon.

Failures in Human Resource Management and Organization. The main failure in this category at Xerox was the rather large gulf that existed between important functional organizations. Product Design and Development and Production Operations prior to 1981 were excessively separated. There was also a large gulf between Product Design and Development and Product Planning. Although these three organizations clearly must cooperate in the product arena, in the Xerox organization prior to 1981 they did not come together until the corporate level was reached in corporate headquarters in Stamford, Conn. The actual operation suffered greatly from this lack of integration. There was far too much tended for product planning to be done and then thrown over the wall to product design and development who tendency to disown it and proceeded with a design that was not adequately responsive to the customers needs. The design was completed and then thrown over the wall to production operations with resulting lack of manufacturability. These splits in the organization tended to accentuate the problems that resulted from the above technological failures. This problem has largely been overcome by the reorganization within Xerox in 1981 and by many other improvements such as employee involvement.

Lack of Cooperation and Systemic Rigidity. This was certainly a serious problem at Xerox. It reinforced the organizational splits that have been noted above. In addition to the division of the organizations, there was little tendency on the part of individuals to emphasize cooperation. Of course, in day to day tasks people cooperated. However, there was little motivation to go beyond one's immediate function to seek cooperation. This became very evident to most employees when Leadership Through Quality was inaugurated in 1984. The Leadership Through Quality activity emphasizes a Quality Improvement Process. The first three steps of the Quality Improvement Process are:

1. Identify the unit of work
2. Identify customers (usually internal customers)
3. Identify the requirements for each customer

As Leadership Through Quality was inaugurated in 1984 and people were trained they started applying all aspects of Leadership Through Quality, including these first three steps of the Quality Improvement Process. It dramatically brought home to most people that they had long been working with little positive seeking of wide ranging cooperation.

Another example of lack of cooperation and systemic rigidity was the relationship between Xerox and suppliers. The relationship was often adversarial and the suppliers were not adequately brought into the design process. There seemed to be little cooperative tendency to try to build upon the expertise of suppliers. Rather, they were simply production houses which would make parts in accordance with Xerox design. Usually there were multiple suppliers for each part. This whole approach has now been greatly changed, starting with an activity in 1982 to reduce the total number of suppliers, involve the suppliers more in the design, and frequently have only one supplier for a part.

From 1978 until 1981 the product development group for copiers in Rochester, New York had a matrix form of management. Prior to 1978 the organization had a strong product orientation. This tended to cause problems with the implementation of the matrix management, which inherently had somewhat less power for product leaders. When the product development activities were reorganized in 1981, the matrix management was eliminated. Although the matrix management form of organization may or may not have had advantages, it seems that a major motivation for going away from the matrix management and to a much stronger product-oriented form of organization was the inability to achieve the levels of cooperation that would have best captured the strong points of matrix organization.

Summary of Proximate Causes. The failures in technological practice were by themselves sufficient to make cost, quality, timeliness, and customer satisfaction weak relative to Canon, Ricoh, Minolta, and a few other Japanese companies. The technological failures were aggravated by the weakness in strategy, human resource management and organization, and cooperation. Of course, these proximate causes are not independent. For example, the other tendencies towards strategic failure in 1975 (failure to respond to Japanese small copiers) were augmented by the perception that Xerox's costs would not be competitive, a technological failure. Xerox started responding in 1979, and has now achieved great cost reduction. Therefore, the 1975 perception was excessively passive and pessimistic. Combined with other factors, it was sufficient to cause a strategic failure.

In summary, these five proximate causes are not orthogonal, and a neat, precise decomposition is not possible. Technological failures were severe, and sufficient to cause major problems. Of course, Xerox was still the technological leader in terms of inventions (advanced development). However, in design, development, and production for specific products there existed the technological failures there have been described. It is difficult to judge if, in the absence of technological failure, the remaining proximate causes would have been sufficient to cause major problems.

Ultimate Cause

In addition to these five proximate causes, there perhaps are underlying causes. Joel Moses of MIT has put forth the thesis that cultural factors make it difficult for us to cope with change. This thesis seems to be supported by the following quotation from David Kearns, the present CEO of Xerox (*Electronics Business*, October 1, 1987, p. 56):

Kearns: To make the changes that are required has been much tougher than I would have guessed. It's not just that the competition continues to improve and that your standards keep going up because I think we understand that very well. But taking a large organization and then having to change measurement systems and change attitudes...The up-front investment and the training required to get people to change is huge. And it's much bigger than I personally anticipated and than I think most people in the company anticipated.

Summary

Xerox certainly should be studied by all American corporations wishing to recover from perceived problems and the threat of Japanese competition. Although much has been achieved, Xerox clearly recognizes that much remains to be done. The strong Xerox improvements coupled with the large drop in value of the dollar have greatly improved the ability of Xerox to compete with the Japanese. However, the Japanese are continuing to improve. Xerox has done well to improve itself, and again have substantial profits in the copier business. Continuous improvement must go on.

Proximate Causes: Summary

Introduction

Copiers, semiconductors, and computers are a far cry from the rust-belt industries that have encountered extremely rough going. There are no rusting factories and mills in these industries. Included are Xerox, Texas Instruments, and IBM; companies that during the past 20 years have been considered among the best in the United States. Still there have been problems, as revealed by serious inroads into market share by Japanese companies. Ironically, in these high-tech industries where the U.S. was long considered the leader, technological failures have been increasingly perceived as a major problem during the past nine years.

Technological Failures

It seems paradoxical. How can the U.S. be the technology leader, but be suffering from technological failures? The answer is that the U.S. is good at invention and other major technological advances, but weak at product realization. Product realization is:

Design

> Identification of customer need
>
> Concept generation and selection
>
> Detailed design for function and manufacturability.

Optimization (Design Improvement)

    Optimization of vital-few design parameters

    Mistake elimination from low-risk design parameters

    Tolerance design (selection of economical precision)

    Optimization of product process parameters

Production

    On-line quality control

    Wasteless production

The U.S. has been found to be weak at all of this when compared with the leading Japanese companies.

Typically U.S. companies have made the major technological advances. These have provided a dominant position for a period of time. The period was roughly ten years for xerographic technology, but much shorter for the other advances. After the period of dominance that was provided by the initial advance, product realization became dominant. This left the U.S. companies vulnerable, to be picked off when the Japanese companies arrived.

Increasing U.S. dependence on major technological advances has coincided with a great increase in venture capital. The change has been quite dramatic. Between 1974 and 1984, annual total venture capital commitments to new U.S. firms rose from $250 million annually to over $3 billion. Venture capital committed to high technology industries behaved similarly. Between 1975 and 1983, annual venture capital commitments to high technology manufacturing companies rose from $75 million to $1.6 billion. Between 1976 and 1983, the number of initial public offerings (IPOs) of U.S. high technology companies rose from $12 million to $1.5 billion. A substantial fraction of these high technology start-ups and IPOs, probably almost one half, were semiconductor, computer, and software firms. Yet during the same period which saw the formation and large scale financing of these firms, many of these firms licensed their technologies to Japanese competitors, and U.S. competitive advantage began to decline steeply in information technology and high technology generally.

This fragmentation has contributed to a more general trend. An increasing fraction of research, development, training, and technology generation is either explicitly available to all as a consequence of university or government policies, and/or is conducted by small start-up firms with little experience in multinational competition. Conversely in Japan government policy, private strategic coordination, and long time horizons combined to generate a strong, oligopolistic industry from an initial position of weakness. The Japanese government protected the domestic infant industry both from imports and from extinction by

IBM Japan, and also provided considerable direct and indirect subsidies to the industry. Both protectionism and direct financial support began in the 1960s, but have continued until quite recently.

In the information technology sectors and possibly several other U.S. high technology arenas, the United States increasingly has a specific place in the international economy. With the exception of remaining strategic competitors such as IBM, DEC, HP, Xerox, and other successful large firms, the splintered U.S. arena provides generic R&D, exports human capital and training services for advanced R&D and management activities, serves as a prototyping and market research testbed, and finally is an open mass market. Conversely, other manufacturing nations, with skill at product realization, long-term horizons, high savings rates, educated workforces, and high levels of governmental and/or private strategic coordination, import U.S. technology services and use them to reduce innovations to practice.

Thus, the U.S. companies' weakness at product realization has been reinforced by the opportunity for the most technically sophisticated people in the U.S. to concentrate on invention (advanced development) and start-up companies, make a bundle, and then move on when the hard slogging of product realization becomes the key to success. This may appear to be short sightedness. From the viewpoint of the total U.S. economy, it is shortsightedness. However, from the viewpoint of the individuals, they have been amply rewarded for sticking to the activity that they know and like, research and advanced development. It is not that they are intentionally being shortsighted. They are simply good at start-up, and poor at product realization. Perhaps if the rewards were changed, they would become good at product realization. However, that is not at all certain, as the required operating styles are very different. It is the mark of the Japanese success that they have attracted innovative intellectual leaders to the product realization process; e.g., Dr. G. Taguchi.

Other Proximate Causes

The technological failures alone have been severe enough to cause major problems. As noted earlier, the five proximate causes are not orthogonal, and precise decomposition is not possible. The other four proximate causes are present, and aggravate the problems that are already inherent in the technological failures.

Strategic Failure. Failures to take Japanese competition seriously enough at an appropriately early time is the main theme in strategic failures. This led to decisions by strong companies (e.g., Xerox and IBM) that were good enough to keep them ahead of domestic competition, but are now perceived as having left them vulnerable to Japanese competition in ways that could have been avoided.

Short Time Horizon. Although often cited, it is not clear that this has directly been a major cause for the industries that are the subject of this report. As noted above, success at research and advanced development (major technological advances), and weakness at product realization has produced an aura of shortsightedness. However, it is more accurate to describe this as technological failure.

As noted in the copier section, higher dividend payouts have been cited by the Asia Advisory Service as the biggest competitive disadvantage of U.S. electronic firms. However, David Kearns, CEO of Xerox, stated that this has not been a significant limiting factor. We are inclined to agree with Mr. Kearns. It seems unlikely that Xerox, Texas Instruments, IBM, and DEC have had shortages of capital as a major barrier to success.

Failures in Human Resource Management, Lack of Cooperation and Systematic Rigidity. Organizational and behavioral habits caused major schisms among major corporate functions; product planning, design, and production. Much has been done to improve this during the past nine years at major companies; e.g., Xerox.

The Japanese government provided assistance in coordination and the maintenance of a nurturing environment. This was clearly helpful, and may have been critical at certain times.

By one accounting reported by Marie Anchorduguy of Harvard Business School, between 1976 and 1981 alone direct Japanese government assistance to the domestic computer industry totaled Y206 billion (roughly $1 billion). Indirect assistance was even larger. Most indirect support came from subsidized loans provided through the Japan Electronic Computer Company (JECC), jointly operated by the government and the major Japanese computer producers. (Every president of the JECC since its creation in 1961 has been a retired MITI official.) Including such indirect sources, government support during the 1976-81 period apparently totaled Y748 billion, or nearly $4 billion. Direct assistance represented 25 percent of private expenditures for R&D and capital investment during this period; total support including loans equaled 92 percent of private sector investment. In earlier periods the relative size of such subsidies was even larger; direct assistance equaled 52 percent of private sector investment during the 1960s.

In addition, the Japanese government preferentially purchased machines from domestic producers. In 1982, 91 percent of the government's installed base came from domestic producers, versus 56 percent of the total installed national base. In that year, the government still represented 18 percent of total Japanese computer demand. In earlier periods, the government's role was more important. In the 1960s, MITI forced IBM to license its hardware patents, prevented other U.S. firms from establishing wholly owned subsidiaries, and forced second-tier U.S. firms to license their technology to Japanese producers in order to gain even modest access to the Japanese market. NEC's mainframe technology derives from licenses obtained from Honeywell in the 1970s; now, however, NEC's technology is superior to Honeywell's. NEC now owns 15 percent of Honeywell and supplies it with NEC's Honeywell-compatible ACOS mainframes and supercomputers.

MITI has not always been right. But it does appear that more cooperation among U.S. corporations on engineering and production processes would be helpful.

Also, the U.S. government appears to have had three policy deficiencies. First, the U.S. government has not ensured adequate supplies of the activities and resources (such as engineering education, foreign language training, and capital investment) necessary for high technology industries. Second, a number of U.S. policies, particularly with respect to tax and financial incentives, appear to favor new venture creation, short-term, and/or paper investments over efficient scale, long-term, productivity-increasing real investments. And third, the U.S. government has generally avoided reaction to foreign strategic behavior (such as Japanese market protection), increasing the likelihood that U.S. firms will choose second-best strategies such as licensing.

Ultimate Cause

As noted in the copier section of this report, Joel Moses of MIT has developed the thesis that behavioral patterns in the U.S. lead to inflexibility and difficulty in coping with change. Moses' thesis is summarized in the remainder of this section.

Why are there so many things going wrong simultaneously in the competitiveness arena? Is this an accident or are the various proposed proximate causes largely derived from one ultimate cause? The thesis is that it is the latter, and that the ultimate cause is related to cultural differences between Japan and the United States.

The cultural values that we claim affect competitiveness are an overemphasis on individualism, competition, and creativity in post-Renaissance societies. In contrast, societies with a larger mix of feudal values (e.g., Japan and, to a lesser degree, Germany) have an overemphasis on cooperation, for example. Each set of values is useful some of the time. Western values lead to better research and Japanese values to better group-oriented development. In principle we ought to be able to counteract the tendencies caused by the cultural values. We have, however, institutionalized them in our organizations, and this makes appropriate behavior extremely difficult, even when one knows that one's actions are suboptimal. For example, promotions, raises, and other incentives for managers in the U.S. are usually geared to rewarding recent actions and thus promote short-term behavior on the part of managers. Such incentives also tend to reward optimization of one's local group or division, rather than the overall corporation.

In contrast, the large Japanese corporations tend to make cooperative behavior a major goal for individuals. Promotions occur relatively slowly. It pays to know many people above you so that they may help in getting you the desired promotion. This leads to a large number of natural links in the Japanese company which is extremely useful when changes are needed in the structure of the organization.

Industry Trends and Future Competitiveness

Integrated Information Industry

A broad long-term process is underway in the entire digital systems sector. This general transformation of systems production and markets might be described as one of continually increasing scale economies and integration requirements, partially counterbalanced by the continuing appearance of new product markets as technical progress renders prior designs obsolescent. The transformation of information technology and product markets induced by the advent of VLSI is one specific case.

Continued growth in demand for information processing, in conjunction with continued progress in the scientific and technology bases which underlie it, imply continued growth and technological progress throughout the information systems industry. For the foreseeable future, semiconductor technology will probably be the largest individual contributor to this progress, though by no means the only one. Other areas undergoing technical change include digital optics and photonics, magnetics, superconducting materials, various communications technologies, software development and products, and pure systems science. The continued development of these technologies will lead to continued digitization of functions previously performed by analog, electrical, or electromechanical systems, and to the creation of progressively more complex digital systems and architectures.

The end result of this process may be more like a single, large digital information systems industry than the separate consumer electronics, computer, communications, copier, semiconductor, and publishing industries we see now. But whether or not there appears a single, integrated information technology sector, the progress of digital integration is already having substantial economic effects. Existing information technology industries are becoming more closely related to each other, more capital intensive, more highly highly automated, and more globalized. Given the comparative Japanese and U.S. structures and behavior described above, these trends will probably cause further deterioration of U.S. performance unless substantial remedial actions are taken.

Mature International Industry

Description. In addition to the trend towards integration, the information industry is becoming mature and international. Therefore, there will be further deterioration in the need for start-up companies that emphasize research and advanced development to capture a domestic market niche for a relatively short period of time.

The technology and cost structure of the systems industry is witnessing a long-term shift in favor of capital intensive flexible automation, high initial design costs, and high fixed costs of research, development, capital systems engineering, and customer service. Much of this transformation derives from the interaction of two trends: the increasing power of systems and their concurrently increasing complexity. Their combined result is the ability, but simultaneously the growing necessity, of using highly capital intensive, but ever more flexible, systems-based automation as a means of managing complexity and improving functionality. Similarly, product markets will be conditioned by tradeoffs between functional specificity, which is associated with high unit costs and high performance in specific applications, and commodity generality which provides flexibility, lower unit costs, and lesser performance in specific applications. The exploitation of computer-based flexible automation in production may shift product markets somewhat towards specialized functionality by reducing the cost penalty of low volume production of customized products. This trend is already visible, for example, in the rise of ASICs in the semiconductor market.

As these considerations become increasingly important, the principal systems technology bases, sectors, and markets—semiconductors, computers, software, and digital communications systems—are converging. All will become increasingly dependent upon capital intensive flexible automation as a design and production technology, and upon complex architectures and standards in product technology. Their technology bases will become increasingly common and interdependent, as similar systems sciences and production technologies, including systems technology itself, come to be employed in the design and manufacture of digital systems such as computers and software products. As these various sectors become more dependent upon architectures and flexible automation, they will remain or in some cases become dominated by the interplay between technical progress favoring new architectures, and learning economies favoring increased usage of existing architectures.

For example, as semiconductor technology continues to progress and the semiconductor market grows, integrated circuits are becoming more like systems. Semiconductor products are increasingly complex, and are progressively more dependent upon architectures and complementary software investments. Initial design costs are increasing; fabrication is increasingly capital intensive, computerized, and automated, yet more flexible as well. The result is increasing concentration of production combined, somewhat paradoxically, with increasing product differentiation within architectures.

Finally, the systems industries are internationalizing—in sourcing, production, markets, technology development, and interim alliances. This process of internationalization derives from several sources, some common to many industries now more global than previously, others particular to informational systems. One, of course, is the rise of foreign markets and competitors in arenas formerly dominated by American production and consumption. Another is the increasing capital intensity of the systems industry and the progressive shift of its cost structure towards initial and fixed costs. This renders global marketing, if successful, more attractive because it reduces long run average costs by permitting large investments to be averaged over large markets. Moreover, the increasing internationalization of other industries which consume systems tends to increase the comparative advantage enjoyed by those able to provide globally uniform products, standards, and service. This consideration also operates within the systems industries: as each globalizes, the others tend to do so in response.

Hence the major systems sectors—semiconductors, computers, digital communications, and software—show similar trends in technology, cost structures, and market behavior. All are becoming heavily dependent upon high initial cost, low marginal cost, capital intensive, highly computerized technologies. Frequently these technologies imply enormous fixed investments while simultaneously permitting greater flexibility in output. As a consequence design, architecture, planning, capital equipment systems, and capacity utilization will soon be the major determinants of premarketing costs. Marginal and direct labor costs will decline in importance, often to insignificant levels. Concomitantly, the boundaries separating various systems product markets will change and often blur. The various systems sectors and product markets will display a continuing process of confluence and re-differentiation, while becoming increasingly dependent upon a large, shared technology base.

These trends, and their interactions with strategic developments examined below, are of sufficient importance that the systems industry may change profoundly, albeit gradually, as a result. The emerging picture is of an industry dominated by three cost categories of fixed and/or initial costs—a) architecture and/or design, b) production systems design, development, and construction, and finally c) customer interactions such as sales, market research, training, consulting, and maintenance.

Data. The concentration, increasing capital intensity, and globalization of the systems sectors are already evident in their aggregate economics. The semiconductor industry has already been discussed, but a few statistical indicators merit review here. According to U.S. Commerce Department data, U.S. semiconductor shipments (i.e. SIC 3674) rose at an 18.5 percent compound annual growth rate (CAGR) between 1977 and 1982. However, total employment grew only 7.9 percent annually in the same period, and the CAGR of production employment was even lower (5.1 percent). Conversely, capital expenditures rose at a CAGR of 33 percent. The industry also continued its internationalization: for example, both imports and exports rose more rapidly than shipments. Other statistical series, for example those compiled by Dataquest and at MIT, support these propositions, as do more recent statistics. The MIT series, for example, indicates that the capital-labor ratio of U.S. based semiconductor production rose by 33 percent between 1980 and 1984. Available statistics indicate that Japanese capital intensity has risen even more rapidly.

Computer markets show similar behavior. While once again statistics must be regarded as approximate, the general trend is clear, and all statistical sources appear to agree. According to U.S. Commerce Department data, between 1972 and 1982, U.S. computer shipments grew from $6.5 billion to $36.7 billion, a compound annual growth rate (CAGR) of 19 percent. But production workers' total employment grew at a CAGR of only eight percent (from 65,000 to 140,000), i.e. less rapidly than shipments, while capital expenditures grew at a CAGR of more than 27 percent. Capital expenditures grew from $213 million (or 3.3 percent of shipments) in 1972 to $2.37 billion (or 6.5 percent of shipments) by 1982. Another statistical series compiled by NBER, primarily based upon Commerce Department data, indicates that between 1980 and 1984, the capital-labor ratio of the U.S. office equipment sector (SIC 3570-9) grew 54 percent.

Hence, while the available statistics are far from complete or wholly reliable, the evidence for increasing scale, capital intensity, and internationalization seems fairly clear. But these changes are occurring on terms unfavorable to the U.S. industries in question.

Product Realization: Key to Success

Introduction. Improved product realization will be the key to success for U.S. companies. Research and advanced development will be able to provide even less cushion (initial success period) than during the past ten years. U.S. companies will have to continue to improve their ability to slug it out on the product realization front.

Research and Advanced Development. The United States has long been, and is by far the largest producer of basic research. In 1973, the U.S. produced 38 percent of the world's scientific and technical literature. By 1982, the percentage had declined only modestly, to 35 percent of world research output. Aside from substantial declines in biology and pure mathematics, U.S. shares changed very little in the eight areas of natural science and engineering research surveyed by NSF in 1985. In contrast, patenting activity tells a very different story. U.S. shares of world patenting activity are declining, and far more rapidly than basic research output. Between 1975 and 1982, the U.S. share of world patent activity declined from 27 percent to 23 percent. Moreover, the U.S. roughly held its share or improved it in only two high technology areas surveyed by NSF, drugs and microbiology. In five others, U.S. shares declined steeply. Between 1975 and 1982, the U.S. share of worldwide new patent activity declined from 28 percent to 14 percent in robotics, from 47 percent to 30 percent in lasers, from 43 percent to 27 percent in integrated circuits, from 27 percent to 22 percent in telecommunications, and from 26 percent to 21 percent in internal combustion engines.

In contrast, Japan's aggregate share of world patent activity rose from 15 percent to 20 percent during the same period. Its share of integrated circuit patents rose from 18 percent to 48 percent; of laser patents, from 11 percent to 37 percent; of robotics patents, from nine percent to 13 percent; of telecommunications patents, 11 percent to 37 percent; of drugs, 16 percent to 20 percent. Japan declined only in microbiology, from 47 percent to 34 percent. Moreover, it is unlikely that Japan's rise can be attributed to any artifact of the Japanese domestic patent system, as has occasionally been suggested. Between 1969 and 1982, Japanese foreign patent applications rose 55 percent, while those of the United States declined 50 percent.

Yet the U.S. trade surplus in license royalties—i.e. net technology exports from the U.S. to other nations—remained very wide, and actually rose in both absolute and ratio terms. Between 1972 and 1982, the U.S. ratio of royalty receipts to royalty payments rose slightly from 8.7 to 9.9. In contrast, Japan's ratio of receipts to payments rose slightly but remained less than 0.7—i.e. Japan remained a net technology and license importer. The fact that U.S. net license exports were increasing even while the U.S. share of world patenting activity was declining rapidly suggests that the United States sells technology more freely than other nations, and that in fact its propensity to sell technology rather than to use it has recently been increasing. The same is not true, however, of Japan. Japan's royalty revenues remained less than one-eighth as large as those of the United States in 1982, and Japan's net technology trade was improving far less than its patent position.

And finally, it is noteworthy that U.S. exports of technology have increased rapidly while U.S. exports of high technology products have not, while again the converse is true of Japan. Between 1972 and 1982, the U.S. trade surplus in high technology products grew rather slowly, from approximately $7 billion to roughly $11 billion (in constant U.S. dollars), and has since become a deficit. Japan's high technology trade surplus grew from $3 billion to nearly $15 billion in the same period, and has continued to increase rapidly since. It is exceedingly unlikely, moreover, that a positive U.S. trade balance in technology could ever compensate for trade deficits in high technology goods.

Hence the picture presented even by the most general, highly aggregate statistics is of two very different national systems. The United States maintains an advantage in basic research; is losing its advantage in innovation; sells its inventions readily; and is losing its comparative advantage in commercial competition. Japan, on the other hand, performs relatively little university or basic research; is rapidly increasing its commercial innovation levels; sells little of its technology; and is increasingly successful in high technology markets.

Other trends in the functional distribution of activities, and in both horizontal and vertical market structure, are consistent with the proposition that investment patterns and incentive structures encourage commercial appropriability in Japan more than in the United States. Not only is a higher fraction of U.S. (versus Japanese) R&D devoted to basic as opposed to applied research, a far higher fraction is also military as opposed to commercial. While there is considerable controversy as to the commercial spinoff of military R&D, military R&D is surely on average much less effective for commercial purposes than explicitly commercial effort. Between 1971 and 1983, United States non-defense R&D rose from 1.7 percent of GNP to 2.0 percent. But Japanese non-defense R&D rose from 1.8 percent of GNP to over 2.6 percent of GNP during the same period. Since Japanese GNP grew far more rapidly than U.S. GNP during this period, absolute Japanese expenditures grew very rapidly indeed. Furthermore, the fraction of non-defense R&D which takes place in universities is larger in the United States than in Japan, where a higher fraction occurs in large firms. This generic U.S. research and human capital production base is readily available to Japanese firms, while Japanese corporate applied R&D is subject to far more strategic control.

Japan has also systematically provided itself with the capacity to use U.S. institutions, research, and knowledge. For example, between 1972 and 1983 the number of Japanese citizens studying in U.S. universities rose from less than 5,000 to approximately 13,000. In fact, the United States is already a substantial net exporter of world-class Ph.D.s in engineering and computer science. Approximately 20 percent of U.S. Ph.D.s in computer science, and 30 percent of Ph.D.s in engineering, are granted to foreign nationals who leave the country upon graduation. Between 1974 and 1983, MIT's total number of Japanese alumni grew from 233 to 475, Taiwanese from 81 to 179, mainland Chinese from 4 to 46, and Koreans from 29 to 67. Impressionistic evidence suggests an acceleration of these trends since 1983. About 25 percent of all corporate members of MIT's Industrial Liaison Program are now Japanese, the Program maintains a Tokyo office, and Japanese firms are widely agreed to be the Program's most sophisticated and aggressive users. In 1986, one MIT summer course in VLSI design had more Japanese than American enrollees.

In contrast, there are fewer than 1,000 U.S, students in Japan. Less than one-tenth of one percent of U.S. technical professionals speak Japanese. The United States graduates less than half as many BSEE's per capita as Japan, and Japan's production is continuing to increase while that of the United States is approximately constant. In many respects, furthermore, the U.S. university system mirrors the fragmentation of the start-up sector. Hence as Japan's interest in advanced research increases, it has begun to invest in, and use, U.S. universities through industrial affiliate programs, research support, and donations of Japanese equipment. The United States system, which by default formerly produced only for itself, now increasingly serves as a source of R&D, technology, technical standards development, and training for the world industry. Research projects, faculty consulting services, industrial affiliate programs such as MIT's Industrial Liaison Program, professional programs available through business schools and engineering departments, publications, and other university services are available on roughly equal terms to all organizations, whether domestic or foreign.

For example, several large software systems for VLSI circuit design and related functions—Crystal, SPICE, Macpitts, Magic, other—were developed at Stanford, Berkeley, CMU, and MIT and are now standard tools in many commercial firms. Berkeley UNIX, developed by U.C. Berkeley with DARPA funds, is available to any UNIX source code licensee for a trivial fee. The X Windowing system developed at MIT has recently become an industry standard for UNIX workstations, and MIT's NuBus architecture is also increasingly popular. The 1984 JTECH Panel report on computer science in Japan noted that BSD 4.2, the then-latest release of Berkeley UNIX, was widely used in Japan. Several recently announced Japanese engineering workstations employ Berkeley code, including its networking support and file system improvements.

A number of software technologies (languages, software development techniques) and novel machine designs have also originated in American universities. Many other architectures and standards were developed by U.S. government agencies, private firms, or standard bodies such as the American National Standards Institute. Most of these are now openly available worldwide, as a consequence of U.S. government procurement policies, standardization conventions, intellectual property law, and industry structure. For a large fraction of the computer and software markets, these standards in effect constitute product specifications available to any imitative manufacturer.

Hence, from the point of view of a Japanese or Korean multinational, a wide variety of activities— personal defections from major U.S. firms, licensing from U.S. start-ups, advanced education, and university research efforts themselves—increase the technology portfolio available on the open market in the United States. And because these activities do not penetrate the Japanese or Korean arenas, they represent little direct risk to potential competitors, either through market competition or domestic strategic disarray in R&D, technology control, personnel training, or government policy arenas.

So by nature of their subsidized efforts, institutional incentives, and fragmented structure, American start-up and university sectors collectively provide R&D, technology assessment, and market research services as worldwide public goods. They also provide access to the technologies and markets themselves, skilled labor, and a variety of information services for would-be strategic entrants. Start-up activities collectively characterize novel markets, their growth rate, potential size, ands relative demand for various product attributes. Entrepreneurial instability lasts until an internal leader emerges, large firms enter, or both. In either case, however, major firms are able to observe the entire distribution of start-up activity.

Then, as the market reaches substantial size, the U.S. and Asian multinationals enter and compete for the mature market; but U.S. firms must contend with the start-up sector and the fragmentation of the American arena as well as with foreign competition. Whereas start-ups rarely obtain strong positions in Japanese and Korean markets, they do sometimes represent significant competitive pressure within the American market. Furthermore, American start-ups are generally more valuable for Asian firms than for American oligopolists such as IBM. Asian entrants, unlike established U.S. firms, often have little previous experience in advanced American systems markets. Hence start-ups provide information and direct assistance which cannot easily be obtained by observing oligopolists such as IBM, as a consequence of their vertical integration and attention to protection of proprietary information.

To summarize research and advanced development:

1) U.S. is still the leader,

2) Japan is moving up fast,

3) A significant part of the U.S. work benefits Japan and other countries.

Product Realization. As the information industry matures, research and advanced development is increasingly unable to achieve major technological advances that increase the performance/cost ratio sufficiently to offset weaknesses in product realization. For U.S. electronic information companies to be successful in the international economy during the period leading up to the 21st century, product realization skills will have to be emphasized.

The product realization process must continuously and rapidly be improved in all of its elements:

- Listen to the voice of the customer.

- Select invulnerable concept.

- Quickly design production-intent product that is superior to all existing designs in function and manufacturability.

- Optimize critical design parameters early to achieve product performance that is robust against noises (unwanted production and environmental variations).

- Select most economical precision level for production processes and components.

- Optimize production process parameters.

- Control quality during production to minimize total cost.

- Avoid waste in the factory. (Waste results from excess space, people, inventory, capital, scrap, rework, and adjustments.)

- Manage the process to achieve holistic actions that prevent problems.

The U.S. cannot expect leadership in research and advanced development to be able to offset weaknesses in the above product realization capabilities. There is no escape. We must slug it out in the product-realization trenches.

Billions of Current Dollars

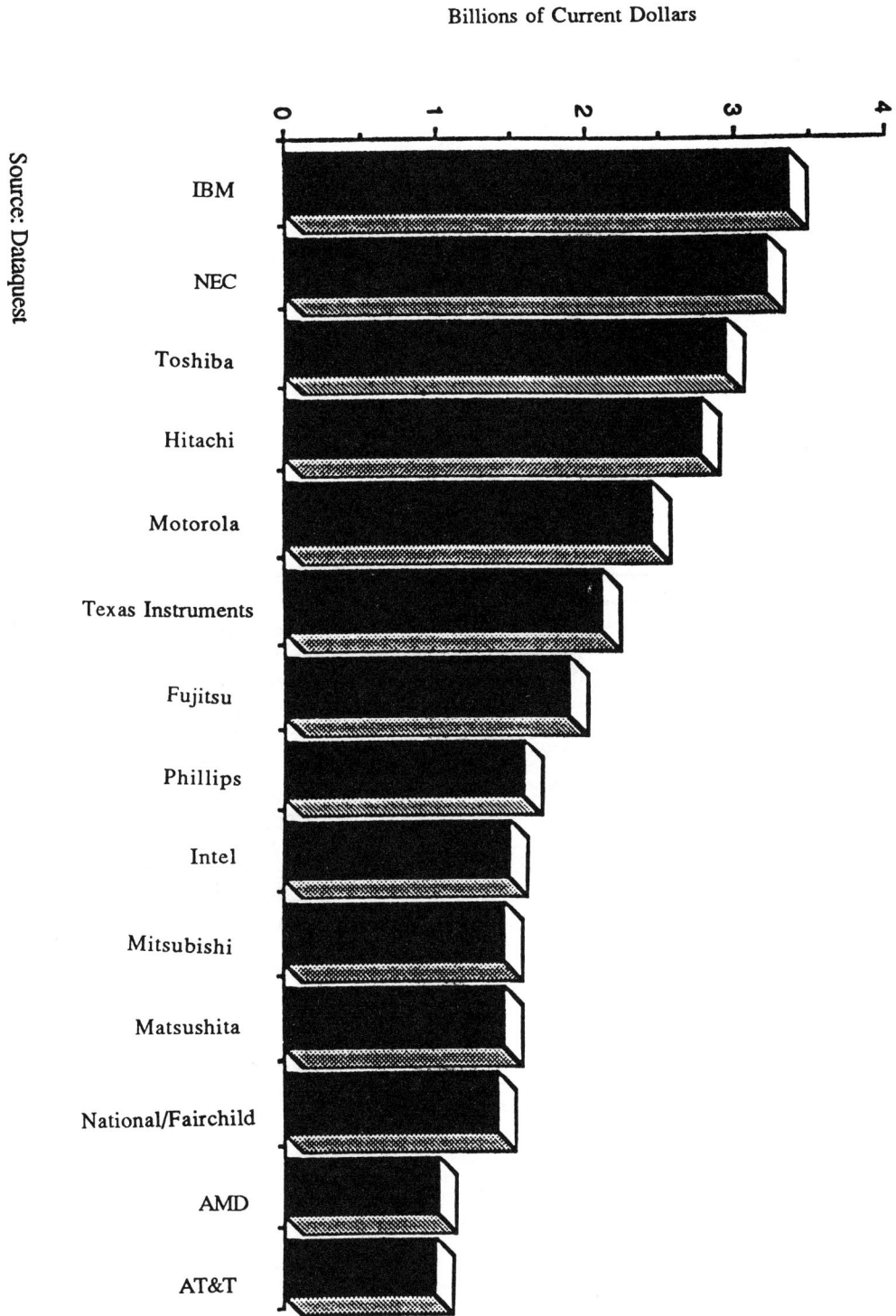

Source: Dataquest

Figure 1. 1987 Semiconductor Production or Revenue by Firm

Figure 2. Productivity: Computers and Semiconductors

U.S. Trends In Total Factor Productivity, Type 2, 1960 to 1985.

■ 3674: Semiconductors and Related Devices
▨ 3573: Electronic Computing Equipment

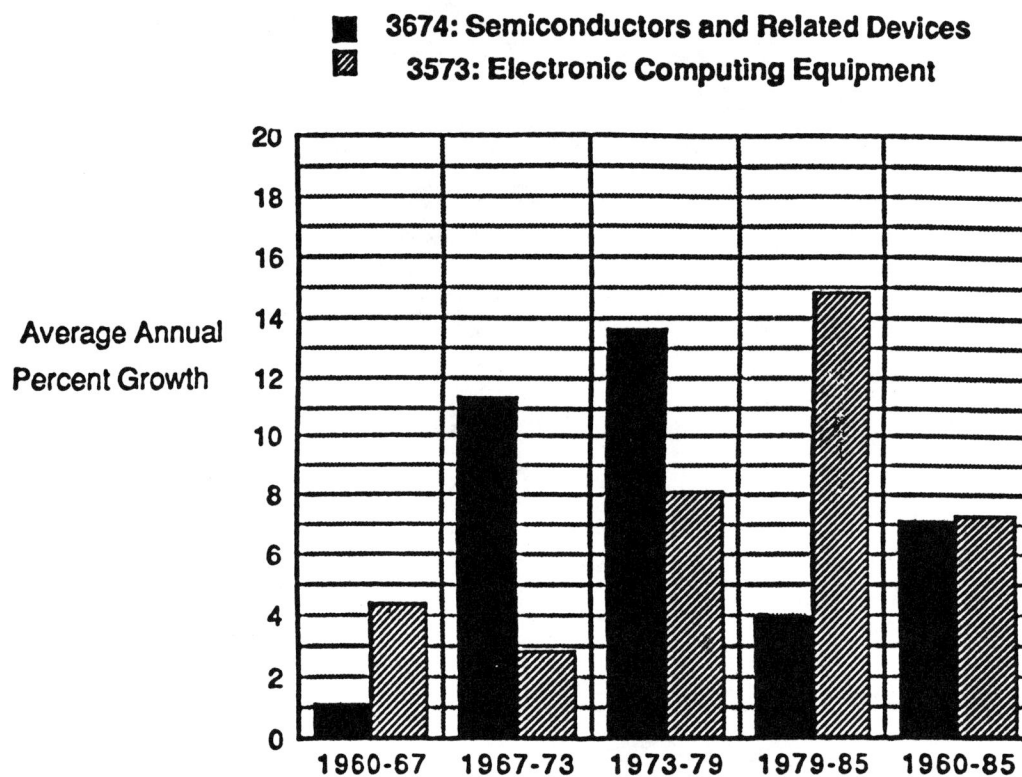

Figure 3. Shipments: Computers, Semiconductors, and Copiers

Value of U.S. Shipments

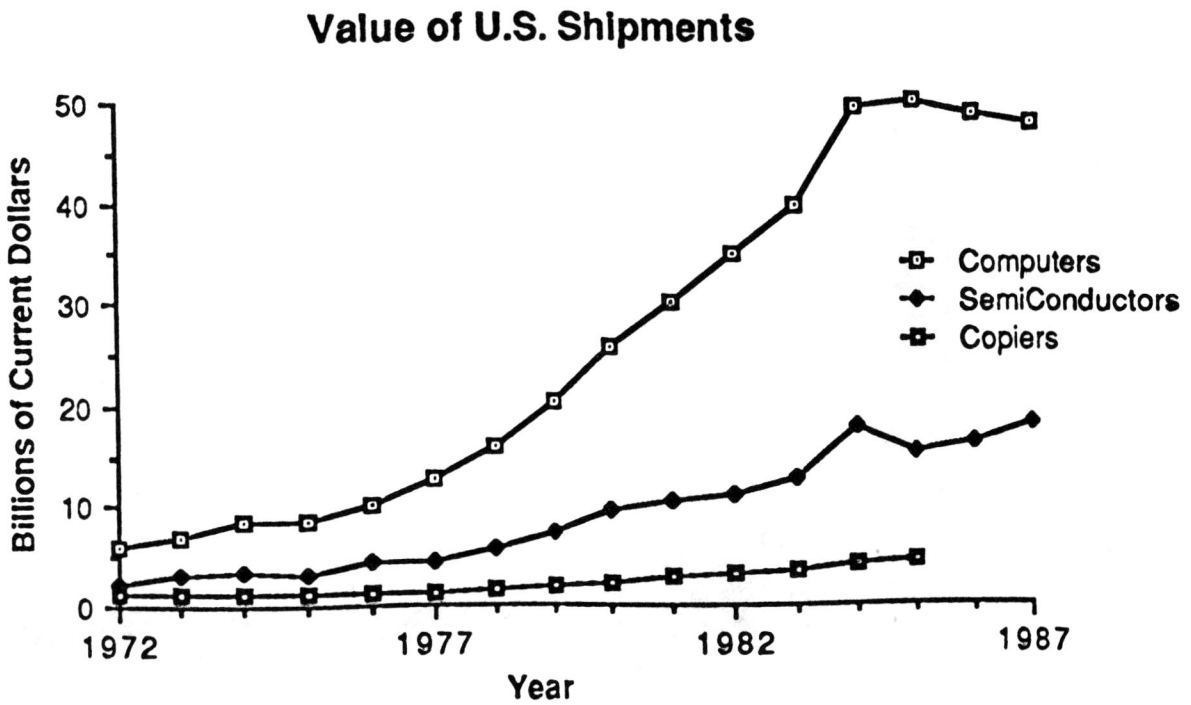

Figure 4. 1986 Total Computer Sales by Company
(including Hardware, Software, and Services)

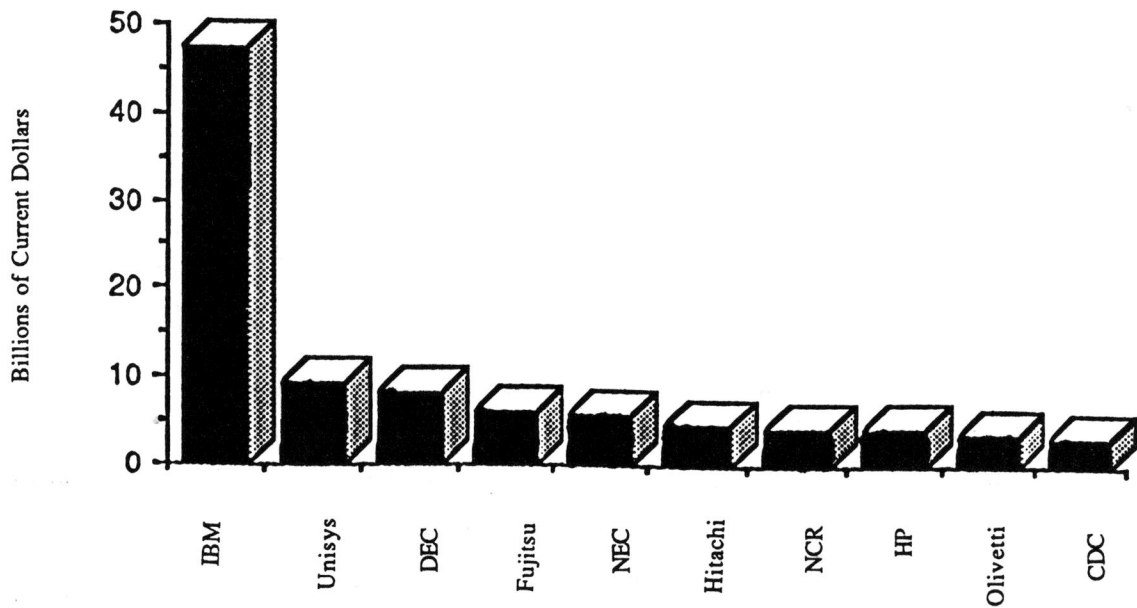

Source: Datamation Magazine

MIT Commission on Industrial Productivity
Working Paper

The US Machine Tool Industry and its Foreign Competitors

Prepared by
Artemis March

for the
Commission Working Group on the Machine Tools Industry

Kent Bowen, Chair
Dimitri Antoniadis
Gabriel Bitran
George Chryssolouris
David Hardt
Eric Von Hippel
Ronald Latanision
Artemis March
Lester Thurow

Research Assistant
John Lin

Table of Contents

List of Tables

List of Figures

Aknowledgments

This report benefitted enormously from numerous site visits, interviews, and conversations. Senior officials promptly returned cold calls, invariably extended invitations to visit their companies, and often spent several hours with the author. Other extremely busy people also gave generously of their time, and shared their experiences, knowledge, ideas, and provided names of other people to contact. Their graciousness and cooperation is deeply appreciated.

In particular, Carolyn Castore provided me with an introduction to the industry and its issues, provided a great many names, and continued an invigorating dialogue as my thinking evolved. Helmut Hammer made it possible for me to attend the International Machine Tool Show in Milan on very short notice. Hans Kief made the frustrating and time-consuming task of setting up a European trip much easier, provided entree to several German builders, and was himself an outstanding informant. Later in the process, Dr. Eugene Merchant engaged in a very stimulating dialogue, shared his wisdom and his international perspective, and gave careful reading and thoughtful feedback on the manuscript.

Several other people who helped me to get a feel for the industry included Howard Greis, Clem McIver Sr., Richard Newman, and Fred Waters. Executives who were particularly gracious with their time included Jim Koontz, Helmut Maschke, Ernst Raiser, Jeurgen Richter, Dick Messinger, and Walt Lewis. Readers who took particular care with feedback were MaryEllen Kelley, Frank Reintjes, Nate Cook, Eugene Merchant, Ralph Cross, and Alex Slocum.

While these and other conversations greatly enriched the report, responsibility for accuracy and interpretation rests with the author.

Introduction

The drastic decline of the domestic machine tool industry has provoked widespread concern, not merely about the industry itself but also about American manufacturing competitiveness in general. The concern is not narrowly economic; the 60 percent drop in industry shipments between 1981 and 1983 is not so unusual for this wildly cyclical industry. What is unusual is that although U.S. manufacturers are again buying capital goods, only half of their machine tool purchases are from domestic builders. The long-term viability of the domestic industry is being questioned; indeed, many have already written it off. But it is not only the survival and competitiveness of the domestic machine tool industry that is being challenged. The lack of international competitiveness of many, if not most, domestic producers has direct implications for the competitiveness of American manufacturing as a whole.

Industry Overview

Scope and Significance of Machine Tool Industry

What are Machine Tools? Machine tools are "power-driven machines, not hand held, that are used to cut, form, or shape metal." Most studies of the industry, including the present one, define the core of the industry as equipment that cuts or forms metal. Metalcutting tools remove metal in the form of chips from the workpiece. They include gearcutting machines and all sorts of grinders, but the high-volume cutting activities are milling and turning. Metalforming tools use large presses and dies to either shear one portion of metal off from another; or to deform, compress, bend, stamp, draw, or extrude metal into new forms. Metalforming alters only the shape, but not the mass, of the metal (i.e., no chips are formed). (See Appendix A for a fuller description of these activities.)

Defining the industry through the type of interaction between tool and workpiece has its limitations for doing research, however. Unless researchers can collect their own data, they must draw primarily from hard data collected by governments and trade associations that has been clustered under metalcutting and metalforming headings, and secondarily from studies conducted by other researchers on specific topics. The aggregate data allow us to track movements of complete machine tool products according to their function, but do not allow us to track more meaningful business and technical distinctions, and fail to capture a broader emerging industry and some of its most significant trends. The studies shed light on some of those trends, and sometimes cluster their data in more meaningful ways (general purpose versus special purpose, standalone versus systems, numerical control versus manual control) than cutting and forming. The present study draws upon both the aggregate data and earlier studies, as well as field work conducted with American and foreign (particularly West German) builders. (Industry definition issues, and the methodology followed by this report are discussed in Appendix A.)

Strategic Importance of Machine Tool Industry. Machine tools turn castings, barstock, or sheet metal into finished components. Machine tools are thus the critical link between intermediate products formed from raw materials and finished discrete components. These components are then assembled either into end products or into yet other machines that will in turn make end products. For example, machine tools are used to mill engine blocks and hone cylinder bores, to grind the slides and ways for other machine tools, and build parts for injection molding machines, textile machinery, or automated assembly equipment. Virtually every manufactured product is built, directly or indirectly, by machine tools.

It is this position at the heart of the manufacturing infrastructure that makes the machine tool industry, small as it is, so critical to a nation's manufacturing competitiveness and productivity. The capabilities of machine tools—their precision, repeatability, reliability, and speed—will determine to a significant extent the quality and manufacturing costs of the users' components built with them. Machine tools that cannot consistently hold precise enough tolerances will produce parts that are not good enough to give the performance required of their end product. Machine tools whose uptime is limited by frequent machine failures, unavailable spare parts, and poor product support will drive up users' costs and drive down their productivity. Machine tools that trade off speed for precision will produce parts that may be too costly for many customers.

Given the intensification of international competition, many users are scrutinizing the performance and productivity of their machine tools as never before. As a result, many domestic manufacturers have turned to foreign machine tool builders for varying combinations of performance, reliability, delivery, cost, and service reasons. Some foreign purchases have been driven by the perception that the requisite performance can only be achieved through using foreign tools. For example, General Motors (GM) has recently ordered 100 new presses, 88 of them from West Germany and Japan, citing their efficiency; die changes, for example, take five minutes instead of eight hours. GM also bought large CNC horizontal milling centers from the West German builder, Scharmann, because of their perceived superior ability to hold tolerances across an enormous range of part sizes, and bought transfer lines for drilling and boring connecting rods from Nabenfabrick Alfing Kessler. Pratt & Whitney has accelerated its purchase of foreign machine tools from ten percent to 25 percent through investments such as $60 million dollars for creep feed grinders purchased from both Hauni-Blohm and Elb in West Germany; no such machines/systems are available from domestic builders. In other cases, the terms (especially delivery and/or price) make the foreign machines more attractive. For example, Pratt spent another $11 million on five-axis milling machines from Japan because it could not get delivery from domestic builders in time to meet its own needs. Kingsbury Machine Tool bought a special grinder from the Italian firm Favretto; although upset that it could not "buy American," Kingsbury would have had to wait two years and pay three times as much for a product comparable to Favretto's from whom it took delivery in four months.[1]

The significance of these foreign purchases is not simply lost sales or lost opportunities for domestic builders. The significance lies in the fact that in many of these and other cases, domestic buyers felt they had no choice but to go overseas in order to get the performance they needed when they needed it. That is, American builders either cannot provide the leading edge equipment that domestic manufacturers believe they need to remain competitive or regain competitiveness, or they are unable to do so within acceptable price/delivery limits. The real twist, however, is that users' international competitors have often had access to the same leading edge equipment a year or two ahead of the American manufacturers. The director of a recent GM study on machine tools laments:

> If you buy the very best from Japan, it has already been in Toyota Motors for two years, and if you buy from West Germany, it has already been with BMW for a year-and-a-half.[2]

The critical implication here is that domestic user industries that are dependent upon foreign machine tools for manufacturing key components will chronically lag their foreign competitors, and perpetually be trying to catch up rather than to lead. If one's machine tools lag, so also will the downstream equipment and products that depend upon them. This, then, is why the machine tool industry is so important to all of domestic manufacturing competitiveness.

Recent Performance of the U.S. Industry

The domestic industry rode a world-wide boom that crested during the 1979-81 period, only to see its orders and shipments plunge dramatically during the next few years of economic recession. What stands out about the 1985-87 recovery is that the U.S. has rebounded less strongly that have any of the other major machine tool producers. This relatively poor rebound belies weaknesses in the domestic industry that predate both the boom and recovery.

Shipments. U.S. shipments are far below their $5.1 billion peak of 1981 (see Table 1). World industry sales recovered to an all-time high of $29 billion in 1986 (current U.S. dollars), but U.S. shipments of complete new tools have recovered only to $2.8 billion (see Figure 1). From being the world's largest producer with nearly 20 percent of world shipments in the 1960s, the U.S. now make less than ten percent of the world's machine tools, most of them sold domestically. When units rather than dollars are counted, the picture is equally or more dismal (see Table 2). Steep declines in units sold cannot be explained away by the greater productivity of newer units (and thus the need for fewer of them), because of the simultaneous rise in imported units.

Consumption. The post-recession market remains far below peak (see Table 1). Although secular shifts in the size of the market are difficult to disentangle from the cycle of boom, recession, and recovery, most observers believe this valley reflects, in part, a permanently shrinking market. Factors contributing to this decline include the loss of domestic metalworking customers who have either closed their doors, gone offshore, or seen their own market share decline; the substitution of plastics, composites, and other materials for metal; improvements in near net shape casting and forging that reduces the amount of machining necessary to bring a part to final dimensions; and the greater productivity of new machine tools that allow a given amount of work to be done by fewer machines.[3] Of these factors, loss of onshore markets has had the biggest effect to date; customers who have gone overseas to manufacture, or whose own sales have plunged or disappeared (e.g., automobiles and consumer electronics) have reduced the domestic market for machine tools. In the future, materials substitutions and alternative processes for creating a finished part will continue to increase in significance, further eroding the domestic base for metalworking tools.

Imports. Between 1964 and 1986, machine tool imports rose from four percent of U.S. consumption to nearly 50 percent. Most of this increase has occurred since 1977, and continued even during the recession. This dramatic change is due largely to the enormous influx of machine tools from Japan since the middle 1970s. Japanese producers now account for over half of American imports (and thus one-quarter of consumption). While Japanese imports have taken market share at the expense of America's European trading partners, the dollar volume of European imports has also continued to rise from their pre-recession highs (see Figure 2).

Deeper inroads have been made into metalcutting, which comprises about three-quarters of the industry both domestically and worldwide, than into metalforming. General purpose CNC Lathes and machining centers—the two export areas first targeted by the Japanese—have shown the deepest import penetration as well as the most rapid (see Table 2). Although metalcutting has been harder hit, note from Table 3 that metalforming penetration has also increased, and that Japan is taking both volume and share from the West Germans.

The axis of import trading relationships has shifted from being overwhelmingly European to predominantly Asian (see Figures 2 and 3, Table 3). America still imports as much and usually more from the Europeans, but it imports still more from the Japanese, Taiwanese, and Koreans. In other words, America imports the same kinds of things it always did—specialized, super-precision machines from the Germans, Swiss, and now also the Italians. But now it also imports products to fill needs it used to fill for itself: from the Japanese, general purpose, standalone numerically controlled (NC) machines for milling, turning, and surface grinding, as well as presses for forming; from the Taiwanese and Koreans, manual and NC lathes, drilling machines and other low-end products.

Exports. The speed at which imports have overtaken the U.S. market has been complemented by its deteriorating ability to export. The U.S. has exported 15-18 percent of its production for most of the past 20 years. But since world shipments have expanded while America's have declined, exports now account for a much smaller part of world consumption and world exports (see Figure 4). Closer examination of the composition of these exports reveals that at least 40 percent are parts rather than new machines (parts were but 20 percent of exports in the 1960s)—a testimony perhaps to the longevity of old American machines but not to success in marketing new ones. One particular factor that has contributed to export declines is the loss of Soviet markets. As Ralph Cross, former chairman of Cross & Trecker, has repeatedly pointed out, the U.S.S.R. does not understand why the U.S. treats it less favorably than other nations in trade matters (i.e., does not apply most-favored nation principles), and denies them use of the Export-Import Bank. The West Germans, Japanese, and Italians, meanwhile, do not irritate the Soviets and help them finance purchases of machine tools and other goods.[4]

Technological and Market Trends

Globalization and International Strategies. Exporting has made the machine tool industry a global one, and success in this global business now requires effective exporting. While less than 30 percent of world production was exported 20 years ago, by 1976, exports were nearly 43 percent of production, and now they are close to half. All the European countries trade extensively—particularly with each other—and the West Germans have consistently led the world in exporting machine tools; the Swiss and Italians also do an excellent job with exporting. The Japanese, now the world's largest producer, is challenging West Germany's position as top exporter (see Table 4). Most of these four countries' imports come from one another, as each country has producers whose outstanding products are difficult or impossible to reproduce at home, whether for technical or economic reasons, or both. The success of these countries in exporting only magnifies the failure of U.S. firms to increase their volume and share of the world market.

Globalization has been brought about through reductions in trade barriers, efforts to counter domestic cyclicality, and European and Asian effectiveness in capitalizing on what they do best. The Europeans specialize in precision-engineered and custom-engineered products whose performance capabilities are outstanding and often unique. The Swiss, for example, were originally driven by their precision watch industry, and now by other precision equipment users; the West Germans developed sophisticated specialized products to meet the demands of diverse engineering industries; the Swedes responded to their ball- bearing manufacturers. Significant world market share is essential if these builders are to have enough volume to profitably produce specialized equipment for their niches. They are therefore driven towards export-consciousness and consistent exporting efforts. The Japanese, by contrast, did not aim for high-performance niches, but for consistent, reliable, low-cost, standard products that many kinds of firms could use. Initially lacking the expertise to develop high-performance equipment, they emphasized different dimensions of "quality"—namely, conformance and reliability.[5] They concentrated on fewer types of general purpose products for higher volume markets, simplified and standardized their designs, and refused to customize their standard products, thereby gaining economies of scale and lower costs, and used pricing policies that capitalized on the cost differentials. The result has been rapid growth in world market share for many of its products.

In the last few years, the Japanese have ceded cost leadership at the very low end to the Koreans, Taiwanese, and Brazilians. These newly industrializing countries (NICs) first picked up production ceded by the industrialized nations of manual, standard tools such as lathes and drills. Increasingly, however, NICs are shifting more and more of their production, and especially their exports, to NC tools.[6]

The resulting international positioning of various countries for the late 1970s-early 1980s is depicted in Figure 5, where technological sophistication is defined in terms of engineering precision and robustness. As will become evident in later sections, the dynamics of the late 1980s—particularly the emerging Japanese strategy—would affect placement on these dimensions, or could suggest other dimensions. The main purposes of these schematics is to point up the lack of a distinctive competitive advantage or international strategy by the U.S. as a whole, and to contrast this with the distinctive advantages that the Europeans, Japanese, and NICs have established in the recent past (or earlier, in the European case).

In addition to exploiting comparative advantages and exporting, international strategies encompass joint ventures and overseas plants. The former have been sought by many American firms, while Japanese and European companies are increasingly establishing overseas plants, particularly in the U.S.

Many U.S. builders and distributors have reacted to the recent Japanese invasion by forming a variety of licensing and distribution agreements. In many cases, the U.S. builder brings in a certain number of foreign-made machine tools per month or year, often under its own name (see Table 5). Such agreements fill out product lines and often bring more profit in the short run than could be earned by selling American machines. In the long run, however, this approach cedes the capability for designing and building low-cost, competitive products.

Increasing numbers of foreign builders have elected to open plants in the U.S. Yamazaki Mazak has a highly automated plant in Kentucky, Hitachi Seiki opened a plant in 1980, and Okuma recently opened a plant in North Carolina. Initially, Okuma is assembling 30 CNC lathes and 15 machining centers monthly from Japanese components, but will move to U.S. up fron production of key components and build long-term relationships with American vendors while moving towards higher production rates and then to cells and FMSs. Miyano Machinery, Ikegai, and Okamoto Corp. are also beginning U.S. operations with assembly and plan to move into fabrication and significant U.S. content. Europeans are also investing in overseas plants. For example, Trumpf, a leading West German producer of flexible sheet metal machining and laser equipment, has opened several overseas plants, including one in Connecticut. Although it has only

2100 employees worldwide, Trumpf is firmly committed to overseas plants as a fundamental part of its strategy, and already has eight.

Implications of Programmable Automation Technologies. The most significant set of technological developments affecting machine tools during the past thirty years has not been advances in machining *per se*, but in the control and environment of machine tools. Beginning with NC these programmable automation technologies have used computers to control the operation of the machines. (See Appendix B for description of NC, CNC, and FMS, and comparisons with manual machining.) This family of technologies has opened up the possibility for flexible automation among batch manufacturers (for whom hard automation was inappropriate). Since 70 percent of discrete parts manufacturing is estimated to be batch production, the great majority of manufacturers are now candidates for at least partial automation of their operations. Because CNC and FMS are reprogrammable, they are particularly useful for certain types of discrete parts manufacturing: small/medium batch sizes, especially if they are run repeatedly; high part variety, especially if they are also technically related; and complex and/or high precision parts.[7]

With this opportunity, however, comes a whole new set of requirements and implications. The mechanical engineering technology base of machine tool builders is no longer adequate by itself. Electronics skills are essential to build controls, interface with the machine, and provide customer support; programming skills are necessary to develop software, and users need sufficient programming skill to program their parts. Whereas most users had been able to maintain their manual machine tools themselves, electronic controls and software are far more complex, and, at first, were far less reliable; thus needs for customer support have skyrocketed. Not only do users require after-sales support, but they look to builders to integrate their system; increasingly, they want "turnkey systems."

These requirements have in turn created new opportunities for responsive builders and for new players from outside the traditional builder structure and technology base. A large set of new players is based in electronics, computers, or information services. Their focus is on the software technology (and sometimes related hardware) that controls and integrates machine tools and other factory automation equipment. They include Allen-Bradley and General Electric (GE), both of whom tried to leverage success with programmable logic controllers to get into NC and CNC controls, and, in GE's case, an overambitious attempt to produce the entire "factory of the future." New electronics-based players also include Digital Equipment Corporation (DEC), now working with Italy's foremost builder, Comau, to link every element of the automated factory; and Big Eight accounting firms who believe their familiarity with information systems allows them to integrate factory systems. These systems integrators can tap resources and skill bases outside the scope of traditional builders, but often lack the indepth understanding of machining and manufacturing to produce products or systems that perform as advertised.

Engineering-based firms have also seized opportunities in service, engineering applications, and systems integration. These engineering-based systems integrators differ from the electronics- and accounting-based systems integrators because they bring extensive experience with manufacturing processes, materials, and equipment to understanding the customer's problem and devising tailored solutions. They put together systems using components from different vendors and provide extensive up front applications work; increasingly, the machine tools in their packages are from the Far East. Although they must move product to make a profit, they see themselves as selling solutions and developing processes rather than selling hardware; traditional builders, by contrast, are still more likely to see themselves primarily as hardware producers. (A minority of traditional builders are, however, also making the shift to selling solutions and providing value-added service with their products.)

Other new players have also capitalized on opportunities that many traditional builders either lacked the foresight to envision, or lacked the resources (in people, skills, and funds) to develop. Some niche players, like Lehr Precision Tool, are developing new processes that compete with traditional machining methods. Lehr specializes in CNC electro-chemical machining (ECM), a process that is cost-effective for complex parts made from hard-to-machine materials (such as titanium components for jet engines) because it eliminates several slow operations. Such work requires a highly technical staff (including chemists, electrochemists, materials scientists, mechanical engineers, and ecologists) who must work together to advance generic ECM development and develop specific customer applications. Few traditional builders have such a spectrum of people, and are unlikely to pursue niches that cut into their traditional machining stronghold.

Several types of players then have understood the opportunities provided by new PATs and moved to fill them. To a large extent, they have come from outside the ranks of traditional builders, although some of the latter are responding as well. These players have diversified their skill base to provide the breadth and depth required to develop sophisticated new processes or to integrate different pieces of equipment for multiple applications. These players have heard the customer who wants a process or a solution, not just a piece of equipment. They have appreciated the importance of value-added services as both a marketing tool for products, and as a potentially profitable, though often risky, venture in its own right. In short, they are building around the remains of the traditional machine tool industry towards a new broader manufacturing process equipment industry.

What Caused the Collapse of the Domestic Machine Tool Industry?

The recent collapse of the domestic machine tool industry has its foundations in a whole system of structural, relational, managerial, and institutional issues. These interrelated factors involve not only builders, but also their customers, American technical schools and universities, and government policies or the lack thereof. Indeed, the roots of the problem are deep within the infrastructure of post-war American manufacturing, education, and culture.

These interrelationships are diagrammed in Figure 6. This map is built around three issues: cyclicality, fragmentation and parochialism, and low rates of product and process innovation. The map is most easily read by starting with those three boxes, and following the arrows that lead to their major sources and results. These three predominantly left-to-right clusters focus on the builders (both as an industry and as firms making choices) and their customers. Around this core, the map represents other key institutional factors that have played an enormous role in the decline of the American machine tool industry: universities, the federal government, and the capital market structure. The organization of this section corresponds to this map. We look first at the basic structure of the industry (fragmentation and cyclicality) and management decisions that grew out of this structure. Then we look at product and process innovation within the industry. As we search for deeper and broader reasons for the industry's decline, we move back and look at the lack of user pull, the short-term investment approach fostered by Wall Street, the absence of supportive commercially-oriented government policies (and the presence of inimical ones), the limited direction of NC product development established in the 1950s to meet military objectives, and the declining interest in and status of manufacturing within both industry and academia.

Industry Structure and Management Decision-Making

Fragmentation and Parochialism. Historically the industry has been populated by hundreds of small firms founded by owner- inventors and geographically clustered around user markets. This pattern developed in the eighteenth and nineteenth centuries, and remains the foundation of the industry even today. Many firms are still family-run or dominated, privately held, and small. The average number of employees is 60, but only 35 percent of domestic builders have more than 20 employees. The number of active firms has been shrinking steadily, and is now less than 500.[8] The industry has become more concentrated, however, at least nominally (see Table 6). By 1982, 12 firms accounted for 85 percent of U.S. production. Their market share increased less from internal growth than through acquisitions of many smaller machine tool companies (see Appendix C). Operations have usually remained unmerged between various machine tool subsidiaries, so that the shift has been more from independent small firm to small firm with parent, rather than from small to large firms.

The mid-sized, family firm still prevails in Europe as well as in the U.S., and its origins are technical. The mechanical technologies and design requirements differed for each type of product. They even varied for high-volume as compared with general purpose equipment of the same general type, such as lathes or milling machines. This led to specialization in narrow product lines for particular markets.[9] For example,

Cross built transfer lines and Gleason gear cutting machines for the auto industry, Bridgeport built milling machines for tool rooms and machine shops, and Hardinge Brothers built lathes for super precision work.

Industry fragmentation was reinforced by production economies that derived from cumulative output of a single model rather than across models, reputations built around particular types of tools, and high switching costs between different manufacturers' products.[10] The resulting industry structure was relatively functional as long as there were few economies of scope or scale to be gained from broader product lines. In the absence of modular design and flexible automation, production economies were not enhanced by broader lines, but rather by standard models and long product life cycles. This design/production paradigm of course worked against product change; this was not a problem as long as product life cycles were long and there was no alternative production paradigm.[11] It became increasingly dysfunctional, however, as new technologies and Japanese production capabilities changed the paradigm and the nature of competition.

The effects of small size and family ownership reinforced the pattern of fragmentation and slow model/production changes: limited resources for reinvestment and research, few links to university research or joint projects, and, very often, a parochial view of competition, and lack of vigor in developing new products or sales growth as long as the family was comfortable. Described by one informant as the "plaything of inventors," these firms were usually staffed by tinkerers and problem-solvers—some of them first-rate mechanics or even designers—but not usually given to sponsoring systematic, long-term development efforts. Indeed, when product life cycles were long and technologies simple enough to be encompassed by a single brain, the inventions of the founder and perhaps of his son(s) could sustain the business for a fairly long time. Sometimes the second or third generation took an active interest in the business and pushed continuous innovation, as at Ingersoll Milling. Very often, however, succeeding generations had limited interest in reinvesting profits for competitively producing the next generation of products; for example, deVlieg, once a highly successful producer of precision boring and jig mills, is one of the builders who failed to bring out new products during the tenure of the second generation. Small, family firms often thought of their competition as the few other firms that specialized in their product/market niche; very often these firms were clustered in the same geographic area. This no doubt contributed to a domestic, even regional, view of competition; few builders thought of themselves as competing in an international market, as needing to export, or needing to take into account what builders and users in other countries were doing. Even when there was an inclination toward sustained innovation, the resources were often not available; as noted by one industry veteran who rose through the ranks to become a plant manager and then vice-president of his company: "In good times, we were too busy getting product out to develop new ones; and in bad times, we didn't have the money or the people."

Although these were the predominant tendencies of small, specialized, family-held firms, we should bear in mind that these tendencies were the results of owner/manager decisions and nondecisions, and thus a contingent rather than a necessary outcome. Further, the same structural features can be a great advantage, as several informants testified. Ingersoll Milling is prospering under the founder's grandson who begins his day by touring the shop. Managers there emphasize the commitment of the owner, the integrity and continuity of the family as the bedrock of the firm's success. The family has consistently ploughed profits back into the business and created a climate for innovation. Almost inseparable, in Ingersoll management's view, is the capability for making responsive decisions quickly, and making major investments because they are "right" rather than whether they can be financially justified. James Koontz, president of Kingsbury Tool, on the other hand, emphasizes the distinction between family-held and privately-held firms, identifying the former with the syndrome of complacency described earlier, and identifying private ownership with the ability to take risks when needed, and make decisions quickly. There is no doubt in his mind, or that of outside colleagues, that it was private ownership that allowed Koontz to turn around Kingsbury in the last few years. That turnaround included several million dollars invested in new equipment to control critical tolerances, and Koontz' assisting anyone in the firm (from janitors to vice presidents) who wanted to get a computer for home use—actions taken because they felt "right" and "smart" rather than because they could be financially quantified or justified.

Industrial Cyclicality. If fragmentation and parochialism have been at the center of one set of issues, cyclicality (the top left-to-right cluster in Figure 6) is the driving force for a second set. The extremity of these cycles is vividly depicted in Figure 7 where we observe 75 percent increases in new orders followed by 50 percent drops. Such dramatic oscillations result from the multiplier effects of customers orders and cancellations in response to the cyclicality of their own markets. Machine tool orders lag as customer business picks up, and lead on the way down, compressing the "good times." In the last two decades, domestic builders have faced three major recessions: 1969-71, 1973-75, and 1981- 83. Narrow product lines have amplified dependence upon the fortunes of particular customer segments. Metalworking customers (autos, aerospace, electrical machinery, nonelectrical machinery, machine shops) respond as well to unstable tax policies that alternately reward and fail to reward capital investment. They also feel pressured by Wall Street to achieve fast paybacks and show quarterly profits, and are unlikely to invest countercyclically.

Cyclicality of machine tool orders has, in turn, had three major types of effects: volatility of cash flow, problems with recruiting and retaining skilled people, and the strategic response of backlogging orders as business rose and paring down the backlog as orders shrank.

Wide swings in cash flow and profitability have decreased builders' willingness to make long-term investment commitments, both because the money is not in fact available and because of high uncertainty about whether it will continue to be available to meet obligations undertaken in more flush periods. Cyclicality makes bankers reluctant to lend, further contributing to industry undercapitalization.

Cyclicality has devastating effects on employment. As shown in Figure 8, it has oscillated between 58,000 and 115,000 during the past two decades. Such cyclicality deters many capable people from joining the industry because of the high probability of periodic layoffs. Builders and machine shop owners agree that it takes four or five years to train a machinist well. Companies that are either willing or forced to train machinists and other technical people are hard-pressed to keep them when orders fall off, and then are short of people when they need to ramp up. For companies, the result is lack of volume flexibility; for the industry as a whole, the result is a serious shortage of skilled younger people to replace the aging cadre of machinists and other craftspeople. The shortages are not confined to shop floor personnel, however. Cyclicality, as well as the industry image of maturity, grubbiness, and noisiness have not routinely attracted the best talent in engineering, manufacturing, or management. This appears to be less of a problem among some of the new entrants described earlier, and among some of the companies that have turned around in the past few years; the quality of people and their energy level was palpably higher than in troubled companies.

Even more significant than cyclicality itself has been the domestic industry's historical response to cyclicality: backlog orders during good times and work down the backlog in bad times in order to keep production and employment levels smoother over the course of the business cycle. This pattern is graphically portrayed in Figure 9; we see shipments lagging orders by as much as five or six quarters during peak periods. While this strategy served the builders, if not their customers, it clearly left them vulnerable, particularly in general purpose market segments, once low-cost, high-quality imports were available and could be delivered quickly. Figure 10 shows that imports have tracked unfilled orders for years, gained a stronger foothold during the late 1970s boom, and then, unlike previous cycles, continued to rise even as unfilled orders dropped. This graph suggests that delivery was an important factor in the early import surge, but that positive experience with Japanese products led customers to keep buying even after the domestic backlog dwindled. This interpretation is consistently supported by interviews with domestic builders and distributors. They acknowledge that rapid delivery and lower prices were the initial openings exploited by the Japanese. Once they had this base, their improving quality, fast service, and (frequently, but not always) generous financing terms consolidated their position.

Did domestic builders have options other than backlogging? They could have expanded capacity, at least of bottleneck operations, to better meet peak demand; this of course would have presented the problem of managing assets and higher fixed costs during downturns. They could have countered domestic cyclicality through exporting.[12] The typical domestic attitude (particularly among smaller firms, but also among some larger firms as well) towards exporting has been to sell in the U.S. when times were good, and try and sell overseas when times were bad. Successful exporting, however, requires sustained effort, and thinking about global markets from the earliest design stage rather than as an afterthought. Such an approach has been the exception. Wayne Moore, the second-generation owner-president of Moore Special Tool, is such an exception; he gets well over half of his business from overseas. Moore emphasizes the importance of continuously drawing upon customers and suppliers world-wide as part of an integral process of designing and modifying products for global markets. A third alternative to backlogging would have been to organize design and production for more rapid delivery. While many domestic builders have now moved toward modular designs and to reorganizing production so that modules can be built to stock, this was not the case prior to the 1980s recession. Jones & Lamson (J&L), for example, had little modularity in their technically fine designs, and built everything to order. Delivery for one of their NC lathes required a minimum of three months prior to the late 1970s boom, and went out to 18-24 months during that boom. When the Japanese commodified NC lathes, and could provide immediate delivery, sales of J&L and other domestic lathes dropped sharply.

Industry structure—particularly fragmentation and cyclicality—has certainly been a significant contributor to the American industry's problems. But we cannot simply blame that structure for those results. First of all, these patterns have been around for a long time; they only became a major problem for domestic builders when foreign competitors provided alternatives. Second, these structural conditions predisposed builders towards certain kinds of management behaviors and patterns of low-risk decision-making, but they did not force those outcomes. And, third, the same structural conditions of small, fragmented, family firms facing highly cyclical buying patterns prevailed in Europe as well as in the U.S. The Europeans have, on the whole, been more successful at coping with these structural conditions.

Both the European and Japanese experiences, as well as analysis of the domestic industry's problems, suggest that inimical industry conditions that are beyond the capacity of any one firm to change require higher-level intervention and policies that produce an environment in which firms can flourish rather than flounder. As will be suggested later, government policies, university programs, interfirm cooperation, industry-university-government linkages all have a role to play here.

Let us now turn to the third major cluster in Figure 6, low rates of product and process innovation. These patterns of behavior, and the reasons behind them, are at the heart of the industry's demise. We will look first within the industry, and then more broadly to users and other institutions.

Product Innovation Among Builders

Lagging Product Innovation. The volume and rate of product innovations has been, in simplest terms, too little, too late. Examples abound. Kingsbury acknowledges that, "We made the same basic dial index machine from 1940 to 1980; sure we added the latest tooling, but we really didn't innovate." Kingsbury has now completely revamped its product line, with an emphasis on flexible, transfer lines for assembly as well as fabrication. It is changing the design and materials of many machine elements to provide greater accuracy and repeatability, and invested in the process equipment needed to achieve it. Bridgeport produced the first of several thousand Series I standard milling machines in 1938; during the 1940s and 1950s, "the Bridgeport" accounted for 95 percent of the company's sales. Over a 50-year period, only minor innovations were made to add horsepower and capacity. Bridgeport is still selling the Series I, but can no longer build it cost competitively in the U.S.; the Bridgeport is now built in Singapore. Cincinnati Milacron acknowledges that, "We ignored the Japanese in machine tools, and now it's late; our attitude has changed, and we're trying not to let the same thing happen in [injection molding machines for] plastics." Milacron has cut development costs for its new plastics machine and its new machining center by 40 percent through using cross-functional teams, reducing part numbers 30 percent through the use of new materials, and paying attention to hundreds of details that provide opportunities for cost reduction. Hardinge designed part of its line to hold super precision tolerances (.0001 - .000050 inch tolerances) and last indefinitely, yet several interviewees referred to its designs as "obsolete." Why? Although the precision-speed tradeoffs implicit in its design parameters have been acceptable in super precision markets (where costs can be passed along in the price), they are not acceptable in the general precision markets (.001 - .0005+ inch tolerances) where speed and price are critical. These tradeoffs are becoming less acceptable in super precision markets as well. Hardinge has since made cost reductions across the company and design changes in its general precision lathes that have increased manufacturing efficiencies and thus made current products more price competitive. It is also bringing out new lathes specifically designed to meet the needs of the general precision market, while enhancing the performance of and support for its super precision lathes.[13]

Budgeted R&D does not reflect the full technical effort of the industry, but it has always been low. Estimates for the 1970s place R&D at about 1.6 percent of sales.[14] That percentage increased at the end of the 1970s, perhaps as much as doubled. (All such estimates may be overinflated, however, due to accounting practices that include applications work in R&D.[15]) True R&D has been concentrated in larger machine tool firms, especially if they have vertically integrated into making their own controls. There is, however, a great deal of engineering and technical effort among builders, particularly those involved in special purpose and customized work.

Why has Product Innovation Lagged? We have already discussed many of the contributing factors that have interacted to limit technology push from the builders: small firm size, waning family interest, volatile cash flows, undercapitalization, complacency, parochial view of competition, lack of contact with international competitors and markets, production economies from long cumulative runs of the same model, and long product life cycles of highly durable products that can be rebuilt to hold their original tolerances. These set of factors may be summarized as fragmentation, parochialism, and complacency among builders. Their negative impact on innovation was also exacerbated by increasing conglomerate ownership of builders.

Several of the industry veterans and analysts interviewed in the course of this study stated unequivocally that conglomerates ruined the domestic industry. While we do not subscribe to such a monocausal theory, we do believe that conglomerates damaged the long-run viability of the industry and destroyed particular companies, primarily through lack of reinvestment. (See Appendix C for examples of merger and acquisition activity.) Profitable machine tool companies looked attractive to conglomerates such as Textron in the 1960s and early 1970s. These profits were typically used to support corporate overhead and other divisions rather than ploughed back into the machine tool divisions. Problems did not show up immediately, because the long product life cycles of machine tools kept revenues coming in for years. But as these products matured, replacements were not forthcoming. In particular, the greater investment required to develop new NC/CNC product lines was not made available by conglomerate owners. As these subsidiary firms began to fall behind and lose money, they were divested. One successful independent builder summarized the feelings and bitterness of many of his colleagues about conglomerates:

> They had no understanding of the product, not any commitment to it. They thought they could make money by selling the same old designs and building them on depreciated equipment—and they did, for a while. These "numbers people" don't like the specialty end of the business—it's too hard to make each job pay off. So they dropped the specials and concentrated on the high volume units. But then they became vulnerable to commodity competition because they don't know anything about manufacturing either.

But builders alone, with or without conglomerate ownership, do not explain limited product innovation. Strong user pull might have jolted the inertia in this system, but user pull was weak.

User Process Investment and Pull

Weak User Pull. User pull is an important stimulus to innovation in many industries; indeed, in some industries, users are the primary source of innovations, developing many right into the prototype stage.[16] User pull is particularly critical for machine tools for two reasons. What is a new product for the builder is new process equipment for the user; a good flow of new products is fundamental to users' remaining competitive in their manufacturing. Second, machine tools are durable, can be rebuilt or even remanufactured, and have long product life cycles. Replacement orders are small. So builders rely on user growth and product change to trigger additions and changes to their [i.e., user's] process equipment as the basis of demand for higher volumes of machine tool orders and for new kinds of tools.

Unfortunately for American builders, user pull has, with some significant exceptions, been quite weak until very recently. The aerospace primes, some of their subcontractors, and certain individual firms have exerted pull for new equipment and technologies, but the domestic automakers (in contrast to their European and Japanese counterparts) have opted for proven technologies even when retooling. In general, metalworking customers allowed their equipment to age continuously after World War II until the late 1970s when retooling for small car production, followed by a defense buildup, began to arrest the pattern. After World War II, the proportion of equipment newer than ten years old kept declining while the proportion 20 years old or more kept rising[17] (see Table 7). Although good comparative data are hard to come by, indications are that relative to other industrial nations, the installed base of U.S. cutting tools is older than that of Japan, the U.K., and Italy, while its forming tools appear to be the oldest of seven industrial nations, and lag the Japanese and the U.K. in particular[18] (see Table 8). In 1973, for example, 60 percent of Japanese machine tools were less than ten years old, while only 33 percent of American machines were that young.[19]

Not only did the installed base of American machine tools keep aging and grow older than that of its foreign competitors, but American users were also slow to adopt programmable automation technologies (PATs) in particular. NC underwent development throughout the 1950s, but there was little adoption until after 1965. For the next decade, NC adoption increased but slowly. By 1973, the U.S. was estimated to have 30,000 NC tools in place, or less than 1 percent of its installed base. The microprocessor was invented in 1972, and solid-state CNC controls became commercially available in the middle 1970s (though not, as we will see, from the two major domestic control manufacturers until 1980). First adoptions of NC/CNC peaked during the 1975-79 period for domestic plants.[20] Yet by 1983, the number of NC/CNC machines had apparently risen only to 100,000, or 5 percent of the installed base.[21] In contrast, 30 percent of the Japanese installed base was NC/CNC tools by 1985.[22]

Not only did the Japanese have several times as many NCs proportionally as the U.S., but their patterns of diffusion differed significantly. NC sales in the U.S. have been concentrated in larger firms; less than ten percent are sold to shops having fewer than 20 employees.[23] It appears that in the U.S. that the larger the plant, the more likely it has been to adopt NC and CNC equipment. Rees et al. found that in the early 1980s, 78 percent of plants having over 1000 employees had some CNC equipment, while that number dropped to 69 percent for plants having 250-999 people, 50 percent for those employing 100-249 people, and 23 percent for plants having fewer than 100 employees. Given that 40 percent of metalworking employees work for firms having less than 100 people, and fully half are in firms with fewer than 500 people, the lower penetration into the broad base of metalworking firms is very significant. In Japan, by contrast, two-thirds of NC and CNC machines are sold to small and mid-sized firms, and over 25 percent to shops having fewer than ten employees.[24]

These three factors—low investment in process equipment in general, slow adoption of NC/CNC in particular, and concentration of NC in larger user firms—all add up to limited user pull from builders for new technology and innovative products. If we ask what lay behind this apparent lack of interest and clear lack of investment in new equipment and technologies, there appear to be three bottom line causes: user complacency, lack of user sophistication, and products mismatched with needs.

Competitive Complacency Among American Manufacturers. In the decades following World War II, American manufacturers vastly underrated the importance of manufacturing excellence to their overall competitiveness. They believed they competed on product performance so that process innovations didn't seem that important, and they failed to appreciate the importance of being competitive internationally, and what that would require, including manufacturing capabilities, in the future. In the aftermath of the war, they were right—there just wasn't anyone else. American manufacturing had ultimately won the war for the Allies. The situation changed, but the perceptions of many, indeed most, American manufacturing companies did not. By "winning" the war in Europe and then not appreciating the changes of the post-war world, American manufacturers have been losing in the battle of global competition.

Thus most users did not exert pressure on builders, or work with them, to develop new products that would strengthen their own productivity, lower their costs, improve their quality, or give them more flexibility. Indeed, they often did quite the opposite. As one builder described the disincentives to innovate:

> If you tried to get a license, the auto companies tried to break it. They didn't want one source so they refused to pay the royalties and the small guys couldn't fight it. That destroyed incentive to innovate because you would only get one-third of the order at most.

GM now acknowledges that its way of doing business with suppliers taught them to sell proven technology rather than new technology. Promotions and bonuses that rewarded plant managers who showed low piece rates and punished those whose innovations failed led to manufacturing managers choosing low-risk technologies with proven track records. When GM sent out for bid its specifications for a new piece of equipment or tooling, the bidders, who had to invest $50,000-100,000 just to work it up, learned to offer what would sell and to come in with the lowest bid.[25]

Low User Sophistication. Users versed in mechanical technologies were frequently ill-prepared to understand and evaluate new, electronically-based technologies. This lack of understanding added an additional level of barriers to the simple business-as-usual attitude when it came to the possibility of adopting such technologies. A few years ago, the Boston University Manufacturing Roundtable sponsored research exploring why people had or had not adopted new manufacturing technologies. They surveyed 57 leading edge users, 38 leading suppliers, and 64 experts. With regard to computer-aided manufacturing, the results show that lack of technical user sophistication, coupled with traditional, short-range approaches to capital investment, was the principal reason limiting adoption. The experts overwhelmingly cited lack of understanding of potential benefits, inability to quantify those benefits, and lack of skills needed to achieve them. Suppliers gave almost identical ratings to the same factors: does not meet investment criteria, unable to quantify returns, wrong people assessing technology decisions, and incomplete understanding of technology. Suppliers believed that most users did not understand either their own needs for CAM, or what such technologies could or could not do for them; user understanding was perceived by suppliers as much poorer with regard to integrated than incremental applications. What appears to distinguish leading edge users from nonadopters is their assessment that waiting posed more risk than going ahead. They knew they would make mistakes, but were willing to learn by doing, and build their in-house experience base. They relied heavily on outside technical assistance to plan and implement their new technologies.[26]

Case studies on FMS implementation by two Boston University researchers illuminate further this lack of understanding of what AMTs involve.[27] They found that most firms did not begin to appreciate the level of involvement required of them, or the breadth of representation needed. Typically they either approached FMS as they would have any other investment, in which case they chose vendors on the basis of past experience, assigned unskilled people to load and unload the system, looked to the vendor for software, facilities people for maintenance, and programmers for programs; or, they left it to advanced manufacturing engineering, and neglected software and systems expertise, early involvement of manufacturing managers and operators, and rethinking work skills and reorganization. Typical results included partial redesigns after operating people pointed out the mismatch between the proposed design and their reality, and poor use of the FMS for new parts.

Lack of user sophistication and business-as-usual are thus two key reasons explaining weak user pull, low rates of process investment, and slow NC/CNC adoption. But a third critical dimension is the institutional factors that charted a course inhospitable to widespread adoption. We will return to this issue in a later section; but before we turn to that discussion, we need to know if builders differed from other users in adopting new process technologies, and what effects those decisions have had on past and future competitiveness.

Builder Process Investment

Lagging Builder Investment. Until the last four or five years, most domestic machine tool builders have themselves been lagging users of new equipment and technology. If we refer to Table 7, we observe that metalworking equipment's (SIC 354) installed base of metalcutting tools aged continuously after World War II—as they did in other industries, but not quite as badly—until the early 1980s. (Metalforming, not shown here, had not yet turned around between the 12th and 13th inventories taken by *American Machinist.*) This recent turnaround among some metalcutting equipment producers is corroborated by plant visits and by Table 9 which shows that, even in current dollars, investment in new equipment declined during the 1967-77 period, accelerated in 1979 and thereafter but had still not picked up in metalforming by 1983. During plant visits, the author found that considerable reinvestment and reorganization of capital assets has taken place during the last five years, at least among the more aggressive builders who intend to survive.[28]

While the recent increases in investment are encouraging, it is not merely the amount of investment but rather the type of investment (as well as its strategic relationship to other equipment and business strategy) that is important. Programmable automation technologies (PATs) are, in theory, particularly appropriate for the kind of small batch, high precision, high variety production by which machine tool components are fabricated. Builder adoption of NC/CNC appears to have been ahead of most user industries, but hardly breathtaking in its pace. According to the 12th and 13th inventories, metalworking equipment producers have lagged only aircraft and nonelectrical machinery (see Table 10). Another national study using 1982 data found a wider spread among industries, but a similar pattern: 68 percent of aircraft firms had adopted some CNC equipment, compared to 58 percent of metalworking equipment producers, 43 percent of construction equipment builders, and 20 percent of farm equipment firms.[29] Note that these numbers pertain to adoption; they say nothing about the degree of penetration of CNC into the firm's operations. If we refer back to Table 10 and divide the number of NC units by total units in industry groups, we find that in 1983, ten percent of the installed base among aircraft firms was NC, 6.2 percent of metalworking equipment, and 5.5 percent of all metalworking users. By comparison, just two years later, fully 30 percent of the Japanese installed base among all users was NC/CNC. Because its builders tend to lead in new process/equipment use, we can safely assume that Japanese builders' use of CNC exceeds 30 percent of their base.

If we move to the next major process steps—flexible machining cells and systems—the gap between American builders and their foreign competitors appears even wider. Although several domestic builders began selling FMSs to customers in the early 1980s, none first installed a system in-house. Ingersoll's first FMS became operative in 1984, Milacron's in 1986; to our knowledge, no other American builder yet has an FMS. By contrast, virtually all of Japan's significant builders had one or more FMSs in-house by the early 1980s; some, such as Hitachi Seiki, had in-house FMSs as early as 1972. Starting with FANUC and Yamazaki, more and more Japanese builders are moving toward integrated automation of the entire factory.[30] The West Germans, although starting later than the Japanese or the Americans, have moved very quickly into flexible manufacturing cells during the past five years. Many builders such as Werner and Kolb have several cells, while Trumpf has highly automated factories. In short, even though the more progressive American builders have taken many steps to reorganize and modernize manufacturing, major foreign competitors may be increasing their lead, and thus the gap, in process technology.

Why has Process Technology Adoption Lagged? The question arises: Why were new process technologies not being adopted by the builders themselves? Why were they not leading new process adoption? Many of the contributory reasons have been cited earlier: undercapitalization, parochial view of competition, small firm size, long product life cycles, etc. Like their customers, many builders were complacent about foreign competition; they did not understand it or the importance of competing through manufacturing.[31] And, like their customers, they lacked the skills and mind-set for understanding and effectively using the new manufacturing technologies being developed from outside of their technology base. A 1985 study of Pennsylvania builders found them to be severely lagging in adopting advanced manufacturing technologies (AMTs). The surface reasons for non-adoption focused around the difficulties of justifying the investment when using short-term payback and ROI criteria. As with the Roundtable study, the underlying reasons had more to do with lack of comprehension of AMT. This led to intimidation, confusion, and failure to buy AMT, on the one hand, and to narrow, nonstrategic purchase decisions and implementation, on the other. When these builders had invested in AMTs, they were making poor use of them. AMT was often seen as a replacement for conventional machines rather than a strategic alteration in the way to do business. Equipment decisions were usually not made as part of a strategic technology and manufacturing plan, and led to islands of automation, and poor integration with other manufacturing operations. In short, the reasons behind slow builder adoption and ineffective utilization are no different than those affecting downstream users.

In addition, as the following section will explain, there have been significant institutional and political barriers to early NC and CNC adoption among the majority of builders and users. One of the most significant effects of these barriers was NC/CNC product development that mismatched the needs of the majority of metalworking users, including builders themselves.

NC Development and Diffusion in the U.S.

Numerical control, considered the single biggest innovation affecting machine tools in the twentieth century, was created in the United States in the 1950s, but its widespread adoption there has been slow, in the view of most observers. While the story of NC and CNC diffusion in the U.S. is complex and far from definitively understood, the story line strongly suggests that the very policies and practices that brought NC into being also established a development direction that later inhibited its broad commercial development. This contrasts sharply with the commercially-oriented approach of the Japanese that has done so much to improve the productivity and flexibility of the entire Japanese manufacturing base.

The Development of NC: Parsons, MIT, and the Air Force.[32]

John Parsons, one of several independent entrepreneurs trying to develop automated machine control in the post-World War II period, sought and gained Air Force support in 1949 to demonstrate the feasibility of a three-axis, automatically controlled prototype machine for milling wing panels. For help in developing the power drive, he went to MIT's Servomechanism Laboratory, based on their past work in analog servo systems. Interested in developing digital servo systems, the Lab became a subcontractor to Parsons.

Following a systems analysis of the problem, the Lab soon redefined the technical approach to be taken. In the view of one author who is highly critical of the MIT role, MIT took the project in an unnecessarily complex direction.[33] In the view of key players from the Servo Lab, Parsons' absolute positioning approach was untenable because it would have required thousands of vacuum tubes for memory (recall that memory was then very expensive, vacuum tubes both large and unreliable), and the Lab actually took a much simpler approach. The Servo Lab's solution—incremental positioning and a master clock pulse oscillator were at the heart of it—made the data processing task manageable and represented a contour solution to a contour problem. (The Air Force's problem—milling of complex contour airfoils—was truly a continuous contour problem, which Parsons' point-to-point system could only have approximated.) In any event, the result was that the more complex problem (continuous path cutting of contours) was tackled and solved before the simpler, point-to-point problem.

The following year, MIT moved into the role of prime contractor with the Air Force while Parsons moved out (or was moved out—accounts conflict) of the program. During the 1950-52 period, the Servo Lab developed an experimental NC system, and held a major demonstration to conclude this phase of the work. The demonstration was just one highlight in a major ongoing effort to familiarize industry with NC—an area in which the Servo Lab took a very active role.

Initial responses among builders ranged from guarded optimism to outright hostility. They were skeptical about reliability, accuracy, economics, and maintenance of electronic equipment. Builders questioned the commercial promise of a technology that was so complex and expensive to customers. Controls might run 40-50 percent of the machine tool's cost instead of the three to five percent for a conventional machine. Both builders and aircraft companies had doubts about the viability of the controls when used at production rates in the harsh environment of the shop floor. The economic concerns stimulated the Lab to undertake a study that tried to compare NC with conventional machining. Although the data were highly imperfect, it suggested that NC per-part machining would be cheaper than conventional machining, but that the programming and tape preparation costs could exceed machining time by factors ranging from 18 to 52. The need to address the programming problem became obvious, and would soon become the next phase of the Lab's work.

By 1954, the Air Force hoped that private industry would underwrite the commercial development of NC, but it did not. Only Giddings and Lewis put its own money into developing an NC machine, subcontracting the development of the director to MIT. Then, in one large stroke, the Air Force assumed financial responsibility for both the transfer of NC from the lab to the shop floor, and for the creation of a market with its "bulk buy." The Air Force had been thinking of stockpiling long lead time machine tools; initially, none were to be NC tools. Discussions between the Air Force and Aircraft Industries Association (AIA) members led to a split NC/nonNC decision, and then, at the last minute, the AIA members decided that all 105 of the profilers and skin mills should be NC. Four of the bid systems met the demonstration requirements and received a share of the business: Cincinnati Milacron/Electric and Musical Instruments, Ltd; Kearney & Trecker/Bendix; GE/Concord Controls/Giddings & Lewis; and Morey Machine Corp./Electronic Control Systems. These machines, which were installed in factories of primes and subcontractors brought the Air Force investment in the new technology to $30 million.[34] With this bold stroke, the Air Force created a market for complex, continuous contour NC machines, and stimulated four builders and four electronics firms to develop products for that market.

The gross inefficiency of manual programming, together with the Air Force concern with compatibility and interchangeability among its primes and subcontractors made the development of a programming approach and language a high priority. It awarded MIT a contract to coordinate such an effort during the late 1950s. The Servo Lab developed the architecture, and divided the development work on particular modules among a dozen members of the AIA to put together the largest software package that had yet been developed, the Automatically Programmed Tool (APT) system.[35] In addition, in 1962, the AIA invited bids to maintain, upgrade, and support APT, and awarded the contract to the Illinois Institute of Technology Research Institute (IITRI). This on-going effort (which included new versions of APT and its offspring) was supported by member fees. As with NC, it was members of the Air Force, academia, and lead users who drove the innovation and the latter two who made it happen.

APT used a three-dimensional vector approach to define contours mathematically. It could accept part geometry descriptions, tool movement instructions, and auxiliary data in an English-like language, and automatically produce a tool tape. First designed for the IBM 704, within a few years it could be used with several other mainframe systems. APT required the user to have a large computer and programming investment, including a mainframe (the 704 then cost around $2 million), compiler, and post-processor, as well as skilled programmers who were then in short supply.

According to members of the Servo Lab, APT was easy to use, a major advance over existing programs which were all in machine language, helped NC economics through reducing programming time and costs, and demonstrated what was possible. According to other interviewees who lived through this period, APT was very difficult to use, very unforgiving, and poorly supported, but nonetheless useful for complex dies or parts. It was very poorly suited to ordinary machine tools and parts, however, requiring more time than manual programming for simple point-to-point problems. Even the savings in programming time for complex parts were not so evident within the data processing realities of the corporate environment which made it take days or even weeks to get a good tape.

What then were the results of APT? On the one hand, the aircraft industry and other large users got early standardization of a software language that could address their complex needs.[36] Once again, MIT, the Air Force, and some lead users demonstrated what could be done. But APT's technical complexity, need for skilled programmers, and hardware investment made it an elite system appropriate for large users who made very complex parts. While in theory it may have demonstrated what others could also do, in practice, it seems to have retarded development of other— i.e., simpler, cheaper—languages that did not demand huge computers and skilled programmers. How did it retard them? First, we need to realize that there was an opportunity cost. By having already absorbed the talents, resources, and interests of the lead users and developers, APT preempted the space for major joint public-private effort. It appears that other companies did propose simpler systems to the DoD, but the latter turned a deaf ear.[37] Second, even when such simpler systems began to appear independently in the early 1970s, large users tended to be so invested in APT that they were not receptive. One interviewee, then working in a key user division of a major corporation, described the attitude:

> When we had time-critical parts, we went to subcontractors who could do them much faster not using APT. When we proposed buying some of these simpler systems, the corporate response was, "Don't bring that up again." They had such a vested interest in APT, they had put so much into making it work, and felt they had already spent enough; they just didn't want to think about something else.

Independent Development Efforts: Proliferation, Incompatibility, and Unreliability. The "bulk buy" strategy had gained the attention of more machine tool builders, but did not lead to the rapid commercial development and diffusion then being hyped by the trade press and some vendors. (Keep in mind that computers were large, expensive, and not all that reliable, that controls were not reprogrammable, that memory required a great deal of floor space and was costly, that transistors did not appear until 1959 and ICs until 1966.) Many of those builders who were not included under the MIT/Air Force/AIA umbrella were dubious about the investment of time and money when the returns were so uncertain, so much electronics expertise was required, and such rapid change was occurring that today's work would be obsolete tomorrow. One early exception was Jones & Lamson (J&L). At the 1955 trade show, J&L was one of a handful of builders who introduced a manual tool it had modified to NC. J&L found interest, but no buyers. It spent two million dollars over the next eight years in an unsuccessful collaboration with one of the entrepreneurial groups formed by ex-Servo Lab people. Then J&L bought the rights to a non-MIT approach, but lacked the capital to develop the market. It was several years before J&L had an NC product line and several customers. Interestingly, it took additional funding from J&L's new parent, Textron, to finally bring J&L's first NC line to fruition. Later, Textron would be less forthcoming.[38]

Unlike J&L, most U.S. builders who developed NC products during the late 1950s and 1960s continued in the direction set by MIT/USAF/AIA. They concentrated on developing complex, sophisticated NC machines that responded to the special needs of milling wing skins, spars, turbine engine airfoils, and other complex contour, super precision, low volume parts for the aerospace industry. Complex NC machine tools were also relevant for some tool and die work, and some shops began to invest. Many suppliers, however, could not afford the $200,000-500,000 for such equipment; Ford, therefore, brought some of its die manufacturing in-house where it was machined on new NC equipment. It also began using NC tools for engine prototyping in 1961. Continuous contour was clearly not what most companies needed, however; by 1970, over 90 percent of the 5,000 continuous contour machines were in aerospace companies, while most small metalworking shops had none.

Several companies did develop point-to-point machines in the 1960s; besides J&L, they included Cincinnati Milacron, Pratt & Whitney, Warner & Swasey, Kearney & Trecker, Burgmaster, and Hillyer. Their unit sales were stronger than those of continuous contour during the 1960s. For example, in 1964, 76 percent of the NC units and 69 percent of their value were point-to-point machines—a good indication of the potential market in this area. But with so little difference between the share of units and dollars, it is obvious that even the point-to-point machines were costly, and their cost-effectiveness therefore difficult to demonstrate. (Recall that the cost of memory and logic chips has dropped drastically since then, and that the microprocessor was still many years away [see Figure 11]) All NC machines, whether contour or point-to-point, required a great deal of new learning, and entailed heavy costs: acquisition, programming, installing, training, part programming, computer support, special tooling, maintenance and repair. But money was not the real problem; in 1971, the Small Business Administration cancelled a low-cost loan program to invest in NC because there were so few takers.

The deeper problem was the mismatch between the complex products (both machine tools and controls) and most user needs. During the 1960s and early 1970s, the capabilities of the machines and the controls continued to exceed the needs of most users. With few exceptions, builders and control manufacturers did not move downward from complex, specialized equipment into simpler two- or three-axis machines with point-to-point software for widespread use by mid-sized and smaller users for diverse applications. Behind this failure was their approach to design—concern with high performance and complex function rather than simplicity and ease of use. It is this failure to understand how to design a generic product for ease of use for which builders and control manufacturers can be justifiably faulted (rather than for factors for which they are often blamed but which were beyond their control).

Notwithstanding this failure by builders, many users were still not interested because of their complacency and risk-aversion in general, and their limited sophistication about computer-aided manufacturing in particular. That made markets seem iffy and dumped responsibility back on the manufacturers. Even when manufacturers did try to better address these markets, early efforts were often unsuccessful. For example, Milacron redesigned its point-to-point system from scratch in the 1960s; even so, it could not sustain its position in the market due to lack of user receptivity. Where does responsibility for this product/market mismatch then lie? Much of it must be shared between complacent users and manufacturers whose design approach blocked their development of more appropriate products. Underlying both of these, however, is the question of a nation's infrastructure supporting or failing to support the adoption of technologies that are critical to its long-term position in the world economy.

Control Manufacturers and Products. While builders and users both have their share of responsibility, a large share of the responsibility for the slowness of NC, and especially of CNC, diffusion can be directly attributed to the control manufacturers. During the 1960s and 1970s, the number of control manufacturers proliferated—and, we might add, were allowed to proliferate (by contrast to the Japanese policy). Led by GE and Allen-Bradley, several firms got into the control business, and many builders also built their own controls—largely because they felt they had to. Because the machines they controlled were complex, and because they had to be versatile enough to control more than one type or model, the controls built by the merchant control makers were themselves very complex and expensive, and not well matched for specific machine tools. Controls could do various things not needed by a particular tool, yet not do some things that tool really needed (or not do them easily). As these early controls were hardwired and no interface standards were developed, incompatibility of controls became a major problem.

The complexity of controls for such complex machines made NC products highly unreliable; lack of reliability was perhaps the single most important deterrent to NC/and early CNC diffusion. It was hard to get the early controls operational, and once they were, the equipment was often down more than it was operating. Lack of reliability was an enormous deterrent to diffusion because uptime is so critical to users, vendors lacked an infrastructure of product support, and users lacked the new maintenance skills they needed. Conventional, long-lived machine tools had always been maintained by users themselves who were very familiar with their functioning. As a result, builders and their distributors had never developed a strong infrastructure of after-sales support. But NCs were a whole new game. New electronic skills were needed, proliferation meant each control was different, and rapid model changes and updates outdated old learning and required new learning. High failure rates and poor service scared away potential buyers, and developed bad reputations for the products and service of many vendors. Builders blamed the control manufacturers, the latter blamed the builders, both blamed ignorant users, and users blamed the builders and the control people. Small users got burned and word got around.

These problems of complexity and reliability carried over into the CNC era. The two major domestic manufacturers of controls, GE and Allen-Bradley, were not especially responsive to either the builders or end users, and kept building very sophisticated controls; indeed, one insider describes GE as seeking to make the "ultimate control," which kept different and non-communicating parts of the organization "fooling around" with exotic materials, lots of board layers, and highly complex software. Such complex controls required extensive applications engineering and support to customize them for each user; an Allen-Bradley official estimates that support costs equaled hardware costs, and kept domestic controls priced way above FANUC's. Not only did customization drive costs way up, but it also drove reliability way down. By contrast,

FANUC refused to customize, selling standard controls that had been extensively tested, and that did only the most important things but did them easily. Part of the complexity and awkwardness of GE controls was in their circuitry; GE remained committed to hardwired controls well after microprocessors became available in the middle 1970s. It did not have a solid state CNC control on the market until the end of the decade.[39] Even then, it changed reluctantly under pressure of losing business to foreign control makers and builders. Again, by way of contrast, FANUC took immediate advantage of Fujitsu's electronics expertise, and moved quickly into solid state controls and then adapted the microprocessor to the needs of NC machine tools. All of this meant that if domestic builders did not choose to put up with hardwired controls or excessively sophisticated controls that matched their machines, they were forced to go overseas or make their own; Milacron, for example, was making its own solid state control by the early 1970s, and was well into microprocessors by the late 1970s. Most of these in-house efforts eventually failed, however, sooner or later driving these builders to FANUC or Siemens, both of whom had successful solid state controls on the market by 1976. FANUC controls were simpler, cheaper, and much more reliable than GE's or Allen-Bradley's, and focused on the high-volume market, while Siemens made high-end controls.

The Effects of Large Institution Domination on Development. The basic development of generic NC was beyond the scope of any one organization. It required the resources and input of users, government, academia, and builders, and it required the kind of driving force that progressive members of the Air Force provided. The complexity of the part geometries posed a sufficient intellectual challenge to the MIT Servo Lab to engage it in a ten-year effort to demonstrate the hardware and software possibilities. Once the Air Force had underwritten the market, the lead users sponsored, co-developed, and enforced the use of a single language whose use requirements effectively restricted it to large users. All of this was a fairly major achievement, at least on its own terms.

What is equally important are the downside effects of this *de facto* consortium, and what neither it nor any other consortium did not do. The United States, through the mechanism of the Air Force, supported only this one major development effort. This effort directed resources and thinking to complex, high-end, sophisticated problems and solutions. It charted a direction and mind-set that was not geared to the simpler needs of the broad industrial base. No comparable singular effort was later devoted to developing standard, simple machine tools and controls that could produce small batches of different workpieces for many, smaller users. No comparable effort was devoted to standardization of interfaces or control of proliferation. No comparable effort was given to rethinking design approaches for simpler tools, let alone for ease of manufacture or to increase volume of components through standardization. Neither the Air Force nor any other part of government intervened when major control manufacturers remained committed to the early technologies, thereby making Americans late in CNC.[40]

It then fell to the manufacturers to independently chart broader commercially-oriented courses. But builders of complex machines and controls failed to redesign them for simplicity when they tried to penetrate other markets. Small builders lacked the electrical engineering base and staying power to develop and promote their own early approaches to NC, and, unlike the Air Force, they could not make a market. They could hardly get the attention of electronics firms who were making controls. Judging from the vulnerability of their eventual NC products to later Japanese imports, they, too, did not know how to design for simplicity of use and for manufacturability. The proliferation of controls without interface standards made it difficult for users to know what to buy and how to integrate their functioning. Incompatibility put strains on user resources (both skills and funds) for training, operating, and maintaining the equipment. Complexity produced poor reliability, and vendors were slow to set up the requisite level of after-sales support.

There is no law of course that says design should always proceed from the simple to the complex. We observe, however, than the Japanese have come to economic domination by just such a route. The state of technology in the 1950s (there were no small computers; no solid state devices; no easy programming languages; memory was costly, unreliable, and bulky; etc.) did not permit simple, cheap, reliable solutions for small users. But, as the technology evolved to permit such solutions, most of the players were so entrenched in their older ways, they neither led the adoption of nor were prepared to take advantage of those changes.

Reasons for Slow NC/CNC Diffusion in the U.S. There are several major reasons why NC, and later CNC, diffusion was slow in the U.S.

Technological constraints. Electronics technology itself did not permit immediate NC application for smaller users.

Competitive complacency. World War II left builders and users feeling confident about American manufacturing and their own competitiveness, providing low incentive to innovate.

Product emphasis. Both users and builders emphasized product engineering over manufacturing competitivenesses, so that users failed to exert strong user pull on builders for process innovations, and builders saw little need to start using the new technologies in their own processes.

Low technical sophistication among both builders and users. Users didn't understand the benefits of the new technology, how to link it to their own operations, how to make it work (either technically or organizationally), how to justify its investment, or continually improve its operation. Most builders' technology base and engineering skills were mechanical only, few had formally trained engineers, and very few were organized to deliver turnkey systems.

Products that were inappropriate for needs of most users. As electronics technologies evolved and made simpler, cheaper, and more reliable equipment possible, builders and control manufacturers moved too slowly to develop more appropriate products that would meet most machining needs of most users. Companies failed to redesign their high-end products for other markets.

Institutional barriers. The initial approach developed and sponsored by MIT/USAF/AIA consumed development resources, limited access to complex standardized software to those with big computers and programming resources, and established a mind-set focused around the high-end needs of one customer set. The military-oriented approach of the Air Force contrasts markedly with the commercial focus of MITI, as we will observe in a later section

Short-term ROI thinking. Users brought a short-term payback/ROI mentality to making NC or other AMT decisions, rather than seeing AMT as providing a technical basis for running the business in strategically new ways. This will be discussed in a section below.

Failure of American Schools of Engineering and Management

While U.S. manufacturers collectively bear major responsibility for the demise of the domestic machine tool industry and their own lack of competitiveness in international markets, they, too, are not alone. In the last thirty years, the values, priorities, and substance taught by many American schools of engineering and of management (or of particular departments within them) have denigrated the importance of process relative to product, of manufacturing relative to other functions (particularly finance and marketing, but also engineering), of making things work relative to their initial discovery or invention, and of making real profits through adding value relative to making paper profits through financial manipulations. Together, the universities and industry have created a reward and status system that draws many of the best students into finance rather than the real product world, and into design engineering rather than manufacturing engineering or even product engineering.

Engineering Schools. Since the 1950s, both design in its fullest sense and manufacturing in all its aspects have been dropped or severely cut back in the science-based curricula at many leading American engineering schools, including MIT. In the wake of Sputnik, many schools, operating under the delusion that future problems could be solved through a combination of computers, physics, and mathematics, moved farther and farther away from the real world of industry and into abstract, mathematical models and elaborate computer programs. At MIT, manufacturing-oriented faculty had to fight department heads and deans to retain a manufacturing lab. (An executive at one builder recalls the time ten years ago when he could not get MIT's lab to even accept major equipment donations.) The results are predictable. Young people move through four years of undergraduate work and then perhaps graduate school, all without knowing or caring how the products they design are made; they have already learned that the prestige and rewards go to the design engineers who create new products, not to those who figure out how to build them, or how to improve them. Students embarking on careers, the faculty who advise them, and the managers who direct their assignments act on the common knowledge that manufacturing is not on the fast track. As a result, the best students have not usually been drawn into manufacturing, let alone into what has been perceived as the mature, conservative, grubby world of machine tool builders.

Instead, manufacturing engineers have been largely drawn from the shop floor. They have tended to be bright, capable, high-school or two-year technical school graduates who showed promise, ingenuity, and problem-solving skills with conventional equipment and operations. They may have been sent back to school by their companies to receive additional training, but they lack the grounding in fundamentals that college engineering can provide. Promoted by management, they have interfaced with manufacturing managers who usually won their stripes and built their careers through effective firefighting. Both the manufacturing engineers and these manufacturing managers may lack understanding of new process technologies, and even be threatened by them. If they do appreciate their potential value, their second-class status means they often lack the clout and communication skills to carry the day within their plant or company.

Thus, while senior managers in most companies emphasize the need for manufacturing engineers to have a mix of professional training and practical experience, most of what they get has one without the other. Some of these managers recall their own intensive exposure to every aspect of their company's functioning when they began 30 or more years ago, and ruefully decry the subsequent closing of manufacturing labs at engineering schools, the decline in status of manufacturing, the absence of an apprenticeship system in the U.S., the gradual retirement of persons like themselves who have broad exposure and also accept new technologies, and the dearth of younger people to replace them.

But there is a broader implication to the absence of a robust manufacturing engineering capability at every level, from the shop floor to senior management. The inadequate skill base and technical comprehension at every level of manufacturing has been a major impediment to the acceptance, diffusion, and successful implementation of advanced manufacturing technologies. The result is user environments that have not, until very recently, demanded the best of their equipment suppliers (or even knew what the best was). The result is users who do not know how to assume the lead role in integrating, installing, and optimizing their equipment, and who are instead dependent upon builders or third parties to assume that responsibility.

While builders decry the lack of manufacturing emphasis at the universities, some faculty extend the self-criticism to design as well, noting, "we don't even teach design; we teach analysis, and a computer could do that." "Design" courses require students to calculate and analyze the stresses and loads, but don't require them to build the product they are supposed to be designing. Departmental focus does not demand that engineers in training learn to span fields, e.g., electrical and mechanical engineering (the minimum for working with today's and tomorrow's manufacturing equipment). Nor does the open-ended, unconstrained approach teach engineers the most fundamental thing they will encounter in the real world, namely, that there are always constraints. Rather than treating constraints as a negative, design-to-targets (simplicity, reliability, manufacturability, cost) needs to be the guiding philosophy of the engineering curriculum.

Management Schools. Several interviewees gave ample blame to business schools and their MBA's for the pervasive short-term mentality that dominates American business. While MBA's are hardly the cause, their contributory effect is noted. There is a deeper and much more serious problem, however, in which some business school departments and parts of the financial community are implicated. And that is the inversion of the roles of product and profit. Whereas most businesses traditionally sought to make a profit through providing a good or service, increasing numbers of greed-minded individuals buy, sell, and often destroy businesses just to make a profit. The machine tool industry has certainly been a major victim of this kind of activity. That some business schools provide both the tools for conducting this sort of activity and the values that glamorize and legitimate it is an appropriate target for indictment.

U.S. Capital Markets and Short-Term Thinking

Even when individuals or groups within user environments are inclined toward new processes and risk-taking, their ability to make those changes is too often vitiated by short-term job assignments, reward systems geared to short-term cost control and paybacks, limited clout within the company, and investment criteria that favor the known over the unknown, the quantifiable over the nonquantifiable, and the short-term over the long-term. Companies that try to fit programmable automation decisions into a rigid capital budgeting framework will, as several analysts have now pointed out, fail to make appropriate decisions in a timely fashion.[41] Short-term thinking was cited over and over again by interviewees as an enormous inhibitor of long-term manufacturing planning and investment and a fundamental problem that pervaded builder-user behavior.

Behind such thinking of course is the structure of American capital markets in which publicly held firms are held hostage to quarterly reports by Wall Street, and, should they not conform to the latter's short-sighted way of doing business, become vulnerable to takeovers by those who would gleefully dismember them in order to further inflate their profits. Interviewees emphasized the importance of actions based on long-term thinking, and the freedom that private ownership had given some of them to do just that.

Whether builder or user, companies who, like Ingersoll Milling, invested early in new manufacturing technology had to put financial justifications aside and make a strategic leap of faith:

> When we went to CAD/CAM, to NC, to FMS, it was hard to prove financially. When we bought our first NC machine, we said, "everyone will eventually be using it, so we better get started." It just made sense, and because we are a private company, we could just go ahead and do it. It was the same with CAD; we said, "This is the way of the future. If you are selling leading edge, you had better be on the leading edge."

Failure of Government Policies

Given the industry structure of fragmentation and cyclicality and its undercapitalization, and given the strategic importance of the machine tool industry, parties other than individual builders needed to take some responsibility for developing a more supportive, compensatory infrastructure. Instead, builders were left on their own to cope with cash flow volatility, training and keeping skilled people, and lack of user demand for new tools. Builders were left on their own to fund and conduct technology, product, and process development, a task beyond their individual resources. Given user complacency about their own competitiveness, the failure of engineering schools with regard to manufacturing and manufacturability, and the uphill struggle against short-term thinking in a quarterly-return-dominated economy, it is too much to expect federal and state governments to have bridged the gap alone. Nonetheless, government, particularly at the national level, bears significant responsibility both for what it did and did not do.

American policy leaders failed to develop a vision of, and political support for, the requirements for the long-term commercial viability of the United States, and the critical role of machine tools to that viability. Leading edge machine tools that are competitive with regard to price, delivery, quality, and service, are essential to downstream American firms' being world-class competitors. Such a vision entails creating an infrastructure that supports, rather than hinders, firms that strive for excellence. That includes simplifying the paperwork and conflicting regulations and multiple regulators that make it difficult for small and mid-sized firms to export. It means intervention that reduces the risk to smaller users who want to try new equipment and technologies, but are overwhelmed by the catalogs and claims of vendors, and by not knowing how to integrate new technologies into their operations. It means making easily available valid comparative performance data on different equipment, and providing technical assistance in translating purchases into effective operation. (Big users demand this assistance in the form of turnkey systems from builders or third parties, and pay for it; smaller users are left on their own.) It means funding for manufacturing research and development. It means supporting, and, if necessary, instigating, collaborative development efforts that bring together users, builders, control manufacturers, universities, private research organization, or whoever else needs to be involved.[42]

What we have had instead are two things: fragmented, inconsistent policies and practices that are not specifically directed at machine tools or manufacturing, but have enormous effects on them; and modest (now shrinking) DoD efforts to stimulate process investment among military contractors. Tax and antitrust laws have had a predominantly negative impact on the machine tool industry. The shadow of anti-trust laws has hung over thoughts of collaborative research essential for this industry, and blocked even such modest efforts as establishing industry standards. Inconsistent tax polices, frequent uncertainty about tax law changes, as well as laws that discourage new investment have all wreaked havoc with investment planning. These laws do not flow from a broad strategic vision, but are the patchwork result of political horse trading. In addition to these inconsistent policies, DoD procurement practices have often exacerbated commercial business cycle problems for builders. DoD dumped a huge number of fairly new machine tools onto the market right after World War II, with a very depressing effect on the industry. Military orders took precedence over commercial during the Vietnam and Reagan defense buildups, pushing out the backlog and making builders more vulnerable to imports with shorter deliveries.

Absent a commercially-oriented industrial policy, it has fallen to the Defense Department, and particularly the Air Force, to try and stimulate process investment among military contractors. Since the usual cost-plus procurement practices do not stimulate contractor investment, special programs and incentives have been created with that aim in mind. The Air Force has assumed a leadership role in trying to stimulate the development and diffusion of new process technologies through its Manufacturing Technology (ManTech) and Technological Modernization (TechMod) programs. Both differ from most government research support in focusing on process rather than product technologies. ManTech supports laboratory development of generic process technologies, and TechMod provides seed money for their application to the shop floor.[43] As a recent pair of National Academy of Engineering (NAE) studies has shown, these efforts have fallen far short of their potential for several reasons. Funding levels have been too low; there have been too many small, narrow, cost-reduction-oriented programs; there has been no coherent DoD policy guiding decisions about which process developments to fund; and funding decisions have not been linked to strategic defense needs.[44]

Even if ManTech fulfilled its potential, it would not be the right tool for the larger task of industrial policy. Any effort to shore up the U.S. industrial base for defense purposes has, by definition, a different objective than that of charting strategic directions for the commercial economy to meet the challenges of the 21st century. The Air Force, or the DoD as a whole, is not the appropriate vehicle for a commercially-oriented industrial policy. We have already seen how development skewed toward military needs were not readily modified to meet commercial needs. An appropriate industrial policy must have a commercial focus, and think about manufacturing as a whole rather than just one or two sectors.

Summary

The collapse of the domestic machine tool industry was not due to any one factor, nor did it happen overnight, nor does responsibility reside in any one quarter. It was the gradual outcome of a complex system of interactions (summarized in Figure 6) which left the industry vulnerable to new forms of foreign competition. The major elements in this system are the following:

1. The industry structure and strategies that were appropriate (or at least viable as long as foreign competition did not challenge it) in the 19th and early 20th centuries became less viable. Long product life cycles, backlogging, fragmentation, underinvestment, and slow rates of change generated sluggishness, inefficient manufacturing practices, a parochial view of competition, and complacency. No third parties intervened to provide an infrastructure that would allow builders who chose to compete to be competitive. Builders failed to understand the dimensions of their situation, and to seek appropriate rather than inappropriate (e.g., protectionist) remedies. The answer is not in import restrictions or tariffs, but in what builders, users, government and academic can do together to enhance the global competitiveness of the domestic machine tool industry. NCMS (see Appendix B) is one important effort in this direction.

2. Like most other manufacturers, builders and control manufacturers failed to understand and accept responsibility for the fact that most costs come from the design, not from labor in putting it together. A recent Ford study, for example, has shown that 70 percent of costs are frozen once the design is set. Builders and control makers did not understand the importance of design simplicity, or that adding special features to a standard/generic design is usually more viable than modifying complex equipment or controls downward.

3. Most users did not understand that process innovation was essential to their remaining competitive, and did not push builders to provide the best equipment. Too often, they discouraged innovation. This behavior stemmed from post-war complacency about their own competitiveness, interlinked to a lack of appreciation for how much their designs (i.e., not for manufacturability or ease of use) and deteriorating manufacturing abilities were contributing to their decline in international markets. In a vicious circle, as manufacturing's status declined, users did not draw their best people into manufacturing, became increasingly ill-versed in process needs, less able to compete through manufacturing, sent manufacturing off-shore, and got even weaker in manufacturing and design. User sophistication deteriorated, and firms were ill-prepared to understand and effectively implement potentially beneficial new technologies and processes.

4. The development path of the most significant technology since World War II (NC/CNC) was directed towards military needs and one subset of users. Builders outside the *de facto* consortium umbrella lacked the scale, the staying power, and the people to mount effective alternative efforts or to gain responsiveness from the control manufacturers. The refusal of GE and Allen-Bradley to move into solid state controls until forced to by competitive pressures hurt builders and users.

5. Engineering schools' turned their backs on manufacturing with several results. They lost touch with practical manufacturing needs, did not provide the applied or fundamental research need to solve problems or improve processes. They did not provide a flow of talent into builders firms, or provide users with well-trained manufacturing engineers who knew about alternative processes for achieving similar ends, knew about or could understand the state of the art, or think about investment strategically rather than piecemeal, or think through the human implications as well as the technical side of new investments.

6. Capital markets fostered short-term financial thinking rather than long-term product/process commitments, exacerbated rather than counteracted cyclicality, and contributed to industry undercapitalization. Piecemeal capital budgeting and unrealistic payback demands were ill-suited to strategic and integrated AMT planning.

7. National and state governments failed to treat machine tools as a critical strategic requirement for commercial competitiveness as well as for the defense industrial base, and to forge an effective set of policies to support that vision.

When these seven interrelated causes are placed against what the rest of the world was doing, the result was inevitable. Let us now look at the two major producer/exporters—Japan and West Germany—in more detail. The Japanese have achieved enormous success during the past decade, while several West European producer—most notably the West Germans, the Swiss, and the Italians—have continued to thrive based on long-standing capabilities in precision engineering as well as recent changes in how they run their businesses. Some American firms are again finding success through repudiating business-as-usual and recasting their way of conducting their operations, while others continue on an already successful path. Let us try and discern what is required for success, and see what lessons could be transferred to or broadened within the American environment.

The Japanese Approach

The Industry

Superficial appearances to the contrary, the Japanese industry is more concentrated than the American or European industries. Japan now has about 70 builders, and the 12 largest publicly-held firms accounted for about $ 2.7 billion, or over 50 percent of 1985 sales (see Table 10). If estimated sales from privately-held Yamazaki and Shin Nippon Koki are added, then fourteen companies account for nearly two-thirds of Japan's machine tool business. The difference between these top dozen and American's top dozen is that most of the latter represent acquisitions of firms whose operations and product lines still remain separate, while the Japanese firms achieved their size through a combination of forced merger and internal growth, and now operate as integral firms. The Japanese consciously and openly rationalized their industry during the 1960s and 1970s through "encouraging" (i.e., forcing) hundreds of family firms to become part of stronger, more successful firms. During the past decade, Japan's largest firms have achieved their present size and market share primarily through internal growth. Only three of Japan's largest 14 firms (Komatsu, Toyota, and Toshiba) are associated with large trading companies; the rest are independent. The large independents such as Okuma tend to make general purpose machines, while the affiliated producers tend to develop and build specialized machines and systems for their affiliated manufacturing divisions.

Industrial Policy

The direction and success of the Japanese industry was charted through industry-government-academic consensus that formed the basis for MITI's highly directive, highly interventionist industrial policy (summarized in Appendix E). Unlike narrow American efforts to improve the defense industrial base, Japanese policy had a bold and broad commercial vision; to improve the performance of all Japanese manufacturers, and most especially to help smaller and mid-sized firms.[45]

Standard Products.[46] This approach directed builders toward developing standard products suitable for a wide range of users. This emphasis on standard products continued even when the Japanese shifted towards emphasizing NC machines at a time when the Europeans held to manual controls and the Americans had still found few buyers for NC. Japanese NC production accelerated sharply from 26 percent in 1977, to 51 percent by 1980, and 67 percent by 1984.[47] Early users of these standard NC/CNC machines included suppliers to the automotive and general machinery industries, followed by suppliers in the electronics and precision machinery industries. NC/CNC brought flexible automation to these small-lot, large-variety, just-in-time suppliers. Between 1970 and 1980, small firms' share of NC/CNC purchases climbed steadily from 28 percent to 64 percent.[48]

Firm Specialization. Not only did Japanese product strategy focus on standard machines, but also on firm specialization in certain product lines. For example, Okuma, Yamazaki, Hitachi Seiki, and Mori-Seiki each have upwards of 70 percent of their production in lathes and machining centers; Okamoto gets 90 percent of its revenues from grinders; and Tsugami, Amada, and Makino have developed specialization in machining centers and EDM equipment for the electronics and precision machinery markets.[49] MITI's push for such specialization was driven by the same thinking that drove industry rationalization: to achieve economies of scale. By the 1982-83 time period, Japanese lathe producers were building between 50-200 CNC lathes monthly, while foreign competitors' rates were 40 at most, and often much lower[50] (see Figure 12). This reduced production costs, as did using simple, modular designs that reduced part count up to 30 percent, and achieved 10-40 percent overlap between models.[51]

Standard Controls. The same focus on standard products and specialization was followed with NC controls. MITI encouraged one supplier, Fujitsu-FANUC, to develop a simple NC control for each type of machine and then supply all the builders. FANUC, which became independent of Fujitsu in 1972, concentrated its heavy R&D around continuous innovation of its core technologies, NC and servomotors, and used a design-to-cost process to develop standard products at reasonable cost. Unlike the American control builders, FANUC quickly exploited solid state technology and microprocessors. Like other Japanese builders, FANUC went after the high-volume markets and achieved a production rate of 4000/month. It gained 80-90 percent of the Japanese control market during the 1970s, and 40-50 percent of the world market by the early 1980s. This strategy left niches too small for financial success for most of the players that had jumped into the market; most eventually got out, or in the cases of Siemens and GE, formed joint ventures with FANUC.[52]

R&D. This approach did not require the most advanced technology. R&D policies focused on licensing, applying, and improving existing—largely American— technologies. Sometimes it included copying and stealing technology, as Yamazaki did with Burgmaster.[53] Later, when breadth and scale required it, major R&D support was provided for cooperative development of a generic FMS, advanced FMS, and ultra-high performance laser production systems.[54]

Reasons for Success

Japanese success in machine tools is based upon a number of interrelated factors. Important as each of them is, their individual contributions are leveraged by their mutually reinforcing integration with each other. It is this congruence in combination with excellent timing and enormous subsidies that explains the overall success of the Japanese industry.

Strategic/Tactical Choices. Industrial policy led the way. MITI coupled a consistent strategic vision with mutually reinforcing and phrase-appropriate tactics. Targets were excellent as were timing of policies and tactical shifts. The Japanese took the lead in commercializing NC/CNC, concentrating on the needs of smaller users and tapping high-volume markets. This gave builders economies of scale and experience with the needs of small users; both served them well as they began to target small American users, a group largely neglected by American builders.[55] This approach strengthened Japanese user industries by improving the quality, productivity, and delivery time of suppliers. Note, however, that the rapid Japanese buildup occurred after the microprocessor and CNC arrived, so that computer costs were dropping and machines were easily and conveniently reprogrammed. These cost and ease of use factors were quite different than those faced by American builders in the preCNC period (see Figure 11).

Simple, Reliable, Nonproliferated Controls. Rapid NC/CNC diffusion was facilitated by MITI's policy of encouraging FANUC to become sole supplier. This approach avoided several of the problems that slowed up NC diffusion in the U.S. during the 1960s and 1970s: incompatibility, unreliability, and complexity. FANUC controls were of course compatible with each other, thereby eliminating interface problems, and reducing user training needs in programming and maintenance. The simple, modular designs achieved good, and later excellent reliability, and FANUC provided self-diagnostics and rapid service to minimize downtime. Builders were relieved of the burden of developing their own controls, and FANUC's concentration on the electronic side of electromechanical products reduced direct competition between FANUC and the builders.[56]

Congruence with Emerging Design/Manufacturing Strengths. The Japanese machine tool product strategy was highly congruent with Japan's emerging strengths in design and manufacturing. The industry did not aim initially for leading edge technology, but rather for applying and adapting licensed or "borrowed" technology into highly reliable, highly consistent products that many people could afford and use. The bases for competition in the emerging market for standard NC tools—reliability, repeatability, cost, and delivery—coincided with what the Japanese were becoming world leaders in doing: simplified designs that reduced part count, fabrication and assembly difficulties; reliability engineering that made sure all the elements worked singly and together, and were unlikely to break; fabrication processes that were in control, so that machine components conformed to specifications within statistical limits, were assembled into machines that were thus nearly identical, thereby engendering consistent performance when used to make customer parts; low unit costs achieved through design and manufacturing methods already noted; and standard products that could be built to inventory and therefore reduce lead time for deliveries. This emphasis on commercializing rather than creating technology, and on "quality" defined as conformance/reliability were consistent with each other, and gave the Japanese a strong competitive edge that differentiated them from the European "quality" product. The latter depended on leading edge technology/high precision/high performance that was hard or impossible to duplicate, but that also often suffered from less than optimal reliability and consistency.

Domestic Base for Exporting. The competitive strengths built by Japanese companies in the 1960s and 1970s enabled them to move from a strong domestic base into exporting in the middle 1970s. They concentrated their exporting efforts on CNC lathes and machining centers for the U.S. These two types of products also began penetrating European markets, but more slowly due to trade barriers, European chauvinism, and the Japanese targeting of the U.S. for its major marketing, distribution, and support efforts. Other Japanese products, such as grinders, EDMs, and presses, also began to be sold overseas.

While the proportion of exports that are NC ran ahead of production, the gap has nearly disappeared as production, too, approaches 70 percent NC.[57]

Exploiting American Builder Weaknesses. Japanese producers gained entree to the U.S. on the basis of low prices and fast delivery during periods of rising domestic backlogs. Japanese lathes, built to inventory and stockpiled at stateside distribution points, were available immediately, while domestic producers had lead times that went out to 18-24 months. As domestic users gained experience with the reliability of Japanese machines, they reordered and spread the word. In many cases, but not all, Japanese builders provided generous introductory offers and financing; "try it for 90 days and see how you like it; if you do, start payments then, and if not, we'll take it back" was typical. Industry observers usually perceive the financial aspects of such offers, but equally and possibly more important are their risk-reducing dimensions. Such offers allowed users to find out how the equipment worked in their own operation—the only real test—rather than forcing them to rely on inadequate and often misleading builder-supplier performance data as the basis for making a permanent investment decision.[58] When service was needed, response was not only rapid, but, according to machine shop owners, typically courteous as well. American users, unhappy with the inadequate service of domestic builders in the face of rising needs for such support, suddenly experienced a new standard by which to evaluate that service. In short, much of the Japanese success in exporting can be attributed to simply doing the basics—product reliability, price, delivery, service—better than anyone else. (It should also be noted that the low price and availability of exports was not totally a result of superior design and manufacturing; huge subsidies played a significant role as discussed below.)

Listening to Customers. Running through the Japanese approach also is an attitude of listening and responding. Several interviewees told stories to this effect: they listened when no one else would. A typical tale is told by one user, then in purchasing, now a value-added distributor of predominantly Japanese tools:

> I had this idea about a control, and no domestic builder would listen. Then I talked to this
> Japanese guy, and the next thing you know, they flew me over there. I met with a whole bunch
> of their high-level people all day, and at the end they said "can do." Six months later, I had it on
> the shop floor.

This raises the question of how the Japanese reconcile responsiveness with refusal to customize their off-the-shelf products. One possibility is that they respond to opportunities they perceive as having broad market appeal, and use such input to generate innovations in their general purpose products.

Gigantic Subsidies. MITI and the builders thus did many things well—standard products, high-volume markets, simplified controls and single manufacturer, accelerated shift to NC/CNC, fast delivery, and good service. One would expect this approach to have lowered their cost structure relative to their foreign competitors and indications are that it did. But it is also the case that the Japanese were able to finance inventory and sell exports at such low prices and on such generous terms because of heavy secret government subsidies. At first, MITI used sugar licenses as a ploy; builders were licensed to import sugar, and then resell it at artificially high prices. When this was discovered, MITI began tapping the pools of cash from gambling on bicycle and motorbike racing. This story was blown open through the efforts of one American attorney who finally got MITI to admit to $104 million per year rather than half a million dollars as it had claimed, and then went on to find documentation that proved the subsidy was $985 million a year.[59]

Long-term Thinking. Both these subsidies and the strong role of banks in the Japanese economy allowed builders and FANUC to take a long-term view. Taxes force individuals to save, providing a large pool of capital for banks to lend. As they are major shareholders as well, banks play an enormously important role in the economy. Because banks take a long-term view of their investments, builders can, like most of their customers, take a long view of capital investment and market development.

Limits to Success of the Japanese Paradigm

While this model has brought the Japanese unparalleled success in the machine tool market, it is not necessarily a blueprint for the future. Although the Japanese remain best at the basics, many American builders are working hard to close the gaps while other Asian producers are taking share at the low end of the commodity markets. The Japanese have permanently raised the standards in commodity machine tools, so that delivering a quality product at competitive prices when the customer wants it will become more and more the "*sine qua non*" rather than a competitive edge in these markets. As the Japanese take their skills at the basics into higher performance and specialty areas, they will force the Europeans and Americans to new standards of reliability, delivery, and price in these areas as well.

Second, the paradigm has rested on huge market needs for standalone and standard machines, but as Japanese builders are the first to recognize, growth in these markets can be expected to slow down. Furthermore, users are increasingly seeking solutions rather than equipment *per se*, systems (or elements that can be configured into systems) rather than standalones, and machines that can be customized to their applications. Insofar as this trend in user demand is greater in the U.S. than elsewhere, it raises questions about the disjunction between the current Japanese delivery system (rapid delivery of standard goods with limited customer interface or engineering applications work) and growing American demand for extensive customer interaction in developing specialized system or in tailoring standard systems to make their parts.

The rate at which Japanese firms are building plants in the U.S. should be a significant cause for concern—not because they get around trade restrictions and exchange rate fluctuations, but because the Japanese are positioning themselves for the next round in which systems integration work, engineering applications, and customer interface will be critical.

Neither can the Japanese continue to rely only on exploiting and improving existing technologies. They have added value to machine tools primarily through applying microelectronics and through design simplification rather than significantly improving machines themselves or developing the foundations for the processing technologies of the future. This approach was ideal for playing catch up, but now they are moving into uncharted territory and must decide in what areas they will seek technology leadership.

Emerging Japanese Strategy

The Japanese are well on their way to charting a new strategy based on factory automation and ultra-precision machining technologies. Leadership in the former, they believe, should include extensive FMS development, flexible automation of builders' own plants, increased standardization and interchangeability of machine modules, the development of interface technologies to link equipment within the company and between the company and its suppliers, and on making significant improvements in the machines themselves, such as replacing castings with other materials that might provide greater thermal stability, less vibration, or other performance characteristics for lower costs.[60] Elements of ultra-processing include high-speed machining, noncontact technologies such as lasers and EDM to process hard-to-cut materials, sub-micron precision processing for products such as laser mirrors and X-ray optics, and new materials processing. Interest in these technologies appears to be linked to targeted user industries such as aircraft, space, electronics, optics, and biotechnology. As noted earlier, the Japanese have undertaken two massive, cooperative research projects in laser processing.[61]

While a U.S. machine tool task force concluded that Japanese technology and manufacturing standards differed little from those in the U.S. in 1980, much of what the task force saw (FMSs in many builders' plants, extensive use of robotics, a good understanding of part families and group technology, a major consortium project in CO_2 laser development) should have led to less sanguine conclusions.[62] Most Japanese builders had already installed or were implementing FMSs in their own factories; unlike U.S. vendors, none attempted to sell FMSs to others before building and learning from at least one in-house system.[63] These systems were often simpler in concept or design than their American counterparts, yet more effective in their operation, and in integrating many kinds of machines and processes. All reports of their utilization rates, number of parts made, and other measurements show that the Japanese are more fully exploiting the potential of these systems for flexible production and maximum utilization than are U.S.

companies. Virtually all observers who have spent time in Japan state the Japanese rate of FMS installation and effectiveness of use is way ahead of the U.S.[64]

Now the Japanese are taking the next step of creating flexibly automated factories. This will allow them to quickly produce modular, specialized machine tools to order. When this capability is combined with fundamental development work in ultra-precision processing, their emergent strategy is clearly one that could decimate European machine tools much as the commodification of standard machine tools decimated the U.S. The Japanese are beginning to challenge the Europeans in their own backyard: excellence in product engineering. The Japanese builders movement into flexible factory automation takes the high ground in shifting competition from product engineering to process capabilities. By offering process solutions/integration as a major product while producing the hardware through the very systems they sell, this strategy integrates their emerging product and process strategies. It therefore puts enormous pressure on the European builders to flexibly automate their factories in order to stay competitive. Secondly, in conjunction with stateside plants that will take on an increasing range of functions over time, it positions the Japanese to deliver the product increasingly sought by American users: integratable cells and turnkey systems. The emergent Japanese strategy thus poses an enormous challenge to a U.S. industry that is still scrambling to catch up to the standards established by the first wave of general purpose Japanese exports. Soon American high-end systems and custom engineering will be challenged by standard Japanese systems delivered through stateside plants.

The German Approach

Machine Tool Industry

West Germany has 350-400 producers, about 80 percent of whom belong to the VDW, the German machine tool builders trade association. Mid-sized firms predominate, and the largest has 2,500 employees. Many of these grew from being small family firms, now have several hundred employees, still have few layers of management, and remain highly responsive to their environment. About 250 export to several countries. Most are independent, few are publicly held, but increasing numbers of them belong to an industrial group.

Because bankers are reluctant to lend to cyclical businesses (the German builders are, however, less cyclical than American), retained earnings have long been the primary source of investment capital. Access to additional capital was one of the major industry weaknesses cited by a recent VDW-commissioned study by the Boston Consulting Group. Given this, and given the practices of German industrial groups towards their subsidiaries, some independents have been seeking corporate parents in recent years. For example, Scharmann, a pre-eminent producer and integrator of large machining centers and systems, recently linked up with Dorries, whose technology base is in turning) when it became part of the Voith Group. In so doing, Scharmann gained a complementary technology, access to more investment capital, and has somewhat more leverage with its very large customers. The attitude and behavior of such industrial groups towards their machine tool companies differs diametrically from that of many U.S. conglomerates. The parent is usually an engineering group in which it makes sense to have machine tools as one component. The group expects to integrate the builder into its total business, make the level of investment needed for the builder to become or remain a technology leader, and have the patience to see it through.

This approach reflects the long-term perspective preferred by German industry. Builders who were interviewed for this study could not explain why they thought this way. Indeed, their slightly taken aback reactions made it clear that it did not occur to them to think otherwise—what other sensible way is there to run a business? This long-term approach was also reflected when builders took on business in which they could anticipate that the engineering work would exceed their fixed price, but they would gain something more valuable than immediate profits: learning.[65] The overall financial results appear to be positive, for the same BCG study found that liquidity, financial stability, and profitability were some of the industry's greatest strengths.

Product Strategy, Innovation, and Exporting

German firms have traditionally produced a limited range of sophisticated machine tools. Historically, a pattern of "cooperative specialization" was fostered by the VDW and the VDMA (the trade group for all machinery producers). Members were encouraged to develop excellence and expertise in a particular set of processes/machines. This effectively reduced the number of firms competing in any one area, but simultaneously fostered fierce domestic competition between subsets of firms, each of whom was technically very strong, and each of whom felt driven to innovate in order to stay ahead or remain competitive. Cooperative specialization facilitated exporting, as trading companies and manufacturers' agents could represent a whole set of noncompeting German producers overseas.[66] Specialization also necessitated exporting in order to improve scale economies, while heavy dependence on exports in turn demanded world-class products designed with world markets in mind.

The overall effect then was to position German firms in high-end niches at the top of many, if not most, machining processes, with every firm having a few excellent domestic competitors yet also being able to cooperate with a wide-range of noncompetitors. Because some of these processes are intrinsically complex—such as gearcutting and grinding—the "high-end niche" could get fairly substantial; the West Germans still have over half of the world's gear-cutting marketing, over one-third of grinding, and one-third of metal-forming.[67] But as Helmut von Monschaw, general manager of the VDW, points out:

You cannot survive on niches alone, however. You have to be highly innovative at the high end
in order to stay competitive, but you can't lose the low end. And, except for those who are very

specialized, we have been starting to feel the effects of the Japanese, especially in lathes and machining centers, but now also in grinders and presses.[68]

The delays in feeling the effects of the Japanese and in Europeans moving into CNC production have several technical and economic bases. Until very recently, the Japanese could not offer direct performance competition in the European strongholds, so the Germans and other Europeans were less pressured to move into CNC production in the 1970s. Gearcutting and grinding are intrinsically more complex than turning and milling, and it took longer to develop NC controls with enough precision to control this high-end equipment. Because there is also much more volume in turning and milling, there was further incentive for European control manufacturers to first develop products for these operations. EEC trade barriers also kept Japanese NCs out, insulating higher-priced, higher-performance European NC controls from price competition. From its somewhat protected position, Siemens, the major European control manufacturer, was not especially responsive or flexible in meeting the needs of European builders. Although Siemens moved to solid state technology in the middle 1970s, it was less innovative than Fanuc The latter continued to innovate the technology, introducing such developments as LSI and bubble memory. While German builders have been even less successful than American in developing their own controls, they have moved rapidly into CNC product lines during the past few years. The rate of NC/CNC production relative to all production has been climbing about ten percent annually, and fully 45 percent of production is now NC/CNC.

User Pull and Relationships

Innovation has also been driven by customers who were themselves technically proficient, and who put technical performance at the top of their purchase criteria. A 1965 survey of British customers found technical considerations to be the leading reason for buying imports, of which West Germany was the leading source. These considerations were technical superiority, machine specifications not available in Britain, and willingness to do specials.[69] Such reasons are very similar to those of present-day American users who feel they must go to Europe to get certain kinds of performance—e.g., Pratt & Whitney and GE going to Hauni-Bloom or Elb for creep-feed grinders, or GM going to Scharmann for large CNC milling centers. While British customers of German equipment may have been technology-oriented, the British, in general, are much less technologically demanding than German customers. A 1984 study comparing British and German users found that 69 percent of the latter rated technical sophistication as being very important, while only 11 percent of the British customers did. German users also found machine power and rigidity to be of much greater importance. Price was secondary to German users, as it was with the British customers in the NEDC study who bought imports.[70]

The importance attached to technical issues by customers of West German builders translates into strong customer pull for product innovation. For example, Burkhardt + Weber's (B+W) customers place a premium on doing all machining operations in a single setup; they will pay the higher costs in order to get fast velocity and flow-through for their parts. B+W has focused a lot of its resources on high value-added hardware that reduces queues and waiting by concentrating operations in a single machine. Their vertical machining centers have heads that can swivel in multiple axes and their horizontal machining centers can machine the workpiece from any angle. While several German companies have developed innovations in automatic tool changing, B+W has chosen an approach in which a robot goes immediately to the tool rather than having to turn the whole tool magazine until the right tool comes to the position opposite the robot— again, the emphasis is on saving time. These design choices are made carefully, for B+W does not sink much money into a new product without having discussed it quite thoroughly with key users. B+W's closeness and responsiveness to customers appears to be more the norm than the exception, at least among specialty producers.

Close relationships with customers are also facilitated by geographic concentration. Half of the German machine tool industry is clustered within 50 kilometers of Stuttgart, the center of the automotive business, making frequent face-to-face contact possible. Coupled with an excellent railroads system and autobahns, Germans can and do make extensive use of ground transportation to meet with one another.

User Sophistication

Greater technological sophistication among users appears to be one of the most important factors differentiating the German from the American industry. It is the thesis of one world expert, Dr. Eugene Merchant, that user sophistication is such a differentiating factor, and one that critically affects the rate at which new manufacturing technologies, especially FMSs, can be implemented. American users, Merchant finds, take little or no responsibility for their own systems, depending heavily on builders (or other third parties) for identifying their needs, specifying their requirements, designing and installing systems, training their people, and providing service. Japanese and European users, by contrast, know a great deal more about their own needs and what is required to fill them.[71]

While several builders declined the concept, they routinely brought out differences that make Merchant's point. Relative to Americans, German users translate their more demanding level of technical requirements into far more detailed specifications. Builders must then address these specifications with very detailed proposals. In response, users know what questions to ask, and ask many of them. Americans, it is often said, just want to know how quickly and at what cost the proposed machine will make their parts.[72] National differences in user sophistication are also reflected in what builders give to users when they deliver their products. One German builder put it this way: "we give five inches of documentation to American firms for every one inch we give to German firms." Recall, too, our earlier discussion of the Boston

University study pointing toward low user sophistication as the greatest cause of delay in adopting new PATs.

The vast gap between German and American production workers is cited over and over by German managers as a, or often as the, top problem of American manufacturers. They say it limits both the kinds of equipment that companies feel they can introduce, and the rates at which they bring it in. One builder said, "U.S. companies hesitate to go to high tech systems because they don't have the people." Another put it more bluntly, "Americans think their people are too dumb to buy sophisticated equipment."

In short, while we would like to examine this issue in much more depth and much more systematically, there appears to be significant anecdotal support for Merchant's thesis. There appear to be fundamental differences between German (or Japanese) and American users' ability to understand their own process needs, turn these into detailed specifications, ask the right questions of bidders, and continually optimize and extend the equipment or system's operation.

Technical and Educational Infrastructure

Underlying greater technical sophistication among German users and their ability to take responsibility for configuring and installing their own systems is an infrastructure of apprenticeship, polytechnical schools, universities, and technical institutes that produce multi-leveled manufacturing expertise among German adults. This educational system provides skilled shop floor people, practical engineers who can make things work and solve problems, and more research-minded engineers who push the limits of process understanding but do so in close association with industry rather than in an ivory tower.[73] These institutions, in turn, are supported by cooperative linkages with industry, trade unions, state governments, the federal government, and trade associations. All invest heavily in education and training. Industry's view is that they are making an investment in the future of the West German economy rather than generating an expense for their individual firms. Dense communication networks, overlapping memberships, and flows of people among these institutions generate wide diffusion of ideas and build consensus about such subjects as collaborative research priorities. The results include the widespread and rapid diffusion of cells and simple FMSs noted earlier, and continuing technical leadership in the mechanical engineering-based industries.

Because a separate Commission study is comparing educational systems, the German system will be described briefly and emphasize aspects most relevant to machine tools.

Apprenticeship. The first level of user sophistication is provided by the apprenticeship system which provides builders and users with shop floor people who have a minimum of three years of technical training. Over half of German young people go through a company-run and funded apprenticeship program following high school. Because of the rapid rate of technology change and the recent acceleration of CNC, the structure of apprenticeship classifications and training was becoming somewhat outdated a few years ago. A slow but thorough reassessment has led to considerable revamping and modernizing of certain apprenticeship areas, metalworking and electric trades being primary among them. One of more visible outcomes of the apprenticeship system, immediately obvious when touring German plants, is that shop floor people work from blueprints while American workers require detailed instructions. German workers also understand feeds and speeds, they understand machining processes, and can work on virtually any machine, NC or manual. Apprenticeship creates a solid foundation among shop floor and technical employees, so that the introduction of new equipment requires their learning only the specifics of the new hardware and software.

Continuing Education. A variety of programs offer ways to maintain, expand, and update skills. They are offered by companies, evening schools, unions, vocational schools, and other organizations. They include the training of master craftsmen (*MeisterSchulen*) who are then entitled to train apprentices, and the deepening of technical skills among those whose have already passed their apprenticeship and had some practical experience (*FachSchulen*). Some of the slowness of the traditional system is compensated for by responsive new systems such as the professional academies (*Berufs akademie*) founded by Bosch, Benz, and Standard Electric several years ago. The idea was to create a practical engineering degree focused around new technologies for people who were already employed. Three-month rotations on the job and in school lead to an engineering (*ing.*) degree equivalent to an American B.S. This program concentrates on NC planning, organization, programming, operation, and maintenance. Many companies give an additional week's vacation to employees who need the time for outside training, most reimburse employees for educational courses they take on their own, and large firms conduct extensive in-house training.

Polytechnical Colleges. German polytechnical colleges, or *FachhochSchulen*, as well as universities offer engineering degrees. Most high-school graduates who go straight into engineering attend a *FachhochSchule*, although, if they have the grades and the inclination, they may go to a university. The former has a more practical, hands-on approach, includes a longer and required practicum, and turns out people who know how to make things work and to troubleshoot problems. Graduates receive a diploma of engineering degree (*Dipl. ing FH*), something close to an American M.S. Up to 90 percent of the engineers in many companies will have gone this route. Polytechnical schools are state- supported, and exist in all major cities. University engineers (*Dipl. ing*) get more theoretical training, and some go on for doctorates (*Dr. ing*), which may take six to eight years altogether. University training stresses the basics (physics, chemistry) in the first two years, but then begins to specialize. Even non-manufacturing majors, however, study manufacturing from the first year. Those who take doctorates often go into company R&D, but retain close connections with sales and manufacturing in their firms.

Technical Institutes. Advanced study in engineering is usually done at or with one of the many technical institutes located at the state-run universities. These institutes, together with the 34 Fraunhofer Institutes, are the focus of generic research, cooperative industrial problem-solving, and advanced technical training. The purpose of all of these institutes is to help industry—the university institutes doing more research, and the Fraunhofer more developmental and applied work, but with considerable overlap. They are driven by applied research; indeed, the charter of the Fraunhofer Institutes is to promote applied research—just as the Max Planck Institutes support pure research. Research programs at different institutes both specialize and overlap; several, but not all, may be conducting work on laser beam machining, or sensor systems for robots, or vibration control. Information about what each other is doing is disseminated formally through the Society of Production Engineers, but informally by dense networks and participation in multiple organizations and processes concerning the development and review of research agendas. The linkages are rich and multiple: being part of a proposal development-review-consensus building process that pulls people from different sectors together; actually working together on applied problems; the institutes' providing people who will assume responsible positions in industry following completion of their studies; selecting institute directors with several years of industry as well as academic experience (and usually from outside the particular university so as to get fresh blood); and by continual communication.

The university institutes gain almost 20 percent of their funding automatically from the states (which support the universities), and over 80 percent from projects. Industry provides about 35 percent and the federal and state governments 45 percent of the total budget; all of these monies are for particular projects. Fraunhofers follow a similar pattern, though their base 20 percent is from the federal government. Over 40 percent of their monies must come from direct, bilateral work with companies. They have much more funding available for equipment than do the university institutes, and a great deal of sharing of equipment goes on between the two. Industry also donates a good deal of state-of-the-art equipment to the institutes.

The sharing between university and Fraunhofer institutes goes beyond equipment. The same professor may wear dual hats and play a parallel role at both institutes at a given geographic location. At Aachen, for example, the same four professors head the parallel subdivisions of the university and Fraunhofer institutes. Many doctoral students do their research at Frauhofers, but their degree must come from the university. Physically, the Fraunhofer may be in the same or an adjacent building as the university institute.

About 20 university institutes are dedicated to machine tools. Each is headed by a different full professor, and attached to a state university. The institute at Aachen, for example, is widely considered to be the best machine tool lab in the world. When asked what has made is so great, German builders and students always talk about the leadership of Dr. Opitz and his four successors (Opitz' chair has now been separated into four). Their names, and those of many other researchers at other institutes, are well known throughout the German industry. Other institutes well known for their machine tool work include Berlin, Hannover, and Stuttgart.

The work program at these institutes are divided into three or four major departments: machine tools (design, automation, and controls); production process technology; production planning and systems; and metrology and quality. Each of these departments has major programs that tend to be relatively stable over at least a 8-10 year period. At Hannover, for example, processing has programs in laser beam machining, abrasive processes, and cutting of super hard materials, nonmetals, and molds, while Aachen has programs in geometrically defined (and in undefined) cutting edges, EDM, metalforming, and gear manufacturing. Each program has multiple projects of greater or lesser duration. Fraunhofers have similar structures for organizing work. In addition, both types of institutes can conduct work that takes a horizontal cut across these departments. For example, processing might be investigating the parameters of a process, while machine tools designs appropriate equipment, and planning considers its sequencing and role in overall operations.

The research agendas of the university institutes are partly self-determining, but most projects evolve from ongoing dialogues with industry and priorities emerge through consensus building. Projects follow one of four models:

1. Basic research proposals are put forth by research groups at the institute to a government agency, the DFG, a group not unlike the American NSF. If approved after review by outside scientists, the project is funded by the DFG from state and federal monies.

2. Individual companies may contract with any institute to solve a particular problem or develop a particular product. For example, a laser manufacturer had trouble with the fifth axis of its six-axis machine, and turned to the institute at Stuttgart, which successfully redesigned this part of the laser. (In this case, it was the Fraunhofer Institute, but the principle is the same.) Institutes serve as consultants and provide technical assistance when asked. Collaborative research follows one of two more complex models. Such projects benefit multiple companies or the entire industry, and are usually more generic or process oriented than product-specific.

3. Working groups among interested companies talk to researchers at an institute, and the ideas get defined and refined. The project idea goes to the VDW, which takes a very active role in spearheading cooperation on generic manufacturing research, and in deciding what contracts should be given. Its technical committees (composed of builder members) meet and decide on the project, and go to the institute to draft the formal proposal. Following revisions this goes to the AIF and outside reviewers. The AIF is a working group of industrial research associations—from textiles to buttons to electronics— whose funds are sought not only for the money itself, but as an expression of broader industry support and interest. The reviewers are from the scientific community and other institutes. If approved, the project is jointly funded by industry (the VDW, using member fees; and the AIF), and the federal government.

4. The last model of establishing agendas and funding is somewhat narrower than the third, but still a cooperative project. These projects are put forth by a horizontal (.e.g., three auto companies) or vertical

(e.g., a steel company, an auto company, and a builder) group of companies to the Ministry of Research and Technology (BMFT). If approved by the Ministry's advisory group, the Ministry supports the institute's share of the work 100 percent, and supports part of the companies' work. Some of this work is done in company R&D labs. Institutes find this type of project to be the most difficult around which to get competitors to collaborate, and conceive their role in part as fostering that kind of collaboration.

In summary, the educational and technical infrastructure is the very foundation of German success in machine tools. Working closely with industry, the university and Fraunhofer institutes provide research, development and technology transfer, carrying out both generic work that no one company should have to do and applying engineering expertise to help companies solve specific problems or implement particular solutions. New engineering talent flows from the institutes and the schools, while experienced industry people teach part-time and provide guidance on the directions research should take. This guidance reaches out beyond the VDW members to the AIF researchers who represent many industries. Overlapping memberships and ongoing dialogues shape and reshape priorities and form a de facto national consensus about generic work.

Industrial Policy

The German federal government has not assumed the highly directive, industry-focused approach of the Japanese, but a much more facilitative, supportive, background role. German builders would not accept a directive industrial policy, as they believe entrepreneurs must chart their own courses. The federal government has encouraged industry standardization, made it clear that it would not retard collaborative research by bringing anti- trust action, strongly supported industry-university relationships, and funded some joint and basic research. It has also channeled bank funds to specialist producers for expansion, and strongly promoted trade with the Eastern bloc.[74] The state governments have supported and funded the joint research and administrative costs of the technical institutes. They have encouraged the industry's focus on incremental improvement and deepened understanding of materials and processes as the foundation for developing ever-better machines.

Changes in Product Design and Production

In the last few years, many German producers have made major changes in their approach to design and manufacturing in order to become more cost competitive and flexible. These changes appear to have been stimulated by several sources, one of which has already been discussed, namely, the needs of lead users. Second, the BCG study strongly emphasized the need for volume in order to be more cost competitive, and the need to use flexible automation (particularly CNC and FMSs) in-house in order to stay competitive with the Japanese. Everyone in Germany with whom the author spoke was familiar with this study, brought it up in discussion, and took its conclusions very seriously. Third, the efforts of builders appear to be part of a larger shift in the German machinery industry toward flexible production of even higher performance/quality products at lower costs. This self-conscious emphasis on flexible production has been adopted by the engineering industries in order to stay competitive in specialized businesses that have short runs of small batches.[75]

Increasingly conscious of the costs of specialized products, German builders are moving toward model reduction, modular designs, and standardized hardware and software. Klingelnberg, for example, a full-line producer and world leader in gears and hobs, has reduced its number of basic models from five to three, gone to modular design, and works from a standard machine which it then tailors for the user. Similarly, B+W has extensively modularized and standardized its designs so that 70 percent of its machining centers' content is standard; this includes 100 percent use of Siemens controls. This is coupled with great depth in tailoring the tooling, fixtures, and software to the customer; over 25 percent of B+W's employees are design and sales engineers who customize standalone equipment and integrate systems.

German builders are also moving rapidly into producing integratable cells and systems, and regearing their own production systems towards flexibility. After a late start, German builders have moved heavily into CNC; many firms produce 80-100 percent CNC products, and the industry average is approximating 50 percent and still climbing. Depending on how one defines "system", between 25 and 50 West German firms are now producing FMSs for customers.[76] Firms like Klingelnberg and B+W have installed machining centers and cells in order to reduce setup and throughput time, and increase flexibility. Like many other German firms that have moved into FMSs, Werner und Kolb started doing standard cells, and then integrating them into systems. Werner has sold 70 FMSs (or cells) in the past few years—30 installed, ten in process, 30 back ordered. Werner is emphatic about offering standardized systems with standardized software; tailoring, it believes, can come later, and with less risk due to accumulated experience with standard systems. Since 1983, the demand for cells and systems has skyrocketed, as has the capability of German builders to deliver them. Trumpf, for example, delivered one system four years ago, four the next year, nine the next, and 16 the next. But it began installing systems in-house in 1981, three years before it delivered one to a customer. Trumpf now has 15 cells and systems in its home plant alone; Trumpf itself has integrated these systems—composed of diverse machines from diverse manufacturers of tools and controls—obviously building an extensive experience base in doing so. Scharmann has taken yet a different approach to flexibility. It has minimized its vertical integration, limiting in-house production to critical components in which it has a clear advantage, while investing heavily in a broad array of talented people who can develop and customize systems.

In summary, the new German approach emphasizes modular design, standardization of both hardware and software, mastering cells before systems, integratability, and learning from in-house experience before making promises to and obvious mistakes with customers. It is the author's impression as well as the impression of virtually all observers with whom she has talked that the German acceleration into FMSs (both selling them and installing them in-house) has been very rapid since 1983, far outpaces the Americans, and is second only to the Japanese.

Success in Machine Tools

Critical Success Factors

Different as their approaches are, the West Germans and the Japanese share certain commonalities that appear to have been critical to their past success in machine tools:

Industry Rationalization or Compensation. Machine tool industries in all countries began as small firms that created highly fragmented industries. As technologies changed more rapidly and there were more of them to master, and as globalization demanded world-class but cost-competitive products, this structure became increasingly dysfunctional. Without a very strong niche, it became extremely difficult for small firms to survive, let alone thrive. The Japanese recognized this thirty years ago and encouraged/forced industry rationalization. This approach fit well with MITI's emphasis on general purpose products that required scale economies. Correlatively, the government took an active role in technology diffusion, and later its development as well, to compensate for what firms could not do on their own. It compensated for small firm size first by licensing and distributing technology, and then by drawing together consortia to develop generic systems and advance their collective understanding of critical new technologies.

The Germans eschewed such a top-down approach, and opted for a bottoms-up and middle-across approach driven by the private sector with government and university support. The limiting effects of small firm size have been counteracted by cooperative and highly active relationships between builders, technical institutes, and users. The technical institutes began over fifty years ago, became permanent centers of technical excellence, and nerve centers for the flow of ideas and people. Overlapping memberships and geographic proximity have helped to nourish the dense communication channels between multiple parties.

Export-orientation. The Germans and the Japanese have led the world in volume and share of exports. The Japanese were, however, more conscious of building world market share and scale economies for standalone commodity products—an example from which the Germans are learning. The new German emphasis on modular building blocks and standard products is aimed at building volume and reducing costs. Builders in both countries also recognize that exporting is needed for more than volume—i.e., that it is also critical for long-term innovativeness and responsiveness to customers. Exporting firms have a different mind-set, constantly gathering input from global suppliers, customers, and their own people that affects how they design and develop products. They are much more likely to know what world competitors are doing, and what kind of production effectiveness and efficiencies they require to stay competitive.

Increasingly, builders in both countries are going beyond exporting to open or expand overseas plants. This strategy does not merely get around trade restrictions and exchange rate fluctuations, but positions such builders for the customization and systems integration work that are the major growth areas for the 1990s.

Long-Term Perspective. Whether privately held (most German firms) or publicly held (most Japanese firms), foreign builders have taken a long-term perspective. They plough funds into long-term development and plant reinvestment. They install FMSs in-house before building them for customers. The take on low profit jobs in order to gain experience. They build overseas plants in advance of sales levels that would make them immediately profitable. This long-term view is, in the Japanese case, fostered by large government subsidies, and the long-term orientation of bankers who encourage a long-term market share/growth orientation over short-term profits. In the case of the Germans, it appears to be endemic to their way of doing business, and is reflected in bankers and investors having more patience than their American counterparts. German banks can take an equity position in companies, and tend to have less inflated expectations than does Wall Street about profit levels. Investment capital is, however, a growing problem for mid-sized builders.

Continuous but Focused Innovation. Domestic users of German and Japanese equipment have viewed themselves as having to compete fiercely in the international arena, and have exerted more pressure on their builders to innovate in order to increase users' own productivity, flexibility, or provide the necessary performance in their products. Innovation has been fostered by close builder-user relationships, and collaborative research projects supported by governments, trade associations, and universities. In conjunction with exporting, product specialization among builders in both countries has placed a premium on each builder continuing to innovate in their own area.

Focus is brought to innovation at two levels—national, and firm. Both countries have mechanisms that develop research priorities for the industry or branches of the industry. Decision-making in Germany is obviously much more decentralized, and sites for priority research multiple and permanent, while MITI pulls consortia together as needed to develop generic technologies and systems in targeted areas. Firms appear to concentrate their resources on high value-added components or technologies—e.g., B+W's focus on heads, Trump's on lasers, FANUC's on servo motors and controls.

Domestic User Sophistication. Both the Europeans and the Japanese provide multiple levels of technical/manufacturing training through their formal educational systems and shop floor experience. Job assignments take engineers into manufacturing, and manufacturing carries high prestige. Together, schools and firms create a manufacturing-competent work force from the shop floor up. The manufacturing competence of the Germans and Japanese allows users in both countries to take on much of the responsibility for identifying their process requirements, configuring systems, implementing them in their shops, and continuously optimizing their operations. While they look to builders for expertise, systems experience, and to take a lead role in systems integration, they are less dependent on them for figuring out what they (the users) need and how to optimize system operation in their own shop. The implications of user sophistication are enormous, because it is the "*sine qua non*" for the rapid diffusion and effective use of FMSs and integratable cells that has been observed in both Japan and West Germany.

Competitive Differentiation. Both the Europeans and the Japanese have built globally competitive machine tool industries based around what they do best. The Europeans are product performance leaders who are now changing their design approach and production systems to be more cost competitive and flexible. The Japanese used their skill in design simplification and manufacturing to commodify a large part of the machine tool market, and gain a greater share of the world market. By leading the way in flexible automation right in their own factories, and focusing development efforts on critical future machining technologies, they are extending their assault from the commodity to the specialty markets, and shifting competition from product engineering to product/process effectiveness.

Rating the American Industry

Do these six factors distinguish countries whose builders have been successful from those that have been less successful? Specifically, do U.S. builders, by and large, fail to meet the critical success factors (CSFs) derived from the West German and Japanese experiences? The short answer is yes, these six CSFs do differentiate between successful and unsuccessful countries. U.S. builders on the whole did not export extensively, and either failed to innovate adequately on their own initiative or found too few takers to sustain their innovation efforts. Had they been more export-oriented, they may have found more interested users. Domestic builders have tended to take a short-term view, again either on their own or due the short term behavior of their customers. Because most of their customers did not push for new technology and lacked the skills for implementing and integrating the new technologies into their business, diffusion has been slow and builders limited in how much they could do because they had to tie up so many of their people resources in each project. Chronically undercapitalized in a cyclical industry (whether because of small size or having to compete for funds from a conglomerate parent), builders were left to sink or swim on their own. They did not build links with other parties, and neither did other parties take initiative to work with them. As a result, most American builders lost competitiveness, or indeed, any distinct competitive advantage.

Responsibility for the results must be shared. Builder decisions and attitudes were shaped in a context in which customers were conservative about early adoption of new technologies, and sometimes actively destroyed builder incentives for continued innovation. Engineering schools dropped their manufacturing engineering programs, shut down their manufacturing labs, and developed engineers who neither knew nor cared about manufacturing. Neither state nor federal governments developed policies to help builders; most policies had the opposite effect.

Recommendations

Machine tools are too essential for competitive manufacturing and a viable economy to just write them off as some people have. Given the systemic causes of the demise of the domestic industry, it follows that systemic changes are required for survivors to maintain or regain their international competitiveness. Changes needs to be undertaken or accelerated at national, industry, and organization levels. Only a few general recommendations are offered here—those that follow most directly from the major themes in the report, and are close to the Commission's charter.

National Vision and Strategy

American policy leaders must develop a vision of, and political support for, the requirements for long-term commercial viability of the United States. That vision must proceed from the fundamental assumption that a manufacturing-based economy is essential, and that leadership in process equipment—the heart of which is machine tools—is essential to manufacturing competitiveness. That vision must refute the dangerous notion that services can be the core of a viable economy. That vision must make it clear that services such as engineering applications or systems integration require a hardware core, without which the services, too, will evaporate.[77]

With specific regard to machine tools, it is obvious that interventions above the firm level are necessary to compensate for the fragmented, cyclical structure and the pressures these create for short-term, nonforward-looking, nonglobal decision- making. Interventions should be linked to an overall strategy regarding the industry segments in which the U.S. can build competitive advantages. Global industry dynamics are pushing the major players (Japanese, West Germans, Americans especially) towards head-to-head competition in systems and high-end standalone products—America's remaining strongholds. But neither can the U.S. afford to completely relinquish general purpose standalone markets to the Far East. Areas in which constructive intervention is needed:

Exports. Consistent policies among different agencies; rational rather than moralistic basis for trade and export policies; simplification of procedures and red tape; technical assistance to small firms who want to export.

Overseas Direct Investments. Increased exporting will not be enough however. Direct investment in overseas plants and engineering will be increasingly essential to global competitiveness. Simplification of procedures, reduction of red tape, information dissemination, and technical assistance are some constructive steps.

Joint Technology Development. Builders cannot be expected to carry the entire burden of research and development. Builders, users, governments, academia, and other research groups must jointly define, sponsor, and conduct fundamental research and generic development in key manufacturing processes, equipment design, and systems control and integration. Areas of joint development should be of common interest and of strategic value to national manufacturing competitiveness; examples would be ultra-precisioning machining, a next-generation controller, or component- oriented programs for next-generation machines. NCMS is pioneering such an approach, and needs to be expanded and duplicated in regional or local areas. The German model (on which NCMS has built) is one that the United States could emulate in building the kind of technical infrastructure required for the 1990s and beyond.

Technical Assistance for Supplier Base. The nation's supplier base is of great strategic importance, but has been deteriorating for many reasons. One reason is that small or modest size constrains the range of technical and staff skills that can be supported, and finances limit the amount of outside expertise that can be hired. Smaller users need technical assistance that provide valid comparative performance data about new equipment, reduce risk in adopting new equipment, provide free or low-cost consulting to choose and implement systems, and financial incentives to invest. The German technical institutes and nonprofit volunteer groups provide two models, while the National Bureau of Standards role could be expanded (e.g., with regard to the providing comparative performance data).

Anti-trust and M&A Policy Changes. Anti-trust policies need to be geared to the 1990s rather than the 1930s, and encourage mergers that increase scale economies and international competitiveness, even if the number of domestic competitors is reduced. Some important manufacturing equipment niches will only support a very few world wide competitors. Merger and acquisition policies need to be developed that prevent greedy arbitrageurs from destroying companies for profit, but encourage rationalization and integration of operations, product lines, and marketing of similar or complementary firms.

Educational Infrastructure

The apparent difference in user sophistication between the U.S. and its major competitors goes to the core of the Commission's inquiry. If we ask, what is the primary cause of this difference, the answer is: the education and training systems of the two countries, and the career and reward patterns within academia and industry. If we ask, what are the implications of this difference, the answer is: much more rapid pace of advanced manufacturing technology diffusion and its more effective optimization in Japan and West Germany than in the U.S. In essence, because fewer of their builder's resources are tied up in each project, they can do more of them. The significance of this difference was brought home to one American builder who attended the 6.EMO trade show in 1985 at Hannover:

> We saw 50 or more FMS vendors, each of whom had shipped at least ten systems that year. We, on the other hand, can do maybe two a year, and have 100 customers waiting. What's the difference? The users. In Germany, users install the systems because they are more technically sophisticated than Americans. They have the manufacturing engineers, the shop floor people, the skills to take responsibility for their systems. We can't do as many systems as their builders— first, because ours are more sophisticated than many of theirs, and second, because our manufacturers don't have the skills. We must rebuild our manufacturing engineering base in this country.

This statement should not be dismissed as the self-serving view of a builder. Rather, it should point us to reallocating more responsibility to metalworking users and the educational system for the effective development, use, and operation of new manufacturing technologies. Only then can manufacturing companies become partners with equipment builders in the massive job of bringing the manufacturing skill base of the United States into global competitiveness.

Technical Education. It is imperative to resurrect and revitalize the technical (i.e., post-secondary) level of education, apprenticeship, and training in the United States. The existing public vocational education system is useless, and it should be scrapped. Enormous efforts are needed, however, to develop technical schools, apprenticeship programs, and community colleges to provide initial post-secondary and continuing education that is relevant for the work and equipment of the 1990s and beyond. Schools need to have access to the latest equipment, although there is a role for learning the "feel" of processes on traditional equipment.

Manufacturing Engineering. Manufacturing engineering programs are badly needed to train new MEs and update current MEs. To make such curricular changes work, major funding of manufacturing research is needed, as are (in most cases) changes in reward and tenure systems so as to make manufacturing, hands-on or interdisciplinary work attractive to younger faculty and students. During the past five years, seed monies from IBM and from the Society of Manufacturing Engineers to inaugurate or redirect such programs have demonstrated what even modest sums, when linked to appropriate guidelines, can achieve. Well-regarded programs are underway at RPI, Purdue, Lehigh, the University of Wisconsin, the University of Rhode Island, and elsewhere.

Manufacturing in the Engineering Curriculum. If the split between manufacturing and engineering is to be bridged, manufacturing must be fully integrated into the undergraduate engineering programs—not an option, an extra, or something for MEs only. Process must be as important as product in the training and retraining of engineers. Engineering schools must rethink their design paradigm so that students design to targets—manufacturability, cost, reliability, ease of use, and ease of maintenance. This means engineering programs that give students much more exposure to reality, through cross-departmental projects, projects with industry, the recruitment of part-time or adjunct faculty rotated or retired from industry, etc. The German Fachhochschulen and technical institutes are one model.

Business Schools. For many years, graduates of the leading business schools have had minimal interest in manufacturing and virtually none in machine tools or manufacturing equipment. Nor do machine tool builders go to business schools to recruit. While more business students are now appreciating the importance of manufacturing, that understanding can be augmented by increasing the centrality of operations and technology management courses, and reorienting the value system from one of profit as the goal to its being a by-product of good products and good working relationships among people inside and outside of the firm.

Continuing Education. Continuing education is required at every level to update disciplinary skills, and provide cross-disciplinary learning. One example is Portsmouth Polytechnical in the U.K. which has a new program that gives a post-graduate masters degree geared to the integration of advanced manufacturing technology.

Builders and Users

The purpose of the foregoing recommendations is not to salvage inept or lazy firms but to give aggressive, capable firms a better shot at success. Some manufacturers have already moved in the directions suggested below, but most have a considerable way to go.

Global and Customer Orientation. American manufacturers need to get more connected with what is happening around the world, and have this consciousness inform their product and manufacturing strategies. While increasing exports is a near-term objective, overseas plants will become a necessity for firms whose products require a lot of customer interface and are application- or customer-specific. Systems do not export well.

Design Strategy. Builders and users must design for manufacturability, which includes simplification of design, reduction of part counts, modularization, early manufacturing involvement, etc.

Manufacturing Strategy and Process. Manufacturing strategies must be developed and modified in concert with business strategies. Flexibility, short lead times, excellent reliability, and competitive cost must all be achieved to remain competitive with Japan's automated and highly flexible factories. This will require that builders use more of the manufacturing process technology that are trying to sell, and that process and equipment choices be strategically based.

Systems Integration and Support. Close' working relationships between builders, control manufacturers, and users are the strongest foundation for effective systems design and integration.

Notes

1   Ralph Winter and Gregory Stricharchuk, "Machine-Tool Makers lose out to Imports due to Price, Quality," *Wall Street Journal,* August 17, 1987; interview with Michael Hasler, former GM manager, and head of a study on machine tool purchasing; September, 1987; *American Machinist*, June 30, 1986, p,5; "P&W Increases Procurement of non-US Tools," *Metalworking News,* June, 1987; interview with Pratt & Whitney, September, 1987; interview with Hauni-Blohm, December, 1987; interview with Kingsbury Machine Tool, September, 1987.

2   Quote in "GM studies U.S. Machine-Tool Firms. One problem: the way automakers buy." *American Machinist*, January, 1986.

3   The first three factors would depress both units and dollar shipments, while the fourth would depress unit sales but not necessarily dollar sales.

4   For example, in remarks to the Manufacturing Studies Board, January 13, 1981; see, e.g. "West Germans give Soviets $2.08 billion credit line," *Wall Street Journal*, May 9, 1988.

5   "Quality" can mean many things, including the high-speed performance and autobahn handling of a BMW or the conformance to specifications and repair record of a Toyota. David Garvin separates out eight dimensions in "What Does 'Product Quality' Really Mean?", *Sloan Management Review*, Fall, 1984; and Competing on Eight Dimensions of Quality," *Harvard Business Review*, November-December, 1987. In machine tools, as in several other products, the Japanese have approached design and manufacturing with an emphasis on conformance and reliability. Good conformance requires processes that are within statistical limits, so that one component is very like another, and the end product itself consistently produces parts that are very similar. Simplicity and standardization of design increase reliability, measured most often as mean time between failures, thereby minimizing machine downtime, a primary concern of users. The dimensions of quality emphasized by Joseph Juran and W. Edwards Deming, and some of the engineering and manufacturing implications of these dimensions, are discussed by Artemis March in "A note on quality: the views of Deming, Juran, and Crosby," Harvard Case Services, 1-687-011.

6   In 1986, 50 percent of the value of Korean exports was NC compared to 31 percent in the previous year; NC production is now one- third of the value of all Korean production. The Taiwanese first specialized in standard lathes and drills, but NC production climbed from 5 percent in 1982 to 20 percent in 1986, and the value of NC exports increased eight-fold between 1982 and 1986. NC lathes and machining centers dominate Taiwan's NC exports, over half of which go to the U.S. Korean Machine Tool Manufacturers' Association, "Machine Tool Industry: Korea, 1987." Taiwanese Machine Tool Builders Association, "The Status of the Machine Tool Industry in Taiwan," 1987.

7   Harvey Brooks and Maryellen Kelley have identified these six technical factors as potentially differentiating factors in user decisions to adopt or not adopt PAT technology in their research proposal, "Technical, Economic, and Organizational Factors Explaining the Diffusion of Programmable Automation in Machining," John F. Kennedy School of Government, Harvard University, 1985.

8   The National Machine Tool Builders Association (NMTBA) estimates than 200 firms closed their doors in the last decade. Although 1000 or more firms are statistically classified in SICs 3541 and 3542, the NMTBA estimates that only half as many are active, operative firms. NMTBA, *Economic Handbook of the Machine Tool Industry, 1986-87* (McLean, Va.: NMTBA, 1986). Hereinafter *Economic Handbook*.

9   David Collis, "The Machine Tool Industry and Industrial Policy, 1955-82," in *International Competitiveness*, ed. by A.M. Spence (New York: Ballinger Books, 1988).

10 C.F. Pratten, "Economies of Scale for Machine Tool Production," *The Journal of Industrial Economics*, Vol. 19, 1970-71, pp. 148-65. Pratten's analysis of British machine tool production in the 1960s demonstrates that the major economies of scale in machine tool production derived from large cumulative output of a single model and fairly large batch sizes for machining. This optimized the amortization of the costs of design, development, jigs, tools, and introducing the model into production, in conjunction with optimizing the costs of setup, paperwork, and supervision while gaining learning benefits. In the absence of modular design and flexible manufacturing, the benefits gained from increasing the range of products appeared limited. Pratten's research implies that the economics of successful machine tool production reinforced small firm size and narrow product lines.

11 The term "paradigm" has come into considerable use since Thomas Kuhn's *The Structure of Scientific Revolutions* (Chicago: University of Chicago Press, 1962 and 1970) put the concept at the heart of its interpretation of the history of science. A fuller and richer term than "framework" and more precise than "system," "paradigms" refer to the invisible and implicit ground rules by which the scientist is socialized into identifying certain questions as appropriate or inappropriate to ask, certain territories legitimate for possible answers, and certain methods sanctioned for seeking the answers. Kuhn argues that science has not been a gradual evolution of the best explanations winning, but an irregular and political process punctuated by the exhaustion of old paradigms' explanatory ability and the existence of a new and more powerful paradigm. The term can be usefully applied to the very different assumptions, thought patterns, linkages, as well as elements in the Japanese approach to world competition.

12 This position is taken by a National Academy of Engineering committee in a study of the industry, *The Competitive Status of the U.S. Machine Tool Industry* (Washington, D.C.: National Academy Press, 1983). *Competitive Status* takes the view that exporting has value primarily as a counter-cyclical strategy; it fails to appreciate that successful exporting must be worked at continuously, not on a stop-and-go basis, or that exporting is a sine qua non of successful participation in a global industry. This study and a companion study, *The U.S. Machine Tool Industry and the Defense Industrial Base* (Washington, D.C.: National Academy Press, 1983) provided the author with an initial orientation to the industry, and stimulated the first rough map out of which Figure 7 eventually emerged. Both studies were invaluable in the early stages of the present study. In the author's present view, however, *Competitive Status* does not give adequate attention to either metalworking customers or other institutions for their contribution to the demise of the machine tool industry. The NAE study places almost all responsibility for the problems of the industry on the builders themselves.

13 Interviews with companies named and "How They Build the Bridgeport," *American Machinist*, August 10, 1970.

14 "Foreign Competition Stirs U.S. Toolmakers," *Business Week*, September 1, 1980, pp. 68-70. cited in *Competitive Status*, 1983, p. 49.

15 National Academy of Engineering, *The U.S. Machine Tool Industry and the Defense Industrial Base*, 1983, p. 16.

16 Eric von Hippel has developed this concept through a series of studies on different industries. Articles include "Users as Innovators," *Technology Review*, 80:3, 1978. *The Sources of Innovation* (Oxford: Oxford University Press, 1988) pulls this body of work together.

17 These statements and Table 7 draw upon the *American Machinist* inventory of metalworking users which is taken every five years. The 13th inventory, conducted in 1983, is the latest for which figures are available. Although its sample is large (12,300 plants), its response rate is low: 7 percent of all metalworking plants, and 24.4 percent of plants having 20 or more employees. These returns are based on a questionnaire mailed to all metalworking plants having 20 or more employees (listed in McGraw-Hill Circulation Market Data Bank) and to a random sample of 10,000 plants from Dun & Bradstreet's list of metalworking plants having fewer than 20 employees. Two follow-up mailings are used. Estimates based on the inventories are therefore to be used with some caution. They are cited at various points in this report for several reasons. The inventories are a basic point of reference for anyone working in this area. Some of the research studies have not done any better with response rate or range of SICs represented in the base. The basic story they tell--aging vintage of equipment, slow adoption of NC--seems corroborated by a variety of observers.

18 These percentages were put together from various sources by American Machinist and are from different years, so some caution must be observed in making comparisons. In addition to international vintage differences, many observers also note international differences in how machinery is cared for; meticulous housekeeping by the Germans makes even their older equipment perform more like newer equipment, while dirty and poorly maintained American and British machines perform worse than their age suggests.

19 Sciberras and Payne, 1985. It should be noted that the size of the Japanese installed base is fully three-quarters that of the American. The Japanese have about 1.5 million tools and the Americans about 2 million (as of 1983). The American base has been shrinking significantly as old tools are thrown out, and replaced by newer tools that are more productive.

20 Hicks found plants of any age to have similar patterns of first adoption: minimal during the 1960-64 period, picking up during the next five years (17 percent), slightly increasing in the early 1970s (23 percent), and peaking in the 1975-79 period (43 percent first adoption). The age of the plant made no difference in pattern of adoption, or likelihood of adoption. Rees *et al.*, however, found a progressive inverse relationship between age and likelihood of adoption; that is, the older the plant, the more likely they were to adopt NC/CNC. Donald A. Hicks, *Automation Technology and Industrial Renewal: Adjustment Dynamics in the U.S. Metalworking Sector* (Washington, D.C.: American Enterprise Institute for Public Policy Research, 1986), pp. 84-89. Hicks' findings are based on data collected at the end of 1982 from 1172 plants in the U.S. Response rate for completed surveys was 15.3 percent. The sampling frame was derived from subscribers to *Modern Machine Shop*, a principal trade publication of the metalworking industries. John Rees, Ronald Briggs, and Raymond Oakey, "The Adoption of New Technology in the American Machinery Industry," occasional paper no. 71, Metropolitan Studies Program, Maxwell School of Citizenship and Public Affairs, Syracuse University, 1983. These national survey results are based on 628 returns, and an adjusted response rate of 19.6 percent.

21 *American Machinist* 13th Inventory, November, 1983. See the cautionary note about this data in footnote 17. But again, while these data alone might be suspect, numerous other sources come to the same conclusion: diffusion of both NC and CNC was slow. David Noble cites a number of these sources, some of them unpublished company reports, in his *Forces of Production: A Social History of Industrial Automation* (New York: Alfred A. Knopf, 1984).

22 Business Research Corp., "Japanese Machine Tool Industry," Investext report number 602938, 1987.

23 *American Machinist* found that eight percent of U.S. NC purchases between 1978 and 1982 were made by firms having fewer than 20 employees.

24 The Japanese Machine Tool Builders Association traced NC sales from 1970-1980, and found a

progressive shift to small users. In 1970, small and mid-sized firms bought 28 percent of NC and by 1980, they bought 64 percent. Quoted in *Computerized Manufacturing Automation: Employment, Education and the Work force* (Washington, D.C.: U.S. Congress, Office of Technology Assessment, QTA-CIT- 235, April, 1984), p. 282. Watanabe reports that 25 percent of NC sales in Japan during 1981 were to shops having fewer than 10 employees. S. Watanabe, "Market Structure, Industrial Organization, and Technological Development: the Case of the Japanese Electronics-based NC Machine Tool Industry." World Employment Programme Research working paper no. WEP 2-22/WP.111 (Geneva, International Labour Office, 1983).

25 "GM Studies U.S. Machine-Tool Firms. One Problem: The Way Automakers Buy." *American Machinist*, January, 1986.

26 Stephen Rosenthal, "Progress toward the Factory of the Future,'" *Journal of Operations Management*, Vol.4:3, May, 1984. Conducted in the 1982-83 period, leading users were surveyed separately from suppliers, while the experts' survey was designed to test some of the preliminary data from the first two surveys. The experts were senior professionals, over half of whom had worked in factory automation for over 15 years. The suppliers were marketing managers of major producers of factory automation technologies. The users were early adopters of factory automation, and required multiple interviewees to cover the range of subjects. The technologies were grouped into four categories: CAD, CAD/CAM, CAM, and factory management and control.

27 Margaret Graham and Stephen Rosenthal studied eight American FMSs in depth, and other sites in less depth. "Flexible Manufacturing Systems require Flexible People," paper presented at TIMS/ORSA, Atlanta, November, 1985.

28 For example, Cincinnati Milacron has thrown out almost 400 machines in the past few years; reorganized plants and equipment through focusing factories, group technology, and work cells; and built a sophisticated FMS for production of parts for its plastics machines. Hardinge now has about 60 NC tools, has spent two years achieving Class A, MRP II user status; with inventory and bill of materials accuracies at 98 percent, Hardinge is using JIT to examine its work centers (i.e., identifying non- value added activity, reduce setup times, lot sizes, etc.) and move to more cellular manufacturing organization so as to reduce inventory, speed up throughput, and give marketing more flexibility. Kingsbury has spent at least $5 million on new equipment to control critical tolerances on key machine parts, and invested in Zeiss gaging equipment to get the accuracy and speed needed for inspecting high-volume (10,000-20,000) parts for customers.

29 Rees *et al.*, 1983.

30 Anderson Ashburn and Joseph Jablonski, "Japan's Builders Embrace FMSs," *American Machinist*, February, 1985. Naoaki Usui, "Yamazaki's Showplace FMS," *American Machinist*, (Date?). Ramchandran Jaikumar, "Hitachi Seiki (A)," Harvard Case Services 0-686-104. Ramchandran Jaikumar, "Yamazaki Mazak (A)," Harvard Case Services 0-686-083. Jaikumar, personal communication, November 25, 1987; interview with Eugene Merchant, November 15, 1987.

31 Philadelphia Technology Management Center, "The use of advanced manufacturing technology in industries impacted by import competition: an analysis of three Pennsylvania industries," 1985.

32 This section draws upon field interviews, and written accounts by two opposing camps: David Noble`s *Forces of Production: A Social History of Industrial Automation* (New York: Alfred a. Knopf, 1984), which is highly critical of MIT and corporate America; and multiple articles, a manuscript in process and interviews, with some of the MIT principals in NC development. Such articles generally take a positive view of the contributions of MIT and the Air Force. Many of the issues in hottest contention between these camps are of little interest to the present study, and need

not concern us. In many, but not all, factual areas, the two sides agree. The gaps in both sets of accounts and their disagreements, together with the limited time and resources for original or comprehensive research in the present study still leave many holes and many important questions unanswered. The interpretation presented here is the author's, based on the current state of her knowledge.

Articles by MIT principals include: John Ward, "Numerical Control of Machine Tools," *McGraw-Hill Yearbook of Science and Technology*, 1968; John Ward, "The Technical Development of Numerical Control," presented at the Society for the History of Technology, Washington, D.C., October, 1977; J. Francis Reintjes, "Crucial Decisions during the Evolution of Numerical Control," presented at the Society for the History of Technology, Washington, D.C., October, 1977; J. Francis Reintjes, unpublished manuscript, chapters 2, 4, and 6, 1988; Douglas Ross, "Origins of the APT Language fdor Automatically Programmed Tools," *ACM SIGPLAN Notices*, Vol. 13:8, August, 1978; and transcripts of interviews by Reintjes conducted with William Webster (civilian chief, Wright Field), 1969; Col. Carter (head of the Manufacturing Methods group at Wright-Patterson, and a key implementer of the "big buy"), 1969; Edgar McFerren (vice president, Giddings & Lewis), 1969. Reintjes was director of the Servo Lab for 20 years, starting in 1953; Ward was project director for APT and later deputy director of the Lab; Ross was the primary architect of APT.

33 Noble, 1984.

34 Noble placed the amount at over $60 million, but Reintjes, based on his interviews with Webster, says that the 105 NC machines cost $30 million, while the total Bulk Buy was for $84 million. Ralph Cross, who was then president of the NMTBA and played a major role in the Bulk Buy, recalls an $80 million total.

35 According to Noble, the Air Force spent at least $33 million (and possibly twice as much) on this effort; MIT participants in the project say this is exaggerated, and that AIA members put up most of the people and money. In any event, the scope of the project was quite large, and some other interviewees believe that $33 is a minimum estimate of what it took to develop.

36 The AIA immediately made APT its standard; by 1974, it had become the U.S. standard for programming metalcutting tools; and in 1978, it was made an international standard.

37 Noble, 1984.

38 Noble, 1984; interview with J&L, August, 1987; *American Machinist* special centennial edition, September, 1977.

39 Sciberras and Payne, 1985, state that GE did not bring out the 1050HTL until 1979-80, and a leading edge user within GE recalls seeing the first solid state prototypes in the middle 1970s. Indeed, Sciberras and Payne believe that the reluctance of GE (and Allen-Bradley) to move to solid state controls is the key to the U.S. lag in adopting CNC, and paved the way for the "Japanese invasion." Efforts to further document this statement have not been conclusive. Most observers believe that GE was late with the right product, but don't emphasize the technology. Allen-Bradley did offer a solid state control by 1973, but it was complex, hard to use, required extensive customization, and was costly. Its effort to simplify the next generation control (in 1982) was rejected by its customers because it did not meet their needs or cost objectives.

40 Only in the past two years has a major joint effort been directed at the generic needs of builders and users. Unlike the 1950s consortium, its needs are commercially oriented. It arose from the shared concerns of members of the Manufacturing Studies Board (MSB) of the National Research Council (NRC), the Department of Defense, and some builders. Their work has led to the formation of a

National Center for Manufacturing Studies (NCMS) described in Appendix B. The top priority emerging from the summer, 1987 meetings of various technical panels is for a generic, second generation controller that would leapfrog present technology and be applicable to a wide range of products.

41   Robert Kaplan, "Must CIM be Justified by Faith Alone?" *Harvard Business Review*, March-April, 1986; Robert Kaplan, "Accounting Lag: The Obsolescence of Cost Accounting Systems," in *Uneasy Alliance*, ed. by Kim Clark, Robert Hayes, and Christopher Lorenz (Boston: Harvard Business School Press, 1985); Bela Gold, "CAM Sets New Rules for Production," *Harvard Business Review*, November-December, 1982; Bela Gold, "Analyzing the Effects of Computer-Aided Manufacturing Systems on Productivity and Competitiveness," in *Managerial Issues in Productivity Analysis*, ed. by Ali Dogramaci and Nabil Adam (Boston/Dordrecht/Lancaster: Kluwer-Nijoff Publishing, 1985). Stephen Rosenthal, "Progress Toward the Factory of the Future," *Journal of Operations Management*, 4:3, May, 1984.

42   This is what the NCMS is now trying to do. Note that the impetus came from concerned individuals at the Manufacturing Studies Board (part of the NRC), the DoD, from among builders and users. But the magnitude of what is needed is much greater than the NCMS can be expected to marshal.

43   These programs, and the deficiencies they are designed to correct, are described by Artemis March in "Note on the Aerospace Industry and Industrial Modernization," Harvard Case Services 9- 687-009, 1987.

44   See National Research Council/Manufacturing Studies Board/Committee on the Role of the Manufacturing Technology Program in the Defense Industrial Base, *The Role of the Department of Defense in Supporting Manufacturing Technology Development* (Washington, D.C.: National Academy Press, 1986); and *Manufacturing Technology: Cornerstone of a Renewed Defense Industrial Base* (Washington, D.C.: National Academy Press, 1987). The studies conclude that present procurement practices do not carry sufficient incentives for contractors to adopt risky technologies, and therefore direct funding mechanisms are needed for developing and diffusing AMTs as one element of a DoD investment portfolio. The committee argues that the deficiencies in the current ManTech programs should not be used to as an excuse to cancel them, but rather to guide the reformation of an advanced techmod program. Such a program should focus on a much smaller, coherent, set of larger, riskier programs that are strategically linked to defense needs.

45   Collis, 1988.

46   "Standard" is used interchangeably with "general purpose" in this discussion.

47   "Machine Tool Industry Reaps Benefits...", 1986. In 1983, the Japanese produced over 24,000 NC machines compared to 4,200 for the U.S. and 7,500 for the FRG.

48   "Machine Tool Industry Reaps Benefits from Product Improvements," *Business JAPAN*, September, 1986. See Footnote 29.

49   Business Research Corp., "Machine Tool Industry Report," Investext Report Number 506995, 1985; Business Research Corp., "Japanese Machine Tool Industry," Investext Report Number 602938, 1987.

50   Japanese production rates may have gone even higher than indicated by Figure 14. Mori Seiki, for example, was said to be building 250 lathes and 120 machining centers monthly in an article by the

senior editors of *American Machinist,* "Japan's Builders Embrace FMSs," February, 1985. Interviews with Okuma/Charlotte indicated that its Japanese partner was building at least 300 lathes monthly in 1987.

51   Collis, 1988.

52   Siemens produces only about 300 of its high-end and specialty controllers per month, while GE has retreated from producing its own NC designs. Gene Bylinsky, "Japan's Robot King Wins Again," *Fortune,* May 25, 1987; Interview with GE/FANUC, 10/16/87; "GE Teams Up with FANUC in Factory Automation," *Electronic Business,* March 15, 1987; Seiuemon Inaba, "My Management," May, 1986 speech.

53   In return for license fees, Burgmaster sent thousands of drawings and much proprietary information to Yamazaki beginning in 1970. Six years later, Mazak began selling an identical machine in the U.S. under its own name and at a lower price. Burgmaster technicians found that Yamazaki's copying had included the mistakes of the original designers. Yamazaki pressured the Japanese government into obstructing investigation by Burgmaster's attorney and ITC officials. Discussed by Marvin A. Wolf, *The Japanese Conspiracy* (New York: Empire Books, 1983).

54   MITI brought together consortia of builders, heavy equipment firms, electronic firms, and FANUC to develop an "advanced FMS" project in 1976. At first planned to be totally unmanned, the FMS was thought to be too sophisticated by industry, and was modified to be more practical. By 1984, the project had developed a demonstration system that ran untended once loaded, completely machined parts for three products (one spindle and two gear boxes), assembled the products with interchangeable robot manipulators, inspected the final product and determined whether it could be shipped. The system was fed by various tool, chuck, and spindle-carrier systems. Naoki Usui, "MITI's 'Super' Manufacturing System," *American Machinist,* August, 1984.

During the same period, MITI began sponsoring another massive consortium to develop an ultra-high-performance, laser- applied multiple production system (participants listed in Table 11). The objective was to develop an automated manufacturing system that applies laser technology to small-lot production of different kinds of products. Recognizing the vast funds needed for laser R&D, MITI has now sponsored a second joint government- private sector project that aims, among other things, to incorporate sensing and monitoring functions into laser equipment, and develop new processing technologies. Industrial Bank of Japan, "Japanese Finance and Industry Quarterly Survey," No. 66 (2nd quarter, 1986). The technical benefits to participants are beginning to be visible; at 7.EMO (the 1987 European-based trade show), for example, several Japanese builders had laser machining equipment, and most of them were manufacturing their own equipment.

55   *U.S. Machine Tool Industry and the Defense Industrial Base,* 1983; National Research Council/Manufacturing Studies Board, "Reactions of Small Shop Owners to the Automated Research Facility of the National Bureau of Standards," April, 1985; interviews with machine shop owners.

56   Dr. Inaba, president and CEO of FANUC, states that he will commercialize only those products based on his core technologies, and that his favored cost structure is 70 percent electronics and 30 percent mechanics. In this way, he says, FANUC gains competitiveness but avoids competition against builders who are also customers. "My Management", 1986.

57   "Machine Tool Industry Reaps Benefits...", 1986; Investext reports 506995 and 602938. In 1981, for example, 70 percent of exports were NC but only 51 percent of production.

58 The problems faced by small shops in this regard are discussed in "Reactions of Small Shop Owners...", 1985, and in interviews with machine shop owners.

59 The incredible story of how the attorney penetrated Japanese secrecy is described by Wolf, 1983, in detail.

60 "Machine Tool Industry Reaps Benefits from Producer Improvements," *Business JAPAN*, September, 1986.

61 See footnote 47 and Table 12.

62 Raymond Larsen, "Japan Exhibits Variety Among Machine Tool Firms," *Iron Age*, May 19, 1980.

63 "Machine Tool Industry Reaps Benefits...," 1986; "Japan's Builders Embrace FMSs," *American Machinist*, February, 1985. Builders with in-house FMSs include FANUC, Yamazaki, Mori Seiki, Hitachi Seiki, Makino Milling, Mitsubishi, Okuma, Shin Nippon Koki, Toshiba Machine Co., Takisawa Machine Tool, Murata Machinery, and Hitachi Seiko. FANUC and Yamazaki are often cited as having the most sophisticated automated factories in the world. See Naoaki Usui, "Yamazaki's Showplace FMS," *American Machinist*, May, 1985, pp. 96-97.

64 "Japan's Builders Embrace FMSs," 1985; Ramchandran Jaikumar, "Postindustrial Manufacturing," *Harvard Business Review*, November-December, 1986; interviews with Eugene Merchant; Anderson Ashburn; Helmut Hammer; Daniel Whitney, Ramchandran Jaikumar.

The Philadelphia Technology Management Center makes a very similar point based upon estimates and evaluations from a variety of (presumably different) industry analysts. All agree upon the basic point: the Japanese are way ahead in FMS implementation. Reported in "The Use of Advanced Manufacturing Technology in Industries Impacted by Import Competition: An Analysis of Three Pennsylvania Industries," 1985, p. 79.

65 This same behavior may be viewed in some quarters as customizing in order not to lose business, and thus a short-run defense of market share. Sciberras and Payne, 1985, are critical of German industry for accepting customization and eroding profits, particularly during the recent recession). Their view of the German industry as profitless conflicts with the BCG study's conclusions about its solid profitability.

66 Gary Herrigel discusses cooperative specialization and the role of the VDMA in fostering it in his working paper, "The Political Economy of the Industry: Mechanical Engineering in the FRG." MIT, April, 1987. The general manager of the VDW confirmed the export facilitation role of cooperative specialization in an October, 1987 interview.

67 *Economic Handbook*, 1986-87 edition, tables on pp.170, 182-83, 191-92.

68 Von Monschaw is also general manager of the machine tool section of the VDMA; machine tools are one of about 10 groups within the larger trade association. His dual hats are symptomatic of the very close and overlapping relationships that pervade German industry and its technical infrastructure.

69 This survey asked British users why they were increasingly buying imported machines; 59 percent cited technical reasons as their primary concern. This 59 percent was composed of: technical superiority, 30 percent; machine specifications not available in Britain, 21 percent; and willingness of foreign manufacturers to meet special requirements, eight percent. Other reasons were quick and reliable delivery, 20 percent: better after sales service, five percent; price, 5 percent; and the prospect of reciprocal trading agreements, 11 percent. The study was conducted by the National Economic

Development Committee, and entitled *Survey of Investment in Machine Tools* (London, HMSO, 1965).

70 Three product attributes--technical sophistication, power, and rigidity--were of much greater importance to German than British users in buying equipment. Percentages were as follows: technical sophistication: 69 percent of German users and 11 percent of British rated this as very important; power, 60 percent versus 18 percent; and rigidity, 60 percent versus 40 percent. The survey was based on responses from 73 British firms and 56 West German. Stephen Parkinson, *New Product Development in Engineering: A Comparison of the British and West German Machine Tool Industries* (Cambridge: Cambridge University Press, 1984).

71 Merchant, retired after a half century at Cincinnati Milacron, now directs advanced manufacturing research at Metcut, a highly regarded engineering consulting firm. His early work on the fundamentals of metalcutting evolved into a theory of chip formation and the mechanics of cutting, regarded by *American Machinist* as "still the best scientific explanation of the metal removal process." Merchant was an early advocate of a computer-integrated, rather than piecemeal, approach to manufacturing. While at the Mill and since, he has traveled extensively, lecturing on manufacturing systems and observing international developments.

72 Another perspective on this would be that German customers are frustrated machine tool builders who get overinvolved in telling builders what gears and bearings to use while American customers let the builder decide how to meet customer performance targets.

73 The tenor of most comments about the technical institutes is positive, but a muted counterpoint says their approaches are too far into the future, and not sufficiently applied.

74 Summary of German industrial policy based in part on Collis, 1988; field interviews, and

75 Herrigel, 1987, discusses this third issue in his paper.

76 By strict definition, many German systems are cells, and less complex than many of the systems built by American builders such as Ingersoll or Milacron (see Appendix B).

77 See Stephen Cohen and John Zysman, *Manufacturing Matters* (New York: Basic Books, 1987) for one development of this thesis.

Appendix A. Industry Parameters and Study Methodology

Defining the Industry

SIC Classification and its Problems. The first step in this study was to determine the scope of the "machine tool industry." Since we were not collecting primary data, we had to accept existing definitions of the industry when dealing with issues such as shipments, exports and imports. All of the primary data collectors (the Census Bureau, other agencies in the Commerce Department, and the National Machine Tool Builders Association) use the standard industrial classification (SIC) framework.

The SIC approach collects data by products, and codes all activities of a firm by its predominant product. Industries become defined as the aggregate of firms having the same primary product. The Census Bureau therefore defines the machine tool industry as composed of firms whose primary products are metalcutting (SIC 3541) or metalforming (3542) tools. Unlike many industries, the overlap between product and industry is very high in machine tools. In 1985, 91 percent of the products shipped by the metalcutting industry were metalcutting machine tools; for metalforming, the corresponding number was 89 percent. The proportion of machine tools made by firms classified as within the industry was also high; the metalcutting industry made 93 percent of such tools, and metalforming made 87 percent of those tools. Much of the remainder is captive production. The three-digit industry group level (SIC 354, metalworking equipment) also encompasses machine tool accessories (3545); dies, molds, and tooling manufacturers (3544); power driven hand tools (3546); rolling mill machinery (3547); and residual metalworking equipment (3549).

But, increasingly, the machine tool industry encompasses more than hardware classified as metalworking. Computerized controls, related software, engineering applications services, and systems integration activities are the major growth areas related to machine tools. One would like to track the level of these activities and who is doing them, but the SIC approach does not allow us to do that. The SIC approach makes it impossible to separate out machine tool-related products or services that have been coded outside of 3541 or 3542. NC controls and software are buried in 3541 or 3542 when shipped as part of the complete unit. If shipped separately, NC controls are classified with "industrial controls" and software according to the primary product of the firm that created it. But neither can these important products and services be unbundled from the machine tool hardware data that is coded within 3541 and 3542. Engineering applications work, after-sales support, systems integration and other value-added services are included, but cannot be unbundled from, hardware products when these activities are performed by builders. When such services are performed by others (distributors, accounting firms, consulting firms), their connection to machine tools is lost. The present study discusses some of these trends, but most of the aggregate hard data it uses has been collected by government and industry associations, and refers to metalcutting and metalforming machinery plus those unbundled products and services performed by builders.

When carried to more than four digits, the SIC code gives detail about traditional products, while collecting many newer products under "cutting, NEC" (not elsewhere classified) of "metalforming, NEC". The former residual "other" category includes machining centers, transfer lines, electrical discharge machining (EDM), electrochemical machining (ECM), and waterjets, as well as shapers, planers, and sawing machines. As more and more functions are performed by single machines (e.g., milling, drilling, boring, and deburring at machining centers), many of these traditional distinctions will become more and more meaningless while new products are inadequately defined. On a more promising note, the SIC schema has begun to develop codes for NC and CNC machines; however, they are set up as alternatives to, rather than inclusive of, specific types of machines.

Data Sources. Data on the industry comes from the Census of Manufactures (every five years), Annual Survey of Manufactures, but have severe time lags. The NMBTA compiles a 300-page handbook annually which draws from these sources, but draws more heavily on quarterly Commerce Department MQ-35W reports as well as its own data on shipments and orders. MQ-35W reports pertain to complete new machine tools only, and their numbers run smaller than tables that include parts, and/or tools that sell for less than $2500. These quarterly reports also collect some data according to whether the products were NC or nonNC controlled. The Commission report draws extensively upon the Handbook.

Meaningful Classification. While the differences between cutting and forming are obviously fundamental, further subdivision by product function leaves the outside observer lost in a sea of detail. More meaningful distinctions are the type of control (conventional, NC, CNC), standalone versus systems, and general purpose versus special purpose. Controls are discussed in Appendix B; the installed base is still predominantly manual (or conventional), but the proportion of NC/CNC is continuously rising, though at different rates according to user and country.

Most machines are standalones: used by themselves, without any peripherals attached. Or they may be linked by materials handling devices into systems. Conventional tools can be linked into dedicated transfer lines for high volume production (i.e., hard automation), and CNC machines may be linked into systems under central computer control (called FMSs, or flexible manufacturing systems).

From a business standpoint, the most significant distinction is between general purpose and special purpose machine tools. General purpose tools are flexible: they can work on many kinds of parts. They include lathes, machining centers, and drills. About 60 percent of the world's metalcutting machines are of this type, and they do at least 60 percent, and perhaps as much as 80 percent of its cutting. Special purpose tools work on a narrower range of workpieces. Their key features are one or more of the following:

1. Precision—very close tolerances are required (.0001- .000001 inch, that is, between "a tenth" and "a millionth"). Examples include jig borers for diemaking or precision machining centers that mill jet engine components.

2. Size—huge machines are required to mill airplane skins or the beds and tables of huge machine tools.

3. Volume—when high volumes warrant, it may be economical to dedicate machines and their tooling to a single workpiece. Transfer lines are examples. Flexible transfer lines (which cost roughly twice as much) can machine a family of parts, e.g., a range of starter engine housings.

4. Complex shapes—some shapes are impossible to make on general purpose machines, or require a very long time; if volumes warrant, special machines are more economical. Examples are gear-cutting machines or milling machines that cut turbine blades and vanes.[1]

General purpose and special purpose tools are not mutually exclusive in some cases. For example, very good general precision machines (.0005-.0002) can, if well handled, be pushed to provide the tolerances of a super precision machine (one tenth or better). Or, a workpiece can in some cases be run for hours on a GP machine rather than for minutes on an SP machine.

Broader Industry Definitions. Initially, the Commission raised for consideration broader topics than machine tools: "machine tools and robotics" or "machine tools and process equipment." This broadened focus was rejected for several reasons. Much of the Commission interest in the industry studies focused on the past: what happened and why? This suggested focusing on the key historical core of process equipment rather than all the emerging trends. Second, no such industry as "process equipment" exists. This would make data collection very difficult, if not impossible. Third, an inquiry into "process equipment" could quickly become impossibly broad since various kinds of process equipment are related to their downstream user industries. No choices on how to set limits seemed satisfactory or clear-cut. For similar reasons, the attempt to look at displacement of metal by newer materials, and of machining by new processing methods seemed beyond the scope of our time and resources.

Basic Metalworking Operations

Metalworking machine tools either surface work metals by removing and cutting material as chips, or change their form by working them hot or cold using presses and dies. The accuracy and consistency of the positioning of the workpiece relative to the tool is critical. This relationship is affected by the accuracy of the workpiece location, accuracy of the tool, and their interface. Positioning devices must rigidly mount and hold the workpiece while it is worked upon, the cutting tool must perform its operations within critical tolerances, and the slippage between them cannot be greater than the product specifications allow. While there is continuous improvement in the understanding of the workpiece-tool relationship, and in the capabilities of machines to perform to stricter tolerances on more difficult shapes and metals, there have been no major changes in these basic machining processes for a long time. The major change in the past three decades has been in how this activity is controlled (see Appendix B.).

Metalcutting. Metalcutting actions include drilling (making holes), boring (enlarging the inside diameter), tapping (adding threads), reaming (widening or tapering a hole), milling (removing metal from one or more surfaces), grinding (imparting a precision finish to any surface), and gearcutting. Metalcutting machines work on one of two types of parts, prismatic or rotational. Prismatic parts are formed by positioning the workpiece (a discrete metal blank) on a table which can move in two or more axes, and allowing the rotating tool to remove metal as chips. For instance, the cutting tools of a milling machine (or its multi-functional, CNC derivative, the machining center) are set into a spindle housed in the head of the machine tool itself. In simpler machines, the spindle orients to the workpiece through only two or three axes of motion; sophisticated machines use five or more axes to achieve complex part geometries such as those found in airfoils. Rotational parts are formed by the rapid turning of the part on its center axis while being presented to the stationary tool. While being turned, the "part" is still a portion of barstock, held in place by a chuck or collet, fed to the tool (a lathe or its [often] multi-spindled, CNC derivative, the turning center), and cut off from the barstock when turning operations are completed.

Metalforming. Metalforming uses presses having thousands of tons of pressure to shape hot metal, or smaller presses and dies to cold-roll changes in the shape or surface of the workpiece at fast speeds, or stamping machines to, for example, stamp out fenders and body panels. Unlike metalcutting, metalforming produces no chips—a major advantage, because chips can land where they should not be, and the speed of cutting operations is limited by how fast chips can be removed.

Study Methodology

The Commission did not have the time or resources to conduct primary research. Our task instead was to pull together existing studies, and supplement this with field work and interviews. An initial overview was formed through studying the NMTBA Handbook, reviewing the two NAE industry studies, the NRC study *Toward a New Era in Manufacturing*, the last several years of trade journals such as *American Machinist* and *Metalworking News*, an assortment of articles and reports yielded by a computer-based search, the Philadelphia Management Center report, the OTA study on *Computerized Manufacturing Automation*, articles such as those by Graham and Rosenthal, Collis, Jaikumar, and others, and talking with knowledgeable people.[2] This work generated the forerunner of Figure 6 (industry map), a list of companies and individuals to contact, and lots of questions.

Field work began with small users, and networked to builders and distributors in the New England area, visits to other U.S. builders, the 7.EMO trade show in Milan, and visits to several leading West German builders and technical institutes. Because of the extreme difficulty of getting a representative sample from such a fragmented, diverse industry, no attempt was made to do so. Instead, several key builders in different product areas were contacted; in addition, other players, users, and experts were contacted. All the builders cooperated by inviting the author to visit. Interviews lasting from one to six hours were held with one or more members of senior management. In small firms, this was often the president or owner; heads of engineering, marketing, or manufacturing were also sometimes interviewed. Plant tours were included in every visit. The interviews covered a set of common issues in variable depth, but no formal questionnaire was used.

In line with the Commission's objectives, the interviews tried to gain an understanding of three things: 1. What happened to the U.S. machine tool industry? 2. What factors appear to distinguish successful firms/nations from those that are less successful? 3. What are the critical trends, changing strategies, emerging players or patterns?

Topics Covered. Interviews with builders focused on multiple topics. Because of the learning process, some questions could be covered more quickly in October than in August, while new issues arose or the salience of particular problems became more evident. Informants also varied widely in their span and depth of knowledge, ability to address questions directly, willingness to stay on the topic, and ability to be specific. The author responded to the informants' strengths and weaknesses by differentially probing or dropping lines of questions. Major areas of coverage were:

1. product policy (what is it, changes, GP vs special, implications for kinds of people-skills and organization);

2. design (modularity, standard vs custom components, use of CAD, responsibilities of engineers, involvement of manufacturing);

3. users (who are they, changes in what want, relationships, differences in technical sophistication among users, customer pull/disinterest re innovations);

4. manufacturing (degree of vertical integration, how and when manufacturing becomes involved, changes in organization of manufacturing, objectives of manufacturing changes, performance improvements);

5. process investment (types of recent investments, reasons for investing, sources of funding);

6. human resources (recruitment and retention issues, training needs, training programs);

7. industry and competitiveness (what happened to various companies and why, diffusion of NC and other innovations, mergers and acquisitions, competitive pressures, after sales support, exporting).

Companies Interviewed and Visited

      Practical Products, Inc.

      D&R Products Co., Inc.

      Clematis Machine & Fixtures

      Methods Machine Tool

      Hardinge Brothers

      Robert Morris, Inc.

      Bridgeport Machine Tool

      Okuma

      Bryant Grinder Corp.

      Jones & Lamson

      Lehr Precision

      Cincinnati Milacron

      Kingsbury Machine Tool

      Penumo Precision

      New England Ball Bearing

      Ingersoll Milling

      Werner und Kolb

      Scharmann

      Burkhardt + Weber

      Trumpf

      Hauni-Blohm

Technical Institutes Interviewed

      Aachen - university and Fraunhofer institutes

      Stuttgart - university and Fraunhofer institutes

      Hannover - university institute

Individuals Interviewed

      Carolyn Castore, NCMS

      Dan Whitney, Draper Laboratories

      Andy Ashburn, former senior editor, *American Machinist*

      Joseph Jablonowski, senior editor, *American Machinist*

      Michael Hasler, former GM purchasing manager

      Eugene Merchant, Metcut

Ramchandran Jaikumar, Harvard Business School

Fred Waters, Portsmouth Polytechnic, U.K.

Hans Kief, author, *Flexible Automation '87/88: the International CNC Reference Book*

Helmut von Monschaw, VDW

Maryellen Kelley, Univ. of Mass, and JFK School of Government

Wayne Moore, Moore Special Tool

---

[1] An excellent discussion of these distinctions is given by Edmund Sciberras and B.D. Payne, *Machine Tool Industry: Technical Change and International Competitiveness* (Harlow, Essex: Longman Group, Ltd., 1985), and it is drawn upon here. Sciberras and Payne further subdivide both general purpose and special purpose tools into standard (built from a high proportion of standard components) and custom (high proportion of nonstandard parts). Rather than using standard/custom to classify tools, the present study takes up this issue under design and product strategy.

[2] Full citations of these studies and some of the more significant articles are given in the text.

Appendix B. Programmable Automation Technologies

Machine Tools and PATs

With regard to machine tools, programmable automation technologies substitute computer control for operator control. The core technology is numerical control, and the term "NC" is widely used to encompass NC, CNC, and the hardware in FMSs.

PATs replace the decision-making and the control of physical movements with computer programs, controllers, and servo motors. Numerical control (NC) uses computerized instructions punched into a tape to control a standalone machine tool. Computerized numerical control (CNC) adds flexibility and reliability by replacing the tape with a microprocessor in the machine tool itself. Programs can be edited or changed easily on the shop floor because the console is right by the machine. Flexible manufacturing systems (FMSs), however defined, tie together standalone CNC machines with automated materials handling and automated tool changing and management under centralized computer control.

NC programs plan the sequence of operations, choice of feeds and speeds, and selection of cutting tools in advance of their use, away from the noise and frequently crowded conditions of the shop floor. The digital instructions are punched into a tape, and are communicated in terms of distances and angles from x,y,z or other axes of workpiece and spindle motion. The program is enacted by servo motors that move and precisely position the spindle and workpiece in relation to one another. Servo motors move more quickly than do cams, and stop their motion more precisely and without first slowing down. NC programs are usually written off the shop floor, separating planning of work from its execution. Because of this physical separation, machine operators are usually excluded from programming.

CNC gets rid of NC tapes and their associated problems of storage, breakage, dirt, as well as their inflexibility once punched. CNCs gain their flexibility from their software. CNC replaces tapes with a microprocessor in the electronic control unit attached to the machine tool itself. The computer memory stores the programs, so they can be called up easily. This makes it possible to edit, make changes, or program another related part on the spot. In contrast to NC, CNC makes it both possible, and apparently more likely, that machine operators will be involved in programming.[1]

FMSs link together multiple CNC machines to complete an entire machining sequence, or even to make a finished part from blanks, with minimal or no human intervention. The configuration of an FMS depends upon the users needs; they may be composed of a wide variety of standard and special purpose machines. For metalcutting, an FMS usually includes multiple machining centers The multi-functional machining centers either perform identical or sequential operations on parts. Automated tool management is an essential part of an FMS. Tool wear and breakage is monitored by sensors and software, and automated tool magazines bring sharp tools to replace identical but worn tools or bring new tools that perform different functions. Workpieces are clamped to special fixtures which are attached to pallets; the pallets are brought to and from the machining center on robotized vehicles. Enough fixtures and pallets are required to load and unload the machines for the desired span of untended operation. FMSs often include equipment for heat treating or washing—i.e. ancillary operations which normally occur between machining operations. Coordinate measuring machines may be included in the FMS so that dimensional testing of the part is completed before it leaves the system. All of these operations are under the control of a host computer and complex software.

FMSs may be distinguished from flexible manufacturing cells (FMCs) by their greater complexity. Cells usually link fewer machines, and the machines are more likely to be identical—i.e., four machining centers. Their span of coverage is narrower. The software is less complex than for a system. Cells can, however, be integrated into systems. Gaining experience with cells before systems is an approach being followed by many users and builders, especially in West Germany.

Comparisons with Manual Control

With a manual machine, the skilled machinist plans the work sequence, sets up the machine, chooses tools, positions the workpiece relative to the tool, controls the cutting or forming operations, sets and reads dials and gauges, checks the tool for wear, and checks the part. Cutting and checking operations may be repeated several times, and each iteration requires stopping the work, making measurements, and starting again. The tendency is to work more slowly as the workpiece approaches final dimensions; that is, the machinist takes a more shallow cut, or runs at a slower feed or speed so as not to cut too much and have to scrap the piece. The setup process also slows down as the machinist adjusts the final positioning of the workpiece. The operator walks to a tool crib (which may be located at some distance from his/her work station) to get initial or replacement tools. Judgement and experience are obviously very important in all of these activities. In some plants or on some lines, the work may be organized so that setups and work sequencing are done by skilled people, and machine operation by less skilled operators.

NC/CNC provides major advantages over both conventional manual tools and "hard automation." Advantages over manual controls are speed, accuracy,[2] greatly reduced setup time, greater productivity, more precise repeatability of operations and positioning, more consistent conformance of parts to specifications, and the ability to do complex parts that are very difficult and slow to do, or even impossible to do manually. Advantages over hard automation center on flexibility. NC/CNC replaces the dedicated fixtures, tooling, and setups of hard automation with flexible fixtures, and reprogrammable instructions that accommodate families of parts and engineering design changes.

NC is particularly useful in certain types of discrete parts manufacturing: small/medium size batches, especially if they are run repeatedly; high part variety, especially if they are also technically related; and complex parts and/or high precision parts. This makes NC ideal for fabricating dies, airframe or aircraft engine parts and machine tool parts, but its potential is far more widespread. Batch fabrication is estimated to be at least 70 percent of all discrete parts manufacturing, parts suppliers report increasing demands for precision in the tenths or millionths (of an inch), and market/product specialization and proliferation is a major trend in almost every industry.

---

1   Maryellen Kelley has found that various institutional (e.g., unionization, seniority system) and management practices mediate the effects of PATs on hourly work force skills--particularly whether they do programming or not. (Many writers on the "deskilling" debate argue that deskilling or upgrading necessarily follows the introduction of these technologies.) One factor relates to timing of adoption. "Early adopters" who started with NC separated programming from shop floor operations and operators, a practice that flows directly from the technology. Even when these firms later adopted CNC, they tended to funnel programming into the pre-existing separation of functions. By contrast, firms who started with CNC were more likely to have operators involved in programming. "Programmable automation and the skill question: a reinterpretation of the cross-national evidence," *Human Systems Management,* Vol.6:3, 1986; "Beyond the Deskilling Debate: A statistical model for explaining the desgin of blue-collar jobs under programmable automation," John F. Kennedy School of Government, working paper, January, 1988.

2   To be more accurate than manual machines, NC machines must have controls capable of repeatability and accuracy at least equal to that of the machine. During the 1960s and 1970s, NC controls from the control manufacturers lagged machine capabilities in some areas such as super precision grinding.

Appendix C. Examples of Acquisitions and Divestitures

Two cases are summarized below. The Textron case concerns a multi-industry conglomerate that bought machine tool companies when they were profitable and divested them when they were not. A smaller conglomerate, Litton Industries, has continued to expand its machine tool base.

Textron

Textron acquired Bridgeport (producer of the highly successful Series I manual milling machine, commonly known as "the Bridgeport") and Jones & Lamson (J&L) during the 1960s percent in an attempt to acquire a portfolio of profitable companies. During the next 10-12 years, these two respected machine tool makers generated a steady stream of income to Textron, most of which was channeled to other less profitable Textron activities rather than to further product or process development of the two builders. This practice did not affect the competitive position and the sales of Bridgeport and J&L until the late 1970s because machine tools had product lives as long as 20 or 30 years.

As their products matured without replacements, and product life cycles shortened, Bridgeport and J&L became less competitive. Due to insufficient development work, these two divisions lacked new lines of competitive products, especially NCs. Cheaper and more efficient Japanese NCs penetrated the traditional Bridgeport and J&L markets and resulted in losses for these two Texton divisions. At the same time, the new CEO Beverly dolan made a conscious decision to renew the conglomerate strategy of the 1960s percent—growth through acquisition and divestitures. New debt incurred from the acquisition of Avco prompted Textron to divest its machine tool businesses.

In 1985 Textron sold J&L to a group of California investors who had acquired Sullivan Machinery a year before. Both Sullivan and J&L filed for Chapter 11 bankruptcy in November, 1986. These two firms are currently managed by a specialist in corporate rescue.[1]

Bridgeport was sold to its top management in a leveraged buy out in 1987. The firm is struggling to meet its debt payments. Bridgeport suffers from inefficient manufacturing, and even its legendary Series I machine is now built in the Far East. It lacks a competitive NC product line, and competitive advantage; it relies on slashing margins to meet lower-priced foreign competition. It also still relies on the Series I, as well as foreign imports such as Yasuda machining centers for most of its income.

Litton Industries

Litton Industries consolidated its eight machine tool-related divisions under the Industrial Automation Systems Group in 1984. The eight divisions are:

New Britain Machine (turning)

Lucas Machine

Landis Tool (cylindrical grinders)

Gardner Machine (disk grinders)

Citco (acquired in 1983)

Landis Lund (UK)

Unit Handling Systems (which included Bell & Howell's robot vehicle business, acquired in 1983, and Taylor Manufacturing Co.)

Kimball Systems (mechanical and electronic identification systems)

In order to expand its presence in the machine tool industry, Litton acquired Lamb Technicon Corp., considered the strongest of the traditional Detroit-oriented builders of high-volume production equipment. This purchase tripled the size of Litton's machine tool business (see Table 6).[2]

---

[1]   "Bankruptcy for Jones & Lamson," *American Machinist*, January, 1987, p.41.

[2]   "Litton forms systems group," *American Machinist*, January 1984, p.35; "Litton to acquire Lam Technicon," *American Machinist*, April, 1987, p.49.

Appendix D. National Center for Manufacturing Sciences (NCMS)

The National Center for Manufacturing Sciences (NCMS) is a not-for-profit, cooperative research organization for U.S. manufacturers. It brings together the suppliers of process technology with their customers to determine important manufacturing research issues, define and fund projects to address them, and share in the benefits. A basic premise of the organization is that the vast majority of manufacturing problems faced by companies across all industries are generic. Only a small percent of processes are proprietary. Further, the supplier base, for a variety of reasons, has not been adequately responding to the problems. Therefore, the basic motivation for customer companies to join is to increase the number of manufacturing problems addressed, particularly those that an individual company would not likely solve on its own. The basic motivation for suppier companies to join is to develop a greater understanding of their customers' problems and support research leading to new products for defined markets.

Background

The NCMS grew out of an October 1985 meeting of machine tool builders at the Manufacturing Studies Board (MSB) of the National Research Council (NRC). The MSB had issued a report for the Department of Defense in 1983 pointing out the need for suppliers of process technology to engage in joint research. Early meetings focused on the deteriorating manufacturing capabilities within the U.S., and the need for a new solution. The concept of cooperating in research to become more competitive was initially met with skepticism. The participants agreed to explore the idea, however. The industry representatives began meeting together, and quickly expanded the discussions to include representatives from the user manufacturing community.

Early Committee Meetings

Early discussions produced a consensus around several issues. First, in order for normally competitive companies or groups to work together, cooperative research had to be concentrated on process rather than product areas. Participants also recognized that process capabilities were American manufacturers' weakest point. Second, overwhelming consensus was achieved on the need to address problems regarding implementation of research results. While no one doubted American capabilities in developing basic research and innovative technology, all had grave concerns about its ability (or inability) to translate those innovations into operational practice on the shop floor. Third, after considerable discussion, participants agreed that a new organization was needed to enable U.S. manufacturers to focus on generic manufacturing processes.

It is worth noting that during the early committee meetings, little consensus developed about the generic nature of manufacturing problems. Virtually no discussion was held in the first year regarding the substance of the work to be sponsored by NCMS. Rather, assumptions about the degree of commonality were borne out only after NCMS participants and other industrial representatives developed the first research agenda late in the summer of 1987. Thus NCMS was born. Initial funding was provided by the National Machine Tool Builders Association (NMTBA). Staff support continued from the Manufacturing Studies Board.

NCMS Membership

NCMS seeks members from all manufacturing industries. Companies must be U.S.-based, and cannot include non-for-profit organizations. The definition of a "U.S. company" has changed over time. For example, NCMS has modified its initial requirement that the majority of research and manufacturing of a member be conducted within the U.S. to that of a large portion of such activities. By October, 1987, the initial target of 80 companies committed to NCMS membership had been reached. The dues structure is based on manufacturing-based sales. Members now represent a wide spectrum of suppliers and customers.

NCMS Charter

NCMS members have developed a national manufacturing research agenda, and continually discuss changes and additions to the agenda. NCMS sponsors programs of generic interest or programs that cannot be undertaken effectively by other organizations, and promotes the dissemination and commercialization of the results. It has developed a licensing policy that allows members to gain the early benefits of research results. The agenda is developed by six Technical Program Committees: Strategic Issues; Manufacturing Data and Factory Control; Manufacturing Operations; Manufacturing Processes and Materials; Production Equipment, Analysis, Design, and Control; and Information and Technology Transfer. By April 198, the first research agenda had been approve and contained over 35 projects. NCMS will not itself perform research. Performers can include corporations, research institutes, and universities. Dissemination will be supported by a resource center whose database is easily accessible to all members.

Decision-Making

NCMS is organized to require significant participation by its members. Members make all of the important decisions. A working board of directors elected by members governs the NCMS. They will soon be aided by an advisory board of trustees. A small staff reports to the Board, and has responsibility for managing operations, membership, and fund-raising, and other activities. A Technology Review Board (TRB), appointed by the Board of Directors, is the focal group responsible for final project selection, overseeing the Technical Program Committees and providing long-term goals for members.

Funding

The NCMS seeks a $50 million annual budget by its third year. The federal government has pledged $15 million in matching funds and has delivered the first $5 million. Members' dues are another source of funding, but larger contributions and endowments are being sought.

Status

As of June 1988, NCMS had over 90 member companies from industries such as automotive, aerospace, electronics, communications, machine tools, and systems integration. It had issued over ten requests for proposals for state-of-the-art assessments. The first permanent Board of Directors has been elected and consists of 16 members. The 13-member TRB has been appointed.

Challenges

Over two years elapsed between the first discussions regarding cooperative research and the establishment of an operational organization. Considerable skepticism remains. NCMS will have a much shorter time period in which to prove its basic concepts. Over the next two years, NCMS will have to demonstrate: 1. that it can attract new and retain current members; 2. that sufficient funding can be found to support significant research; 3. that the process by which research projects are selected insures that "common" problems are defined; and 4. that the NCMS process substantially increases the likelihood that research results will be incorporated into factory operations.

Appendix E. Japanese Industrial Policy re Machine Tools

Phase I: 1956 - Early 1970s

Assumption:	Machine tools (MT) a priority industry
Objective:	Become competitive in standard manual markets
Actions:	**MITI:**

-Loans and tax breaks

-Differential tariffs to force targeted specialization

-Foreign capital not allowed

-Technology flows controlled via license approval

-Industry rationalization forced 100s of small firms to merge into 70; accomplished

    through anti-trust relaxation and 5&20 rule: make product only if have five percent

    market share in Japan and product exceeds 20 percent of firm's output.

Firms:

-Adapted and innovated licensed technology from France and U.S.

-Broadened and then rationalized product lines

-Developed competence and scale economies in particular standard products.

Phase II: Early 1970s - Early 1980s

Objective:	Retain focus on standard tools and product specialization but shift from manual to NC; goal of 50percent NC production by end of 1970s.
Actions:	**MITI:**

-10-15percent R&D subsidies (loans, tax credits, direct subsidies).

  Focus: application of NC to machine tools

-Tariffs cut on standard tools but kept on NC

-Foreign capital and factories accepted if licensed their NC technology to Japanese

-Encouraged FANUC to become sole supplier of control units for entire industry.

Industry

-Simple, low-cost CNC lathes and machining centers

-Industry-wide standards for tool-changing mechanisms, size increments, etc.

Firms:

-Concentrated on one type of CNC tool, achieving economies of scale

-Developed simple, modular, highly reliable designs

-FANUC concentrated on control and servo-motor technology, developing simplest Control unit for each type of MT.

Phase III: 1976-present

Objective: Add R&D support for cooperative development of generic advanced technologies and financing support for installation.

Actions: **MITI:**

-Funded $60 million advanced FMS project; technology available to all participants

-Low-interest loans for financing FMS installation

-Funded ultra-high performance laser production system project

-Funded second joint laser project to incorporate sensing and monitoring functions.

TABLE 1. UNITED STATES PRODUCTION, IMPORTS, EXPORTS, & DOMESTIC CONSUMPTION OF NEW MACHINE TOOLS (a), 1963 TO 1985
(Thousands of Dollars)

Year	Production	Exports	Imports	Domestic Consumption
1963	$ 946,083	$ 185,443	$ 37,679	$ 798,319
1964	1,185,380	254,511	36,364	967,233
1965	1,429,650	222,437	56,293	1,263,506
1966	1,680,014	208,909	117,748	1,588,853
1967	1,826,432	224,672	178,205	1,779,965
1968	1,722,727	216,552	163,576	1,669,751
1969	1,692,188	242,427	156,122	1,605,883
1970	1,551,777	292,086	131,826	1,391,517
1971	1,057,870	251,532	90,085	896,423
1972	1,269,302	238,135	113,998	1,145,165
1973	1,787,850	325,494	167,057	1,629,413
1974	2,165,937	410,510	270,740	2,026,167
1975	2,406,082	536,659	317,578	2,187,001
1976	2,178,265	514,942	318,304	1,981,627
1977	2,453,423	426,729	400,904	2,427,598
1978	3,142,594	533,094	715,282	3,324,782
1979	4,064,045	619,111	1,043,768	4,488,702
1980	4,812,349	734,135	1,259,802	5,338,016
1981	5,111,253	949,553	1,431,457	5,593,157
1982	3,804,250	574,567	1,217,718	4,447,401
1983(r)	2,144,849	359,037	921,083	2,706,895
1984(r)	2,423,263	373,457	1,318,964	3,368,770
1985(p)	2,729,330	400,453	1,688,693	4,017,570

p - Preliminary. r - Revised.

(a) Production figures are those reported by domestic manufacturers in the MQ-35W. Import and export figures are taken from the Department of Commerce's "IM 146" and "EM 522" reports. These figures reflect data for machine tools of all values but do not include the value of used and rebuilt machines.

Source: NMTBA. `Current Industrial Reports; Metalworking Series, MQ-35W`, U.S. Department of Commerce Trade Statistics.

TABLE 2. SELECTED U.S. IMPORTS BY PRODUCT CATEGORIES
(unit sales, dollar sales in millions dollars, and average price per machine)

YEAR	1966	1972	1974	1976	1978	1980	1981	1982	1983	1984	1985
LATHES											
Shipment:											
– Units		12,295	19,305	14,085	13,557	17,937	16,904	4,508	3,695	4,300	3,831
– Dollar value ($ millions)		203.2	370.2	430.3	535.9	827.0	816.8	507.3	320.9	310.3	318.6
– Average Price ($ thousands)		16.5	19.2	30.6	39.5	46.1	48.3	112.5	86.8	72.2	83.2
Imports: (excluding vertical turret lathes)											
– Units	14,819	5,578	8,187	7,801	12,280	16,710	15,445	11,141	6,662	9,019	11,938
– Dollar value ($ millions)	37.2	22.9	73.1	77.0	219.3	380.0	479.8	338.6	165.7	268.1	350.3
– Average Price ($ thousands)	2.6	4.1	8.9	9.9	17.9	22.7	31.1	30.4	24.9	29.7	29.3
Import penetration: (% of dollar consumption)					33.1%	36.0%	41.3%	45.9%	38.6%	51.4%	57.7%
GRINDING & POLISHING MACHINES											
Shipment:											
– Units					110,202	97,004	91,548	58,362	56,864	60,189	51,044
– Dollar value ($ millions)					348.6	555.8	615.4	486.7	280.8	335.6	413.5
– Average Price ($ thousands)					3.2	5.7	6.7	8.3	4.9	5.6	8.1
Imports:											
– Units	4,966	4,791	7,500	11,500	3,261	3,698	5,334	4,530	3,282	5,249	6,746
– Dollar value ($ millions)	12.7	12.7	32.4	31.0	68.1	138.6	137.2	117.6	89.6	118.5	147.9
– Average Price ($ thousands)	2.6	2.7	4.3	2.7	20.9	24.3	25.7	26.0	27.3	22.6	21.9
Import penetration: (% of dollar consumption)					33.4%	23.4%	22.6%	22.6%	28.9%	30.1%	29.9%
MACHINING CENTERS (new classification after 1979)											
Shipment:											
– Units					1,486	2,132	2,081	1,396	1,005	1,237	1,093
– Dollar value ($ millions)					246.0	413.0	482.7	357.6	182.9	213.2	218.4
– Average Price ($ thousands)					165.3	193.7	232.0	256.2	182.0	172.4	199.8
Imports:											
– Units						957	2,007	1,873	1,936	2,911	4,188
– Dollar value ($ millions)						93.4	195.7	188.9	164.9	248.0	330.0
– Average Price ($ thousands)						97.6	97.5	100.9	85.2	85.2	78.8
Import penetration: (% of dollar consumption)						20.8%	31.3%	36.9%	49.3%	56.0%	62.6%
PRESSES											
Shipment:											
– Units					16,655	20,428	18,030	11,765	9,665	10,747	9,140
– Dollar value ($ millions)					350.9	440.8	429.6	344.8	160.8	212.4	253.6
– Average Price ($ thousands)					21.1	21.6	23.8	29.3	16.6	19.8	27.7
Imports:											
– Units										366	466
– Dollar value ($ millions)										22.8	31.9
– Average Price ($ thousands)										62.2	68.4
Import penetration: (% of dollar consumption)						16.0%	11.6%	12.4%	29.3%	29.9%	28.5%

Source: NMTBA, The Economic Handbook of the Machine Tool Industry, McGraw-Hill Inc.
pp. 103, 106, 108, 111, 116, 126, 131, 133, 150, 151, 153.

TABLE 3. IMPORT PENETRATION (%) & IMPORTS (in $ millions)

YEAR	IMPORT PENETRATION (%)			IMPORTS ($ millions)		
	1976	1980	1984	1976	1980	1984
Metal Cutting						
West Germany	24.3%	14.1%	13.0%	59.7	150.2	137.1
Switzerland	9.2%	6.2%	6.3%	22.5	65.9	66.1
United Kingdom	11.3%	9.8%	5.8%	27.8	103.8	60.8
Japan	22.3%	40.7%	52.1%	54.8	433.4	550.6
Taiwan	5.2%	8.7%	9.2%	12.8	93.1	97.3
5 largest total	72.4%	79.5%	86.3%	177.6	846.4	911.9
Metal Forming						
West Germany	38.9%	36.6%	22.9%	27.0	85.7	68.6
Italy	6.1%	4.0%	4.3%	4.2	9.3	12.8
Canada	9.4%	8.0%	7.8%	6.5	18.8	23.5
Switzerland	8.8%	6.7%	4.1%	6.1	15.7	12.3
United Kingdom	7.3%	5.8%	4.6%	5.1	13.6	13.9
Japan	13.7%	25.0%	44.2%	9.5	58.6	132.7
6 largest total	84.1%	86.2%	88.0%	58.4	201.7	263.8

Source: NMTBA, The Economic Handbook of the Machine Tool Industry 1986-87, page 129.

TABLE 4

COMPARATIVE PERFORMANCE: U.S., WEST GERMANY, JAPAN

	1968	1972	1976	1980	1984	1985	1986
USA							
share of world production	26.3%	14.2%	16.3%	18.2%	12.0%	12.4%	9.7%
exports / dom. production	12.6%	18.8%	23.6%	15.3%	15.5%	16.6%	19.8%
imports / dom. consumpt'n	9.8%	10.0%	16.4%	23.3%	38.0%	43.4%	49.2%
total shipments ($ millions)	1722.8	1269.3	2178.2	4812.4	2412.5	2717.8	2830.0
share of world exports	10.0%	7.6%	8.5%	7.3%	4.8%	4.7%	4.1%
West Germany							
share of world production			18.3%	17.9%	14.0%	14.5%	17.8%
exports / dom. production	68.3%	55.7%	70.2%	62.6%	59.6%	62.2%	60.2%
imports / dom. consumpt'n	21.4%	22.1%	27.7%	32.8%	35.3%	23.3%	34.8%
total shipments ($ millions)			2450.0	4750.0	2803.8	3168.6	5210.1
share of world exports	28.9%	27.4%	28.5%	24.8%	22.3%	20.3%	22.9%
Japan							
share of world production	7.5%	7.5%	7.9%	14.5%	22.3%	24.3%	24.2%
exports / dom. production	10.6%	13.4%	34.9%	37.9%	38.9%	41.1%	41.3%
imports / dom. consumpt'n	18.6%	12.2%	9.3%	8.5%	6.2%	6.6%	5.6%
total shipments ($ millions)	488.9	675.6	1058.9	3830.3	4474.6	5316.7	7081.6
share of world exports	3.6%	7.6%	7.2%	13.2%	21.5%	22.6%	21.4%

Source: NMTBA, The Economic Handbook of the Machine Tool Industry 1986-87. pp. 126, 162, 163, 167, 188, 190, 198.

TABLE 5. EXAMPLES OF JOINT VENTURES

Date	Venture Partners	Product(s)	Comments
12/82	Bendix Corp[1] Toyoda Machines	Machining Centers	Bendix secured exclusive rights from Toyoda to manufacture and to market a full line of MCs in North America. (Terminated when C&T acquired Bendix from Allied in 1984.)
1984	Kearney & Trecker[2] Ikegai	Machining Centers	K&T will replace its low-end MC line with Ikegai horizontal MCs at about 100 units a year. All Ikegai MC must use K&T controls.
8/85	Cincinnati Milacron[3] Hitachi Seiki	CNC Lathes	The Mill will market Hitachi's CNC lathes as the its (private-label) low-end machining centers.
8/85	Bridgeport[4] Yasuda Industry Co.	Machining Centers	Bridgeport initiated and concluded a marketing agreement to market Yasuda MCs under its own name.
8/85	Hurco Manufacturing[5] Nippei Toyama Corp.	Machining Centers	Hurco will market Nippei vertical NC lathes as its own MCs at 20-30 units per month.
1/87	General Electric[6] Fanuc	Industrial Controllers	GE will focus on programmable-logic controllers (PLCs) and local-area networks (LANs) and discontinue its computer numerical control (CNCs) line. Fanuc will concentrate on CNCs.

1 "Bendix, Toyoda in Machine Tool Pact", American Metal Market Metalworking News, December 13, 1982.
2 "K&T Plans to Expand its Line of Imported Machine Tools", American Metal Market Metalworking News, September 17, 1984.
3 The Japan Economic Journal, October 19, 1985, page 11.
4 "Yasuda and Bridgeport Join Hands in Machine Tool Business", The Japan Economic Journal, August 13, 1985. p. 11.
5 "Nippei to Supply Hurco with Machining Centers", The Japan Economic Journal, August 20, 1985. p. 12.
6 American Machinist, March 1987, pp. 17.

TABLE 6. LARGEST AMERICAN MACHINE TOOL PRODUCERS IN 1985, 1986

Company Name	Machine Tool Sales ($ millions) 1986	1985	% Change between 1985-1986	Comments
Cross & Trecker	417.6	423.3	-1.3	Overseas sales doubled.
Cincinnati Milacron	391.6	325.8	+20.2	The Mill has diversified into the field of plastic machinery.
Ingersoll Milling Machine	300.0	165.0	+81.8	Largest privately held builder in the US. The estimated sales did not include its tools and consulting services divisions.
Oerlikon Buhrle	273.8	170.0	+61.1	Part of a $2.6 billion-sales Swiss conglomerate.
Lamb Technicon	250.0	225.0	+11.1	This privately held firm was acquired by Litton Industries earlier this year.
Litton Industries	128.0	145.0	-11.7	Its machine tool division includes Gardner, Landis Tool, Lucas, and New Britain.
Amca International	134.8	180.0	-25.1	The Canadian firm owns Gidding & Lewis.
Gleason Works	160.0	137.7	+16.2	
Wean United	90.7	NA	—	

Other large American machine tool builders are Textron (which acquired Ex-Cell-O and divested Bridgeport and Jones & Lamson,) Newcor, Monarch Machine Tool, Colt Industries, Acme-Cleveland, and Met-Col Systems.

Several Japanese machine tool builders have opened significant operations in the US and would be larger than some of the American top ten: Okuma, Mori Seiki, Makino (LeBlond Makino), Toyoda, and Hitachi Seiki.

Source: "C&T, Milacron again top list of machine-tool producers in '86", American Machinist, September 1987. p. 125. "Cross & Trecker and Cincinnati Milacron top list of machine-tool producers in '85", American Machinist, September 1986. pp. 59,61.

TABLE 7. PERCENTAGE OF METALCUTTING MACHINE TOOLS UNDER 10 YEARS OLD
Selected User Industries Between 1925 and 1983

INDUSTRY	1925	1930	1935	1940	1945	1949	1953	1958	1963	1968	1973	1978	1983
Farm machinery	35%	42%	40%	31%	45%	50%	50%	28%	27%	22%	25%	28%	33%
Constrn, mng, matl hdlg		51	26	27	52	52	42	36	26	30	31	36	39
Metalworking													
Special ind machry	44	55	24	29	55	57	40	38	37	40	39	34	37
General ind machry	48	53	25	26	46	56	45	34	31	33	30	28	29
Fabricated metal pdts	41	51	30	24	53	55	48	41	36	37	33	29	32
Off & business machs								43	40	40	47	39	43
Service ind machry		47	27	31	42	52	47	34	31	30	32	30	30
Electrical equipment	55	49	35	30	53	63	49	43	41	39	27	30	34
Communications equpt								58	61	52	46	30	38
Household appliances		54	40	31	53	62	57	34	20	26	25	27	27
Motor vehicles & parts	73	73	45	37	63	44	43	54	32	33	32	24	36
Aircraft & parts		97	87	71	98	84	50	50	42	30	30	24	36
Precision instruments			39		64	65	55	41	44	41	29	38	38
Metalcutting Average	**56**	**48**	**33**	**27**	**62**	**57**	**45**	**40**	**36**	**37**	**33**	**31**	**34**

Source: "The 11th American Machinist Inventory of Metalworking Equipment 1973", American Machinist, October 29, 1973, pp. 151, 152. "The 12th American Machinist Inventory of Metalworking Equipment 1976-78", American Machinist, December 1978, p. 136. "The 13th American Machinist Inventory of Metalworking Equipment 1973", American Machinist, November 1983, page 118.

TABLE 8.

COMPARISONS OF MACHINE TOOL VINTAGE IN SEVEN INDUSTRIAL COUNTRIES

Metalcutting Machines

	Year	Units (thousands)	0-2 yr	0-4 yr	0-9 yr	15 yr & up	20 yr & up
United States	'83	1,703.0		14%	34%		32%
Canada	'78	149.4			41		37
West Germany	'80	985.0		15	34	48	
France	'80	584.0		16	35		32
Italy	'75	408.3			41[3]		29[5]
Japan	'81	707.0	15		35[2]	37[4]	
United Kingdom	'82	627.9		41[1]			27

Metalforming Machines

	Year	Units (thousands)	0-2 yr	0-4 yr	0-9 yr	15 yr & up	20 yr & up
United States	'83	490.0		9%	18%		37%
Canada	'78	61.4			23		26
West Germany	'80	265.0		15	34	48	
France	'80	177.0		16	35		32
Italy	'75	133.0			29[3]		25[5]
Japan	'81	211.0	18		41[2]	38[4]	
United Kingdom	'82	146.8		48[1]			28

[1] 0-5 years old; [2] 0-7 years old; [3] 0-8 years old; [4] 13 years & up; [5] 18 years & up.

Sources: US, "13th American Machinist Inventory", American Machinist; Canada, "Survey by Canadian Machinery and Metalworking"; West Germany, "Survey by Verein Deutscher Werkzeugmaschinenfabriken"; France, Bureau d'Informations et de Provisions Economique; Italy, "Survey by Unione Construttori Italieni Machine Utensile"; Japan, survey by Ministry of International Trade & Industry; United Kingdom, survey by Metalworking Production.

Reproduced from "The 13th AM Inventory", American Machinist, November 1983. p. 116.

TABLE 9.

NEW CAPITAL EXPENDITURES
IN THE MACHINE TOOLS INDUSTRY 1954-83
(millions of dollars)

Year	Total	Metal Cutting Industry			Metal Forming Industry		
		Total	Structures and Additions	Machinery and Equipment	Total	Structures and Additions	Machinery and Equipment~
1954	NA	$ 37.7	$11.2	$ 26.5	NA	NA	NA
1955	NA	44.0	NA	NA	NA	NA	NA
1956	NA	49.2	NA	NA	NA	NA	NA
1957	NA	39.7	NA	NA	NA	NA	NA
1958	$ 30.5	18.8	.9	16.9	$11.7	$ 3.8	$ 7.9
1959	31.9	22.2	NA	NA	9.7	NA	NA
1960	37.4	24.8	NA	NA	12.6	NA	NA
1961	26.4	18.7	NA	NA	7.7	NA	NA
1962	39.3	26.6	NA	NA	12.7(a)	NA	NA
1963	39.6	28.8	5.4	23.4	10.8	2.1	8.7
1964	71.7	41.7	11.0	30.7	30.0(a)	7.5(a)	22.5(a)
1965	74.2	53.7	10.2	43.5	20.5	4.4(a)	16.1
1966	102.5	74.9	17.1	57.8	27.6	6.2(a)	21.4(a)
1967	104.9	78.7	19.3	59.3	26.2	5.7	20.5
1968	90.9	62.3	9.1	53.2	28.6	7.7	20.9
1969	105.0	75.5	21.8	53.7	29.5	7.7	21.8
1970	72.7	49.3	11.7	37.6	23.4	7.8	15.6
1971	39.1	28.7	4.6	24.1	10.4	1.6	8.9
1972	52.7	35.2	7.2	28.0	17.5	4.7	12.8
1973	65.9	38.4	7.3	31.1	27.5	4.0	23.4
1974	93.3	58.9	10.6	48.3	34.4	8.6	25.9
1975	76.1	52.2	7.9	44.2	23.9	4.0	19.9
1976	93.5	65.2	11.2	54.0	28.3	10.8	17.5
1977	132.4	107.9	19.1	88.8	24.5	2.6	21.9
1978	142.4	102.0	22.4	79.6	40.4	5.8	34.6
1979	199.4	147.6	31.8	115.8	51.8	9.7	42.1
1980	241.0	171.6	39.8	131.8	69.4	14.5	54.9
1981	296.2	233.2	52.3	180.9	63.0	12.8	50.2
1982(r)	190.3	152.2	32.8	119.4	38.1	4.3	33.8
1983	132.9	104.8	18.6	86.2	28.1	4.6	23.5

NA - Not Available.   r — Revised.

(a) Standard errors exceeding 15%, not consistent with other Census data in metal forming.

NOTE: Change of definition of machine tool industry makes comparisons before 1957 difficult.

Source: U.S. Bureau of the Census, "Census of Manufactures," 1963, 1967, 1972, 1977, 1982, 1983; U.S. Bureau of the Census, "Annual Survey of Manufactures."

Reproduced from: NMTBA, The Economic Handbook of the Machine Tool Industry 1986-87. p. 260.

TABLE 10. AGE OF EQUIPMENT BY USER SEGMENT, 1978, 1983
Part A — Metalcutting Machines

1978

SIC	Industry	Plants with	Total units	Change since '73	0-4 yr	5-9 yr	10-19 yr	20 yr & up	NC units	as % of 0-9 yr
25	Metal furn, fixtures	87%	14,300	-22%	13%	23%	32%	32%	< 50	0.1%
33	Primary metals	78	92,200	-29	11	19	33	37	700	2.5
34	Fabricated metal pdts	94	374,300	-9	9	20	34	37	4,900	4.1
35	Non-Electrical machy	96	843,000	-13	11	22	35	32	28,900	9.0
354	metalworking machy	97	222,300	-13	10	24	36	30	6,900	8.1
36	Electrical machy	91	222,000	-21	11	22	42	25	4,200	6.2
37	Transportation equipt	92	298,500	-9	9	15	33	43	8,900	12.0
371	Motor vehicles, equipt	94	141,000	-13	9	15	31	45	900	2.6
372	Aircraft & parts	93	124,100	-13	8	16	35	41	7,300	23.4
38	Precision instruments	92	110,800	-21	13	25	37	25	2,200	5.3
39	Misc mfg industries	78	31,400	-54	11	26	35	28	300	1.8
	TOTAL	93	1,986,500	-16	10	21	35	34	50,100	7.4

1983

SIC	Industry	Plants with	Total units	Change since '78	0-4 yr	5-9 yr	10-19 yr	20 yr & up	NC units	as % of 0-9 yr
25	Metal furn, fixtures	81%	10,778	-25%	11%	23%	44%	22%	253	6.8%
33	Primary metals	83	88,515	-4	10	20	32	39	2,413	9.2
34	Fabricated metal pdts	93	325,995	-13	12	20	34	35	10,841	10.6
35	Non-Electrical machy	96	714,760	-15	15	21	34	30	50,698	19.7
354	metalworking machy	97	187,873	-4	15	22	34	29	11,713	16.8
36	Electrical machy	88	177,942	-20	15	21	36	27	9,415	14.6
37	Transportation equipt	94	248,579		14	16	30	40	14,397	19.4
371	Motor vehicles, equipt	96	118,998	-16	11	14	31	44	3,708	12.3
372	Aircraft & parts	96	85,883	-31	18	18	34	30	8,450	27.4
38	Precision instruments	88	91,257	-18	16	22	36	25	4,434	12.6
39	Misc mfg industries	74	45,007	43	22	25	31	22	1,561	7.4
	TOTAL	92	1,702,833	-14	14	20	34	32	94,012	16.1

Source: "The 12th American Machinist Inventory of Metalworking Equipment 1976-78", American Machinist, December 1978. p. 136.
"The 13th American Machinist Inventory of Metalworking Equipment 1983", American Machinist, November 1983. p. 118.

TABLE 10. (cont'd)
Part B— Metalforming Machines

1978

SIC	Industry	Plants with	Total units	Change since '73	0-4 yr	5-9 yr	10-19 yr	20 yr & up	NC units	as % of 0-9 yr
25	Metal furn, fixtures	88%	22,500	-12%	10%	22%	36%	32%	100	1.3%
33	Primary metals	54	25,100	-24	7	19	31	43	50	0.2
34	Fabricated metal pdts	85	257,300	4	8	17	37	38	700	1.0
35	Non-Electrical machy	72	117,000	-13	11	20	36	33	800	0.5
354	metalworking machy	65	19,800	5	10	23	39	28	< 50	0.3
36	Electrical machy	82	117,100	-1	10	23	41	26	500	1.1
37	Transportation equipt	82	62,600	-14	8	15	33	34	200	1.2
371	Motor vehicles, equipt	88	36,900	-25	8	15	33	44	100	1.0
372	Aircraft & parts	75	15,100	-17	6	13	34	47	100	2.2
38	Precision instruments	69	21,700	-8	14	24	36	26	300	3.3
39	Misc mfg industries	61	19,900	-53	11	30	31	28	100	0.1
	TOTAL	75	644,200	-8	9	20	36	35	2,750	1.2

1983

SIC	Industry	Plants with	Total units	Change since '78	0-4 yr	5-9 yr	10-19 yr	20 yr & up	NC units	as % of 0-9 yr
25	Metal furn, fixtures	83%	15,870	-29%	7%	14%	41%	38%	351	11.1%
33	Primary metals	63	29,320	-17	9	20	39	33	249	3.0
34	Fabricated metal pdts	84	192,923	-25	8	17	35	40	3,622	7.7
35	Non-Electrical machy	69	90,529	-23	11	19	35	34	1,843	6.7
354	metalworking machy	60	14,122	-29	10	20	37	33	85	2.0
36	Electrical machy	77	67,731	-42	12	19	38	31	1,357	6.5
37	Transportation equipt	84	54,400	-13	11	16	32	41	887	6.0
371	Motor vehicles, equipt	88	34,249	-7	9	17	31	44	423	4.9
372	Aircraft & parts	76	11,825	-22	16	13	35	37	332	9.7
38	Precision instruments	70	18,300	-16	12	21	37	30	440	7.3
39	Misc mfg industries	58	20,848	4	8	15	30	46	541	10.9
	TOTAL	74	489,921	-24	9	18	36	37	9,296	7.0

Source: "The 12th American Machinist Inventory of Metalworking Equipment 1976-78", _American Machinist_, December 1978. p. 136.

"The 13th American Machinist Inventory of Metalworking Equipment 1983", _American Machinist_, November 1983. p. 118.

TABLE 11. LARGEST JAPANESE MACHINE TOOL PRODUCERS IN 1984, 1985

Company Name	Machine Tool Sales ($ millions)		% Change between	Comments
	1985	1984	1984-1985	
Amada	468	432	+ 8%	Owns 20% of 9th ranked Sonoike.
Okuma Machinery Works	374	263	+42%	
Mori Seiki	283	229	+24%	
Komatsu	244	164	+49%	
Makino Milling Machine	224	206	+ 9%	
Toyoda Machine	222	152	+46%	Toyoda Machine founded Toyota Motors. The company is now owned by Toyota Motors with 25% of stock. It is the recipient of the prestigious Deming Award in 1985.
Hitachi Seiki	209	168	+24%	This builder is different from the smaller Hitachi Seiko owned by the electrical and electronics giant Hitachi.
Sonoike Manufacturing	208	167	+25%	
Toshiba Machine's	166	148	+12%	
Aida Enginering	165	137	+20%	
Wasino Machines	134	107	+25%	
SUBTOTAL	2,697			
Fanuc*	684		+20%	World leader in machine tool controls and robotics. Its production is highly automated with an industry-high labor productivity of $521,000/worker.

The two privately-held Japanese machine tool makers, Yamazaki (known as Mazak in the US) and Shin Nippon Koki, should rank among the top three and among the top dozen respectively. No financial data was available for privately-held corporations. The 14 largest Jp. MTBs accounted for approximately $3.3 to $3.5 billion or 62 to 64% of the $5.3 billion MT production.

* Fanuc sales are excluded from subtotal to avoid doublecounting of Fanuc controls used in Japanese machine tools.

Sources: "Japan's Machine-Tool Builders Enjoy Sales Gain in Past Fiscal Year", American Machinist, January 1987. p. 47. "Japan's Machine-Tool Builders Enjoy Sales Gain in Past Fiscal Year", ibid. January 1986. p. 53.

TABLE 12. Japanese Institutions Participating in Research for Ultra High-Performance Laser-Applied Multiple Production System Sponsored by MITI of Japan

Subject of R&D	Research Institutes/Commissioned Organizations
1. Total System	Research Association for Laser-Applied Multiple Production System Technology
2. Cutting & Processing Technologies	Toshiba Machine Makino Milling Machine Hitachi Seiki Yamazaki Mazak Yaskawa Electric Mfg. Co. Okuma Machinery Works Shin-Nippon Koki
3. Material Processing Technologies	Government Industrial Research Institute, Kyushu Ishikawajima-Harima Heavy Industries Kobe Steel Mitsubishi Heavy Industries Aida Engineering
4. Automated Assemblying Technologies	Toyoda Machine Works Yaskawa Electric Mfg. Co.
5. Laser Application Technology	Mitsubishi Electric Toshiba Matsushita Research Institute Sumitomo Electric Industries Horiba NEC Corp
6. Automated Diagnosis Technologies	FANUC Okuma Machinery Works Shin-Nippon Koki
7. Planning & Control Technologies	Oki Electric Industries

Source: Industrial Bank of Japan. QUARTERLY SURVEY—Japanese Finance and Industry, No. 66, 1986 II. page 7.

FIGURE 1

MACHINE TOOL SHIPMENTS OF LEADING NATIONS:
Japan, West Germany, United States, and Italy

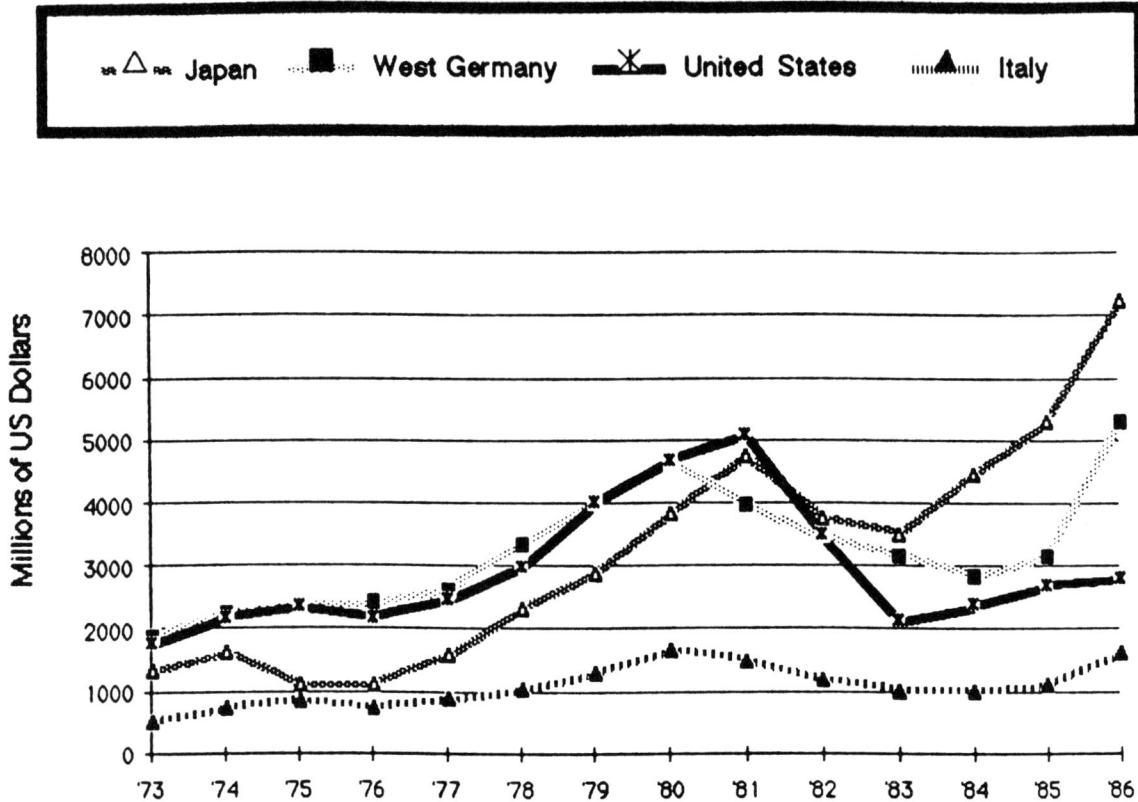

Note: The figures are significantly affected by the exchange rates between the US dollar and foreign currencies. Examples of major differences:

	1985 total (1985 exchange rates)	1985 total (1986 exchange rates)
Japan	$5317mm	$7536mm
West Germany	3167	4301
Italy	1116	1431

Source: "Europe Gains in Machine Tools", <u>American Machinist.</u> February 1987. p. 65, 67.

FIGURE 2

US Machine Tool Imports From W. Germany and Japan

— West Germany	-- Japan

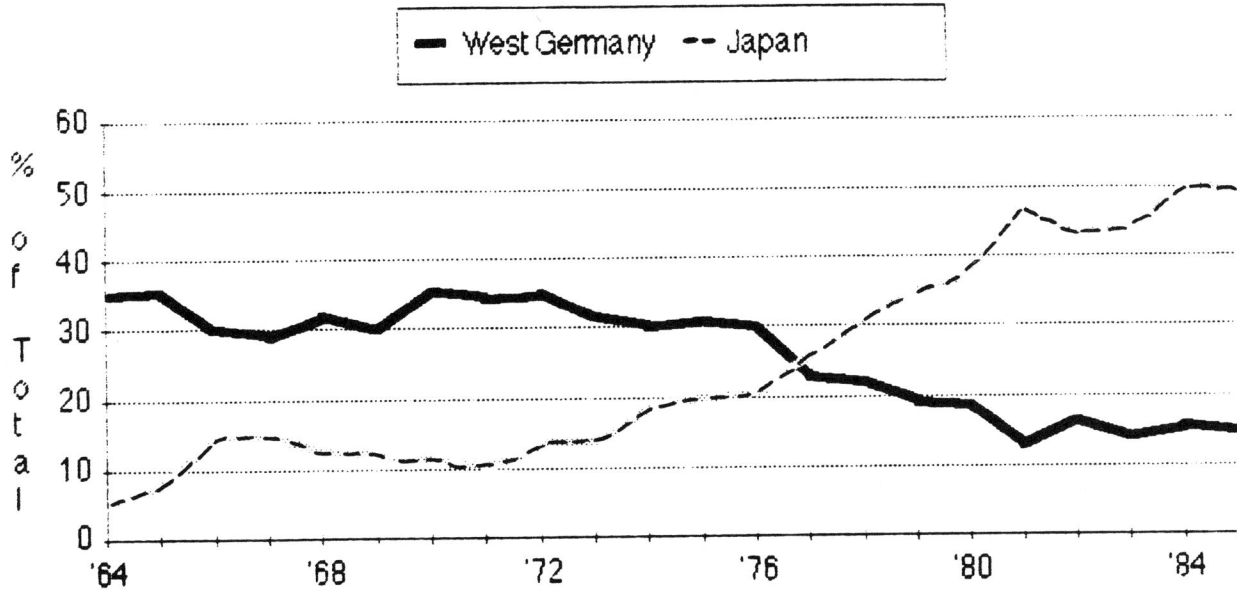

US Machine Tools Imports From UK, France, Italy, and Switz.

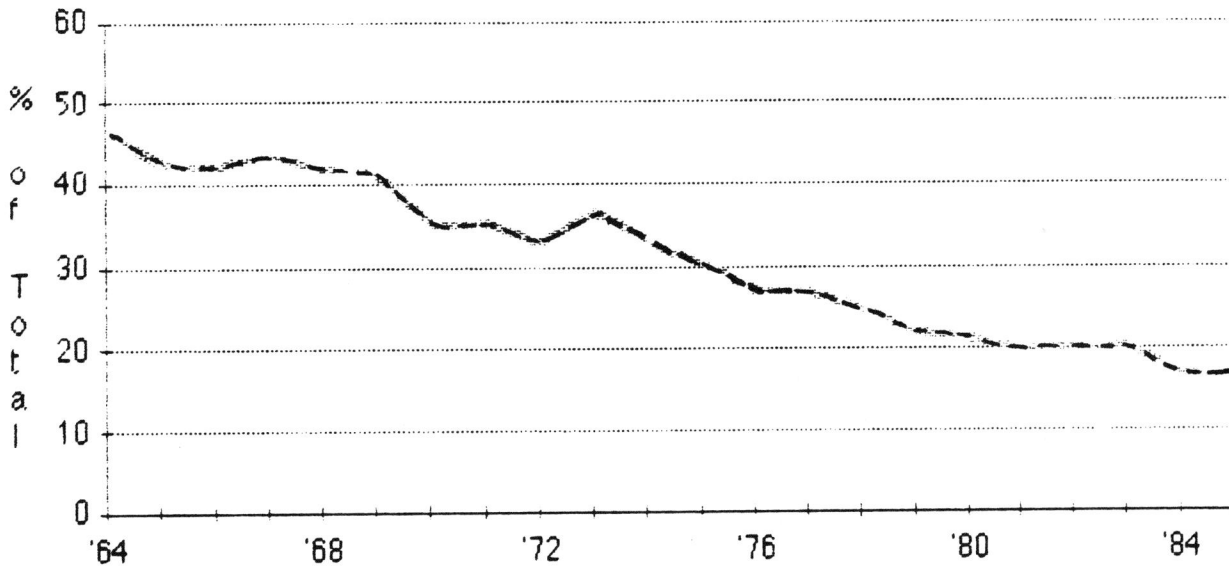

Source: NMTBA, The Economic Handbook of the Machine Tool Industry
           1986-87, page 134.

FIGURE 3

U.S. MACHINE TOOL IMPORTS BY COUNTRY OF ORIGIN

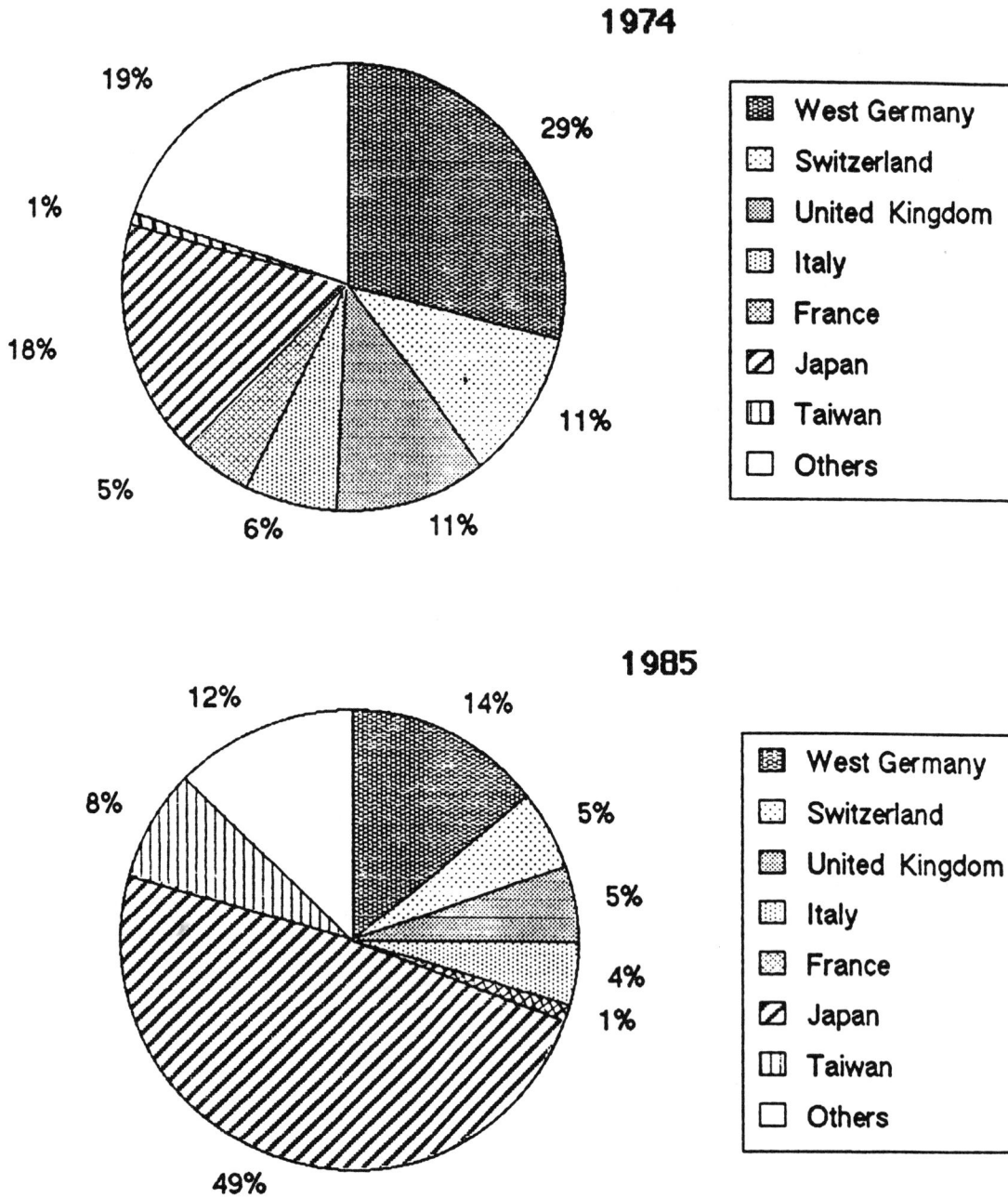

1974

▨	West Germany
▨	Switzerland
▨	United Kingdom
▨	Italy
▨	France
▨	Japan
▥	Taiwan
☐	Others

1985

▨	West Germany
▨	Switzerland
▨	United Kingdom
▨	Italy
▨	France
▨	Japan
▥	Taiwan
☐	Others

Figures include "Used and Rebuilt" but not parts.

Source: NMTBA, The Economic Handbook of the Machine Tool Industry
1986-87, page 126.

FIGURE 4

**US Machine Tool Exports as a
Percent of World Machine Tool Consumption**

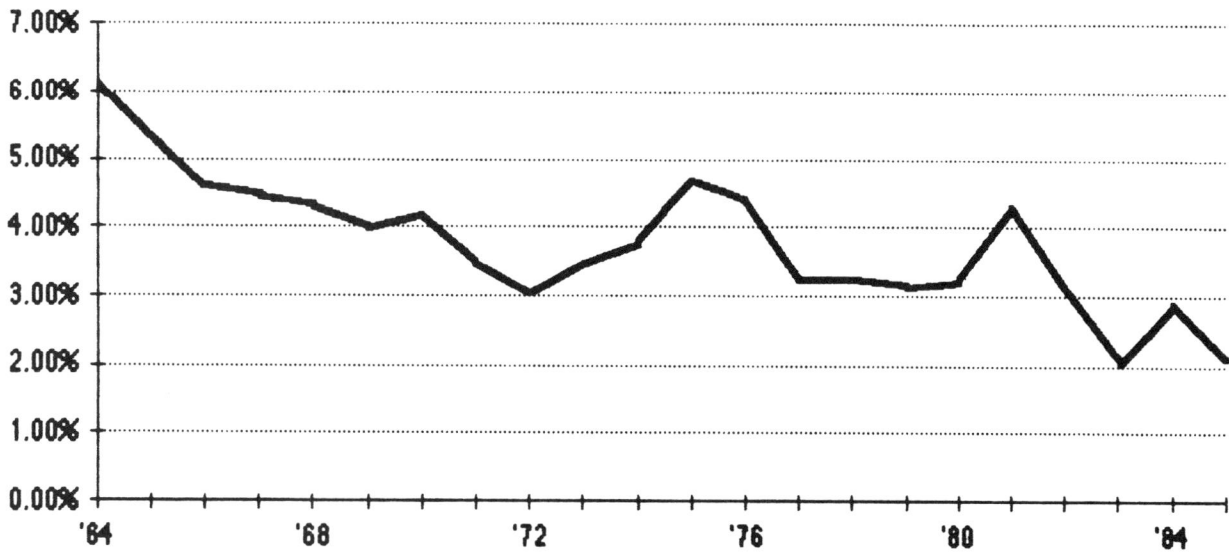

**Share of World Exports
(Machine Tool Exports as a % of World)**

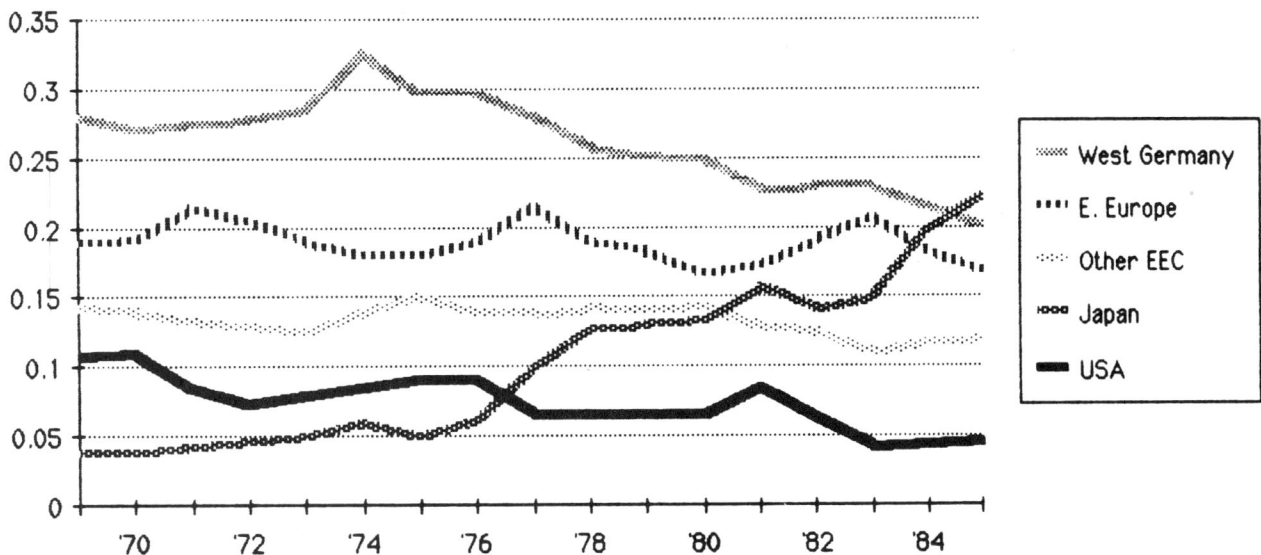

Legend:
- West Germany
- E. Europe
- Other EEC
- Japan
- USA

Source: NMTBA, <u>The Economic Handbook of the Machine Tool Industry
1986-87,</u>   page 135,167.

FIGURE 5.

SCHEMATICS OF INTERNATIONAL POSITIONING:

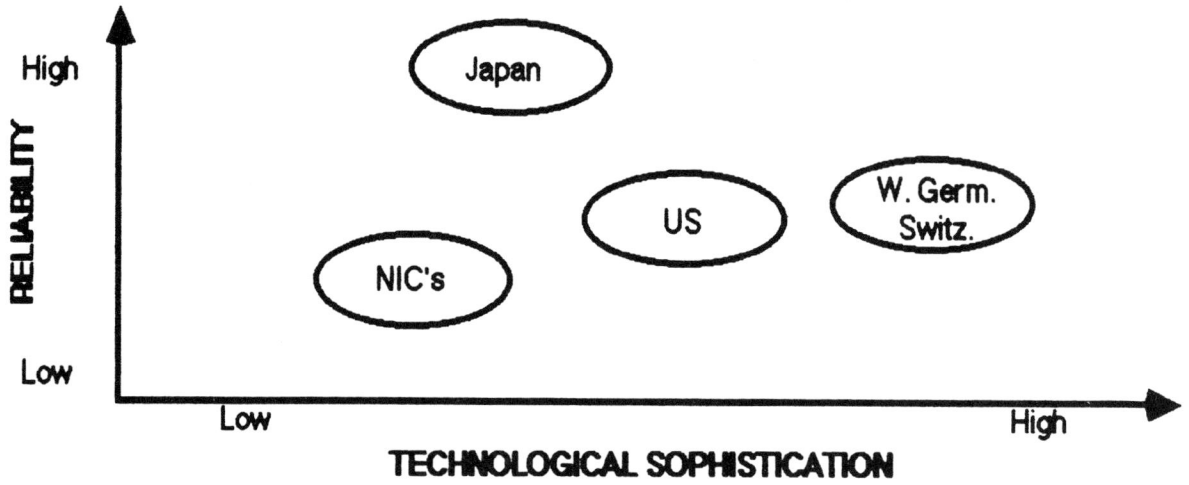

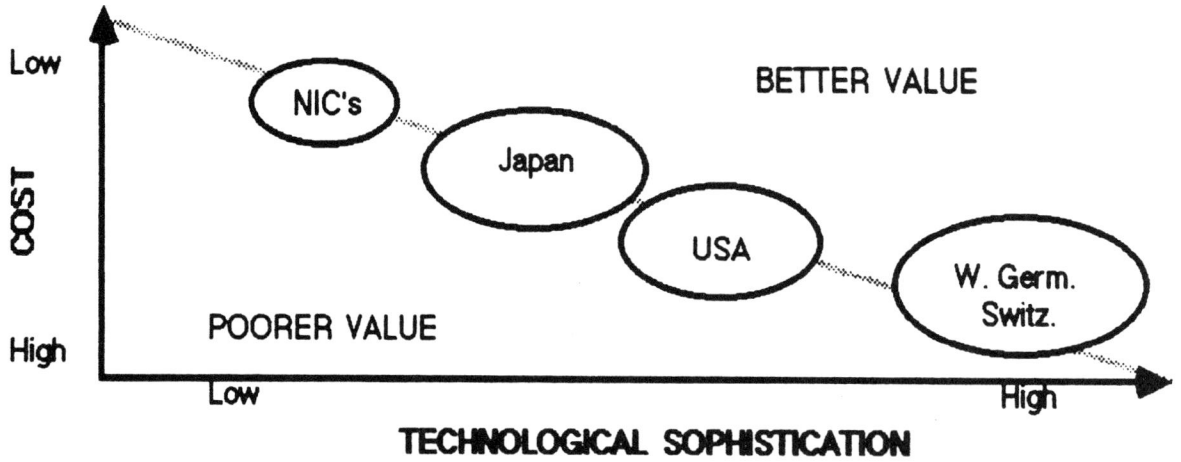

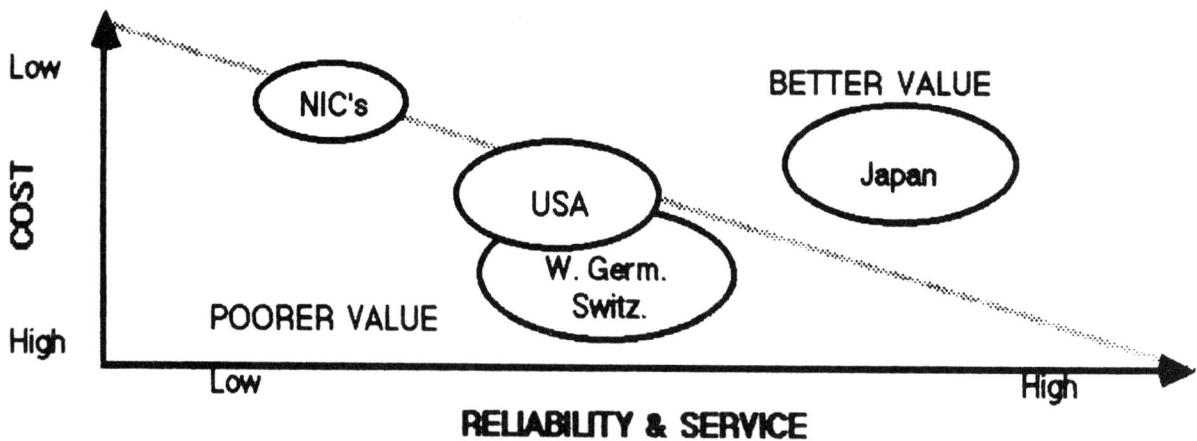

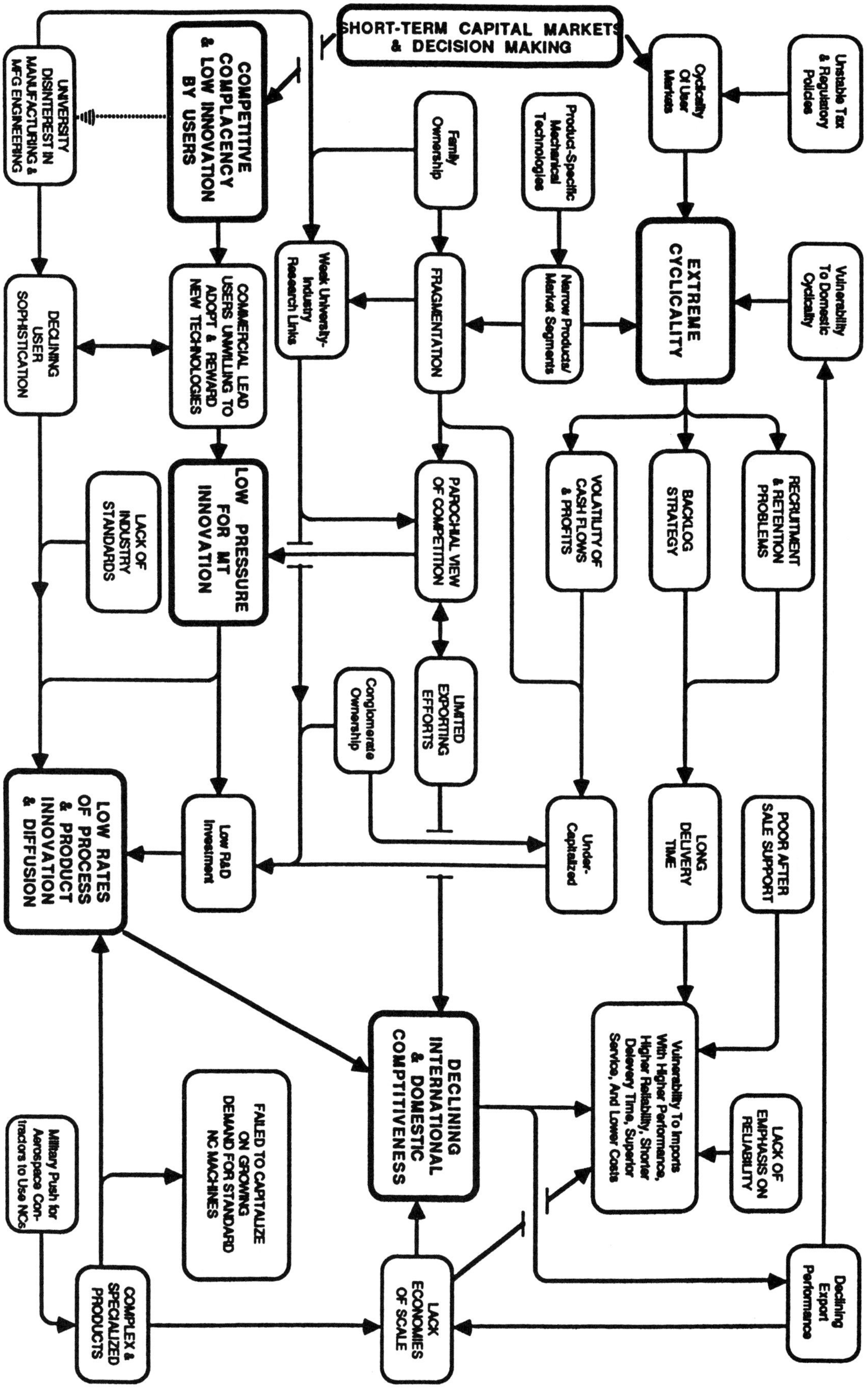

103

FIGURE 6. US MACHINE TOOL INDUSTRY: STRUCTURE & BEHAVIORS LEADING TO DECLINE

© Artemis March 1987

FIGURE 7.

YEAR-TO-YEAR CHANGE IN
REAL NET NEW ORDERS OF MACHINE TOOLS
1957-82

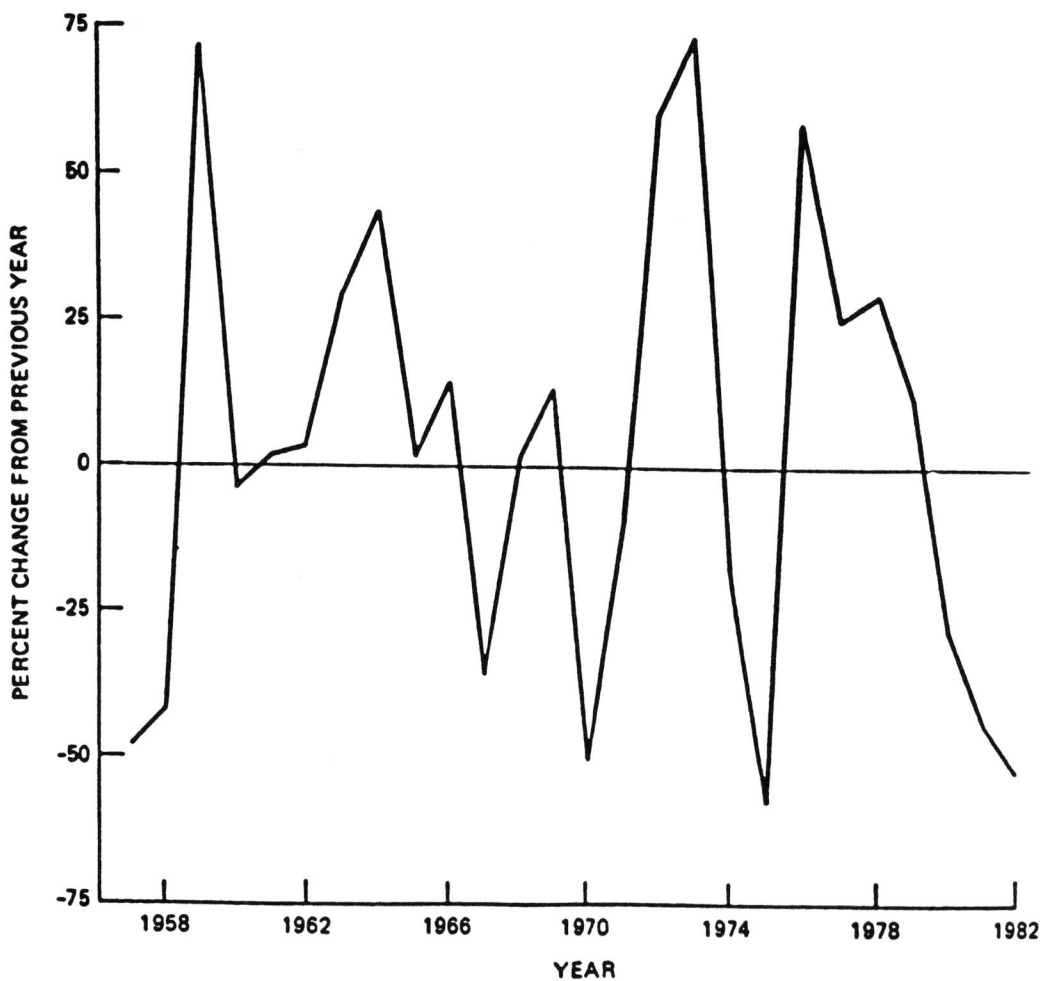

Sources: NMTBA, The Economic Handbook of the Machine Tool Industry, 1982-83;
NMTBA, "Industry Estimate of New Orders, Cancellations, Shipments and
Backlog" (monthly).

105

FIGURE 8. EMPLOYMENT IN THE MACHINE TOOL INDUSTRY (1958-1984)

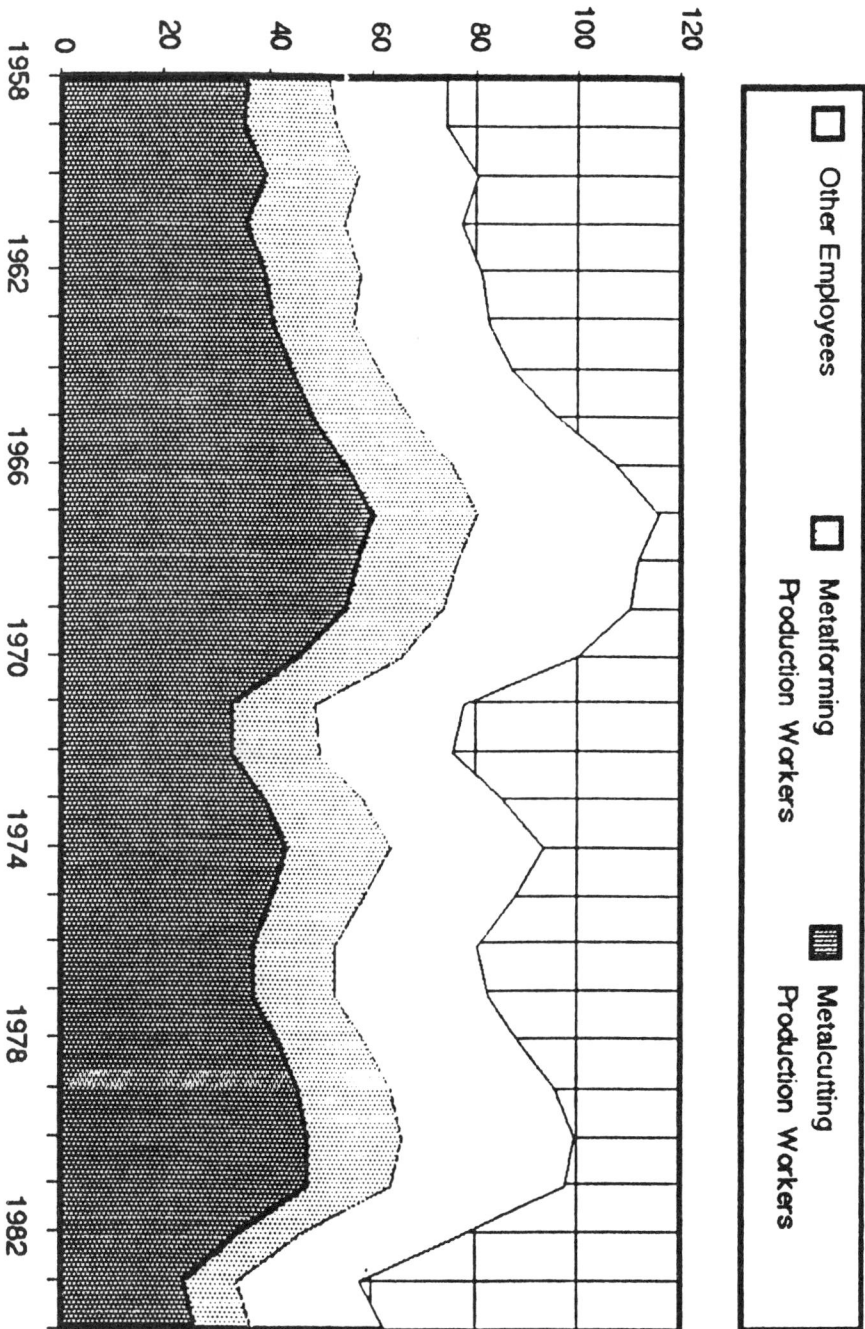

☐ Other Employees   ☐ Metalforming
Production Workers

▦ Metalcutting
Production Workers

Source: US Bureau of Census, "Census of Manufactures" and "Annual Survey of Manufactures".
Reproduced from: NMTBA, The Economic Handbook of the Machine Tool Industry, 1986-87, P. 250

FIGURE 9. DOMESTIC SHIPMENTS VS. ORDERS, BY QUARTER, 1956-86.

Metal Cutting Machine Tools

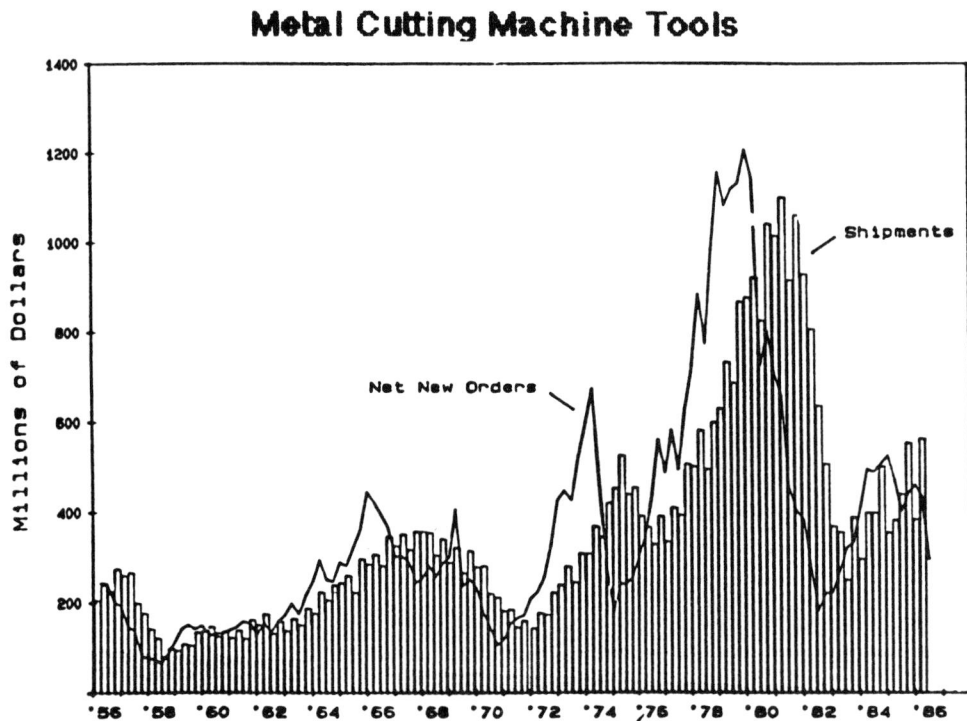

Metal Forming Machine Tools

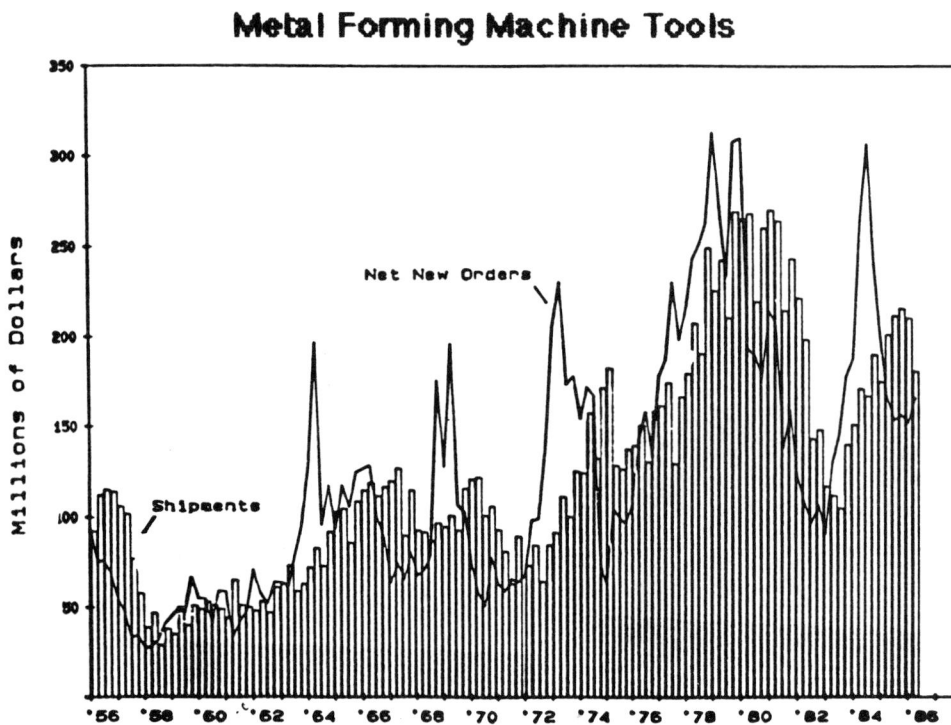

Source: NMTBA, <u>The Economic Handbook of the Machine Tool Industry 1986-87</u>. p. 83.

FIGURE 10.

Machine Tool Unfilled Orders and Imports, 1963-85

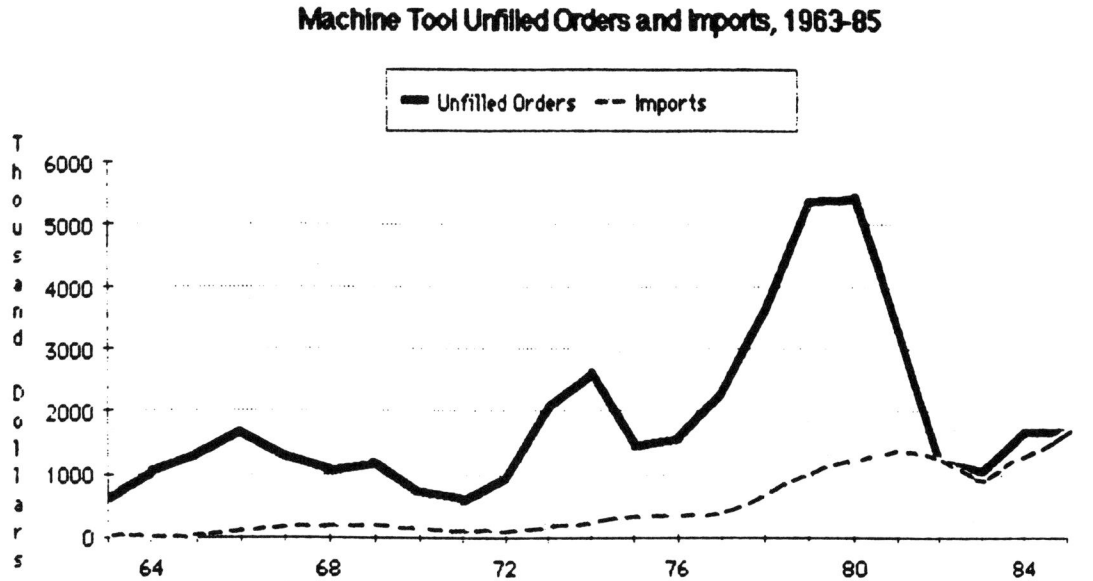

Machine Tool Industry Indices of Unfilled Orders & Imports
(1976=100, Ratio Scale)

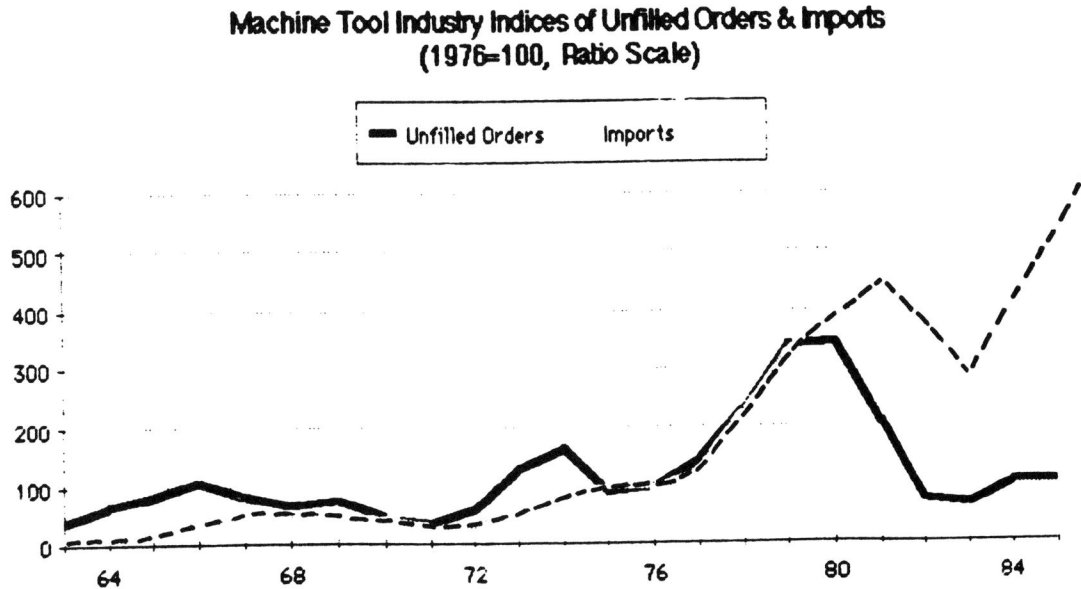

Source: NMTBA, The Economic Handbook of the Machine Tool Industry 1986-87. p. 79, 130.

FIGURE 11.

IMPACT OF ELECTRONICS DEVELOPMENT ON COSTS OF NC CONTROLS

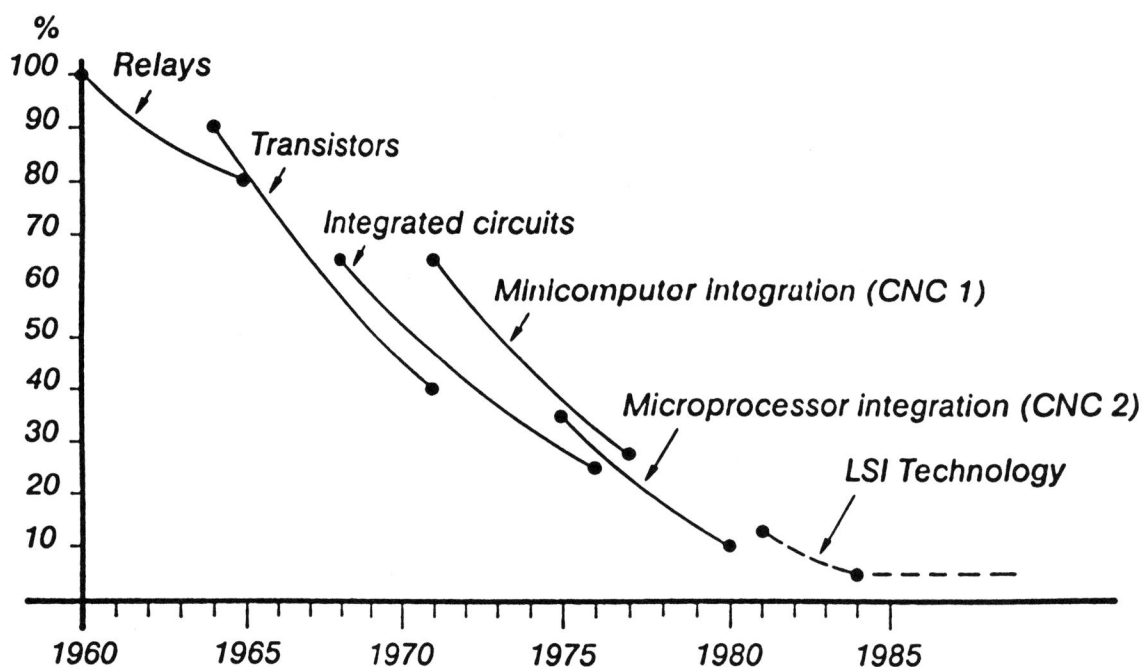

Figure 3: Price development in numerical controls of approximately equal specifications as a result of innovations in the electronics sector.

Source: Hans Kief, Flexible Automation '87/88: The International CNC Reference Book. (Havant, U.K.: Becker Publishing, 1987.)

FIGURE 12.

RANGE OF MONTHLY PRODUCTION FOR MAJOR MACHINE TOOLS, 1982-83

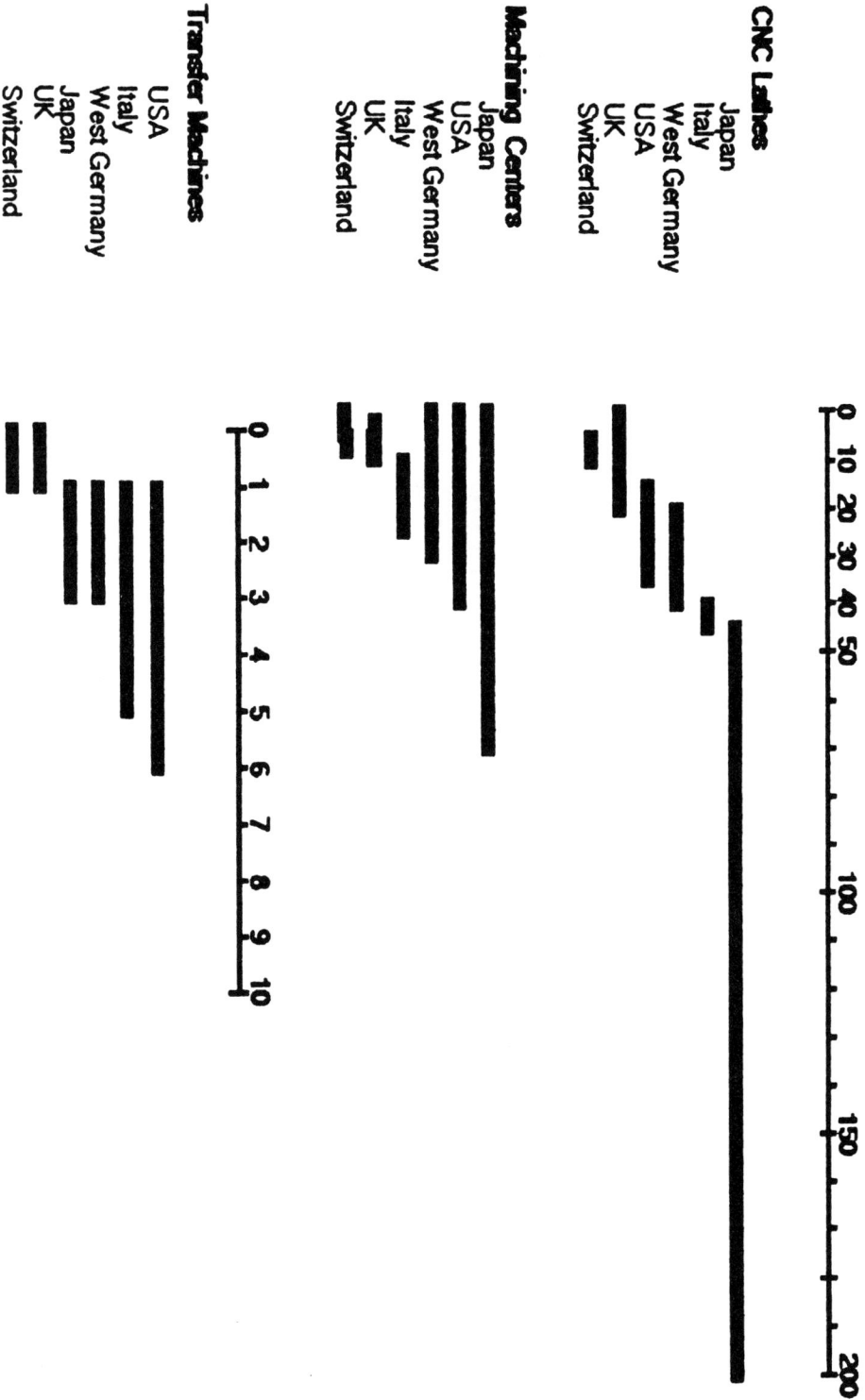

CNC Lathes
Japan
Italy
West Germany
USA
UK
Switzerland

Machining Centers
Japan
USA
West Germany
Italy
UK
Switzerland

Transfer Machines
USA
Italy
West Germany
Japan
UK
Switzerland

Source: E. Sciberas and B.D. Payne. Machine Tool Industry — Technological Change and International Competitiveness . (Harlow, Essex: Longman Group Ltd., 1985.) Page 90.

MIT Commission on Industrial Productivity
Working Paper

The Future of the US Steel Industry in the International Marketplace

Prepared by the
Commission Working Group on the Materials Industries

Merton Flemings, Chair
Joel Clark
Morris Cohen
Thomas Eager
John Elliott
Timothy Gutowski
Lester Thurow
Harry Tuller

Graduate Research Assistant
Barbara Masi

Table of Contents

List of Tables

List of Figures

Executive Summary

The domestic steel industry in the United States, once the largest, most modern, and most technologically efficient in the world, has suffered in the last decade from declining demand for its products, loss of home market share, declining production and employment, and low or negative earnings.

The fate of the industry has serious ramifications for the national economy, because the steel industry provides input to related industrial sectors, including the important defense sector, in addition to being a major employer.

In 1987, just when most analysts were about to lay the industry to rest, many firms reported significant profits, and, for the first time since 1974, the industry as a whole surpassed the average financial rate of return for all manufacturing industries.

The two major segments of the domestic steel industry—integrated producers and minimills—have had different histories and now have different outlooks. The integrated producers, who operate blast furnaces, coke ovens and steel-making facilities, suffered the most severe economic setbacks, and are now recovering. The minimills, non-integrated producers who make carbon and low-alloy steels in electric furnaces, using scrap as a raw material, continue to prosper, on the whole, as they have for the last 15 to 20 years.

A number of factors explain the economic difficulties experienced by the integrated producers in the early 1980s, including a lack of technological foresight, a shortage of available cash to invest more efficient equipment, poor labor-management relations, maintenance of inefficient plants, and federal government interference.

Over the past 25 years, U.S. integrated producers lost their technological lead when they failed to adopt quickly the newest technology, including the basic oxygen furnace (BOF), continuous casting, and computer controls, as they became available. Some of the smaller U.S. firms were among the first to adopt the BOF and continuous casting, but most U.S. integrated firms lagged behind foreign producers, in particular the Japanese, in their willingness to adopt the newest technologies.

The unwillingness of U.S. firms to make technological changes has been attributed to the mature, relatively inflexible organizational structure and management of the integrated firms. The attitudes of the integrated carbon steel producers are compared dramatically to the U.S. specialty steel segment, which has encouraged technological development and in the 1960s even adopted a state-of-the-art specialty steelmaking process (the AOD process). This technology is currently used in virtually 100 percent stainless steel processing, and has future implications for the processing of low carbon steels.

Certainly, the late advent of the steel industry in Japan assisted in the relatively fast rate of adoption of process technology by the integrated steelmakers. Moreover, the uniformity of operations, the structure of the industry, and government-industry cooperation facilitated a transfer of information among companies and plants. The product mix was kept narrow, and the largest of the six firms had no more than four times the steel production capacity of the smallest. As well, the firms were able to improve their performance jointly by purchasing raw materials and coordinating the production and sale of steel in the international market through the trading companies.

In the U.S. it was difficult for the domestic industry to generate the capital needed to deploy the most modern technology. Only twice since 1960 has the rate of return of the U.S. steel industry exceeded the average of all manufacturing industries.

Another burden for the domestic industry has been the hostile, antagonistic tone of labor-management relations. Through its unions, labor won major concessions from the steel industry in wages, benefits, and work rules. The consequent higher labor costs were blamed for the increased imports from foreign nations, where producers still paid less for labor per ton of steel. However, the recent financial strains of the steel industry have softened union demands—labor has agreed to a reduced hourly rate and more flexibility in work rules. In addition, lay-offs in the labor force (both blue and white collar), the closing of the older inefficient plants, and a reversal of exchange rates have favored U.S. producers and made their labor costs competitive with all but the developing countries.

The steel industry has been troubled, as well, by its relations with the federal government. The confrontation between President Kennedy and the United States Steel Company in 1960 established de facto price controls on steel for more than a decade, in the opinion of many observers. The steel industry was unable to raise prices during this period of high demand, and its subsequently limited profits restricted the amount of capital available for modernization.

Even inter-firm cooperative efforts to economize were thwarted by the inconsistencies in Federal anti-trust policy that kept these attempts at a minimal level, since the U.S. Department of Justice was unconvinced that consolidated operations did not unfairly restrict competition in the domestic market. Hence U.S. companies were not able to work together as were the Japanese companies. The recent receptivity of the Department of Justice and the Federal Trade Commission to mergers and joint research projects by steel firms has encouraged these ventures, but the policy is subject to discontinuance at any time.

The structure of the domestic steel industry has changed dramatically over the past 20 years. Although the actors remain the same, the roles and market shares of the integrated firms, minimills, and imports have been transformed, with the integrated producers losing market share to both domestic minimills and imports.

Minimill managers and investors used advances in electric arc furnace technology during the 1970s to move into low-grade steel areas, such as small structural and bar products. Subsequently, the more aggressive plants have moved into direct competition for products in the high-quality end of the market. At the same time, the minimills have developed a formula for success that relies on constant marketing updates and customer contact, weekly production schedules to ensure synchrony with market changes, changes in the production mix to match the market (even if the steel grade demanded had never been made previously), and substantial sales to steel service centers, which provided reliable information on any changes in the needs of customers.

The typical minimill has taken advantage of the inherent flexibility of electric furnaces, which allow for fast product changeovers from one type of steel to another. Incremental improvements in production are more easily implemented using a simple process flow and a limited number of products instead of a complex integrated system. Finally, the better minimill managers search world-wide for the best steel-making technology before investing in new equipment. Some of these mills represent the best that the U.S. as well as foreign equipment suppliers have to offer.

The world-wide forecast for the consumption of steel products anticipates decreases or stagnation in developed countries concurrent with increases in developing countries, especially Taiwan, China, India, Korea, and Brazil. It is unlikely that U.S. integrated firms will develop a long-term export position in the growing markets of developing countries, but if the dollar remains weak while developing countries build their industrial base to produce high quality steel, U.S. firms could temporarily expect increased exports to this market.

Moreover, the market share of carbon steel products produced by the integrated firms, such as bars, structurals, rail and pipe, that is held by foreign steel firms continues to be significant. U.S. firms have responded to this trend by shifting their product mix to increasing amounts of high-value-added sheet products, which are produced only in small quantities by most developing countries. Another significant trend is seen in the growth of joint ventures between U.S. producers and steelmakers from other countries.

In the years since 1982, the integrated carbon steel industry has undergone a painful restructuring that has greatly improved its competitive position. Labor productivity and average product quality have been improved by the closing of a number of outdated and high-cost facilities.

And while the industry is to be applauded for the great strides made by integrated firms to improve their competitive position, the problems that remain—product quality, customer service, and labor-management relations—must still be addressed. It is the ability of the integrated producers to make improvements in these areas that will determine the long-term competitive position of the industry.

Introduction

The domestic integrated carbon steel industry in the United States, which once was the world's largest, most modern and technologically efficient, has experienced a series of problems in the past ten years characterized by declining demand for its products, loss of home market share, declining production and employment, and low or negative earnings. However, just when most analysts were about to lay the industry to rest, many firms reported significant profits in 1987, and the average rate of return on equity of the industry exceeded that of the average of all manufacturing industries for only the second time since 1960. This is an encouraging statistic, even if one recognizes that this ratio was inflated by the industry's severely eroded equity caused by previous losses.

In spite of this financial turnaround, the problems of the domestic integrated carbon steel industry are still disturbing, for several reasons. First, the industry remains an important contributor to the economic and military security of the country. The steel industry is still reasonably large, with annual sales in the range of $50-$60 billion, and gross final assets of $30-$40 billion. The steel industry is also a major employer, although total direct employment by the industry has declined from 600,000 in 1979 to slightly over 200,000 in 1988.

In addition, the industry makes important inputs to other industrial sectors of the economy, including: 1) manufacturing (particularly the automotive industry); 2) construction; 3) suppliers of equipment and raw materials to the steel industry; and 4) the approximately 20,000 metal fabricating plants that the steel industry supplies. It has been estimated[1] that multiplying the direct employment figure of the steel industry by a factor of four would equal the number employed each year by industries directly dependent on it for business.[2] This estimate is probably high since some indirect employment will exist at the same level whether steel is domestically produced or imported.

Steel is unquestionably important to the nation's defense-related industries. Almost every item of military hardware contains some form of steel, and no other material exists that can provide the required properties so cheaply. Moreover, industries that provide for the military's need for equipment, transport, and support also depend on steel.

The national security and the industrial economy are interdependent, and the economic stability of the manufacturing sector depends upon a continuous and adequate supply of steel. However, the United States has no compelling reason to adopt policies that would maintain a domestic industry capable of supplying 100 percent of peak demand.

Numerous reports and books published in the past decade address the issue of the competitive status of the U.S. steel industry. Although this report will draw upon the information in these publications, it will not attempt to cover old ground comprehensively. It will identify the causes for the decline and subsequent revival of the domestic industry, focussing primarily on the large carbon steel segment, and attempt to assess the future prospects of the industry.

The report is organized as follows: Section 1 contains a brief introduction to the report. Section 2 provides an overview of the steel industry, including its structure, and a short discussion of the technology of steel production. Section 3 discusses the technological performance and the costs of production of the domestic producers and their major international competitors. Section 4 provides an overview of the markets for steel products. Section 5 discusses the competitive position of the domestic steel industry, together with the proximate and fundamental causes for its decline. Finally, Section 6 assesses the current status and future of the industry.

Industry Structure and Steel Making Technology

The domestic steel industry has two important segments: 1) integrated producers, who operate blast furnaces, coke ovens, and steel-making facilities; and 2) non-integrated producers (minimills), who operate electric furnaces using scrap as the primary raw material.

Each segment can be subdivided into producers of carbon steel and producers of specialty steels. Carbon steel is a tonnage commodity containing small amounts of carbon, manganese, and other elements. Specialty steels include alloys and stainless steels, and are used in applications where more expensive materials can be justified by special requirements such as corrosion resistance and high strength-to-weight ratio.

The flow sheets for integrated and non-integrated producers are shown in Figure 1.[3] An integrated plant, which includes equipment to handle and convert raw materials (ore, coal, and limestone) to iron and then to steel and finished products, is more complex and capital intensive than a non-integrated plant, which uses scrap steel as a starting material. The start-up of an integrated plant would require an investment on the order of $1,000-$3,000 per annual ton of production, compared to about $200-$400 per annual ton for a new non-integrated plant.

Since 1950, only two new integrated plants have been built in the United States, and many domestic plants are outdated compared with our international competitors. Annual domestic capacity is about 90 million net tons of finished steel.

The total capacity of the minimill segment is about 15 to 20 million tons per year. Plant sizes range from about 200,000 to one million annual tons capacity. Markets served tend to be local, and products are narrowly concentrated on such items as wire rod, concrete reinforcing bars, and small shapes.

A typical non-integrated specialty plant has a capacity of 100,000 to 300,000 tons of alloy and stainless steel per year. The total U.S. annual capacity in this segment is about five to seven million tons. However, specialty and integrated firms are not always distinguishable, as alloy and stainless steels are also produced by some large integrated carbon steelmakers.

An integrated steel plant uses three principal raw materials: iron ore, coal, and limestone. The ore is iron oxide containing impurities such as silicates. The coal, which must be converted to metallurgical-grade coke for use in the blast furnace, should have lower sulfur content. The limestone combines with silicates to form a slag.

The ore, coal, and limestone are charged into a blast furnace, a roughly cylindrical structure up to 20 stories high with a volume of 5,000 cubic meters, through which vast quantities of air are blown from the bottom to the top. The blast furnace is run continuously, with periodic changing of raw materials at the top and the tapping of molten pig iron from the bottom once or twice daily. Typical production rates are several thousand tons of pig iron per day. This type of furnace is very difficult to shut down, and it is inefficient to operate at reduced capacity.

Due to the tremendous size of the blast furnace, the iron ore and coke must have great strength and the proper particle size to prevent collapse and plugging of the air passages between the raw materials. Many ores without the proper composition, size, or strength, are ground to powder and baked into small, hard pellets before use.

Coal is converted to coke, a strong, porous, carbonaceous solid, before it is used in the blast furnace. This is done at high temperatures in an air-free retort, called a coke oven. Coke ovens run on a semi-continuous basis, and are even more difficult than blast furnaces to remove from production during periods of recession.

In the blast furnaces, the carbon in the coke combines with the iron oxide in the ore, and produces carbon monoxide gas (later used as a by-product fuel) and cast iron (molten iron saturated with about three to four percent carbon). The cost of producing the cast iron is 50 percent of the final cost of a simple steel product.

To improve the ductility of the carbon-saturated iron, most of the carbon is removed to produce steel which typically contains 0.20 to 0.40 percent by weight of carbon. Prior to 1960, carbon was removed from cast iron in open hearth furnaces. Today, this is done in a basic oxygen furnace (BOF), using pure oxygen to burn carbon from the iron. The BOF process takes only 30 minutes, compared to 12 hours in the open hearth.

The BOF furnace can use 10 percent to 30 percent scrap steel along with its charge of molten iron. Electric arc furnaces and open hearth furnaces can handle any ratio of solid scrap to molten iron.

The amount and quality of the scrap iron has a great influence on the quality of the final product. The steel made from the BOF is usually low in impurities such as tin, copper, and arsenic, and can be used to make high-quality sheet steel. The large amount of scrap used in the electric furnace produces steel with more impurities, and this steel is usually limited to bar, wire, and plate products.

At this point in the process, the steel is cast into solid forms. In the older ingot process, a series of large, individual blocks of steel are cast into ingot molds. In the newer, continuous casting process, liquid steel is poured into a water-cooled sleeve emitting a continuous ingot from the bottom, which is then cut and rolled. Continuous casting produces less scrap and is used by most of the efficient, high-volume mills today.

In the older technology, after solidifying, the ingots were reheated to rolling temperatures in the soaking pit furnaces. Some continuous casting mills now roll most of the steel directly after casting, before it has cooled, to save a part of the energy costs of producing steel.

The final plate, sheet, wire, bar, pipe, or other shapes may later be coated (with zinc, lead, tin, paint, etc.) to improve corrosion resistance, or heat-treated to improve strength, toughness, or wear resistance. These final treatments are as varied as the many forms and products that are made from steel.

Comparative Technological Performance and Production Costs

In 1950, the U.S. steel industry produced almost half the world's output of steel, whereas the Japanese steel industry accounted for only three percent of world production. In the last three decades, the U.S. producers' share of the world market has declined steadily, and reached a low in 1982 (Figure 2). Over the past 20 years, the domestic industry has produced an average of 120 million tons of raw material annually; 1973 was the industry's best year, when it produced in excess of 150 million net tons. From 1960 to 1974, raw steel production in the U.S. grew at an average annual rate of three percent, but since then it has been declining. Table 1 shows declining U.S. raw steel production and capacity from 1975 to 1986. In 1987, production capacity declined substantially as outdated facilities were closed. However, both output and capacity utilization increased by a healthy margin. In terms of sustainable steel capacity, the U.S. industry is currently ranked third in the world, behind the Soviet Union and Japan.

The U.S. currently exports little carbon steel directly, although it is an important exporter of steel in the form of finished products. In both forms, however, the U.S. is a significant net importer. Table 2 shows that in 1986 net U.S. demand for steel was 96.3 million tons, that 18.6 million tons of steel were directly imported, and that 17.2 million tons were indirectly imported (in the form of finished products such as automobiles).

Labor Productivity[4]

In 1975, the U.S. steel industry was troubled by a low rate of productivity, compared to Japanese and West German rates. The standard operating rates (defined at 90 percent of theoretical capacity utilization) for man-hours per ton of steel shipped were 11.85 in the U.S., 10.54 in Japan, and 9.7 in West Germany. By 1986, the U.S. rate was 6.4, only slightly higher than Japan, which had a rate of 6.03, and well below West Germany, at 7.21 (Table 3). The dramatic increase in domestic labor productivity since 1975 is a reflection of massive layoffs by the larger steel companies, as well as the effects of improved technology. Bethlehem Steel cut its steel hourly work force by 15 percent and its salaried work force by 47 percent between 1983 and 1986, for example.

Table 4 lists man-hours per ton for 26 plants from various countries, and shows that even mills within the same country vary widely in productivity. The three most efficient are Japanese, and the least efficient are in the plants in the developing world. However, labor costs in the developing world are still low; they averaged $3 to $3.50 per hour, compared to $24 in the U.S. and $16 in Japan in the mid-1980s.

Production Costs

Table 5 compares production costs for 1978-1987 in five countries, and indicates that the U.S. has improved its position relative to all foreign competitors except the U.K. In the U.S. in 1978, a finished carbon steel product mix cost $411 per ton to produce in an integrated mill at 85 percent capacity utilization; the same product cost Japan $384 per ton, at a 209 yen-to-dollar exchange. By 1987, the U.S. cost had risen to $511 per ton at 60 percent capacity utilization, but Japanese costs had risen even higher, to $535 per ton at a similar utilization rate.

This dramatic increase primarily reflects the change in the dollar-yen ratio. Even at Japan's currently low operating rate, Japanese steel would still be cheaper than U.S. steel, using the 1985 exchange rate. However, the declining dollar has made the U.S. steel price competitive (at least in the U.S.) with all major producers except Korea, Brazil, and Canada.

The relatively low wages paid in Korea give the country a significant cost advantage. For example, as shown in Table 6, the cost to produce hot-rolled sheet per short ton is $252 in Korea, compared to $334 in the U.S., $399 in Japan, and $306 in Canada. However, shipping costs from Japan or Korea to a U.S. West Coast port add another $50-$60 per ton.

As the changing Japan-U.S. exchange rate has slowed the decline of the U.S. integrated steel industry, so might a change in the Korean-U.S. exchange rate. The exchange rate has dropped from 860 won per dollar to 800 since January 1987, and may drop to as low as 500-600 per dollar. Table 7 shows how a decrease in the exchange rate would affect the price of Korean hot-rolled sheet compared to U.S. sheet, barring changes in either technology or input factors over the next two years.

Markets for Steel Products

This section will briefly review the important determinants of steel demand, and present conditional forecasts of steel consumption in the years 1985, 1990, and 2000. To project national and international supply/demand balances, and to understand how each forecast will affect the domestic industry, requires an understanding of what determines the national and international demand for steel.

The two important factors that affect aggregate steel consumption in developed countries are declining intensity of use and capital investment expenditures. Figure 3 depicts the intensity of use (steel consumption and gross national product (GNP) in the United States, Japan, and West Germany from 1950 to 1980. Although there are fluctuations in the ratio of steel consumption/GNP, and the United States shows the strongest and earliest trends, all three countries used less in the 1970s.

Steel usage has declined for four reasons. First, in a maturing economy, the percentage of output represented by the manufacturing sector diminishes relative to the service-oriented sector. A decreased need for steel-intensive investments in infrastructure (e.g., manufacturing plants, heavy equipment, roads, bridges, railroads) becomes apparent as the industry develops, and consumer preferences change as affluence increases.

Second, as technology becomes more sophisticated, changes in manufacturing methods and equipment lead to a relative decrease in steel consumption. For example, electronic manufacturing processes are significantly less steel-intensive than traditional mechanical methods. Computer-controlled machine tools are more efficient than their manually controlled counterparts and increase the output per unit of steel contained in the product.

Third, as product design and technology improves, steel is used more efficiently in manufactured goods. For example, the downsizing of automobiles by U.S. manufacturers led to a 25 percent decrease in carbon steel consumption over the period 1971-1981. Developments in casting and container technology have led to dramatic reductions in the wall thickness of engine blocks and the gauge of metal sheet used in beverage cans, respectively.

The development of more efficient design systems, together with vastly superior grades of steel, has, in many cases moved the emphasis from tons to quality and from cost to value added. For example, the Eiffel Tower required 9500 tons of steel when it was built a hundred years ago. If it were replicated today, only about 3000 tons would be used.

Fourth, carbon steel will experience intensified competition within industrial sectors. By 1983, aluminum had already captured 85 percent of the market in beverage cans. Some steel producers foresee aluminum cans and plastic pouches as formidable competitors in the container market of the future.

In the automotive market, polymeric materials are particularly competitive for parts where weight, corrosion resistance, formability, and consolidation are important. High-strength steels have been developed, some with excellent formability, that may compete in the near-term with polymers. However, carbon steel will also be competing with lighter high-strength, low-alloy steels and dual phase steels in these applications.

Table 8 shows historical data for steel consumption by region, from 1960 to 1985. Table 9 lists forecast of world steel consumption for the years 1985, 1990, and 2000 made in 1984 by three different sources. These forecasts show a slow growth in the aggregate world consumption of steel to the end of the century. The members of the "Materials Working Group" think these forecasts are optimistic, particularly where the U.S. market is concerned. Even if the forecasts are correct, the implications for U.S. producers are not encouraging. There is, however, a place and a need for the integrated carbon plants in the U.S.

Table 9 shows an annual consumption of 120 million metric tons of raw steel from 1990 to 2000, which translates to 96 million metric tons, or 150 million short tons of finished steel consumption, assuming an 80 percent yield of semi-finished to finished steel. Today, this yield is actually higher, 86 percent.

If finished steel imports increase to 30 percent of the market in the 1990s (as forecast by *World Steel Dynamics*), and another five million tons of steel is imported in semi-finished form, shipments from domestic producers would amount to 69-70 million short tons. (Even less optimistic forecasts show domestic shipments of 55-64 million short tons, *World Steel Dynamics*.) Either scenario implies a need for less capacity in the domestic market than now exists.

Causes of Changing Patterns of Competition

Technological Leadership and Adoption of New Technology

This chapter will focus on the root causes of the recent problems of the integrated firms, which are facing the most severe problems. However, it should be noted that the competitive situation for the specialty and minimill segments of the domestic steel industry differs from the integrated producers.

U.S. firms face overcapacity in the world steel market. The dynamics of the world steel market are determined by factors such as: 1) government investment in steel plants, particularly in developing countries; 2) subsidies to steel plants that increase output and reduce the probability of plant closure; and 3) a policy of protectionism in the domestic markets for steel.

In the past 20 years, the market for steel products has been depressed three out of four years. Depressed world markets have contributed to a poor record of profitability for domestic producers, especially in recent years. The recent decline in profitability can be attributed to the advanced age of production facilities, high labor costs, costs of compliance with safety and environmental regulations, and relatively extended capital depreciation schedules. As well, the combination of price controls and a reluctance on the part of domestic producers to engage in supply-demand pricing have kept revenues down.

The recession of 1982 forced major structural changes in the domestic steel industry. Industrial capacity was decreased when older plants were retired, wage and work practice concessions were offered by United Steelworkers of America, and pricing policy was changed from cost-plus (i.e., production cost plus a profit margin) to supply-demand, based on international market conditions. The first two factors are expected to contribute to a domestic industry that is more cost-efficient and better able to profit from a recovery when it occurs. The third factor will induce domestic producers to compete with imports on the basis of price, but may decrease revenues.

Major factors that have been identified as contributing to the shifts in the competitiveness of domestic integrated producers include:

- Rate of Adoption of New Technology
- Adoption of Computer Controls
- Industry-Customer Relations
- Labor-Management Relations
- Industry-Government Relations
- Strategic Management Issues

Each of these is discussed in the following sections.

There is no doubt technological leadership has been lost by the U.S. in the past 25 years. The reasons for this shift are two-fold: 1) the failure of the U.S. industry to adopt the most modern technology in a timely fashion, and 2) an inability to generate the capital necessary to deploy modern technology.

History of Adoption of the Basic Oxygen Furnace. As shown by Figure 4, there is little doubt that U.S. firms lagged behind their foreign counterparts in the adoption of the most modern steelworking technology. While there is much anecdotal evidence that puts the majority of the blame for the slow rate of technological change on the organizational structure and management of the integrated firms, there are little hard data to support this view.

Smaller U.S. firms such as McClouth and J&L were the first to adopt the BOF. McClouth was also the first U.S. firm to adopt continuous casting and acid tower pickling. One reason, perhaps, is that these smaller firms were not slowed or encumbered by the many layers of bureaucracy that existed in the larger U.S. firms.

It also appears that a great deal of internal pressure was maintained on the larger U.S. steelmakers to keep the technical status quo. Upper management in these firms had a large financial and technical stake in the open hearth process, and builders of open hearths applied pressure on the steel firms not to adopt the BOF.

The decision to adopt the BOF was opposed by engineering firms that built and often helped to design new plants because they lacked expertise in the technology, and their business would be hurt by BOF adoption. Adoption was also slowed by the fact that no U.S. refractory firm produced or was willing to research new types of refractory brick necessary to build a BOF furnace.

In contrast to the U.S. firms, the Japanese firms made an intensive search for alternatives: they visited foreign plants, scanned international technical literature, and built pilot plants over an extended period of time. Furthermore, MITI and the trading companies fed the firms additional information and made available the capital needed to adopt the new technologies.

Finally, the homogeneity of the Japanese steel industry affected the speed of adoption. A narrower product mix was produced, and the largest of the six firms had no more than four times the steel production capacity of the smallest. All the firms bought their inputs and sold their steel internationally through the trading companies. The uniformity of operation and the structure of the industry enabled a ready transfer of information from plant to plant.

History of Adoption of Continuous Casting. The U.S. industry was also slower than its foreign competitors in adopting continuous casting technology. However, in contrast to the BOF, the benefits of continuous casting were not initially obvious.

Although Western Europeans experimented with continuous (slab) casting in the middle and late 1950s, U.S. producers were scarcely interested in these small-scale (250,000 to 300,000 ton) efforts. However, by the early 1960s, U.S. integrated producers began to experiment with pilot plants, and by the mid-1960s, the technology was adopted by some domestic and foreign plants despite ongoing problems with design and operation. In fact, the slab and billet-casting machines installed in the U.S. between 1963-75 came from sixteen different equipment manufacturers, each with designs that had to be modified over time.

By the early 1970s, it was clear that continuous casting was a viable and commercially feasible technology. A 1973 *Iron and Steel Institute Journal*[6] article listed the advantages that were to be derived from slab casting over ingot casting: 1) reduces by 25-40 percent fixed capital investment in equipment; 2) reduces plant space more than 35 percent; 3) reduces direct energy costs by 30-75 percent; 4) reduces labor costs by eliminating material handling and ingot preparation; 5) improves yield up to ten percent; and 6) improves output surface quality, eliminating labor-intensive surface repairs.

The short-term economic feasibility was still questionable in existing plants, particularly if slab casting replaced ingot casting on an incremental basis. Incremental replacement meant production flows had to be planned and coordinated in duplicate, which led to cost increases in some plants. Moreover, operations planning was complicated by the need to divert production scheduled for the continuous casting machine to the ingot caster in case of unexpected difficulties.

Adoption of Computer Controls. The BOF and continuous casting cases are examples of major innovations, but most technological innovations are not major. Technological advances consisting of gradual improvements in the production process contribute greatly to technological advancement.

The incremental improvements that were seen to develop in the efficiency of the BOF or continuous casting process are examples of the general form; such advancements included process R&D, changes in material flow, product scheduling, facility scale-up, and auxiliary equipment purchases. Computerization represents another example of a general form of technological advance.

In the past, top management in the U.S. waited for managerial and technical specialists from within an operating area to generate proposals for technological improvement, proposals that were intended to meet their own performance criteria. Proposals were then compared and selected by upper management on the basis of expected benefits.

The "from the bottom-up" approach to computerized control started with process controls for selected individual operations and then integrated controls for operational sequences; this approach required programs to be redesigned frequently to be sure they were integrated with each other. Moreover, coverage was sporadic because of the changing pressures and initiatives generated by different operating units. In the absence of an overall development program, coverage lost momentum in the delay between the completion of one project and the initiation of the next.

In Japan, upper management supported the computerization of the steel industry nationwide. In choosing to implement an integrated network of computers, the three goals that guided upper management were: 1) to decrease dependence on foreign technologies; 2) to emphasize long-term performance targets over short-term criteria; and 3) to implement company-wide comprehensive planning and centralized control.

According to Gold (*Iron and Steel Engineer*, April 1978), engineers in Japanese firms are pushed harder than U.S. engineers. Head office and plant engineers are expected to keep increasing the capacity and efficiency of all facilities and equipment by 3-5 percent per year, through developing modifications in design, tooling accessories, and operating methods. It was within this context that long-term programs for computerization arose.

In Japan, computer systems were designed to encompass all company operations, and their design defined the conceptual constraints for all hierarchical levels of application, assuring compatibility with the larger system. Systems design and computer specialists became an integral part of the team assigned to design new plants. Capacity, process, equipment, and lay-out decisions were integrated with the computer system from the start, instead of being retrofitted. Steelmaking specialists and production personnel were trained in systems analysis and computerization methods. Computer specialists were trained in steelmaking. Therefore, the production personnel on the team formed from this group were less likely to be skeptical about the new technology.

The attitude taken by U.S. upper and production level management towards computer process control can be seen in the example of the BOF. Once the BOF technology was being used, management found that new process controls were needed to accommodate the more complex technology. Specifically, the shorter tap-to-tap time required immediate results from the tests of the metallurgical quality of samples taken from the BOF vessel. The most obvious control was by computer. However, U.S. management backed off from this solution, citing the difficulty of developing sensing devices that could withstand the extreme conditions in the BOF vessel and the problems of developing software. Even as late as 1980, there were no genuine control-feedback systems used on U.S. BOF plants.

More recently, domestic integrated producers have been understandably reluctant to invest the capital needed to modernize technology. Figure 5 makes it clear that the U.S. steel industry has experienced a low rate of return on equity over the past 25 years, when compared with the average of all other manufacturing industries. In fact, since 1960 its rate of return has exceeded the average only twice. As mentioned earlier, however, it is encouraging to note that 1987 was an excellent year for the U.S. steel industry. The industry as a whole recovered nicely from the disastrous period of 1982-1985, surpassing the average rate of return on equity of all manufacturing industries for the first time since 1974.

Today, it is widely sensed there is a revolution underway in the U.S. steel industry with respect to computer process control. This development, in the eyes of many competent observers, has had greater technological impact on the industry in the last few years than any other single technological innovation.

The Argon-Oxygen-Decarburization Process. The AOD process was invented by William Krivsky at the Union Carbide Corporation. In 1954, immediately after earning his PhD in process metallurgy from MIT, Krivsky was attempting to resolve the differences between two published studies of the relationship of chromium to carbon in conventional steel refining. His major discovery was that by diluting the oxygen with argon during one stage of the stainless steel refining process, the carbon content of the melt could be reduced in a simpler and more cost-effective manner.

In the conventional stainless steel refining practice, the charge (consisting of Fe, Ni, and a small amount of chromium) is melted in an electric furnace. Oxygen is blown into the furnace at a high temperature (about 3000°F), and later the majority of chromium is added in the form of low carbon ferrochromium. The entire process takes place in the electric furnace vessel.

In the AOD process, the charge is melted in an electric furnace, transferred by ladle to a separate refining vessel that is similar to a Bessemer converter with two or more tuyeres in the bottom through which oxygen and argon are blown through the molten bath. No low carbon ferrochromium additions are necessary. The differences between the two processes for producing a standard stainless steel grade, containing 18 percent Cr and eight percent Ni, are summarized in Table 10.

It was recognized early that the new process had the potential to be economically competitive even though it involved more process steps than the conventional technique. There was a growing market for extra low carbon (ELC) grades of stainless steel, but they were expensive because the high finishing temperature (3300°F) of the conventional process resulted in low refractory life. Moreover, the ELC products made with the conventional process were not easily reproducible. The lower temperature (3100°F) required by the AOD process led to better refractory life, and the process did not need the addition of expensive low carbon ferrochrome.

A number of difficulties were encountered during the scale-up of the laboratory-size 100-pound furnace, however. These included developing effective refractories and lances, coatings for the lances, and gas dispersal throughout the bath. The major problem arose when Union Carbide decided it needed a stainless steel producer to complete the commercial scale-up of the new process. None of the larger companies was interested, and only after a long search did Union Carbide convince a small producer, Joslyn Stainless Steel Company, to participate. Moreover, after a joint development contract was formed between the two companies in 1960, the initial tests on a 15-ton furnace were failures.

At that time, it was thought that the argon and oxygen mixtures should be applied directly in the electric furnace so as not to require another step and item of capital equipment in the process. However, after much experimentation, it was finally realized that argon distributed in a separate refining vessel added only a small fraction of the cost of an electric furnace, and could actually double the steel output of a given furnace. Therefore, it represented a cost-effective way to increase capacity.

By 1968, Joslyn had built the first commercial AOD production unit, and converted its entire melt shop to AOD process technology by mid-1969. Subsequently, the company found that, in addition to lower capital costs, the variable costs were also reduced. The additional cost associated with operating the refining vessel was more than offset by the reduction in raw materials costs, as well as the elimination of the refining and finishing stages from the electric arc furnace.

Once the improved process had been demonstrated, Union Carbide mounted an aggressive marketing campaign to license the AOD, contacting practically every major stainless steel company in the world, and arranging for demonstrations of the technology at Joslyn and elsewhere. By 1970, two additional companies, Electralloy (U.S.) and Illsa Viola (Italy) licensed the process from Union Carbide. Seven years after the first commercial product was made, Union Carbide had sold 60 licenses worldwide. By 1978, the AOD accounted for about 75 percent of world stainless steel production, and in 1988 it holds virtually 100 percent of the world market.

The AOD process could also be significant in the future for making some types of steels other than the stainless variety. Currently, some companies such as Jorgensen Steel use the AOD process for high quality carbon and low alloy steels for heavy section forgings. USX has used the AOD process on an experimental basis to produce ultralow carbon ferritic stainless steels, which are usually made by vacuum melting.

The real growth of AOD in the future could be in foundries, with one to two ton vessels producing low sulfur, high quality castings. On a more speculative basis, the AOD could be used by integrated producers to produce ultra-low-carbon alloy steels, such as the ultra-low carbon bainitic steels developed by AMAX 15 years ago and now being used by the Navy for high strength ship plate. In addition, the AOD might find application with ultralow nitrogen steels or "interstitial free" steels, which are currently made by using microalloy additions.

On the other hand, it is probable that in most cases various other processes will fill the role of AOD more economically for producing ultra-low-carbon bainitic and high strength low alloy (HSLA) steels. For example, a two station ladle refining unit can convey the steel at proper chemistry and temperature to a tank degasser. There, under vacuum, argon and oxygen are bubbled through the ladle to reduce carbon and remove other impurities in a fashion more suited to large heats of carbon and HSLA steel than the AOD process.

Technology—Summary. It is evident from the previous sections that the U.S. has for many reasons lost its clear technological leadership in the production of carbon steel in integrated mills. It is also evident that there has been significant progress within the last few years, and that U.S. firms are quite capable of making major technological advances such as the AOD process.

The industry has been characterized as mature. This is probably true in a financial sense, but not necessarily in a technological sense. The annual volume produced in integrated carbon steel mills will not increase significantly in the U.S. in the foreseeable future. However, there is not only room for technological developments in the steelmaking process, but an actual need for continuing process improvements in order to maintain international competitiveness.

Industry-Customer Relations

On average, stamping costs are higher in the U.S. than in Japan, due to the lack of joint R&D projects between steel makers and automakers, and the lack of technical assistance by steelmakers for steel stamping. Automakers have not been able to optimize the use of new coatings on steel sheet, or the HSLA (high-strength, low-alloy steels) in terms of stamping efficiency, part, or tool design. Moreover, the Japanese maintain an advantage in the lower cost of dies and faster die change-over times.

U.S. steelmakers are beginning to invest in the improvement of steel stamping processes and tool design, and have initiated several research projects, under the leadership of the American Iron and Steel Institute. An important one concerning tooling design and tooling costs is being worked on at the University of Michigan.

Steel suppliers have organized Product Application Centers (PACs) to address a significant deficiency within the steel industry, which is the inadequate communication between marketing, R&D, production, and quality assurance groups. The common goal of the PACs is to offer technical assistance to auto firms during the soft-and-hard-tool tryouts of new part prototyping. By now, all of the larger steel firms have sales offices/technical centers in Detroit to assist with prototyping. In return, the auto firm promises to use the products of the steel firm that participates in developing the new part.

For the steel industry to meet auto industry demands is not simple, mainly because the auto firms do not easily agree to cross-industry supplier/user standardized material tests, or any other system. For example, although the auto firms agreed on the need for laser-readable bar codes for inventory, the firms could not agree on one standard. The problem of standardization has also been evident in the corrosion tests used by the three U.S. auto firms and the largest integrated steel suppliers.

Chrysler, Ford, and GM do not have effective supplier rating systems that would help suppliers know where they stand relative to their competitors or what the quantifiable problems with their materials are. All three auto firms say that they are working to form such a system. Ford has begun to implement the Japanese automaker's policy of directly observing the quality control system used in steelmaking plants in order to generate suggestions to improve it.

Steel suppliers find it difficult to implement just-in-time inventory systems because the automakers vacillate in their demands. According to an executive from USX, U.S. automakers do not freeze the design specifications for a part even when the part has moved from prototype to full production. An executive at Chrysler agreed that this was a problem. Because design changes continue throughout the production lifetime of the part, production schedules at the stamping plants vary as often as automakers change their orders. According to this executive, Japanese automakers freeze a design long before it reaches production so that Japanese automakers can order steel three months in advance.

In Japan, steel suppliers actively sought out customer feedback on product defects or qualities. A survey of Japanese steel suppliers showed that over 50 percent of all new product ideas originated from the customers. Firms that were not aggressive in the marketing area did not seek out customer complaints, but waited for customers to call with complaints.

Collaborations between the steel companies in the United States and automotive companies are making progress. For example, intensive joint studies have been carried out on automotive stamping operations. Worth noting in this connection is the drop in rejection rates for poorly manufactured steel auto body panels. It is now below one percent, down from three to six percent just a few years ago. Along the same lines, the AISI/Northwestern University Steel Resource Center is well along in studies ranging from steel surfaces to expert systems to customer-supplier relationships. This center has an advisory board that includes representatives from the university, the industry, and major customers and is accomplishing major advances in research leading toward increased U.S. steel industry competitiveness.

Labor-Management Relations

The nature of labor-management relations in the U.S. steel industry has been characterized by a hostile, antagonistic tone. Labor, through its unions, fought for and won major concessions from the steel industry in wages, benefits, and work rules. The higher labor costs resulting from these negotiations have been blamed by many for the rise in imports from foreign nations whose producers enjoyed a lower labor cost per ton of steel.

The effectiveness of labor in wage negotiations can be inferred from the dramatic comparison between hourly total compensation of production workers in steel companies compared to workers in all manufacturing industries. These data are tabulated in Table 10 and shown graphically in Figure 6.

Two conclusions are reasonably clear from these data. First, fringe benefits, including paid holidays, retirement pensions, unemployment benefits, and health and life insurance account for a major proportion of domestic steelworker employment costs. Benefits in the United States currently average about 75 percent higher than benefits in other countries. (However, this differential may not be as large as noted since many benefits abroad are paid publicly rather than privately). Second, domestic steel workers' wages have been rising much faster than the average manufacturing wage since 1971. The U.S. steelworking wage exceeded the average manufacturing wage by 76 percent in 1987 (in 1982 the premium was 89 percent). Steelworkers in other countries also earned more than the average manufacturing wage, but the difference was much less pronounced.

The higher wages paid to U.S. workers immediately following World War II were offset partially by the higher rates of productivity (man-hours per ton of steel) shown by U.S. manufacturers. When the

Japanese and European steel industries rebuilt in the early 1950s using the newest technology and more efficient plant layouts, dramatic gains in productivity were made. However, the United States still enjoyed a productivity advantage into the 1970s. By 1979, although the United States still compared favorably with France and the United Kingdom, Japan and West Germany were producing better at both standard and actual operating rates.

Although the U.S. lost its position as the most efficient steel producer, it still is one of the world's leaders. The financial burden stems from higher labor costs, not labor productivity. Labor rates in the U.S. steel industry rose sharply in the 1970s, both in absolute terms and relative to other manufacturing wages, even though cheaper imports were already an obvious threat. In 1978, U.S. steel workers were paid 25 and 40 percent more per hour than their West German and Japanese counterparts, respectively. The effect of the strong dollar on exchange rates in the early 1980s exacerbated this trend. By early 1983, U.S. labor was more than twice as expensive as Japanese and West German labor, despite a recent agreement with the U.S. steelworkers' union that had reduced wages and some benefits.

Throughout the 1950s, there had been an increasingly hostile tone in labor negotiations between the U.S. steel industry and the United Steelworkers of America (USWA). The industry-wide strike that lasted 116 days in 1959 ushered in a new era of net steel importation by the United States. Although there has not been another prolonged general strike since, labor negotiations in a number of years (1965-1969, 1971) went down to the wire before a settlement was reached. Dramatic increases in imports occurred in these years as consumers built contingency inventories and established alternate sources of supply in anticipation of another extensive work stoppage.

To avoid these periodic import surges, which they feared had the potential to establish long-range business between foreign producers and U.S. consumers, U.S. steelmakers tried to mollify their labor unions. In March 1973, an agreement between the USWA and ten principal steelmakers stabilized inventory build-ups. The USWA gave up the right to strike nationwide in return for a guarantee workers would not be locked out during labor negotiations. As well, this agreement guaranteed workers a minimum annual real wage increase of three percent, a cost-of-living clause as a standard feature of future agreements, and a one-time bonus payment for each covered worker. This agreement brought labor peace.

The Experimental Negotiating Agreement (ENA) of 1973 was amended for the 1977 and 1980 negotiations. In the eyes of both the steel companies and the USWA, the ENA was a success in 1974 and 1977. Delicate issues were resolved without going to arbitration. The absence of a strike threat eliminated strike hedge buying, which had swelled inventories and imports in the past. But, by the early 1980s, the sharp increase in hourly wages and benefits produced a large gap in labor costs between U.S. and foreign producers, which encouraged a continuing increase in steel importation by the U.S. In the 1983 bargaining season, at a time of great financial stress for the industry, wages on an absolute basis were actually reduced. Today, ENA appears to be history.

In recent history, through 1983, the steel industry (with a few exceptions) engaged in triennial industry-wide collective bargaining with the USWA. That very important situation changed dramatically in 1986, when each company bargained individually. Since ENA implies an industry-wide pact to avoid an industry-wide strike, the ENA would no longer be relevant. Moreover, there are several other very important economic reasons why the ENA was allowed to lapse. Today, each steel company bargains separately, even possessing different contract expiration dates, so a "prolonged general strike" is no longer a real possibility.

As a result of financial strains on the steel industry, the picture is changing somewhat. Recent concessions by labor have reduced hourly compensation and introduced more flexibility in attitudes towards work rules. In addition to these changes, reductions in the labor force (both blue collar and white collar), the closing of old, inefficient plants, and the dramatic change in exchange rates have made the labor costs of U.S. producers more internationally competitive.The exchange rates in effect in March 1988 (i.e., 128 yen/$, $1.69DM/$) make the relative labor costs per ton of steel in the three countries approximately equal.

The relatively stabilized labor costs of U.S., Japanese, and West German steel producers provide little hedge against the major advantages in labor costs that developing countries currently maintain. Labor costs in most developing countries are in the $2 to $4 per hour range ($4 per hour in Mexico, $3 per hour in Brazil, and $2 per hour in Korea). When labor comprises 20-40 percent of the cost per ton of finished steel (depending on the product type and shape), in the long-term it will be difficult for industrialized countries to compete in integrated carbon steel facilities.

Industry-Government Relations

A major constraint was placed on the steel industry as a result of the confrontation in 1962 between President Kennedy and Roger Blough, the President of U.S. Steel. Following a labor agreement more or less mediated by the Federal Government, U.S. Steel apparently violated an implied understanding and announced price increases. President Kennedy, fearing that others in the industry would follow suit and that a round of inflationary price increases might occur in other sectors, forced Blough to rescind the increases with a show of government power. Many observers saw this move as establishing de facto price controls on steel for the 1960s and early 1970s. The inability of the steel industry to raise prices in periods of high demand limited profits, which, in turn, restricted the amount of capital available for modernization.

The industry has also faced an apparent lack of consistency in federal anti-trust policy. Domestic firms willing to economize through inter-firm cooperation have not been able to convince the U.S. Department of Justice that their efforts to consolidate operations would not unduly restrict competition in the domestic market.

For instance, the Department of Justice opposed the merger in 1983 of Republic and LTV, a decision that was criticized by the Executive Branch and the Secretary of Commerce. Although the decision was later modified to allow the Republic-LTV merger on the condition that some stainless steel operations be sold, the criteria for approval of mergers and acquisitions remains unclear.

Also noteworthy was the earlier Jones and Laughlin-Youngstown Sheet and Tube merger, turned down by the Justice Department staff but approved by the Attorney General, and earlier attempts, for example Bethlehem-YST, that were rejected. The steel industry today could have a very different shape had our anti-trust policy been different 20 years ago.

In another case, U.S. Steel and National Steel announced a plan for a merger in January 1984 that would have increased the capacity of the nation's largest steelmaker by about six million tons (the same as the announced closings by U.S. Steel in December, 1983), and allowed it to shift its product mix more toward the flat-rolled products desired by the auto and consumer appliance industries. However, because of apparent opposition from the U.S. Department of Justice, and the precedent of the initial Republic-LTV decision, U.S. Steel decided not to pursue the merger. As a result, National Steel was forced to look elsewhere for needed capital. In April 1984 NKK (Nippon Kokan) purchased 50 percent of National, the seventh largest U.S. producer.

In a separate incident, another foreign company, Nisshin Steel, Japan's sixth largest, purchased ten percent of the financially troubled Wheeling-Pittsburgh company with $35 million in capital, and the two firms agreed to build a coating mill in the Ohio Valley for rust-proofing flat-rolled products. Anti-trust approval was not required because the deal was not a merger or acquisition.

More recently, the Department of Justice and the Federal Trade Commission appear to be more receptive to mergers and joint research projects by steel firms. However, it is unclear if this policy will continue.

Management Issues

In the late 1940s, the integrated segment of the domestic steel industry dominated world steelmaking. Contrary to popular opinion, in the 1960s and early 1970s, the U.S. spent amounts equal to Japan's expenditures for research and new equipment (Table 11). In that period, however, it appears in retrospect that U.S. integrated steelmakers made a number of mistakes in their investments in research and plant and equipment. As well, the top management of the U.S. integrated-mills in the 1960s failed to anticipate the competition emerging from imports and the U.S. minimills.

U.S. integrated firms found themselves unprepared for rising import levels; facilities were outdated, and production costs were higher than the more modern plants of foreign competitors. Extensive modernization programs begun in the 1960s were cut short in the 1970s. Hence, the integrated firms ended up with partially modernized facilities that were often out-of-balance with respect to the capacity of the coke ovens, blast furnaces, BOFs, casters, and mills. To make matters worse, in countries where steel plants were not cost competitive, subsidies by host governments and dumping in the U.S. market allowed others to increase their market share. Consequently, in steel, as in other high fixed cost industries, managers became preoccupied with stabilizing price and volume. They minimized short-term losses by avoiding price-cutting and deferring large capital investments.

A look at the expansion strategies of Japanese steel firms in the 1960s shows that the influence of MITI led to a vastly different, highly controlled business environment for Japanese steelmakers. Facing the same problems as the U.S. industry—overcapacity, high fixed costs, and uncertain price and demand—MITI created an environment conducive to plant modernization.

MITI took command on several fronts. Imports were practically prohibited. Then, MITI coordinated investment, production volume, and pricing decisions on an inter-company basis. In fact, this coordination was crucial to the tremendous growth of a small number of Japanese firms as well as their financial ability to completely scrap old plants to build new ones, a pattern characteristic of the Japanese steel industry. MITI pressured the firms to coordinate by giving building and new equipment funds only to firms with the new required levels of productivity. A policy like this could not be practiced in the U.S. Most importantly, since the Japanese steel firms were able to complete modernization plans, their plants were well-balanced and modern throughout, not the piecemeal old-and-new of U.S. plants.

Today, a comparison of product quality from U.S. integrated steelplants and newer mills in Japan, Korea, and Germany indicates a technological gap, particularly among products such as high-grade arctic line pipe, high performance light and heavy plates and sheet products. The quality of flat-rolled sheet is improved by continuous casting, continuous annealing, vacuum degassing, and computer controls. No U.S. firm has incorporated all of these techniques, though most Japanese firms have. This technological gap explains how the U.S. industry allowed major segments of its market to be taken over by foreign producers and by competing materials.

Although an imbalance in capacity partially explains why U.S. steelmakers were not cost competitive in the 1970s, it is still not clear why firms were willing to invest heavily in equipment, but did not take advantage of new ideas, processes, and products being developed in the U.S. and elsewhere. Today, samplings of the most advanced methods and processes are represented in many domestic plants, but there is no plant in the integrated industry that is as thoroughly modernized as the better Japanese plants.

However, technological pre-eminence is not always equated with economic leadership. For instance, the specialty steel division of the domestic steel industry has led the world in both process and product development, largely because of the stringent performance demands of the U.S. defense, aerospace, and energy industries. It has simultaneously been suffering economically, in part because of the importation of stainless and tool steels that are sold at prices allegedly below full costs of production (including an "adequate" return on investment), or below the exporting nation's own domestic prices. These imports have seriously eroded domestic profits by reducing the utilization rates of our specialty steel mills.

Among the integrated firms, Inland and Armco appear to lead in the incorporation of advanced steelmaking techniques. In 1986, Inland showed the lowest cold-rolled coil cost (though the gap was only a few dollars). By 1987, when Inland and Armco brought their new vacuum degassing systems on line, the cost of their galvanized sheet for the auto industry, reputedly a superior product, had risen $40/ton higher than other U.S. steel suppliers.

Current Situation and Future Prospects

The structure of the domestic steel industry has changed dramatically over the past 20 years. Although the actors remain the same, the role and market shares of the integrated firms, minimills, and imports has undergone a transition, as shown in Table 12. In addition to data for 1980 and 1985, the Table includes a gloomy forecast for U.S. integrated mills with which the Working Group does not agree.

Minimills

Minimills used advances in electric arc furnace technology during the 1970s to move into low-grade steel areas, such as small structurals and bar products. At the same time, the minimills were developing a formula for success that relied on constant marketing updates and customer contact, weekly production schedules to ensure synchrony with market changes, changes in the production mix to match the market, and substantial sales to steel service centers—because service centers were better predictors of slight changes in customer needs.

The flexible manufacturing systems of the typical minimill allowed for fast product changeovers from one type of steel to another. The simplicity of the process flow meant incremental improvements in production were more easily implemented than was possible in complex integrated systems. Finally, minimill management searched worldwide for the best steelmaking technology before investing in new equipment. Today, some of these mills represent the best either the U.S. or foreign equipment suppliers have to offer.

The low production costs and market-oriented production planning of minimills has allowed them to gain substantial market shares of various steel products in the U.S. These shares amount to about 13 million tons or 20 percent of the total U.S. market for steel (Table 13).

Today, of the approximately 50 minimill firms in the U.S., two-thirds produce less than 600,000 tons per year. Because of the increased output by minimills, the percentage of steel made by electric furnaces in the U.S. has risen to 38 percent in 1987, up from 36 percent in 1986.

Minimills have the advantage of producing a few related, highly specialized products in long production runs. Minimill plants use a simple technology with fewer process steps than integrated firms. In the average mill, the process line is electric furnace to continuous caster to rolling mill. The production capacity of each section is balanced with the other sections to achieve maximum efficiency, rather than maximum scale. As well, capital costs are low because the mills are built for a short economic life, and the most profitable mills plan for additional new or replacement equipment in the annual budget.

The lower labor costs in the minimills have contributed to their success. Man-hours per ton continued to fall in the 80s, from five in 1972 to 3.5 in 1981 to 1.8 in 1987. In most cases, they use non-unionized labor, without restrictive work rules, at a rate of $17-$22.50 per hour. Barge costs average $5/ton, while rail or freight costs average $25/ton. However, the mills have kept freight costs down by selling within a 300-mile radius of the mill, on average. This factor gives a minimill selling within that radius a strong advantage over another that is located outside the range. At least 30 percent of all production volume is sold to service centers.

Table 14 shows the 1985 cost of reproducing wire rod, reinforcing bar, and seamless tube at a representative mill at 90 percent utilization of capacity. However, factor imput efficiencies and costs have changed recently. While labor cost is the same, man-hours per ton now average two, and the most efficient minimills, Nucor and Chaparral, have lowered this value to 1.6. Average scrap costs increased to $78 per ton in 1987, and have risen further in 1988. Furthermore, reinforcing bar capacity utilization averages 85 percent, not 90 percent. Even with such changes, minimills have decreased the cost of making reinforcing bar from $233 in 1985 to $200 in 1987. The current market price of rebar ranges from $240 to $270 per ton, depending on the geographic region.

The most profitable minimills purchased the latest technology from around the world. Ladle metallurgy (i.e., refining in the ladle as compared to the furnace) decreases steelmaking costs by an average of $20/ton, while bottom tapping decreases costs by $10/ton.

In the future, the improved competitive position of the integrated firms could affect the minimills. In fact, it appears that a shake-out has already begun. Because of geographic price differences, the larger minimills are shipping products beyond the 300-mile radius and thereby depriving the smaller mills of their regional market niches. Furthermore, the market for reinforcing bar (rebar), a major minimill product, is expected to decrease substantially in the near future, and the majority of minimills have not adjusted their product mixes. Mills that did not anticipate the current degree of competitive pressure are now short of capital to invest in the equipment required to enter new product markets. Imports from foreign minimills are just beginning to enter the U.S. market and could increase. Rebar imports were .402 million tons in a 4.1 million ton U.S. rebar market in 1985 and in 1986 constituted .43 million of the same size market.

Some of the larger, aggressive minimills are expanding into higher value-added products, such as seamless tubing and large structural shapes, and decreasing output of reinforcing bar. Others are moving into downstream fabrication facilities to guarantee captive markets for products and to achieve better profit margins. Meanwhile, the larger mills are using flexible production and new equipment to improve the efficiency of their facilities.

Minimills that are expanding their mix are careful to choose products that are still experiencing market growth and that still offer the production advantage of long runs on a few related products. The near-term new market focus is on large structurals of greater than 14" width. In fact, while steel demand has decreased for most products, demand for large structurals increased from 4.4 to 4.5 million tons between 1985 and 1986. Imports fell from two to 1.7 million tons. Today, only Northwestern Steel and Wire can produce a product wider than 14" among the minimills. Nucor has formed a 51/49 percent joint venture with Yamata Kogyo. Together they are building a 70,000 ton per year facility to produce 24" width beams.

Another near-term market for new minimills is in flat-rolled products, though current technology only allows low-grade products. Thin-slab casting technology needs to be improved before the product will be competitive in high quality sheet markets. Nucor has built a new $250 million plant with a capacity of 800,000 tons in Utah, but so far it is the only investor.

The integrated firms are now actively protecting the market in large structurals from the minimills, whereas they had allowed the minimills to take over reinforcing bar, wire rod, and light structurals without resistance. The integrated sector has maintained competitive costs by investing in new equipment for continuous casting and renegotiating labor contracts. Clearly, minimills will not as easily enter new markets as they did during the 1970s.

Integrated Firms

Foreign firms initially concentrated on low-value-added products but Japan soon moved to obtain a significant market share in the higher-value-added products, such as flat-rolled products and coated sheet.

Initially, imports gained a foothold in the U.S. market during periods when domestic supplies were limited by labor problems or during periods of peak demand. By the 1970s, imports were competing on the basis of cost, quality, and service. A primary factor in the declining competitive position of the domestic industry was the slow rate of adoption of new technology. In the cases presented here—BOF, continuous casting, computer process control, problems were identified as: 1) inflexibility in the structured relationships between upper management, R&D, and production; 2) the lack of emphasis on process innovation; 3) the lack of support from either materials and equipment industries, or government and universities; and 4) the strong influence of short-term financial concerns on upper management decisions.

The PAC centers are currently being used to improve the auto/steel relationship, and labor-management participation teams are being used to improve management/labor relationships. Although U.S. steelmakers are helping auto firms to design entire systems so that the strength and economics of steel can be optimized (compared to plastic), steel firms must also become involved in tool design, stamping, and assembly to have any real affect on plastic competition.

Unfortunately, traditional design-to-manufacture in U.S. auto firms is compartmentalized, and this tradition resists change, although the auto firms realize they need to combine these functions for optimal design-to-manufacture.

In industrial relations, the success of labor-management teams is limited by the mistrust of the labor unions and the unwillingness of management to lose control. Even before the severe steel market downturn in 1982, management employed a productivity improvement policy based solely on "losing heads" to improve man-hours per ton. In turn, U.S. labor unions maintain an unduly restrictive focus on short-term goals, such as protecting job security and job classifications, increasing wages, and ensuring consideration of health issues. Labor and management clearly have not held common goals.

The relationship between Inland Steel and Honda, in Ohio, is an example of a redefined auto/steel/labor relationship; Inland is allowed to work jointly with Honda on production and quality problems, and Inland permits Honda management to visit the Inland plant to run sessions with Inland steel workers on quality improvement. Honda, in turn, allows Inland personnel to suggest improvements in the auto part-stamping process. Inland's shipment rejection rate to Honda has decreased from 50 percent to five percent. The firms have benefitted by taking the time to be educated in each other's technology.

Barnett (1986) predicts that U.S. minimill production will account for 50 percent of all U.S. steel production by the year 2000, and that minimills will hold increasing shares of the semi-finished slab, cold-finished bar, plate, rail, sheet, and pipe markets in the U.S. This prediction seems fairly optimistic. Many opposing forces are already slowing the fast growth of this sector—including integrated sector production using the minimill concept, foreign minimills imports, flat market growth, and lack of investment capital. Only the largest mills will be strong enough financially to sustain significant growth, and to enter new product markets simultaneously with the concomitant investments in new equipment that are required.

In the future, it appears that worldwide consumption of steel products will follow a stagnant or declining trend in developed countries while increasing in developing countries, especially China, India, Korea, and Brazil. It is unlikely that U.S. firms will develop a strong export position in these growing markets over the long-term. In the short-term, while the dollar remains weak and developing countries are in the process of building industries to produce high quality steel, U.S. firms could increase their exports.

These firms are now in a position to compete internationally because the integrated carbon steel industry has undergone a painful restructuring process that has greatly improved its competitive position. Labor productivity and average product quality has been improved by the closing of a number of outdated and high-cost facilities. While the industry is to be applauded for the great strides made by integrated firms to improve their competitive position, the ongoing problems cannot be ignored. More improvements still need to be made in the areas of product quality, customer service, and labor-management relations. The ability of the integrated producers to make these changes will determine the long-term competitive position of the industry.

Notes

1 Arthur D. Little, Inc., *Environmental Policy for the 1980s: Impact on the American Steel Industry*, Report to the AISI, 1981.

2 National Research Council, *The Competitive Status of the U.S. Steel Industry*, 1985.

3 D. Barnett and R. Crandall, *Up From the Ashes: The Rise of the Steel Minimill in the United States*, The Brookings Institute, Washington D.C., p.4., 1986

4 The data used in this section have been drawn from various sources. Each source has its own basis (standard operating rate, exchange rates, etc.). The data are thus not comparable from one Table to another. No attempt has been made to put them all on a common basis. The data are quoted as found in the reference and are internally consistent within each individual table.

5 The standard operating rate is obtained as the man-hours per ton at 90 percent plant utilization. The actual operating rate is the man-hours per ton applicable to the nation and year in the table.

6 S.K. Morton and F. Weinberg, "Continuous Casting of Steel," *Iron and Steel Institute Journal*, Vol. 211, Part 1, 1973.

TABLE 1. U.S. RAW STEEL PRODUCTION AND CAPABILITY
          (MILLIONS OF NET TONS)

YEAR	CAPACITY	PRODUCTION	UTILIZATION
1975	153.1	116.6	76.2%
1976	158.3	128	80.9%
1977	160	125.3	78.3%
1978	157.9	137	86.8%
1979	155.3	136.3	87.8%
1980	153.7	111.8	72.8%
1981	154.3	120.8	78.3%
1982	154	74.6	48.4%
1983	150.6	84.6	56.2%
1984	135.3	92.5	68.4%
1985	133.6	88.3	66.1%
1986	127.9	81.6	63.8%
1987	112.2	88.5	78.9%
AVERAGE 1975 - 79	156.9	128.6	82.0%
AVERAGE 1982 - 87	140.3	84.3	60.6%

SOURCE: AMERICAN IRON AND STEEL INSTITUTE ANNUAL STATISTICAL REPORT,
        VARIOUS ISSUES.

TABLE 2. DEMAND FOR STEEL IN THE UNITED STATES
(MILLIONS OF NET TONS)

YEAR	SHIPMENTS (NET OF DIRECT EXPORTS)	+ DIRECT IMPORT =	APPARENT CONSUMPTION	+ INDIRECT IMPORTS =	TOTAL DEMAND	- INDIRECT EXPORTS =	NET DEMAND
1975	77	11.8	88.8	8	96.8	9.5	87.3
1976	86.8	14	100.8	8.3	109.1	10	99.1
1977	89.2	19	108.2	9.8	118	9.3	108.7
1978	95.5	20.7	116.2	10.2	126.4	9.6	116.8
1979	97.4	17.2	114.6	10.3	124.9	9.6	115.3
1980	79.8	15.3	95.1	9.6	104.7	9.5	95.2
1981	85.6	19.1	104.7	9.7	114.4	9.5	104.9
1982	59.8	15.9	75.7	9.6	85.3	8.3	77
1983	66.4	16.2	82.6	10.5	93.1	7.2	85.9
1984	72.8	24.6	97.4	13.8	111.2	8.8	102.4
1985	72.1	21.8	93.9	16.1	110	8.7	101.3
1986	69.3	18.6	87.9	17.2	105.1	8.8	96.3

SOURCE: TEMPLE, BARKER, SLOAN REPORT TO THE AMERICAN IRON AND STEEL IN-
STITUTE.
IMPORTS ADJUSTED TO AVOID DOUBLE-COUNTING OF SEMI-FINISHED.
DATA FOR 1986 DIRECTLY FORM AISI.

TABLE 3. Major Mills Man-Hours per Ton Shipped[1]
===

	Standard Operating Rate			Actual Operating Rate		
	1975	1981	1986	1975	1981	1986
USA	11.85	9.76	6.4	12.47	9.92	7.04
Japan	10.54	7.18	6.03	11.35	9.48	8.54
W.Germany	9.7	7.78	7.21	13.04	10.15	7.79
U.K.	19.36	9.96	6.49	24.9	14.18	9.13
France	16.17	9.91	8.07	17.66	10.86	8.88

---

1 The standard operating rate is obtained as the man-hours per ton at 90% plant utilization. The actual operating rate is the man-hours per ton applicable to the nation and year in the table.

TABLE 4. MANHOUR PER TON RANKING
==

		SLAB	RANK	HR COIL	RANK	CR COIL	RANK	CR COIL SHIPPED
1	JAPAN 1	1.52	1	2.57	1	4.19	1	5.37
2	JAPAN 2	1.6	2	2.67	2	4.29	2	5.54
3	JAPAN 3	1.72	3	2.8	3	4.43	3	5.63
4	EUROPE 1	1.83	4	3	4	4.67	4	5.67
5	CANADA 1	1.97	5	3.2	6	4.81	5	5.76
6	U.S. 1	1.98	6	3.16	5	4.91	6	5.86
7	U.S. 2	1.98	6	3.44	13	4.95	7	5.95
8	U.S. 3	2.14	8	3.37	9	5.01	8	5.96
8	U.S. 4	2.19	11	3.34	7	5.01	8	5.96
10	EUROPE 2	2.14	8	3.34	7	5.04	10	5.99
11	U.S. 5	2.15	10	3.37	9	5.06	11	6.01
11	U.S. 6	2.26	14	3.66	20	5.36	17	6.01
13	U.S. 7	2.21	12	3.42	12	5.12	12	6.07
14	U.S. 8	2.26	14	3.56	15	5.18	14	6.13
15	CANADA 2	2.25	13	3.52	14	5.21	15	6.16
16	EUROPE 3	2.26	14	3.4	11	5.14	13	6.24
17	U.S. 9	2.33	20	3.64	18	5.34	16	6.29
18	U.S. 10	2.26	14	2.62	17	5.36	17	6.31
19	U.S. 11	2.43	21	3.68	21	5.37	19	6.32
20	U.S. 12	2.29	18	3.6	16	5.37	19	6.32
21	U.S. 13	2.25	12	3.64	18	5.39	22	6.39
22	CANADA 3	2.6	22	3.9	22	5.61	21	6.56
23	U.S. 14	2.69	23	4	23	5.74	23	6.69
24	U.S. 15	2.79	24	4.16	24	5.91	24	6.86
25	DEVELOPING WORLD 1	2.9	25	4.37	25	6.49	25	7.94
26	DEVELOPING WORLD 2	3.99	26	5.8	26	8.33	26	10.53

Source: World Steel Dynamics, P. Marcus and D. Barnett, Paine Webber, February, 1986.

TABLE 5. COMPARATIVE PRODUCTION COSTS - $/ NET TON
         ACTUAL OPERATING RATE
==

	USA	JAPAN	W.GERMANY	U.K.	FRANCE
1978	411	384	418	436	433
EXCHANGE RATE		209	2	0.52	4.5
1980	523	431	502	615	546
EXCHANGE RATE		219	1.83	0.43	4.23
1982	671	452	474	505	555
EXCHANGE RATE		227	1.82	0.57	6.51
1984	547	417	378	372	424
EXCHANGE RATE		237	2.84	0.75	0.73
1986	518	540	452	415	503
EXCHANGE RATE		168	2.16	0.68	6.9
1987	511	535	517	428	592
EXCHANGE RATE		155	1.84	0.65	6.1

SOURCE: STEEL COSTS FROM WORLD STEEL DYNAMICS, STEEL STRATEGIST #13,
        PAINE WEBBER, MARCH 30, 1987.

TABLE 6. COMPARATIVE LABOR COSTS - JANUARY 1987
===

$/SHORT TON TO PRODUCE HOT ROLLED SHEET

	USA	JAPAN	KOREA	CANADA
MAN-HOURS PER TON	3.7	4.3	6	4.4
OPERATING RATE	60%	60%	100%	80%
LABOR $/HOUR	23	16	4	18
TOTAL LABOR COST $/TON	85	69	24	79
TOTAL COST/$ NET TON	334	399	252	305
TOTAL U.S. COST DISADVANTAGE		($65)	$82	$29
EXCHANGE RATE/ 1987		155	860	1.25

SOURCE: STEEL COSTS FROM WORLD STEEL DYNAMICS, STEEL STRATEGIST #13
        PAINE WEBBER, MARCH 30, 1987.

TABLE 7. EFFECT OF KOREAN CURRENCY EXCHANGE RATES ON TOTAL STEEL
         PRODUCTION COSTS
==

HOT ROLLED SHEET $/TON	EXCHANGE RATE (WON/$)	
$252	860	JANUARY 1987
$271	800	JULY 1987
$361	600	1989 HIGH
$434	500	1989 LOW

SOURCE: STEEL COSTS FROM WORLD STEEL DYNAMICS, STEEL STRATEGIST
         #13, PAINE WEBBER, MARCH 30, 1987.

TABLE 8. WORLD STEEL CONSUMPTION: HISTORICAL DATA
(MILLIONS OF METRIC TONS OF RAW STEEL EQUIVALENT)

	1960	1970	1978	1980	1981	1982	1985
USA	91	127	145	118	128	88	121
JAPAN	19	70	67	79	72	79	80
EUROPEAN ECONOMIC COMMUNITY	82	124	102	109	101	101	105
OTHER INDUSTRIAL COUNTRIES	30	55	56	61	61	58	60
DEVELOPING COUNTRIES	14	38	91	99	98	102	128
TOTAL MARKET ECONOMIES	236	414	451	466	460	428	494
PLANNED ECONOMIES	107	176	260	256	250	255	265
TOTAL	344	590	711	722	710	683	759

NOTE: **Other Industrialized Countries** include Western European countries other than EEC countries and Canada, South Africa, Australia and New Zealand

Developing Countries include Latin America, Africa (except South Africa), Middle East, and Asia (except Japan, China, and North Korea).

SOURCE: INTERNATIONAL IRON AND STEEL INSTITUTE, 1985.

TABLE 9. COMPARISONS OF FORECASTS OF WORLD STEEL CONSUMPTION BY
COUNTRY GROUP (MILLIONS OF METRIC TONS OF RAW STEEL EQUIVALENT)

	1985	1990	2000
USA			
NRC (1985)	121	121	118
MUELLER (1982)	133	137	143
BARNETT AND SCHORSCH (1983)	122	129	136
JAPAN			
NRC (1985)	80	80	80
MUELLER (1982)	80	85	95
BARNETT AND SCHORSCH (1983)	91	91	91
EEC			
NRC (1985)	105	105	105
MUELLER (1982)	111	114	119
BARNETT AND SCHORSCH (1983)	123	125	136
OTHER INDUSTRIALIZED COUNTRIES			
NRC (1985)	60	65	70
MUELLER (1982)	64	68	75
BARNETT AND SCHORSCH (1983)	27	30	45
DEVELOPING COUNTRIES			
NRC (1985)	128	163	241
MUELLER (1982)	113	131	176
BARNETT AND SCHORSCH (1983)	136	164	205
TOTAL MARKET ECONOMIES			
NRC (1985)	494	534	614
MUELLER (1982)	501	535	608
BARNETT AND SCHORSCH (1983)	499	539	613
PLANNED ECONOMIES			
NRC (1985)	265	270	285
MUELLER (1982)	262	269	282
BARNETT AND SCHORSCH (1983)	260	260	277
TOTAL			
NRC (1985)	759	804	899
MUELLER (1982)	763	804	890
BARNETT AND SCHORSCH (1983)	759	799	890

SOURCE: STEEL INITIATIVE- HEARING BEFORE THE COMMITTEE ON
SCIENCE AND TECHNOLOGY, HOUSE OF REPRESENTATIVES, JULY 17, 1985.

Table 10.
The Argon-Oxygen-Decarburization (AOD) Process

CONVENTIONAL	AOD
1. Melt charge in electric furnace a) 4 % Cr charge normal; less Cr charged for ELC grades	Melt charge in electric furnace a) 18 % Cr charged even for ELC grades b) deslag melted charge transfer charge; to AOD vessel

2. Lance with oxygen; end point
    3300°F
    2 % Cr
    0.02 % C
	Blow with oxygen-argon mixture; end point
	    3100°F
	    17 % Cr
	    0.03 % C

3. Recover 1/2 of Cr (1 %) in slag with FeCrSi or FeSi add'n	Recover 0.75 % Cr from slag. Pure argon injection

4. Add 15 to 17 % Cr as low carbon FeCr to final specification
Final Composition:
    Cr-18.5 %
    C-0.02 %
	No low carbon FeCr addition necessary
	Final Composition:
	    Cr-18.5 %
	    C-0.01 %

Source: W. A. Krivsky, "The Linde Argon-Oxygen Process for Stainless Steel; A Case Study of Major Innovation in a Basic Industry", *Metallurgical Transactions*, Volume 4, June 1973, p. 1441.

Table 11. Hourly Labor Costs in the U.S. Steel Industry and All Manufacturing, 1961-1987

YEAR	HOURLY EARNINGS		TOTAL COMPENSATION		FRINGE BENEFITS	
	STEEL	ALL MFG	STEEL	ALL MFG	STEEL	ALL MFG
1961	3.24	2.32	3.99	2.95	23.15%	27.16%
1962	3.33	2.39	4.16	3.06	24.92%	28.03%
1963	3.39	2.45	4.25	3.16	25.37%	28.98%
1964	3.43	2.53	4.36	3.29	27.11%	30.04%
1965	3.54	2.61	4.48	3.35	26.55%	28.35%
1966	3.64	2.71	4.64	3.50	27.47%	29.15%
1967	3.66	2.82	4.76	3.68	30.05%	30.50%
1968	3.86	3.01	5.03	3.94	30.31%	30.90%
1969	4.12	3.19	5.38	4.20	30.58%	31.66%
1970	4.24	3.35	5.68	4.50	33.96%	34.33%
1971	4.57	3.57	6.26	4.78	36.98%	33.89%
1972	5.22	3.82	7.08	5.03	35.63%	31.68%
1973	5.69	4.09	7.68	5.39	34.97%	31.78%
1974	6.55	4.42	9.08	5.95	38.63%	34.62%
1975	7.23	4.83	10.59	6.66	46.47%	37.89%
1976	8.00	5.22	11.74	7.22	46.75%	38.31%
1977	8.91	5.68	13.04	7.83	46.35%	37.85%
1978	9.98	6.17	14.30	8.47	43.29%	37.28%
1979	11.02	7.13	15.92	9.00	44.46%	26.23%
1980	12.11	7.75	18.45	10.00	52.35%	29.03%
1981	13.43	8.52	20.16	10.60	50.11%	24.41%
1982	14.06	8.50	23.78	11.50	69.13%	35.29%
1983	13.63	-	22.21	12.10	62.95%	
1984	13.73	-	21.30	12.60	55.13%	
1985	14.27	-	22.81	13.91	59.85%	
1986	14.63	-	23.24	14.36	58.85%	
1987	14.53	10.77	23.71	14.55	63.18%	35.10%

Source: Steel - Selected Issues of American Iron and Steel Institute Annual Statistical Report Which Contains Bureau of Labor Statistics and AISI Data. All Manufacturing Data from Bureau of Labor Statistics.

Table 12. U.S. and Japanese Steel Equipment Investment, 1960-87

===

	BILLIONS OF DOLLARS		
	1960s	1970s	1980s
US	$16.3	$23.0	$13.0
JAPAN	$7.8	$29.6	

SOURCE: INDUSTRIAL ECONOMICS REVIEW , 1980.

Table 13. Market Share of Carbon Steel Industry (Percent)

Year	Integrated Sector	Imports	Minimills
1980	69.7	16.5	13.8
1985	53.8	25.2	21
1990 Proj	43.5	25	26.5
2000 Proj	30	30	40

Source: D. Barnett and R. Crandall, *Up from the Ashes:The Rise of the Steel Minimll in the United States*, The Brookings Institute, Washington, D.C., 1986

Table 14.
Minimill Share of U.S. Market by Product-1987

Product	Percent Share
Structural bar (<3")	94
Reinforcing bar	94
Wire rod	70
Hot-rolled bar	50
Small structural (>3")	30
Cold-finished bar	10
Mid-sized structural	5

Source: American Metals Market, 1987

Table 15. Cost of Producing Wire Rod at a Representative Minimill, 1985

Item	2.4 man-hrs per ton Input per ton of output	Operating cost
Electric furnace and continuous casting		$/ton
Scrap	1.1 tons @ $85	93.5
Labor	.9 man-hr @ $17.5	15.75
Electricity	520 kwh @ $.045	23.4
Natural gas	.27 thousand cu.ft. @ $4.5	1.2
Fluxes and alloys		8
Electrodes	9 lbs at @ $1.2	10.8
Refractories	38 lbs @ $.25	9.5
Supplies		9
Misc.		8.2
Total raw steel cost		179.35

Rod Mill

Item	Input	Operating cost
Yield loss	.06 @ $179.35	10.75
Scrap credit	.045 @ $85	-3.85
Labor	.85 @ $17.5	14.9
Electricity	160 kwh @ $.045	7.2
Natural gas	2.25 thousand cu.ft. @ $4.5	10.15
Supplies		6.5
Misc.		4
Total rod mill cost		49.65
Sales, Overhead, Shipping		15.05

Financial costs

Item		Operating cost
Depreciation		9
Interest		12
Taxes		2
Total financial cost		23
Total cost of finished steel		267.05

Cost of Producing Concrete Reinforcing Bar and Seamless Tube

	$/ton	
Item	Reinforcing Bar	Seamless Tube (5.5" diam, .275" thick)
Labor	31.5	80
Scrap	93	106
Energy	40	52
Misc.	60.5	223
Depreciation	4	100
Interest	3.5	70
Taxes	1	9
Total	233.5	640

Source: Up From The Ashes, Barnett and Crandall, 1986.

Figure 1. Steel Production Processes

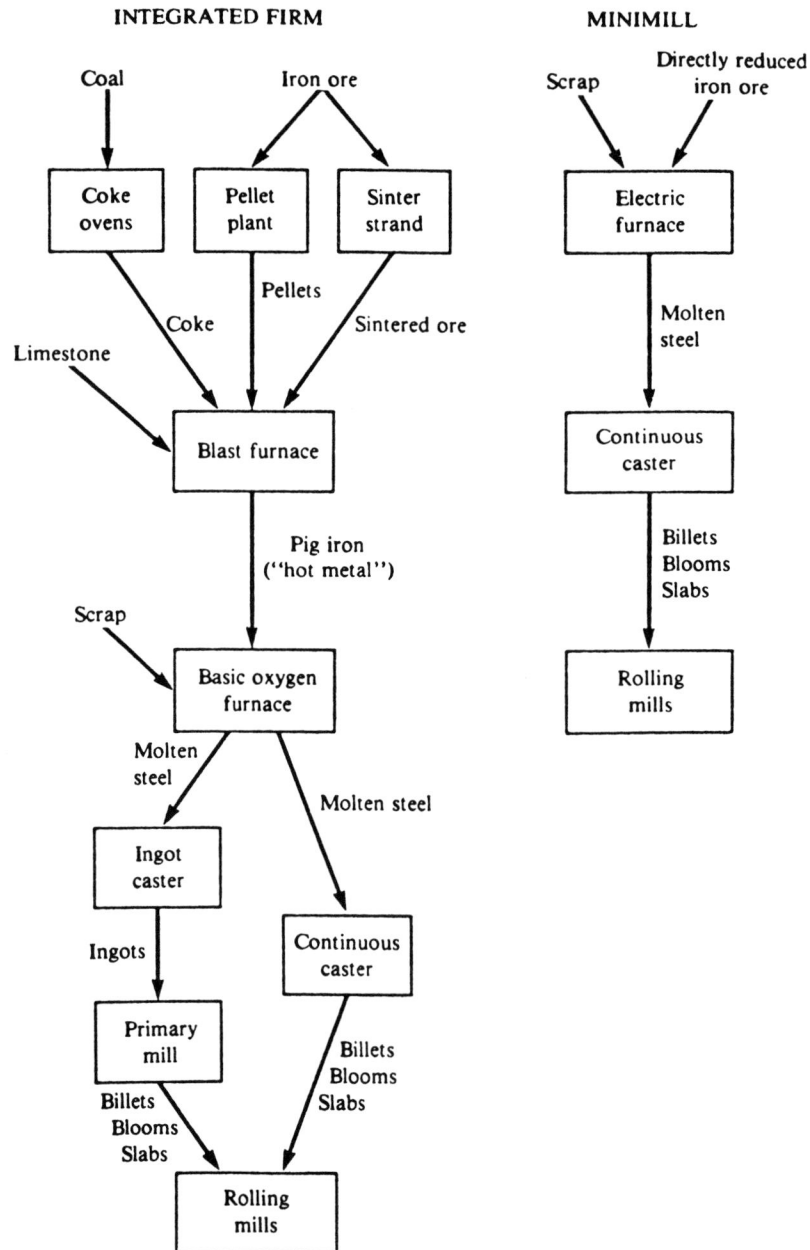

Source: D. Barnett and R. Crandall, *Up From the Ashes: The Rise of the Steel Minimill in the United States*, The Brookings Institute, Washington D.C., p.4., 1986

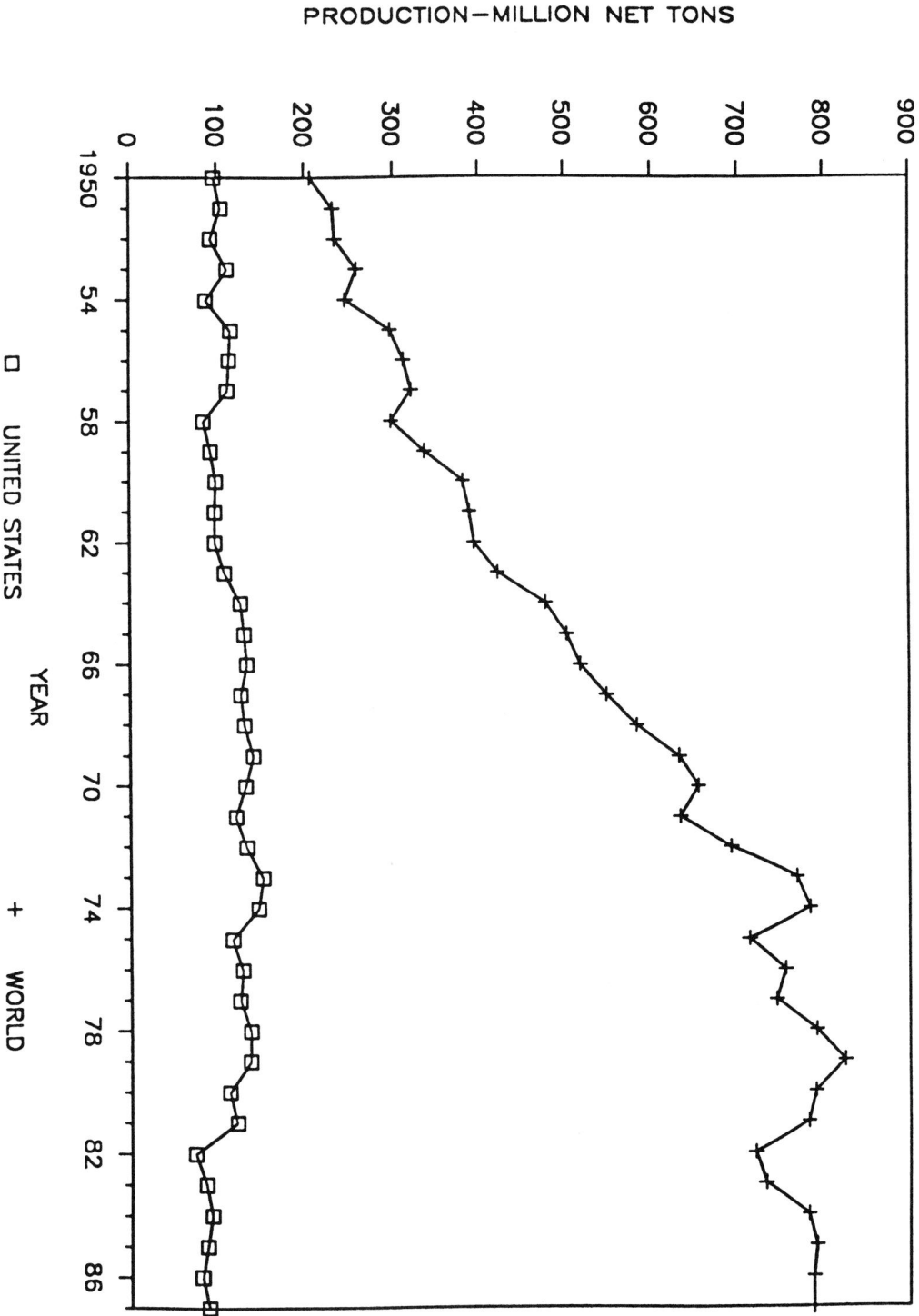

WORLD PRODUCTION OF RAW STEEL 1950 — 87

FIGURE 2.

MILLIONS OF NET TONS

PRODUCTION—MILLION NET TONS

YEAR

□   UNITED STATES   +   WORLD

Source: American Iron and Steel Institute Annual Statistical Report, various issues

Figure 3. Finished Steel Consumption Relative to Real GNP: Japan, U.S., West Germany

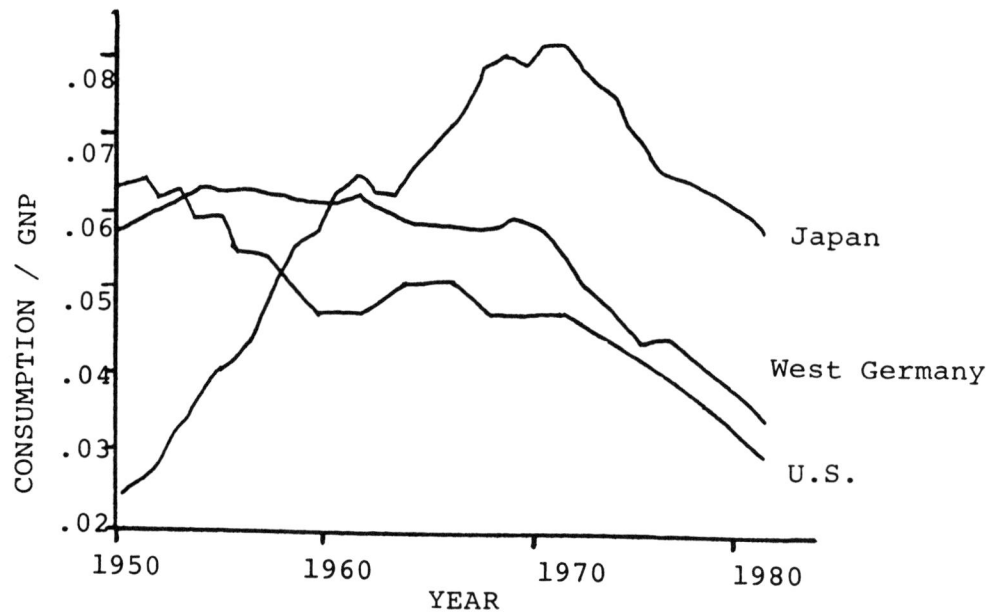

Source: *Steel: Upheaval in a Basic Industry*, D. Barnett and L. Schorsch, 1983.

47

PERCENT OF CRUDE STEEL
PRODUCED BY OXYGEN PROCESS

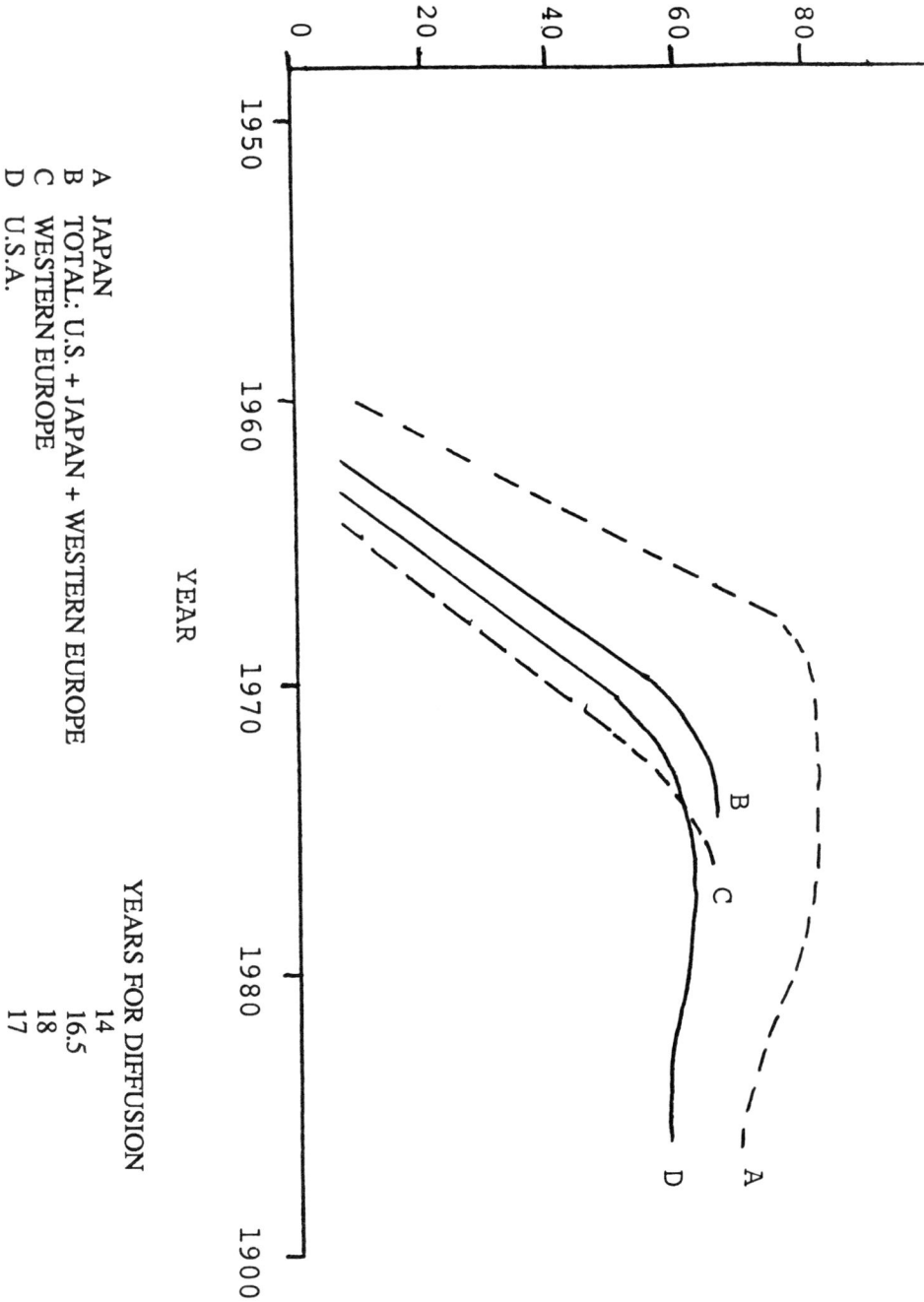

Figure 4. Adoption of Basic Oxygen Furnace Steelmaking

		YEARS FOR DIFFUSION
A	JAPAN	14
B	TOTAL: U.S. + JAPAN + WESTERN EUROPE	16.5
C	WESTERN EUROPE	18
D	U.S.A.	17

Source: "International Diffusion of Steel Technologies," by K.Z. Poznanski, *Technological Forecasting and Social Change*, p.23, 1983.

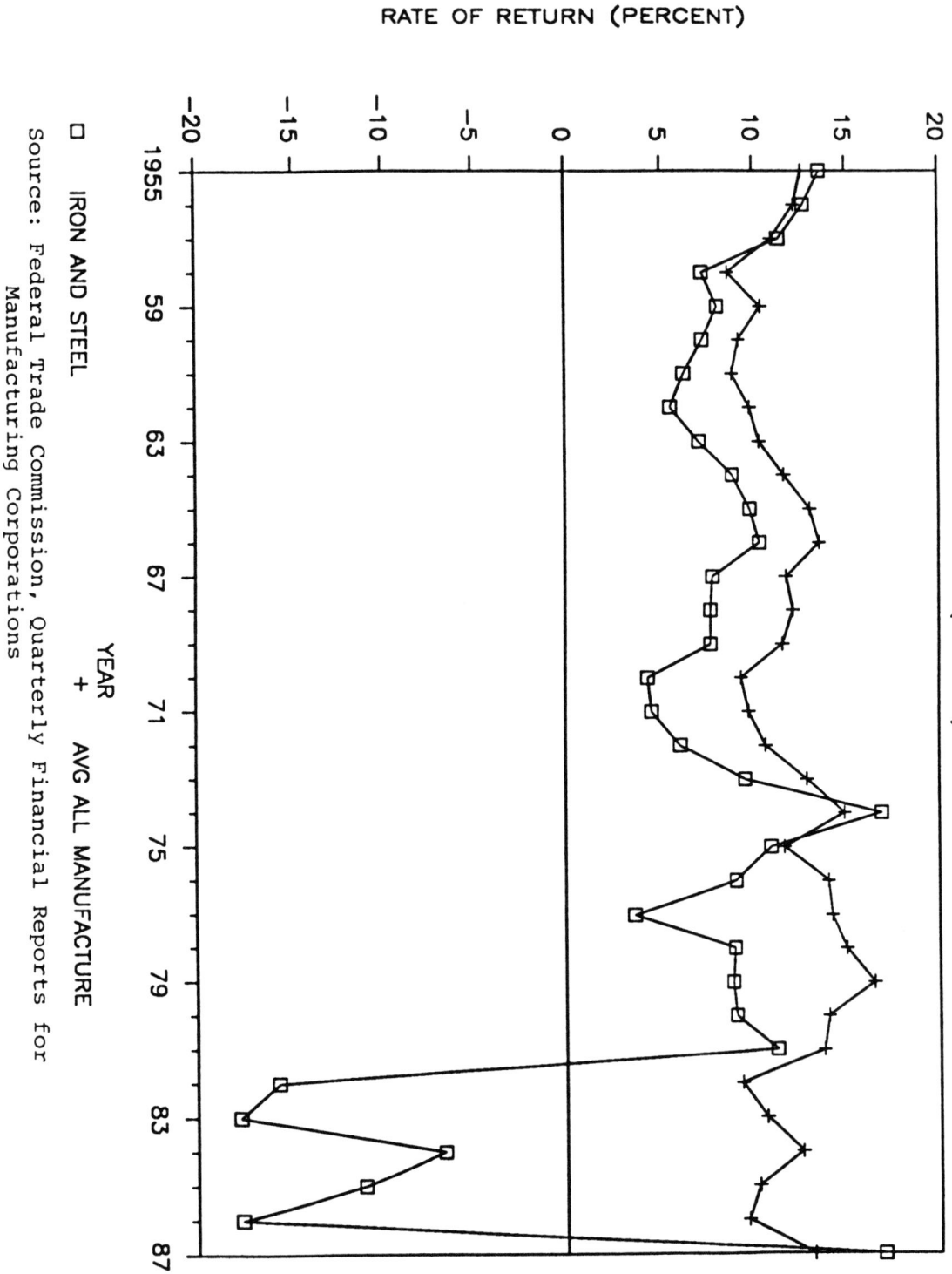

FIGURE 5 .

RATE OF RETURN ON EQUITY AFTER TAXES
(PERCENT)

RATE OF RETURN (PERCENT)

YEAR

□ IRON AND STEEL   + AVG ALL MANUFACTURE

Source: Federal Trade Commission, Quarterly Financial Reports for
Manufacturing Corporations

TOTAL COMPENSATION FOR STEEL PRODUCTION

WORKERS & ALL MANUFACTURING INDUSTRIES

DOLLARS PER HOUR

FIGURE 6.

□ STEEL   + ALL MANUFACTURING

YEAR

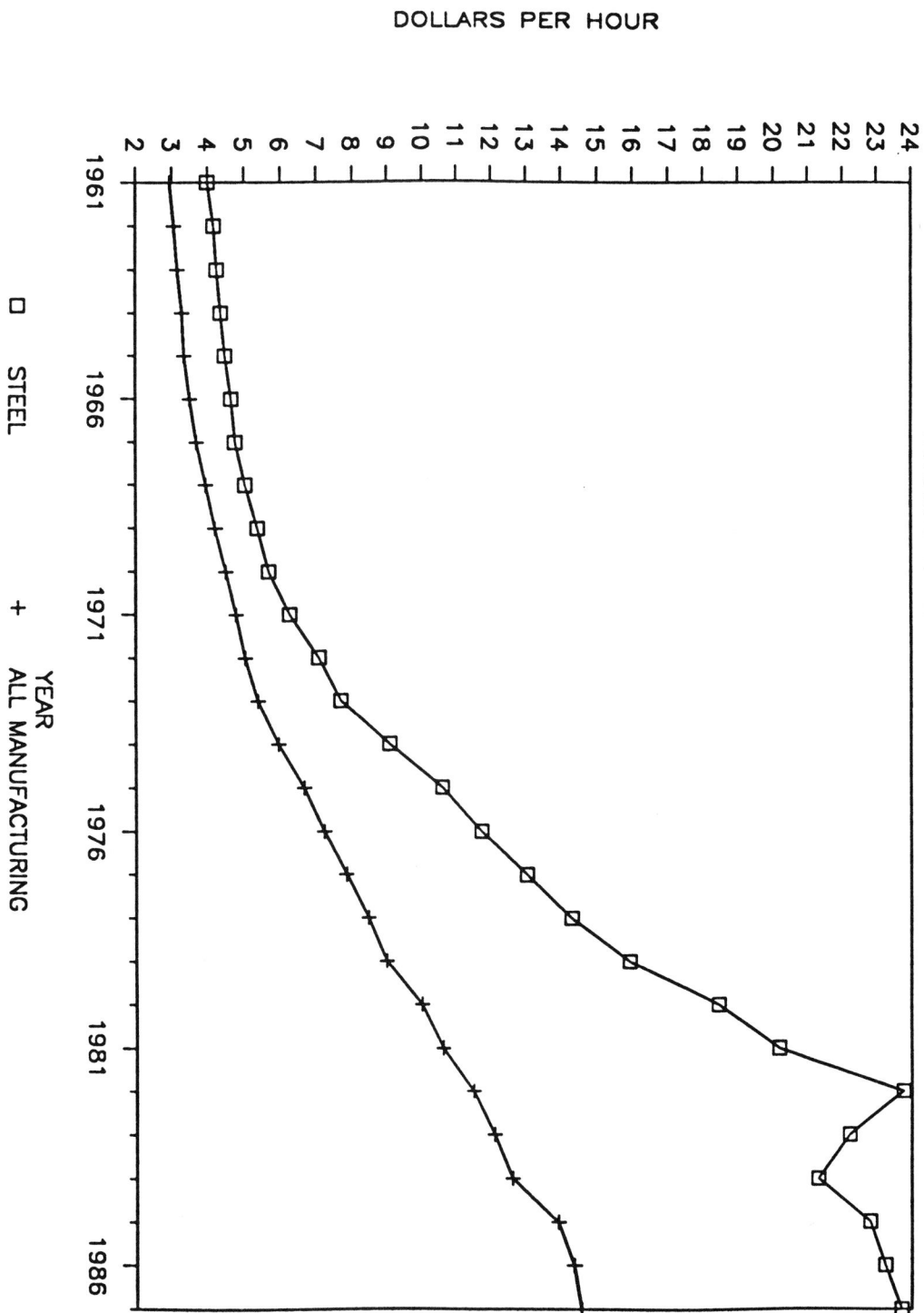

Source: U.S. Department of Labor, Bureau of Labor Statistics,
unpublished estimates, January, 1985 and March, 1988.

MIT Commission on Industrial Productivity
Working Paper

The US Textile Industry: Challenges and Opportunities

Prepared by the
Commission Working Group on the Textile Industry

Members
Suzanne Berger, Chair
Stanley Backer
Cathie Jo Martin
Michael Piore

Graduate Research Assistants
Christopher Erickson
Richard Kazis
Richard Locke
Wayne Nelson

Table of Contents

List of Tables

List of Figures

Acknowledgments

In the course of the research carried out by the Working Group on the Textile Industry, over 150 interviews were conducted in the United States, France, Italy, West Germany, and Japan. The names of many of those who devoted time to helping us in that endeavor are listed in Appendix I. There were, however, a few individuals who deserve special mention for their willingness to spend hours, even days, opening up a world that for most of us in the group was a new one. In Italy, Paolo Ferla in Biella, senior managers at GFT and Marzoli, and trade unionist Mario Agostinelli organized plant visits and long hours of discussion. In Japan, Ronald Dore, Kuniyuki Shoya, and Yoshioka Hisatoshi arranged introductions without which our access to the textile network would have been impossible. In the United States, the senior executives at Dupont, Milliken, and Russell organized day-long plant visits and discussions which were very valuable. One of our MIT colleagues, Charles Sabel, deserves special mention for the ways in which his own research on flexible specialization and on textiles in Germany shaped our ideas on these subjects.

This report focuses on the textile industry, one of the oldest sectors of the US industrial economy. The analysis presented here focuses above all on two questions: first, how and why the best textile firms in the high-wage industrial societies of Western Europe and Japan (and some outstanding US textile firms) succeed; and second, why the patterns that make for success are not more widely diffused throughout the textile sector.

As the technologies on which this industry relies have spread around the world, and as the textile goods manufactured by low-wage foreign workers flood into US markets, the US textile sector faces competitive pressures that many see as fatal. With the emergence of dynamic export-oriented textile industries in such newly industrializing countries as Hong Kong and Korea, and with the specter of an expansive, modernized Chinese textile industry on the horizon, many have come to believe that there is no competitive solution for US textiles. Much current scholarly and popular writing describes textiles as a "sunset industry," condemned by the new international division of labor to an increasingly marginal and vulnerable situation in advanced industrial societies.

If US textiles can no longer compete in world markets nor even in an open domestic market, the only way to save the industry is with tariff and quota protection. Such remedies might provide social and political benefits, but at high cost to American consumers and at great risk to the long-term competitiveness of the industry and the stability of an open international trading order. Some conclude that preserving jobs and the well-being of the regions and communities in which textiles are concentrated in the US is so important that the price of protection ought to be paid. Other analysts and politicians draw the opposite lesson: the efficient solution for the economy as a whole is to shrink labor-intensive, low-tech industries like textiles and to transfer capital and labor into new activities.

Our research suggests that this perspective and the two contradictory sets of policy recommendations that follow from it are seriously flawed. They build on a conventional view of a traditional, technologically stagnant textile sector, while in fact major parts of the US industry have in recent years had rates of productivity growth as high or higher than the national average. The stereotype of textiles as low-tech obscures both the actual experiences of some of the most successful US and foreign textile firms with microelectronics and the prospects for more far reaching automation of some of the most labor-intensive activities in the sector. The conventional view focuses on labor costs as a cause of the US industry's troubles, but neglects the extraordinary successes of textile firms in countries with wages and rates of unionization higher than the US. The West Germans, for example, are the world's third largest exporter of textiles, despite high wages. Indeed some of the outstanding textile successes of the past decade are to be found in high-wage economies, where textile workers earn on average more than they do in the US This is the case in West Germany, Italy, and Switzerland. [1]

Finally, the conclusion that textiles must be protected from competition or die is refuted by examples of flourishing US and foreign textile firms in all segments of the industry--fiber, mills, apparel, and industrial uses. Indeed in the early 1980s the US textile industry invested heavily, doubling capital expenditure per worker between 1975 and 1981. The rate of productivity growth in textiles in this period was faster than in any other manufacturing industry. From the mid-1970s into the early 1980s this productivity record contributed to a positive trade balance in textile mill goods, a marked improvement on the deficits of the past. [2] In the textile machine industry--in an advanced state of collapse in the US--the successes of Swiss, German, Italian, Japanese, and French firms suggest that the US outcome was hardly inevitable. [3] The performance in domestic and export markets of those firms that implement best practice (in market strategies, technological choices, and relations with suppliers and customers) shows a high potential for productivity growth and competitiveness in this sector.

Textiles thus represent a kind of critical case for the work of the Commission on Industrial Productivity, as the Commission considers how different industries might contribute to future economic growth. Even in textiles, an old, relatively labor-intensive industry now globally-disseminated, the best US and foreign textile firms demonstrate that competitiveness depends on strategic, structural, and technological choices that are still possible in the US.

We explore these issues in the following fashion. Section One provides a general overview of the US textile industry. Section Two considers the principal factors that account for high productivity and competitiveness in US and foreign textile firms. Section Three then explores major obstacles hindering the diffusion and generalization of factors and patterns that produce successful performance. Section Four considers the future evolution of the industry.

The research reported here was conducted from April 1987-October 1987 by the MIT Commission on Industrial Productivity's textile sector study group: Professor Suzanne Berger, Department of Political Science, chair; Professor Stanley Backer, Department of Mechanical Engineering; Professor Michael Piore, Department of

Economics; Dr. Cathie Jo Martin, Commission staff; Richard Kazis, Richard Locke, Wayne Nelson, Chris Erickson, graduate research assistants. It involved a review of the extensive literature on this industry in the United States and abroad as well as site visits and interviews in the United States, Italy, Japan, France, and West Germany. We conducted over 100 interviews with managers, union representatives, government officials, and scholars; and visited over 50 firms. (See Appendix 1).

I. An Overview of the US Textile Industry

Components of the Textile Complex

The textile complex is composed of four primary segments: fibers, textile mill products, apparel and other end uses (household and industrial applications), and associated industries (such as textile machinery). Although this cluster of industries does not correspond to any single set of census categories (i.e., the standard definition "textile and apparel" consists of both SIC 22-Textile Mill Products and SIC 23-Apparel and Other Textile Products), we are examining the entire textile complex because of the interdependence and linkages among industries in this complex.

The textile industry is a complicated network of interdependent segments. Textile fibers are used to make fabric; fabric to make apparel, household goods, or industrial applications; textile machinery to both create fibers and weave fabric. Despite tight linkages among them, the four main sectors differ greatly with respect to firm size, levels of corporate concentration, and rates of capital investment. Competitive performance and strategies vary across segments as well. Figure 1 illustrates the linkages between segments.

Fibers. The fiber industry is divided into two sectors--natural (cotton, wool) and synthetic fibers. The synthetic fiber industry consists of a few large multinational firms: the top ten firms account for 90 percent of US production, with Du Pont and Celanese at the top. [4] This high degree of industrial concentration is due in part to the capital-intensive nature of synthetic fiber production. [5] The United States remains the leading world producer of manmade fiber. Overall production almost doubled between 1970 and 1984, reaching 3,050 tons. [6] Synthetic fibers now account for nearly 75 percent of all textile mill fiber consumption in the United States. Notwithstanding these increases in domestic consumption and production of synthetic fibers, the US share of the total world production has decreased from 32.5 percent in 1970 to 24.9

4

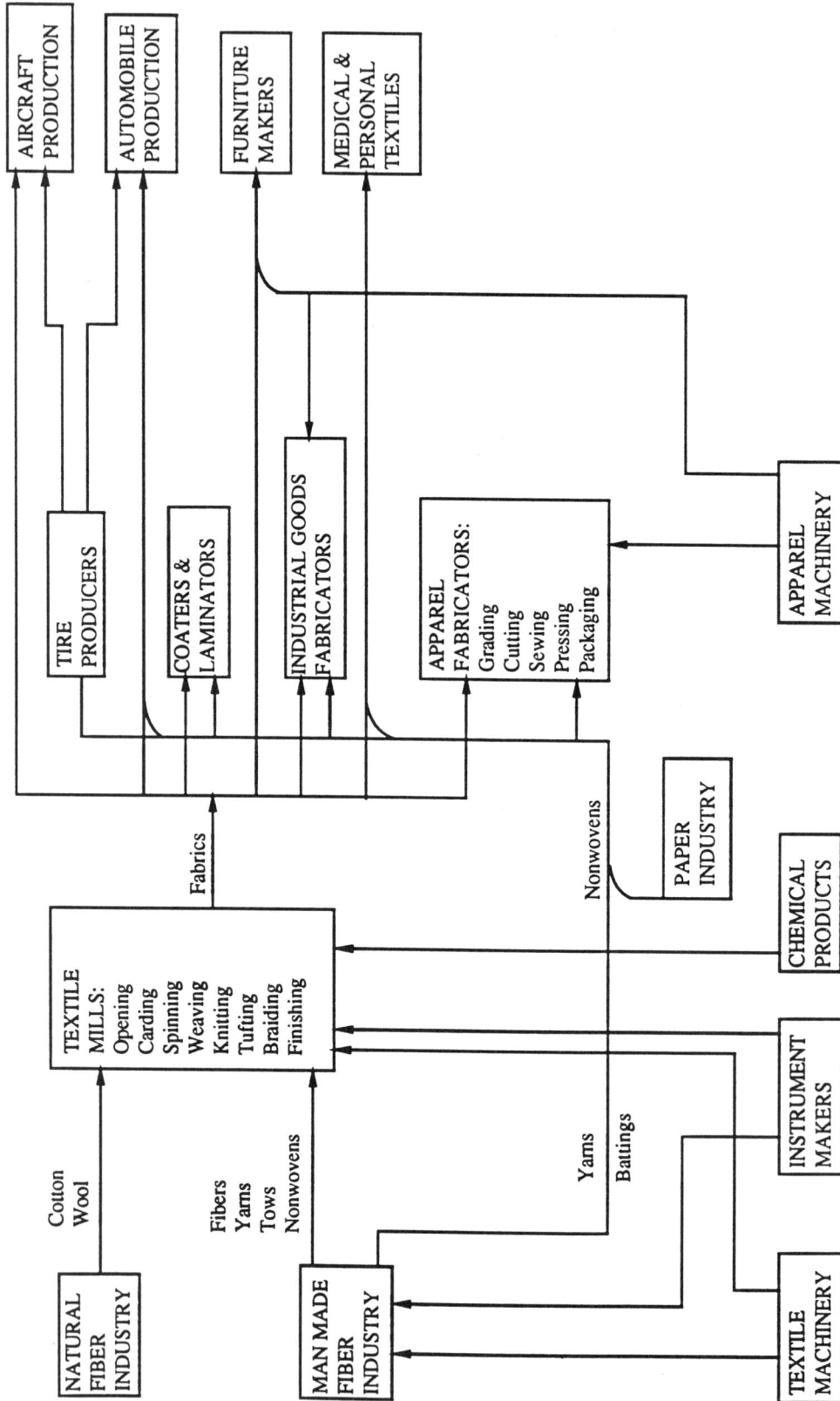

Figure 1. Fiber, textile, and apparel industry complex

ASSOCIATED INDUSTRIES

percent due to increased competition from Japan and various newly industrialized countries. [7]

Cotton fibers dominate the natural fiber consumption and production in the United States. Cotton fibers account for 90 percent of natural fiber consumption in the United States. Wool production and consumption in the United States is insignificant, amounting to only 1.5 percent of domestic fiber consumption and only 1.5 percent of total world production of wool fibers. [8]

Yet cotton fibers, which did account for 80 percent of total domestic fiber consumption in 1940, has now dropped to 25 percent [9] and US exports have declined from 76,300 tons in 1978 to 23,390 tons in 1984. [10]

The US cotton fiber industry has a fragmented structure, consisting of approximately 270 small firms which trade and compete with one another. [11] Concentration in this sector is low and stable, at about 20 percent, and nearly all cotton fiber production occurs in the Southern or Western states of the US.

The American fiber industry (both natural and synthetics) has competed by producing standard fibers in high volume at low cost. This strategy, however, seems to be seriously challenged by changes in production technologies, the nature of demand for the industry's products and the growth of competition from abroad. A tension appears to be growing between competition based on low cost and that based on flexibility. [12]

Textile Mill Products. Textile mill products are the second major group in the textile complex. This sector of the industry includes all operations that are involved in converting fiber to finished fabric and the production of many nonapparel consumer products. Although the 12 largest companies (including Burlington Industries, J.P. Stevens, and Milliken) produce approximately 26 percent of total sales dollars, most production in this sector is carried out in small and medium-sized firms. [13] There are about 450 weaving, 500 knitting, and 300-400 tufting mills. [14] The rivalry among these producers is high. All fight for market shares in a low growth market, where expanding market share for one firm means decreasing shares for others. This situation is further exacerbated by increased competition from textile mills abroad and subsequent decreases in world market shares of US producers.

For example, US imports of cotton fabric increased from 267 million pounds in 1974 to 463 million pounds in 1984. Similarly, imports of fabric made from manmade fibers increased from 82 million pounds in 1974 to 159 million pounds in 1984. [15] On the other side of the coin, US exports of cotton fabric decreased from 217 million pounds in 1975 to 65 million pounds in 1984, while US exports of manmade-fiber fabric declined from 184 million pounds in 1975 to 154 million pounds in 1984. [16] For textile mill products as a whole, the US trade balance in the decade between 1974 and 1984 went from a surplus of 43 million dollars to a deficit of 2.49 billion dollars. [17]

Textile mill products have three major end uses--apparel, home furnishings, and industrial and speciality products. Historically, apparel has dominated consumption; but this is no longer the case. While apparel's share of fiber consumption remained at approximately 37 percent between 1979 and 1985, the share of home furnishings grew from 31 to 38 percent and industrial textile products consume a stable 20 percent of fiber production. [18]

Apparel and Other End Uses. Apparel production is carried out primarily in small firms: 15,000 firms with 21,000 plants. Over 70 percent of these establishments employ fewer than 50 workers. [19]

Traditionally, the apparel industry made three kinds of products: fashion products--ten weeks, 35 percent of total; seasonal products--20 weeks, 45 percent; and basic products--all year, 20 percent. Men's and children's clothing fall into the basic products category with few style changes from year to year. Such products are better suited to large-scale production. Women's clothing is distributed in fashion and seasonal cycles.

The retailing of apparel products is undergoing major changes. Department stores, traditionally a major outlet for clothing, are in decline. Recently, however, new sales formats such as mail order shopping, specialty boutiques, and discount stores have become popular vehicles for apparel retail. [20] Relations between manufacturers and retailers are changing, with garment makers moving into retail sales: Benetton of Italy is a forerunner in this respect.

The US apparel industry is gravely threatened. Tariffs, the Multifiber Arrangement, and other complex attempts at protection have not stemmed the flood of imported textile and apparel products. Measured in square yards, 48 percent of the US apparel market was imported in 1985--more than double the share in 1975. [21] This rate of erosion of domestic market share shows no sign of diminishing. According to the Office of Technology Assessment, "if penetration of US apparel markets were to continue at the pace of the past decade (measured in terms of volume), domestic sales of US apparel firms would approach zero by the year 2000." [22] Such problems are compounded by America's comparatively insignificant apparel exports. For example, in

1980, when US apparel exports reached an all-time high, they amounted to merely three percent of domestic apparel production. [23]

Associated Industries. In this sector we include industries integrally related to the other three sectors, such as textile machinery and non-woven fabrics. While there is evidence which suggests that non-woven industries and industrial uses of other fabrics and fibers are growing, trends in the American textile machinery industry are consistent with developments in the other sectors of the textile complex. [24]

There are some 500 firms in the textile machinery industry, manufacturing machinery, parts, and accessories used in the production of textile mill products for apparel, home furnishing and industrial applications. Most US producers specialize in machinery for one stage of the textile production process, although a few market a range of textile machinery. Many produce only parts and accessories for textile machinery. [25]

US producers of textile machinery have fallen far behind the international state of the art. For example, the United States produces none of the advanced shuttleless looms that are revolutionizing weaving. As a result, their overall share of the domestic market has fallen from 93 percent in 1963 to 55 percent today. What remains of the industry is not particularly encouraging. Over 92 percent of the export sales of domestic textile machinery firms went to supply replacement parts. [26] US producers are also at a disadvantage in overseas markets. They are unable to match the international marketing networks that European and Japanese manufacturers have developed over the past two decades. This shortcoming, along with high production and product liability costs, combined to undermine this industry. US textile machinery shipments have declined steadily in real terms by an average of 4.7 percent annually since 1974--before and after the appreciation of the dollar in the early 1980s. [27] (See Figure 2).

The reasons for this decline are due to the developmental patterns of the industry in the US. Prior to World War II, textile machinery firms in New England dominated the mill industry. With a few exceptions mills were small, dependent for their technology on machinery producers, and unable to exert pressure for machinery improvements. Machinery producers operated in stand-alone configuration, limiting their interaction with supply firm infrastructures while maintaining a level of industrial secrecy which minimized technical communication with the external engineering professions. It was a recipe for intellectual stagnation. Machine companies failed to underwrite adequate research and development activities and to devote sufficient

Figure 2. Textile machinery industry annual shipments

Billion$

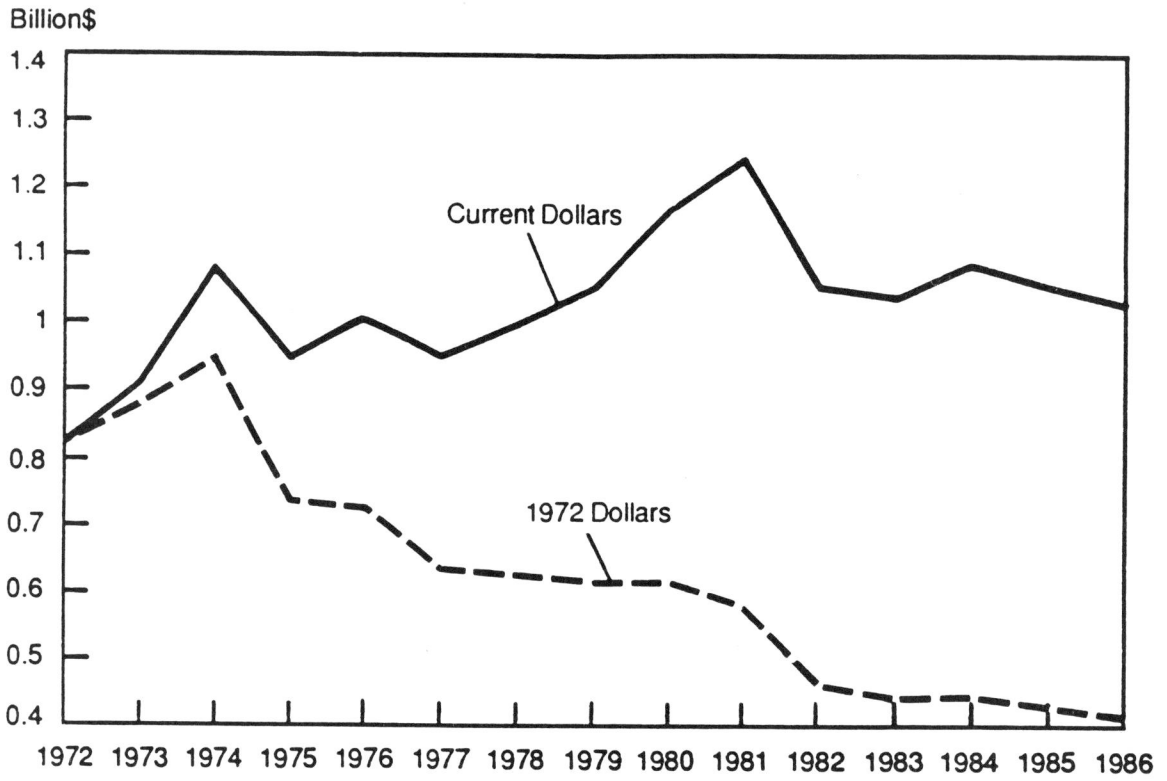

Source: US Department of Commerce: Bureau of the Census, Bureau of Economic Analysis, International Trade Administration

investment to plant facilities and staff development. Extensive patent litigation between mill and machinery companies often led to elimination of once-held competitive edge.

During and after WWII, mills in the South started to expand, consolidate, and merge, thus changing the mill-to-machinery industry relationship from a configuration of subservience to one of dominance. Such mill groups soon found European machine offerings provided higher quality, reliability, and ultimately, service.

In contrast to the European scene (particularly Germany), the US lacked the regional institutions, supported jointly by government and industry, to provide training for industry personnel from machine operator to research engineer. Just as critical was a lack of broadly trained engineers working on process development and evaluation.

Employment in the Textile Industry

Jobs and Unions. The textile industry is one of the largest employers in the manufacturing sector. In 1985 there were 1.1 million employees in apparel, 700,000 in textile mill products, and 64,000 in fibers. The textile industry is an important employer of women and minorities. While manufacturing overall had an employment profile that was 32 percent female in 1980, it was 51 percent for the textile industry. Whereas minorities held 11 percent of manufacturing jobs overall in 1980, they represented 20 percent of textile manufacturing employment. [28] The industry is also a major employer of immigrants.

Employment in the industry has been falling: from 1980 to 1985, 282,000 jobs were lost in apparel and textiles. Apparel employment dropped 11 percent; textile employment, 15 percent. [29] The problem of unemployment in the textile and apparel sectors stands out in contrast to the average for all manufacturing industries. In 1985 the manufacturing average unemployment rate was 7.7 percent; textile mill products, 9.9 percent; and apparel, 11.4 percent. The tendency toward unemployment predates the recent import invasion. In 1965 the unemployment in all manufacturing was 4.0 percent; in textile mill products, 4.3 percent; and in apparel 7.3 percent. [30]

The damage that job loss brings to individuals and families can be significant since many of the workers affected are minorities, women, and/or those with little education and few jobs. In many cases, there may be little or no severance pay to displaced workers. Because of the low level of wages, it is unlikely that a displaced individual has much in the way of savings. Furthermore, displacement may mean the erosion of traditional forms of organization or community. For instance, while union membership is concentrated primarily in the North-East and Mid-West in this sector, overall membership has declined dramatically. And even in the South, where entire towns and regions are dependent on this industry, plant closings and job displacement can be ruinous to local communities.

Wages in Textiles. Although labor costs have been cited as responsible for the surge of imports in textiles and apparel, wages in these sectors are quite depressed. A comparison with the average for all US manufacturing sectors confirms this point. Apparel wages dropped from 62 percent of all manufacturing in 1970 to 52 percent in 1985. [31] Table 1 displays the difference in average hourly earnings between textiles and all manufacturing over a 20-year period.

Table 1. Average Hourly Earnings in US Manufacturing, 1960-80 [32]

Year	Manufacturing	Durable goods		Non-durable goods	Textiles
1960	2.26	2.42	2.05	1.61	
1965	2.61	2.79	2.36	1.87	
1970	3.36	3.55	3.08	2.45	
1975	4.81	5.15	4.37	3.42	
1976	5.22	5.58	4.70	3.67	
1977	5.68	6.06	5.11	3.98	
1978	6.17	6.58	5.53	4.30	
1979	6.69	7.13	6.00	4.66	
1980	7.27	7.76	6.53	5.07	
percent change					
1960-80	222	246	219	215	

A cross-national comparison of textile wage rates demonstrates a wage gap between the United States and its third world competitors. US labor costs are, however, comparable with or even below those of many European countries. In 1985-6 with the high dollar exacerbating the wage differential the United States still ranked ninth in textile labor costs. In 1980 it was only eleventh, after highly successful competitors such as West Germany and Italy. [33]

Productivity Performance of US Textiles

The US textile industry has overall had good productivity growth relative to other US manufacturing industries, measured in terms of output per person hour. Aggregate productivity performance over time and relative to other sectors has continued to increase during the slow-down of the 1970s and early 1980s. Between 1975 and 1985 productivity levels in the textile mills increased 5.6 percent per year. Total manufacturing levels only increased 2.4 percent per year during that period. Even in apparel, productivity growth for the decade was 2.7 percent per year. [34] (See Figures 3 and 4.)

Martin Bailey's micro level study of four industries substantiates this view. Unlike the other sectors examined, the textile industry experienced no productivity slowdown after 1973. The chemical sector's multifactor productivity increased 3.09 percent per year from 1965-1973; 1.73 percent from 1973-79; and 0.98 percent

Table 2. Werner Textile Labor Cost Comparison (Winter 1985/6, US Dollars)

Ratio	Country	Wages'86	Rank'86	Wages'80	Rank'80
128	Norway	11.06	1	9.62	6
126	Switzerland	10.84	2	9.65	5
118	Belgium	10.08	3	11.82	1
116	Denmark	10.07	4	9.12	8
113	Holland	9.76	5	11.68	2
111	Sweden	9.61	6	10.43	3
103	West Germany	8.88	7	10.16	4
101	Austria	8.71	8	6.42	10
100	USA	8.66	9	6.37	11
98	Canada	8.50	10	6.25	12
95	Italy	8.22	11	9.12	7
95	Japan	8.20	12	4.35	17
86	France	7.44	14	7.91	9
69	UK	5.90	16	5.75	13
41	Spain	3.54	18	4.90	16
21	Hong Kong	1.81	26	1.91	21
18	Taiwan	1.60	29	1.26	25
18	S. Korea	1.57	30	0.78	32
7	India	0.61	42	0.60	33
2	China	0.20	52	NA	NA

Figure 3. Total factor productivity of textile mill products, SIC #22

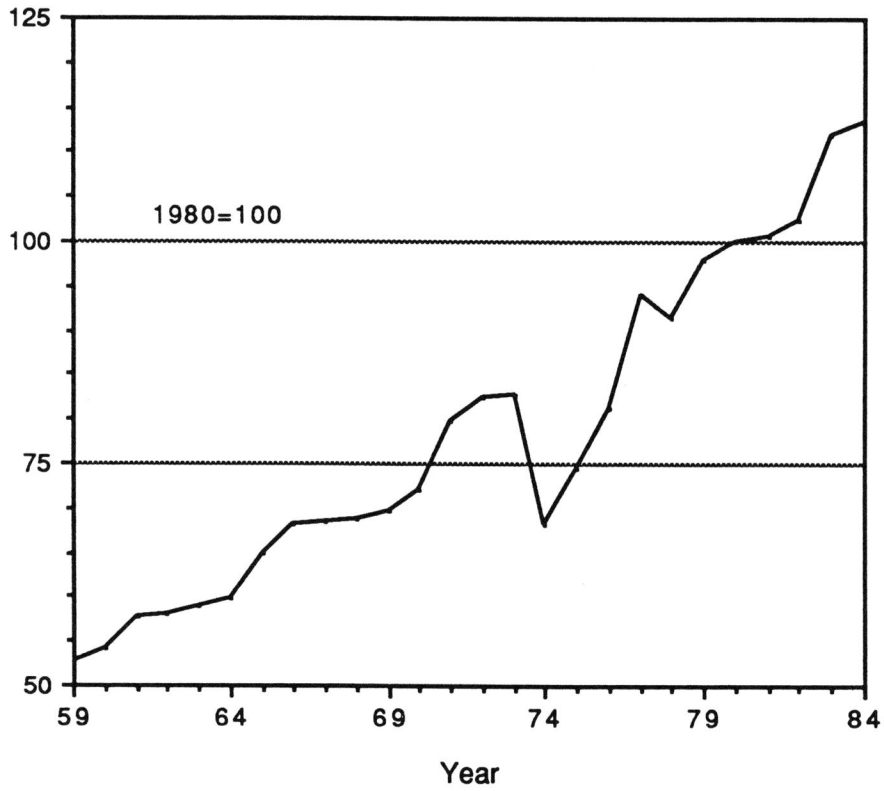

Figure 4. Total factor productivity of apparel products, SIC #23

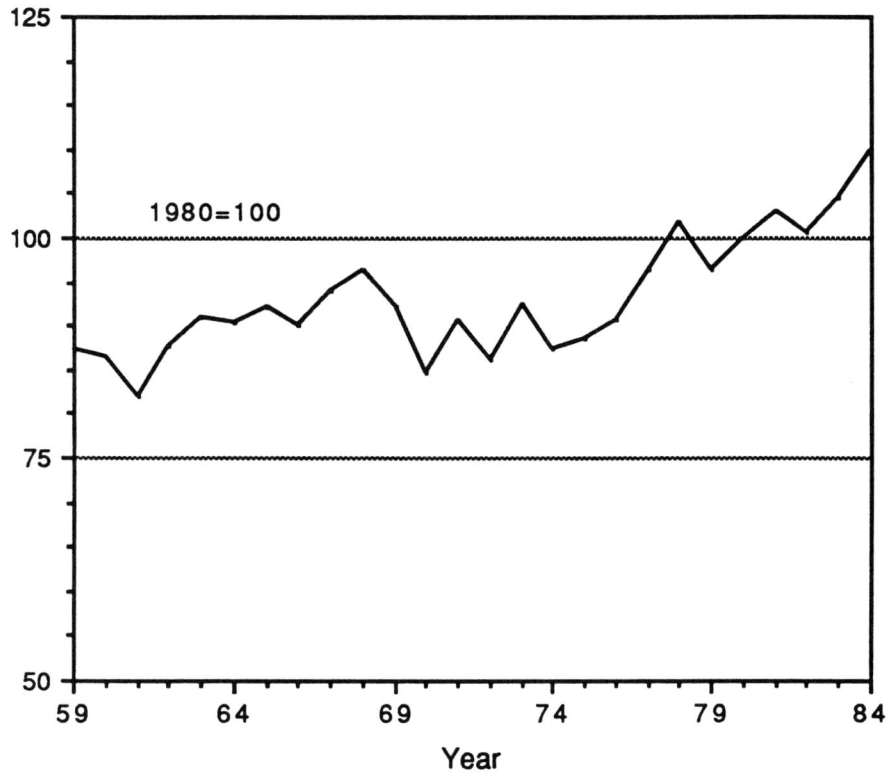

from 1979-83. By comparison multifactor productivity growth in textiles improved during this period: It increased by 2.61 percent per year from 1965 to 1973; 3.37 percent from 1973 to 1979; and 3.18 percent from 1979 to 1983. His data also suggested that textile equipment was being utilized at close to full capacity. The adjusted figures are: 2.73 percent annual increase from 1965-73; 3.56 percent from 1973-79; 3.58 percent from 1979-83. [35] A recent article in the *New York Times* claimed that this trend has continued and that US mills are now operating at full capacity. As a result of these productivity increases, as well as other factors like trade agreements in 1986 and the fall of the dollar, the last two years appear to signal a turnaround for certain segments of the US textile industry. [36]

Industry sources explain that, faced with high labor costs, the industry in both the United States and Western Europe has competed by enhancing productivity. While we were unable to find a reliable and recent international comparison of productivity for the textile industry as a whole, American industry representatives claim that US firms are the most efficient in terms of productivity. Part of this success seems to be related to quite high levels of capital investment. The US textile industry spends about $1.5 billion a year in new plant and equipment. [37]

Market Share Changes

Despite high rates of productivity, large parts of the US textile and apparel industry are gravely threatened by international competition. This has helped the US balance of payment deficits. The trade surplus in man-made fiber increased from $3.8 million in 1968 to $823.6 million in 1981. Fiber firms' major concern has been that the decline of the domestic apparel industry will threaten the market for fiber consumption. This to some extent has been lessened with the shift in the end use of fibers during this period. Man-made fibers were increasingly used in home furnishings and industrial products rather than in apparel. Thus, in 1974 38 percent was used for apparel, 30 percent for home furnishings, and 29 percent for industrial products. By 1984 27 percent went toward apparel, 35 percent toward home furnishings, and 36 percent into industrial products. North America's share of world textile production dropped from 21.7 percent in 1963 to 20.2 percent in 1980. [38] Apparel imports have risen more dramatically: only two percent of domestic consumption in 1963, today imports have captured over 50 percent of the domestic market (see figure 5). [39] About one-third of the imports coming into the US market are brought in by domestic apparel firms

Figure 5. US apparel imports, exports, and trade balance

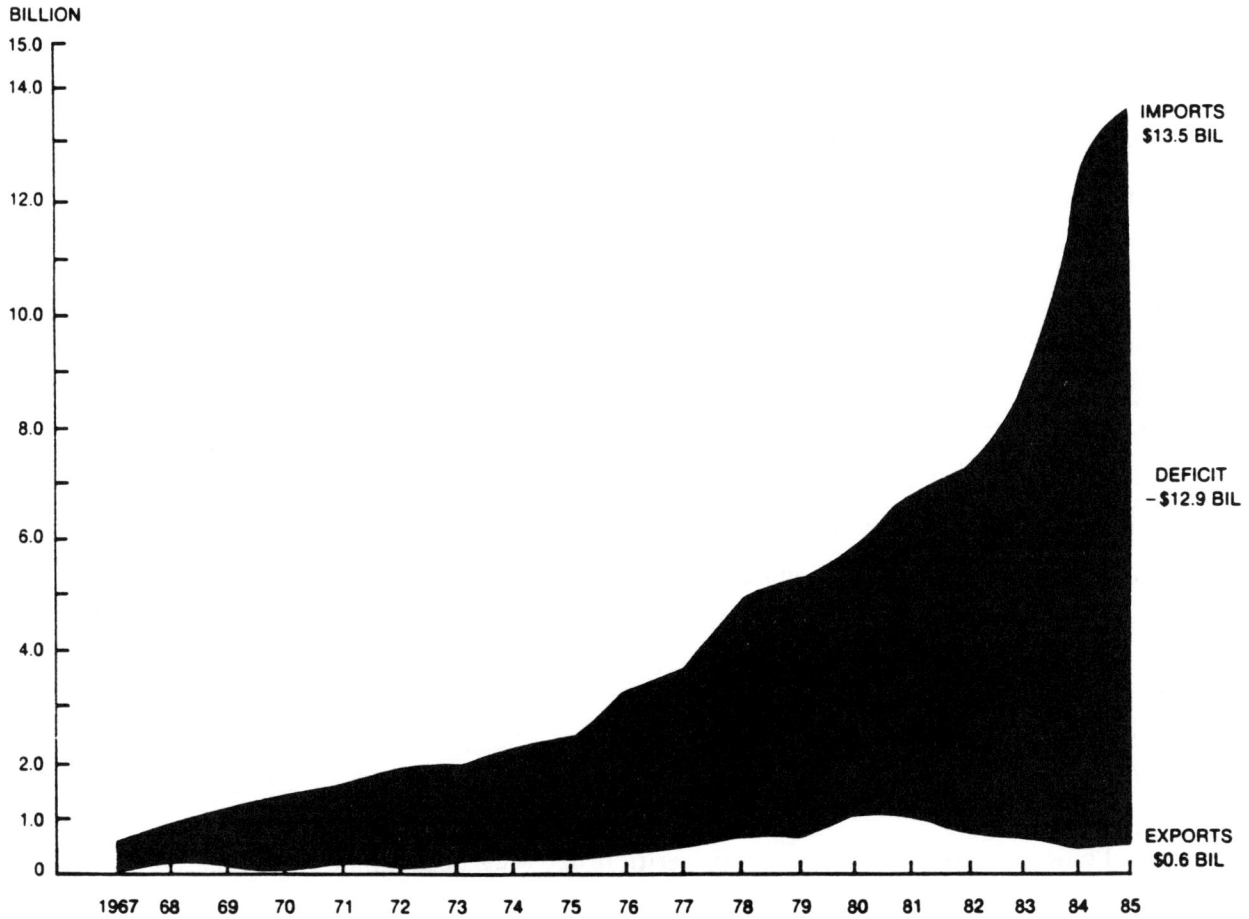

Source: Office of Textiles and Apparel, US Department of Commerce

through offshore sourcing. One-third are imported directly by American retailers and one-third are brought in by importers. [40]

How can we account for this paradox: high rates of industrial productivity but decreasing international competitiveness? What is required is a closer look at the industry. For instance, US producers have remained competitive at the extremes of the domestic market for textiles and apparel. Import penetration is relatively low for basic items like home furnishings, which have an extremely low labor content, and for items like basic men's wear, where styles change slowly and domestic production is highly automated. US producers are also doing well in such industrial products as automobile upholstery, where the cost of textiles is a small fraction of total selling costs and where the risks of dealing with low-cost producers abroad are often not worth the small direct savings.

In contrast, foreign penetration is highest in seasonal products, particularly private label products. Market uncertainty and virtually no tradition of concern with production technology mean that domestic labor productivity in the seasonal product sectors is relatively low.

Industry analysts anticipate that as the dollar becomes weaker again, textile products will become comparatively less expensive, enhancing their competitiveness in world markets. Several of the countries which have succeeded best in US markets have currencies tied to the dollar; so its decline will not much affect their chances in the US.

Protection in Textiles

Because textiles and apparel were one of the first manufacturing industries developed by industrializing nations, international competition has long been intense. Protectionism of some sort has been an established part of every developed nation's textile trade policies.

In the United States, the textile and apparel complex is regulated by 37 bilateral textile agreements. Over 1300 quotas are enforced on individual textile products. Textiles and apparel are subject to the highest *ad-valorem* tariff rates of all US industries. Compared to an average US duty rate on imported commodities of roughly 3.7 percent during the years 1982 through 1985, imported textiles and apparel articles face an 18 percent tariff rate. In addition, many textile and apparel items are ineligible for duty-free treatment under the US Generalized System of Preferences.

European and Asian nations are parties to the same international trade agreements-- the GATT and the Multifiber Arrangement--as the United States. A 1983 OECD report concluded that while there are differences in tariff structures and apparent levels of protectionism among the OECD nations, the effects of national tariff systems cannot be definitively established. For fabrics, post-Tokyo Round weighted tariffs differ little: tariffs average 11.5 percent in the US, 9.4 percent in Japan and 10.6 percent in the EEC. In addition, widespread exceptions to the Generalized System of Preferences for textile and apparel products are not limited to the US: They are common in the other 18 OECD countries that adopted the GSP system in the 1970s. [41]

The non-tariff regulation of trade in textiles and apparel has grown more and more pervasive and complex since the 1950s and is now the key tactic of developed countries to restrict imports from low cost producers. (According to the OECD, however, tariff barriers and exceptions to tariffs remain key factors in shaping trade in textiles and apparel between countries with similar cost structures.) The history of the evolution of the current quota system reads like a case study in trying to plug a crumbling dike.

In the mid-1950s, President Eisenhower initiated negotiations with Japan that culminated in a five-year agreement to restrain voluntarily the flow of cotton textile exports from Japan. A similar agreement was negotiated with Italy. It did not take long before the slack from the Japanese limitations was picked up by Hong Kong, which became the second largest exporter of cotton textiles by 1960. Hong Kong resisted US pressure to enter into a voluntary restraint agreement. By 1961, with Korea and Taiwan now emerging as major exporters to the US, and with European nations feeling similar pressure, momentum grew for an international agreement on textile and apparel trade. That agreement, the Short Term Arrangement, was a one-year agreement among 18 importing and exporting countries. It established formal mechanisms for voluntary restraint agreements and established a GATT Cotton Textiles Committee to oversee negotiation of a Long Term Arrangement, which was signed in 1962. This marked a clear departure from the GATT in its provision for detailed product-by-product quota agreements. The LTA covered textiles containing more than 50 percent cotton by weight or value. It permitted bilateral quotas on terms consistent with the LTA goal of five percent per annum import growth. Imposition of unilateral quotas by importing countries was allowed but only at levels not less than actual imports during the previous period.

The STA and the LTA only covered cotton textiles which, in the early 1960s, were the only real threat. However, by the mid-1960s, manmade fibers were capturing a growing share of the textile and apparel market: US imports or man-made fiber goods increased tenfold from 31 million pounds to 329 million pounds. Like wool, synthetic products were not covered by the LTA. Japan, Hong Kong, Taiwan, and Korea shifted much of their production out of cotton--and the scenario of growing import penetration played itself out again in the US and, even more dramatically, in Europe.

In 1971, the Nixon Administration strong-armed the Japanese to extend voluntary restraints to wool and synthetic products by tying the textile issue to negotiations over the return of Okinawa to the Japanese. The Japanese conceded and the US negotiators then won similar agreements from the other three key Asian exporters. European countries followed suit. Since these agreements violated the LTA, a new international system of regulation was needed. After several years of international negotiations, the Multifiber Arrangement was agreed to and entered into effect in 1974.

The MFA permits industrialized nations to negotiate bilateral agreements with developing countries in order to manage the rate of growth of imports from each country. Specifically, the goal of the MFA is to give an importing country the right to limit imports from another country when its domestic market is disrupted by that country's imported products.

The MFA has been renewed three times: in 1978, 1982, and 1986. Covering imports of manmade fibers and wool (and, in MFA IV, products of silk, linen, ramie and a variety of blends), the MFA has created the machinery for bilateral agreements designed to minimize market disruption in importing nations while enabling export growth among developing countries. The MFA targeted annual growth of imports to around six percent a year and provided three types of "flexibility" provisions that made it possible for that quota to exceed six percent in the short run. In 1979, the Carter Administration, feeling pressure from the textile industry which linked its support for multilateral trade negotiations to further relief from imports, tightened restrictions on bilateral agreements. MFA IV has been seen generally as favoring the importing nations. In addition to extension of coverage to linen, silk, and ramie, the 1986 Protocol of Extension makes it easier for developed nations to negotiate lower than six percent growth rates for quotas, and makes it easier to apply especially restrictive quotas on the dominant textile suppliers.

The implementation of the MFA is structured and administered differently in the US and the EEC. US textile policy--and trade policy generally--is heavily influenced by the State Department and the Office of the US Trade Representative, who make sure that textile and apparel policy dovetails with US foreign policy priorities. Sometimes this interferes with development of an economically coherent textile policy. In Europe, the Council of Ministers make the major decisions about when to place "calls" and to pursue quota cases. This complicated layer of bureaucracy, requiring approval from each EEC country, makes the EEC slower to act and more reticent to issue a call. At the same time, though, it makes the EEC more determined to make agreements that will not need to be renegotiated quickly. US decisions about the administration and enforcement of MFA agreements are made by the Committee for Implementation of Textile Agreements, an interagency body with representatives from the Department of Labor, the Department of Commerce, the Office of the Trade Representative, the State Department and the Treasure Department. In effect, the Trade Representative is the swing vote. (State used to have the power to veto any decision on foreign policy grounds. This is no longer the case, but State still has significant influence--e.g. Philippines quotas after Marcos was deposed; dealing with China.)

The US has a very complex system of setting product categories. In Europe, product categories are fewer and broader. US categories are very specific. Thus, the EEC is primarily concerned with eight Group I product categories that accounted for 56 percent of the EEC's import volume of MFA-covered products. These categories are cotton yarn, cotton fabrics, synthetic fabrics, T-shirts and knit shirts, jerseys and pullovers, trousers, blouses, and men's woven shirts. By contrast, the same products are covered by 75 different categories in the US.

It is often argued that the trajectory of the US and European industries in the past ten to 15 years can be explained in terms of levels of protection, changes in exchange rates, and differential wage rates. The above description shows that the tariff and nontariff regulatory structures in the US and Europe are not very different, although administration of the rules has differed. We consider below the claim that greater effective protection explains European and Japanese success.

Finally, one provision of US tariff legislation that permits outsourcing should be considered in some detail, for it has major implications for US producers. Under paragraph 807 of the US tariff schedules, an apparel company is allowed to cut fabric into garment parts, ship these parts to a foreign country for assembly, and reimport the assembled garments at a reduced tariff duty. Duty must be paid only on the value added to the cut pieces, not on the value of the entire garment. This allows for offshore stitching at labor rates that average about 20 percent of the US apparel wages. The net difference on the wholesale price can easily be ten percent, compared to wholly domestic production.

807 production has increased in recent years, climbing from $300 million in 1983 (7.8 percent of total US imports) to $435 million in 1985 (8.5 percent of total imports).

Almost all of this production is in Mexico and the countries of the Caribbean Basin Initiative. The leading 807 exporters are: Dominican Republic (23 percent in 1985); Mexico (22 percent); Haiti (17 percent); Costa Rica (eight percent).

The advantages of 807 production are clear: lower labor costs on garments requiring needle-intensive stitching and ornamentation; a return time that allows for quicker turnaround that Far East production allows. The disadvantages are first come, first serve (each country has a quota); risks of late delivery; the scarcity of skilled labor; customs problems; political insecurity; telecommunications problems; and above all, problems of quality control.

When domestic producers turn to 807, they are more likely to use US fabrics than when they subcontract to the Far East, and they are more likely to be able to sell service and speed to retailers. 807 facilities also enable the domestic manufacturer to run its US facilities at full capacity and use the 807 sourcing to meet market fluctuations. The cost differential vis a vis domestic production can be seen in the following comparison of production of men's shorts (8.9 lbs. per dozen; 1.8 standard labor hours per dozen).

Table 3. Cost comparison of domestic versus 807 production of men's shorts ($/dozen)

	Domestic	*807*
fabric, trim cutting	22.95	22.95
assembly, labor, overhead	19.97	6.90
freight, duty	-----	6.90
807 savings		6.15
percent savings		14.3%

807 production cannot, however, compete in many lines, particularly those with uncomplicated and little stitching and those for which domestic fabric is not available or competitive. A cost comparison similar to the one above but calculated for men's outerwear jackets shows 807 production to be 89 percent of domestic production, but Far Eastern production to cost only 78 percent of on-shore production. In general, more men's wear than women's wear is produced under 807.

Significant Technological Innovation

This section focuses on process productivity in the Fiber/ Textile/ Clothing (FTC) complex. As noted above, productivity growth in US textile manufacturing has been double the average productivity growth of manufacturing as a whole for over a decade; and the US textile industry has been investing in new technology at an unprecedented rate. US firms are not alone: the past two decades have been a period of dramatic technological innovation in textiles. All over the world, firms have been forced to invest in increasingly productive new equipment in order to keep pace with competitors. As a recent government report states, "Little of the technology that allowed for increased productivity was developed by US based enterprises. The same advanced technology is available to firms throughout the world, including those in nations that pay workers a small fraction of the US minimum wage. [Consequently]...Technology alone may not be able to salvage major parts of the industry."[42] While technology alone may not secure the FTC, in the absence of technological advance, the industry's case becomes hopeless. Prospects for maintaining a structurally balanced and healthy US textile industry complex depend to a major degree on the development of process technologies with productivity levels *exceeding* those of actual or potential competitors.

In this section, the focus is on mechanical processes used to manufacture yarns, fabrics, and garments. These mechanical processes are by no means limited to the traditional textile mill. As Figure 1 indicates, several other industries employ similar or identical processes. As a result, improvements in any one of these processes will simultaneously help raise productivity in several segments of the FTC. For example, the fiber producer, the integrated textile mill, the throwster, the cordage mill and the tire-producing plant all twist yarns to alter their geometry and properties. The fiber industry's radically new production methods for making nonwoven sheet structures find functional equivalents in the "dry process" of textile mills or the "wet process" of the paper industry.

The technological basis for increased productivity in the FTC can consist of: better equipment construction; improved machine design; improved feed material; radical process innovation with the same product; and new process/product combinations. Of these five factors, the first two (better construction and improved machine design) generally permit or lead to *incremental* increases in process speeds. The last three have more often led to *step* increases in production output in individual machine or process units. The remainder of this section will summarize recent significant technological innovations of both types in the different sectors of the textile industry. (See Appendix 2 for a list of definitions of textile operations.)

Improvements in Fiber Production. The textile and associated industries use both natural and manmade fibers. "Manmade" fibers include rayon (chemically modified or regenerated natural cellulose available since the turn of the century) and truly synthetic fibers.

Nylon, the first complete synthetic fiber, was developed at the Du Pont Company in the mid-1930's, in time to substitute during World War II for silk previously imported from the Far East. Acrylic fibers developed at Du Pont and modacrylics developed at Union Carbide became available in 1950. Polyester, developed in England, was licensed and produced commercially in the US in 1953. Soon afterwards, olefin fibers were developed in Italy. Synthetic elastomers (Spandex) were developed at Du Pont in 1958. In subsequent years, numerous chemical variants and modifications of these synthetic fibers have been developed.

Most of these new polymeric fibers made possible faster processing speeds. In addition, blends of these stronger nylon and polyester fibers with natural fibers allowed for greater production efficiency in the spinning and subsequent weaving or knitting of finer yarns and lighter weight fabrics.

The early synthetic fibers, however, suffered various shortcomings. For instance, spin-extruded nylon, polyester, and polypropylene came in the form of straight round cylinders suitable only for weaving or knitting thin, flat-lustrous fabrics with restricted markets (i.e. linings, dress fabrics). To overcome this drawback, fiber producers were forced to alter permanently the geometry of the fiber to simulate the natural twisting convolutions of cotton or the reversible helical geometry of wool. This required filament or yarn texturing, which was a burdensome extra process for the textile industry.

The earliest texturing method for manmade fiber producers was gear crimping, which adapted synthetic fibers to permit their use on traditional carding and spinning equipment. Research in Japan and in the US during and shortly after WWII revealed that fiber self-crimping could be acheived, without extra processing steps, by spin extruding two different polymers into a single filament. Because of property differences across the fiber section, the filament would bend and curl into helical form when subjected to heat and/or moisture. In the late 1960s fully synthetic bicomponent fibers were developed by Du Pont in the US and ICI in England.

Another important fiber innovation designed to improve both product and process was the development of fibers with differential dyeing characteristics. Whereas fabrics made with fibers or yarns of different colors (e.g. heather fabrics) had in the past required separate dyeing processes, it became possible to blend batches of the same polymeric fiber with different dye affinities and impart multiple color to the final fabric in a single bath.

The fiber industry soon moved from production of straight circular (fiber) rods to varying cross-section shapes, mostly to improve product appearance and performance, but also to improve process efficiency in the textile mill. Improved feed yarn materials (i.e. fibers for uses in the textile and associated industries) were developed.

The fiber industry also developed machines and processes for synthetic fibers. A breakthrough in the use of conventional textile equipment by the fiber producers took place in the early 1960s when Bunting and Nelson developed the interlace process which impacted a high pressure air jet against a fast moving continuous filament yarn to cause filament entanglement. Such entanglement eliminated the need for major plant areas devoted to conventional textile twisting and made possible yarn processing at as much as six times the speed of the large expensive textile twisting machines. Since the original development, over 100 patents relying on the jet entanglement process have been filed worldwide. Many are used in textile mills today, in particular in piecing or splicing, or in the joining of false twist yarns.

Other fiber developments used air streams to create yarn texture. One such system was the Taslan (US) process which took "flat" continuous filament yarns and converted them into rough, bulky, and somewhat staple-like yarns suitable for apparel or industrial use. The effect on productivity was obvious in that a staple-like yarn was produced without the usual five or six textile mill operations of opening, carding, etc. A second important jet technology was the jet treatment of continuous filament carpet yarns to impose random crimping of fibers, adding bulk and softness to carpet pile. This process (now widely emulated around the world), along with US-developed tufting process, account to a great extent for domestic producer dominance in the US floor covering market. Still another important application of jet technology by the fiber industry was in the use of hydraulic impacting of nonwoven webs to create fabric-like patterns as in the case of "Spun-lace" materials used for such products as curtains and medical gowns.

The fiber industry has played a significant role in the growth of nonwoven applications. In the early 1970s Du Pont developed a series of nonwoven structures which are now widely used in geotechnical applications, in the construction industry, as carpet backings, and even as non-tearing Federal Express envelopes. These products with significantly improved mechanical properties were based on radically different production procedures, wherein spin-extruded continuous filament fibers were spread onto moving belts and moved forward to heated rollers for consolidation and "welding".

Numerous variations of the process have followed in the textile, medical supplies, and paper industries.

Innovations in Textile Mill Processes. *Opening and Picking.* Fiber is delivered to the mills in baled form with every effort having been made to select bales of equivalent fiber (of the same grade, degree of cleanliness, staple length, regional origin). Before 1970, it was customary to open the bales manually and to load portions of several bales at a time into a large hopper where it was churned and then carried on belts for blending. Since the introduction of automatic bale openers in the early 1970s, this process is carried out virtually without manpower. Figure 6 indicates the spread of automatic bale opening machines in the US industry.

Fibers used to be either belt-conveyed or blown through large pipes from the blending process to the opening/picking operation, which essentially consisted of beater bars which separated the fibers from dirt and carried them by air stream to screen cylinders. In earlier years these fibers were then built up into a rolled batting which was later transferred to the carding machine. Starting in the 1970s the process was modified to allow blowing of the opened and "picked" fibers directly to a large feed chute at the carding machine. Figure 6 reflects the spread of this innovation through the US textile industry.

The harsh beating action of earlier opening and picking systems is being replaced in some firms by wire wound rolls providing more gentle opening action. In the opening system of the US machinery maker Hollingsworth, an optical sampling system allows calculation of trash content and thus control of output quality.

Chute feeding of carding machines has been accompanied by automatic weighing of the input to the card. In addition, many modern cards of the 1980s are provided with linear density measuring devices for feedback control or for production monitoring. Under OSHA pressure the textile and the textile machinery industries have been forced to enclose all cotton opening and carding processes to minimize escape of cotton dust, the basic cause of byssinosis (brown lung).

Preparation for Spinning. Carding, a process in which cotton tufts are sheared between fast moving metallic wire-covered cylindrical surfaces, is designed to open further and to clean the fibers and to provide initial fiber straightening and parallelization. For many years carding outputs were increased linearly by component design improvements

Figure 6. Diffusion of improvements in textile processing

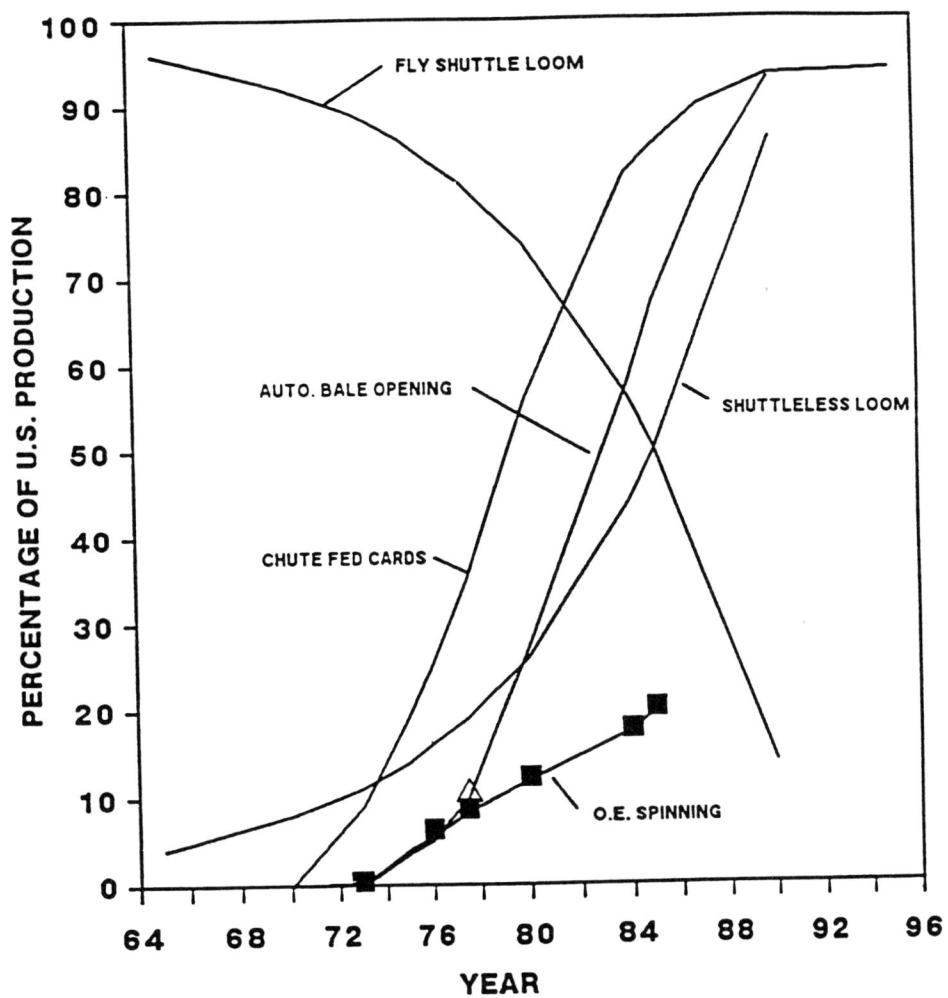

Source: Franklin S. Looney (1984)

(metallic teeth, roll crushing of residual trash, improved feeding elements, improved coiling devices, and large output cans for sliver). The most advanced carding machines in the US provide continuous sliver flow to downstream processes through automatic movement of sliver cans. Prior to 1960 a continuous automated spinning system was designed and built in Japan, capable of moving card sliver output directly and continuously to the subsequent draw process. This more efficient production method was never accepted in the US industry due to lack of flexibility for mill operations.

Card speeds are now at about 80-90 lbs/hour. This calculation excludes nonwovens, since nonwoven producers are often concerned primarily with speed and output and do not have to worry about fiber straightening and parallelization required for drawing and spinning of conventional fibers. Thus entirely new carding sytems or web production units have been developed in the US by nonconventional machine manufacturers and by the major producers of nonwoven materials, including fiber producers and the group termed Medical and Personal Textiles in Figure 1.

While most advanced carding systems exhibited at the 1987 Paris International Textile Machinery Association (ITMA) Exhibit were the product of European machine makers, Hollingsworth displayed a radically new carding system which treated both sides of the web with multiple carding cylinders in contrast to the conventional cards' one-sided treatment. This system is purported to provide 300 percent more carding action as well as better cleaning and parallelization. Carding production was reported by the manufacturer to reach 200 lbs/hour with web quality equivalent to that obtained by conventional machines. Programmable logic controls were included to control production rates and move output cans.

The drawing process feeds off multiple slivers from the carding process. It extends and attenuates the loose assembly of fibers which constitute the the sliver output, slipping fibers past one another in the same way that one spreads a deck of cards on a flat surface. Drawing also orients and straightens fibers and uncurls fiber hooks as the sliver is run through a succession of ever faster rotating rolls. The principle was patented in England in 1730, but increases in process output have been steady and significant as engineering design and construction have improved. Application of feedback control systems, use of intermeshing fluted rolls instead of round cylinders, and development of improved high speed coiling systems with large sliver output cans have been the basis for production rate increases from 250 meters/minute in the late 1970s to about 800 meters/minute at present. At the 1987 ITMA show, some manufacturers claimed output rates as high as 1300 to 1600 meters/minute.

The combing operation, which serves to further align fibers in the sliver and to remove shorter fibers to improve product quality, has been improved incrementally. Its speed has been gradually increased to three times that of 25 years ago. However, no US machinery firm produces this equipment.

Roving--further drafting of the sliver and addition of a slight twist in preparation for the spinning frame--has also been improved incrementally. Automatic doffing, automatic tension compensation, and computer monitoring and control, have made operation of today's roving machines virtually labor-free. In some cases, roving output is transferred automatically to the spinning frame.

Spinning. Spinning takes the roving output and converts it into usable yarn for subsequent weaving, knitting, or other processes. Here, innovation has been radical. The industry workhorse during the first 75 years of this century was the ring-spinning frame, which combined a set of drafting rolls with a vertical bobbin-bearing spindle. A flanged ring was positioned around the spindle and provided with an automatic tension and winding control device. Impressive incremental gains in process output were made over the years through improved fiber control in the draft rolls, improved bearings for the spindle, controlled pressure of the draft rolls and improved, stronger synthetic fibers. Spinning was the first textile process to receive serious study by applied physicists and mechanical engineers.

Radically new approaches developed in the last five years were required to break through the output ceiling of the late 1960s. The first was the development in Japan and Italy of automatic yarn air splicers and the use of smaller bobbins and rings at much higher speeds, with automatic bobbin doffing. A second innovation (by SKF in Sweden) has been the development of individual controllable motor drives for each spindle with improved bearings. This seemingly simple modification permits a decrease in energy consumption (of 50 percent) and a stepwise increase in spinning efficiency (in ends down per spindle hours) at the higher speeds possible with the smaller bobbins.

Ring frames are now being linked to winding machines. This is viewed as the major innovation of 1987. All major producers now offer robot-effected linkages between spinning and winding and between winding and twisting processes. The most radical innovation in yarn spinning has been open end spinning, or rotor spinning, developed in the 1960s. Figure 6 indicates the diffusion of this process. The entry material is broken into separate fibers which are air impelled into the circumferential groove of a high speed rotor. A lead yarn is allowed to touch the rotor base and, by friction, it is then rotated in crank-like fashion causing it to twist and entangle with the fibers along the groove. As the yarn is withdrawn, new fibers entangle in its end, providing continuity of yarn formation.

Yarn produced in this radically new system has different geometrical and mechanical properties than ring-spun yarn. The range of fineness in rotor spun yarns is limited to the somewhat coarser end of the spectrum. In the US, however, cooperative efforts between fiber producers and mill operators (e.g. Russell) have promoted improved fiber quality and finish at the higher speeds of open end spinning.

Nonetheless, when the first rotor machines were introduced at about 25,000 RPM, they were 25 percent to 50 percent faster than available ring-spinning systems. At present, rotor spinning has reached speeds of close to 100,000 RPM while ring-spinning limits are still below 25,000 RPM. Relative performances are shown in Figure 7. Most modern rotor machines are of German, Italian, or Czechoslovakian origin.

Another spinning innovation is air-jet spinning. If the drafted bundle of fibers is twisted by a rotating air jet stream instead of by the ring-traveller-spindle combination, the result is a fasciated yarn with fairly straight inner fibers and with periodic wrapping of outer fibers. Du Pont produced considerable quantities of fasciated acrylic yarns for the US and European market using this process. However, when Du Pont concluded that the venture was not a commercial success, the company abandoned the process and machine prospects.

Some years later, Murata in Japan developed a similar double jet-spinning system for *short* staple fibers (i.e. cotton rather than acrylics) and currently offers it for use in the textile industry. The system, which operates at 150 to 200 meters/minute, is capable of producing extremely fine yarns. Comparison of the air jet-spinning production rate with that of the other systems is shown in Figure 7.

Other radical innovations in spinning systems include the friction system, the spin wrap system, the self-twist (Repco) system, and the laminate (Bobtex) yarn system. A review of the patent record in the field of spinning machinery reveals a low flat rate of patent issuance for ring spinning over the last 20 years, a rising rate for open end systems between the late 1960s and late 1970s and a noticeable increase for "other" systems in the early 1980s. (See figure 8.)

The above spinning processes refer to staple fiber (i.e. cotton spinning which requires drafting, twisting, and winding). Synthetic fibers, produced by spin-extrusion and drawing of filament, always requires some form of texturing. The most common

Figure 7. Increases in process output

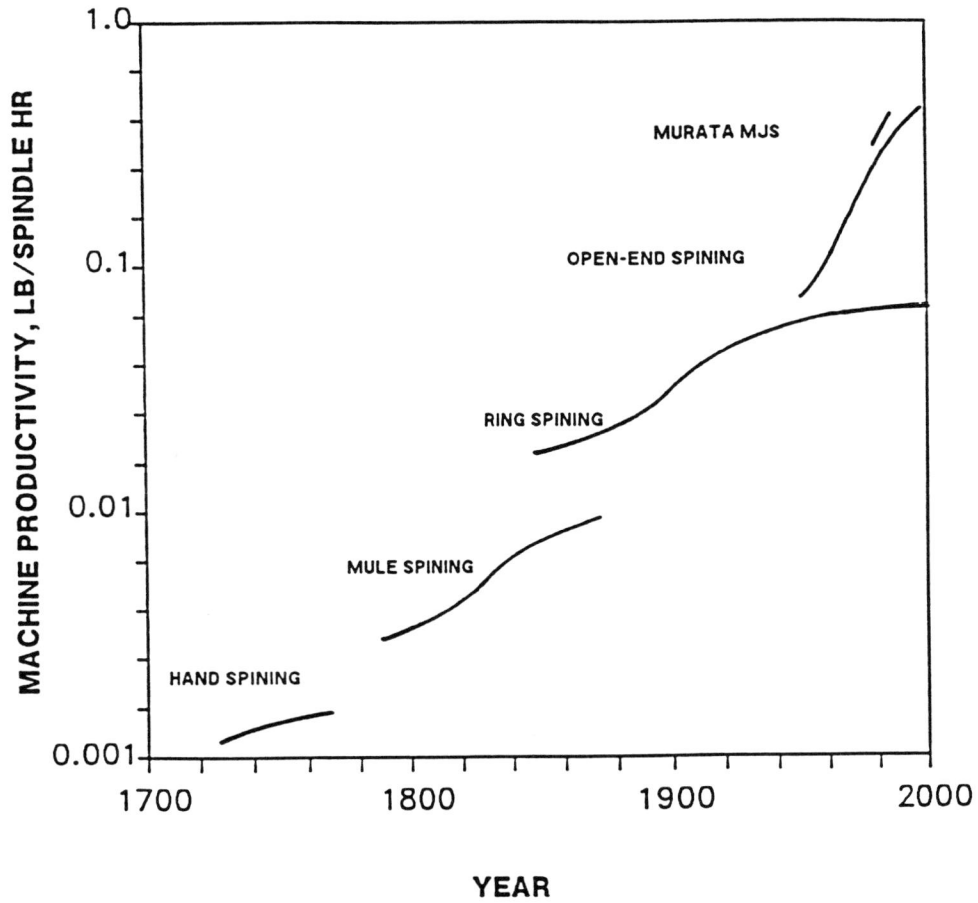

Source: Peter Lord, "Air Jet and Friction Spinning," *Textile Horizons*, Vol.7, No. 10 (October 1987) pp. 20-24. (Figure 3).

Figure 8. Inventions in spinning machines per five-year period

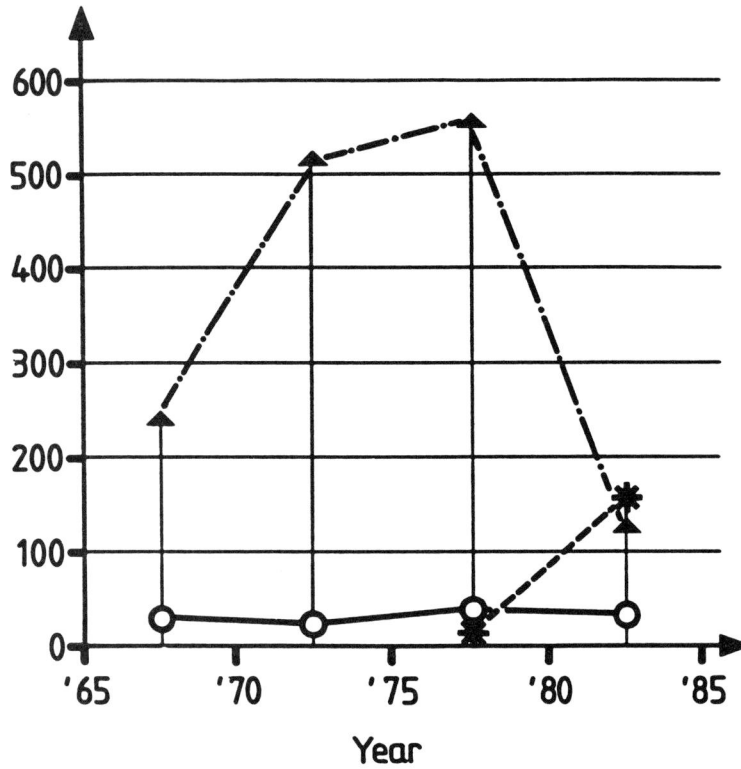

O Ring Spinning
▲ Rotor Spinning
✳ Alternative Spinning

Source: H. Locher, "The Link between Innovation and Investment" in *World Textiles: Investment, Innovation and Invention*, Manchester: The Textile Institute, 1985. (Figure 6).

method of texturing for apparel applications is the false twist process where continuous filament yarns are temporarily twisted at high speeds, heat set, and then untwisted. Yarn throughput speeds for this process were about 100 meters/minute in the late 1960s when pin spindles were used. With the introduction of friction in the mid-1970s, speeds rose to 350 meters/minute. Today, machines operate at 900-1000 meters/minute with yarn rotation at over 1.5 million RPM.

For a considerable period, US-built machines dominated the domestic-texturing industry. Now, there are no domestic machine makers and the market is dominated by German, Japanese, Swiss, and Italian machines. This decline can be traced to the lack of aggressive US research and development in texturing, as well as a series of drawn out patent suits between US textile mills and US machinery makers which undercut America's patent position.

Weaving. The general decrease in weaving labor per unit output since the industrial revolution is shown in Figure 9. With the introduction of projectile shuttleless looms in the early 1950s by the Swiss firm Sulzer, production speeds rose dramatically, as shown in Figure 10. Figure 11 shows that patents for shuttleless looms are on the rise as compared to the rather stagnant development of shuttle looms. While Figure 6 pictures the easing out of the shuttle looms by the shuttleless variety, the pattern of innovation in this field is shown in figure 12.

The basic principles of weaving (which accounts for 70 percent of the fabric used in the US) have not changed since the industrial revolution. What have changed radically are the principles of executing the individual actions of weaving. This, along with availability of stronger, longer fibers, accounts for the marked increase in weaving productivity reflected in Figure 10. Modern looms are also equipped with extensive controls for warp inlet and fabric winding, for detection of missed picks, and in some cases for the automatic removal of broken picks. All of these innovations have contributed to increased productivity.

Presently there are 70,000 shuttleless looms in the US, mostly of the rapier and projectile types. Water jet looms appeared commercially in the late 1960s while air jet looms (developed in Finland decades ago) appeared in the 1980s. The water jet looms are faster but cannot be used on some yarns. The air jet looms are more flexible.

Projectile looms shown at the ITMA 1987 exhibit weave up to four color selections at an insertion rate of 1100 meters/minute with full automation in loom stoppage, pick finding and color selection. Rapier looms are viewed as the conventional

Figure 9. Reduction of human labor

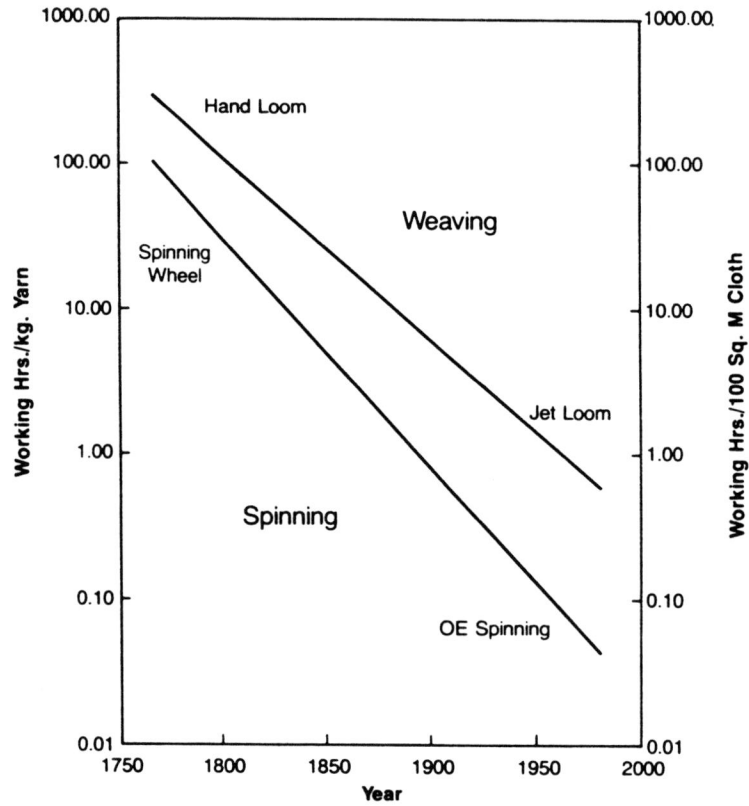

Source: Prof. H. W. Krause, as reproduced in
J. A. Krol, "The Global Outlook on Marketing and
Research" in *World Textiles: Investment,
Innovation, and Invention*, Manchester: The Textile
Institute, 1985. (Figure 8).

**Figure 10. Trends in maximum loom speeds
demonstrated on commercial looms**

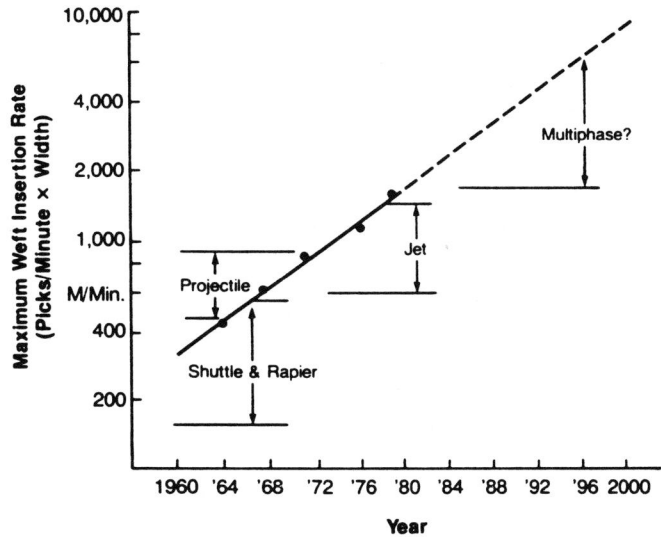

Source: J. A. Krol, "The Global Outlook on
Marketing and Research" in *World Textiles:
Investment, Innovation and Invention*, Manchester:
The Textile Institute, 1985. (Figure 7).

Figure 11. Inventions in weaving machines per five-year period

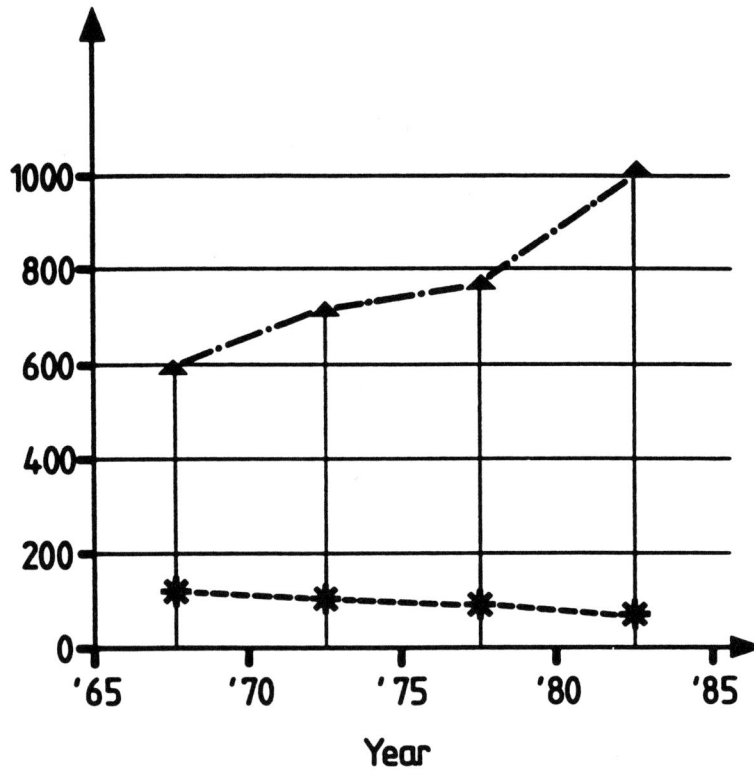

✳ Shuttle Looms

▲ Shuttleless Looms

Source: H. Locher, "The Link between Innovation and Investment" in *World Textiles: Investment, Innovation and Invention*, Manchester: The Textile Institute, 1985. (Figure 7).

35

Figure 12. Textile industry innovation chronology

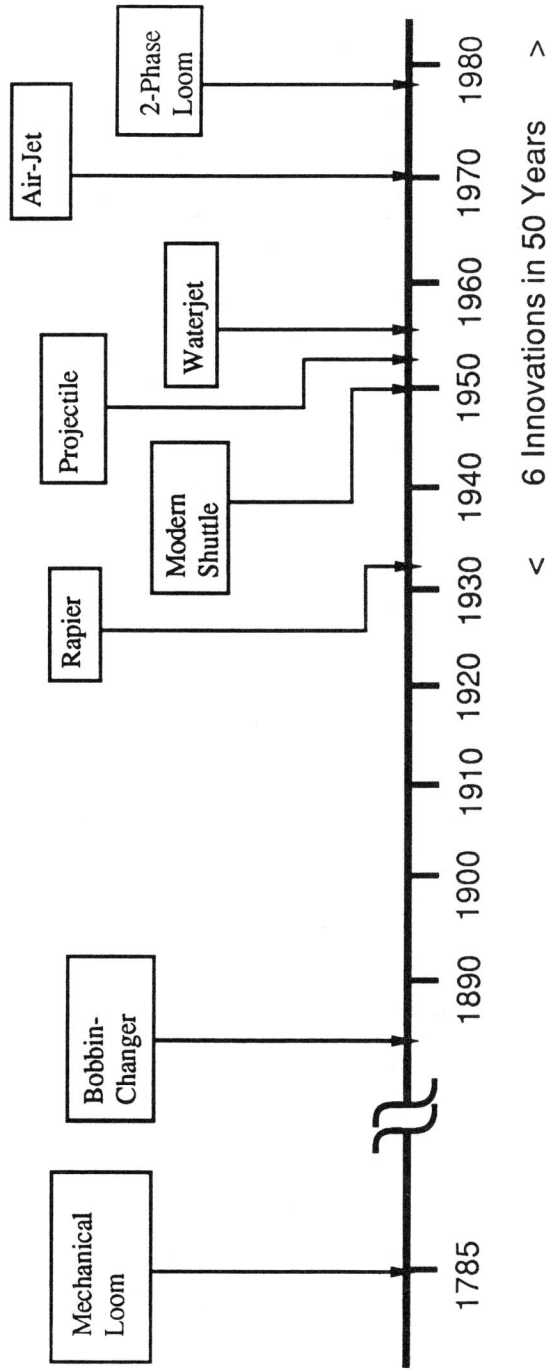

Source: H. Locher, "The Link between Innovation and Investment" in *World Textiles: Investment, Innovation and Invention*, Manchester: The Textile Institute, 1985. (Figure 5).

looms of the future due to their flexibility. Insertion rates are up to 1000 meters/minute with up to 12 colors.

The Swiss projectile loom (the "daddy") was licensed to Warner and Swazey for many years, while the Draper Company developed and produced modern flexible rapier looms in the 1960s and 1970s. When North American Rockwell's purchase of Draper did not lead to expected expansion of its air loom business, Rockwell let Draper wither away.

No US companies produce jet-weaving machines. The first jet machines were developed in the 1960s by Investa (Czechoslovakia). The Swiss firm Ruti entered the field in 1971, followed by the Japanese firms Nissan, Toyoda and Tsudakoma in 1979. Sulzer-Ruti now produces an air jet weaving machine operating at 1760 meters/minute with one, two, or four colors and fabric width from 55 to 158 inches. A further development in weaving technology is the multiphase loom which permits simultaneous insertion of multiple fitting gains and varied beatings at different locations along the fabric width. These looms were first developed in Czechoslovakia and show great promise for the future.

We say nothing further about fabric production, except to recognize major innovations in the field of knit fabric patterning, sliver knitting and warp knitting. Indeed the combination of warp knitting superimposed over layers of filling yarns or even loose battings provides for a range of woven-like materials produced at speeds far exceeding that of conventional looms.

This brief survey of the textile industry's production rates leads again to the inevitable conclusion that US-based enterprises developed little of the technology responsible for greater productivity. In fact, certain advances in processing attributed above to US firms were actually developed by their European subsidiaries (e.g. the case of advanced carding machines).

However, the question remains whether the US textile industry can maintain a productivity lead versus overseas textiles producers if all of its process technology is imported. For lower wage countries have been able to acquire the same advanced technology and to apply it with vastly reduced labor costs.

This question was put to a number of fiber and textile industry executives and the initial answers were generally in the affirmative. The qualification was added that good communications with overseas machinery makers was essential to ensure early trial and evaluation of new developments in process and product. It is worth noting that in follow-up discussions some of the affirmatives were reversed as certain managers acknowledged the desirability, if not the need, for close collaboration between fiber plant or textile mill staff and the development engineers of machine companies. It was pointed out that such collaboration inevitably suffered from separation distance and from language differences.

Whether the making of primary textile machinery in the USA is in the realm of possibility is a question difficult to answer. Many think not, but the TMA (Textile Machinery Association) is actively advocating a program of industry revival, building on the relatively few firms which have been successful in competing with overseas machinery makers, both in the USA and abroad.

There are selective US examples where clever and unique developments have occurred in the process area. One example is a rope company near Puget Sound which has designed and built from the ground up a radically different braiding machine complete with improved tension controls and computer monitoring of the entire rope-making operation.

A final note in terms of equipment development has to do with quality control equipment for process monitoring, in other words, textile test instruments. Here we must acknowledge the superiority of Swiss-made instruments for continuous measurement and recording of yarn strength and uniformity. The Japanese have of late dominated the "hand" measurement area with a sequence of well engineered instruments based on the decade of studies by Kawabata. At the same time, certain US instrument makers successfully compete (both in US markets and abroad). As examples we note Instron's servo-controlled (screw) testing machines and servo-hydraulic impact and fatigue machines, or Lawson's TYT test machine for the texturing industry, or CTT instrument for the staple yarn mill. The likelihood of expanding this special area of textile industry equipment is certainly greater than for the making of primary process equipment. However, if sound technical concepts are combined with a motivation towards directed applications, as at Puget Sound, the results may surprise the industry.

Research and Innovation in Apparel Technology. The apparel industry is extremely labor intensive. Unlike the capital intensive textile industry the production process in the manufacture of clothing has not changed radically in the last 50 years. Research has been virtually nonexistent. Various obstacles slow greater automation of apparel manufacture. One problem is scale: The predominance of small firms with limited resources restricts the market for expensive automated machinery and automation systems. Another is technical: To date, there has been little success in designing and commercializing automated systems for sewing the limp materials used in clothing. Yet, given the weight of labor costs in the sector of the industry, and the advantages this gives to imports from low-wage economies, innovations here would be very important for the competitiveness of the entire sector.

There are signs of change. Microelectronics-related innovations are making possible automation of certain steps of the apparel manufacture process that were either too expensive or too difficult to automate in the past. [43] There have been significant advances in the pre-assembly stages. Currently, efforts are underway in the US, Europe and Japan to achieve a breakthrough in automated sewing--a breakthrough that would have significant implications for the clothing industries in developed and newly industrializing nations and for patterns of world trade in apparel in the coming decades. Little of this research takes place in individual firms, with a few exceptions like the Russell Corporation, a privately-held, highly integrated manufacturer that goes from fiber to finished garments. Rather, both the US and the Japanese projects in automated sewing research and development involve collaboration between government and industry and, in the US case, labor, in cooperative research ventures. These are the $(TC)^2$ project and its spinoffs in the US and the Automated Sewing System project in Japan.

Before turning to these two research projects, it is useful to describe the steps of apparel manufacture: pre-assembly, assembly and finishing. Pre-assembly consists of four steps: inspection of fabric; grading of patterns for the individual components of the garment for the various sizes being produced; preparation of the marker from the graded patterns; and cutting of the cloth. In the past ten years, there has been much technological change in these four steps. The most important changes have been the introduction of Computer Assisted Design (CAD) systems and the introduction of computer-controlled cutters. These systems are mainly restricted in use to the larger firms, since a US-made CAD/cutter system can cost about $1 million--quite a commitment for firms used to capital investments per worker of about $1500 (for sewing machines). Some foreign-made CAD/cutters (e.g. Lectra, Investronica) are smaller and less expensive, hence better suited to the needs of the average apparel firm.

In the assembly phase of production, the components of a garment are sewn. In general, this work is broken down so that machine operators, using function-specific machines, perform sewing tasks that are simple and quick. Recent years have seen increased computerization of the sewing machines, and automated transfer systems and materials-handling systems are beginning to make inroads in the largest firms. But it is this phase, in which the fabric may move through dozens of sequential steps, with materials handling between each, that has been the most resistant to automation in the past and that is the subject of much automation research today. The final phase, finishing, involves pressing and packaging of the sewn garments.

(TC)^2, the US project in automated sewing research and development, began in 1979 as a collaborative R & D effort among labor, industry, and government.[44] The initial focus of the acitivity reflected the special concerns of the founders. The union, the Amalgamated Clothing and Textile Workers Union (ACTWU), is heavily concentrated in the tailored men's clothing industry, and it has a history of good working relations with the manufacturers. John Dunlop, former Secretary of Labor and Harvard professor, who knew both the unionists and the manufacturers, took the initiative in obtaining government support for the project. The US Department of Commerce provided half the $450,000 funding for the first year, and the union and three firms, Hartmarx, Genesco, and Palm Beach, provided the rest. The aim was to reduce labor costs, since they represent about 35 percent of manufacturing expense of US-made garments. The union accepted the need for cutting costs in order to maintain and restore US competitiveness in apparel manufacture.

The first task chosen was to develop equipment to automate the assembly of the sleeve of a man's coat. Sleeve assembly is complex and labor intensive. If computer-driven automation techniques and equipment could be developed for sleeve assembly, they could be applied to other aspects of apparel manufacturing. As Professor Frederick Abernathy, a Harvard engineer associated with the project from the outset, recounts, the organizers recognized that this project would have to produce concrete results rapidly to keep the sponsors interested, and that this constraint ruled out any basic research option. The main technical challenge was the movement and manipulation of fabric. By 1985, Draper developed a prototype system. It consists of modular units: an automatic loader to insert parts to be assembled into the transfer line; a viewing table that allows the automated vision system to recognize the parts; a robot that folds and aligns edges; a transfer door that slides the parts to the sewing station; a sewing unit with feed belts and a sewing machine under complete automatic control.

The prototype has been transferred to Singer Sewing Machine Company for development on a commercial basis. No equipment manufacturers had been associated with (TC)^2, and the choice of Singer--which no longer manufactures any sewing machines in the US--brought in a company primarily focused on robotics and aerospace. Singer has not yet sold any robotics systems to the apparel industry, but only to automotive upholstery and sheet and towel firms. It is unclear how successful Singer will be in marketing machines developed from the $(TC)^2$ prototype. Companies that have automated some part of sewing operations are large firms like Levi Strauss and Russell, with highly repetitive, long runs of quite standard goods. For this they use stand-alone, dedicated machinery. The $(TC)^2$/Singer concept is more flexible, but whether it can become cheap enough to find users is open. At this point, the prototypes are being tested in two large men's clothing manufacturers.

Over the past nine years, $(TC)^2$ has changed significantly in membership and focus, from participants drawn mainly from highly unionized parts of the industry that produce shorter runs of more labor intensive garments (tailored men's suits) to segments of the industry that are nonunionized and produce long runs of less skill-intensive goods, such as sweatpants and jeans. Executives from the textile mills and fiber companies now play a larger role in the group. The new projects focus on sewing pants, an item of interest to the larger long-run manufacturers. Government support for $(TC)^2$ rose to $3.3 million in 1984, which was matched by industry.

The benefits of $(TC)^2$ in bringing together parts of the textile/apparel industry that had previously had little contact or even hostile relations may well outweigh the actual technological and economic results. In an industry characterized by extreme segmentation and mutual suspicion, heightened by regional (New Yorkers vs. Southerners) and ethnic (Jewish, Chinese, and Italian apparel manufacturers vs. Southern WASP textile mill operators) differences, the contacts at $(TC)^2$ among people from different parts of the industry has contributed to the creation of new collective ventures--the Quick Response program, the Crafted with Pride in the USA Council. Intra-industry linkages, which play a large role in recent changes in the sector, build on new networks formed in the $(TC)^2$ advisory committees.

The conception and course of the Japanese automated sewing project show striking differences from $(TC)^2$. [45] First, on the side of industry, the equipment manufacturers are among the key players, and much of the experimentation is taking place within their own firms. Industry contributes very little of the funding of the project, although certain costs have been incurred because the project has been carried out in its initial phases within the companies and will only be assembled within a national laboratory at a later stage (1988). The unions as such do not participate. Second, government's contribution to the program is more substantial than in the US. It provides about $7 million a year, which is funneled to a private research company and then distributed to the 28 companies carrying out the research.

Finally and most interesting, the task has been conceived and organized in quite different fashion in Japan. Despite pressures from industry for rapidly marketable innovations, MITI insisted on a long-term development perspective and on a more integrated approach to the problem. They started with an analysis of the entire cutting, sewing, and pressing process, and divided work up among four groups. The first works on developing automatic fabric inspection and cutting; the second, on processing of such parts as cuffs; the third on the main sewing process, in particular, on side and back seams and sewing the sleeve to the body; and the fourth, on pressing garments.

The technologies being considered involve a radical break with flat sewing. They are trying to develop three dimensional sewing, using machines with moving heads, working on garments that are draped around dummies. The Japanese are continuing to focus on developing flexible machinery that would be capable of sewing various garments and of transforming the entire process of production of these clothes in contrast to the American shift towards more dedicated machinery for longer runs and the continued focus on particular segments of the production process. The active participation of equipment manufacturers in Japan suggest that there are likely to be many fewer practical barriers to commercialization, in contrast to the uncertainties which still hang over the ultimate fate of $(TC)^2$ products. (From the perspective of American apparel manufacturers, the involvement of Japanese machine makers in the MITI automated sewing project may well have positive outcomes, since the machinery to be developed will apparently be available for sale abroad as well as within Japan.)

The technical difficulties that the Japanese project still faces, the paring down of $(TC)^2$'s original ambitions, and the very spotty record of microelectronics application to date in the apparel industry suggest that automation is not likely soon to lower total labor costs across the advanced industrial societies. [46] Moreover, given the structure of the industry, it seems unlikely that small firms can take advantage of these innovations. Technological innovation in this part of the textile sector would have the greatest possible impact on future economic and employment prospects in the industry as a whole. But a review of current research efforts does not suggest technical break-throughs in the near future of a sort that could be used by the firms that today make up the apparel sector.

As Section I has sought to demonstrate, increases in productivity of certain sectors of the textile complex notwithstanding, the US textile industry has suffered dramatic reductions in market share both here and abroad. As a result, wages and employment levels in this industry have also suffered. Even significant technological innovations in product and process, once an area of American primacy, now originate for the most part in Europe and Japan. What innovations continue to be either developed or widely diffused in the US either reinforce existent patterns in the industry (i.e. process technologies which enchance efficiency in the production of standardized goods) or are unavailable to large segments of the industry (i.e. (TC)^2. The next section seeks to better understand these shortcomings by considering those factors which account for success, both in the US and abroad.

II. Explaining Success: Factors that Account for High Productivity and Competitiveness.

The lessons that might be learned from the best practices of successful foreign firms are often explained away by the conventional wisdom about textiles in advanced industrial states. Confronted with examples of profitable and dynamic European and Japanese textile companies, Americans frequently take refuge in the comfortable notion that these firms succeed for reasons having little to do with superior productivity and much to do with governmental intervention and regressive social practices. Before considering the lessons for US productivity that might be gleaned from these countries, one must first consider the claims that their success derives from better state protection from foreign competition or from residual societal backwardness--in the form of lower wages, or poorer working conditions, or ineffective tax collection, or unregulated environments--all of which would cheapen the cost of production.

Restricting Imports: Do the Europeans and Japanese
Succeed Because of More Effective Protection?
The different outcomes in the United States and West Europe with using the Multifiber Arrangements of 1974, 1978, 1982, and 1986 (MFA I, II, III, IV) to limit textile imports suggest that European nations have been more effective in the 1980s stemming the arrival of textile products from the largest and most sophisticated exporters: Hong Kong, South Korea, and Taiwan. Annual growth in US imports of most quota items has been above six percent in the past five years, while growth in the EEC countries has been much less--and imports to the EEC from the dominant MFA suppliers has declined nearly five percent over all and over seven percent in the sensitive Group I category

(cotton and synthetic fabrics, cotton yarn, T-shirts, woven and knit shirts, jerseys, trousers, blouses).

The critical period was the early 1980s, the years of MFA III. From 1976 through 1981, imports into the US grew, but at rates that were tolerable. In Europe, disagreements among EEC member countries over textile policy led to piecemeal implementation and to serious import surges during MFA I. High levels of imports in a period of slow demand growth cost the EEC countries about 430,000 jobs between 1971 and 1978. EEC countries then pushed for more restrictions in MFA II and III. Between 1981 and 1986, as Europe was gaining some control over the rate of textile and apparel import growth, the dam burst in the US. Imports soared, growing at an average annual rate of over 15 percent (33 percent increase in 1983; 24 percent in 1984). The evidence suggests that this change reflects two concurrent factors: 1) the impact on trade flows of the overvalued dollar in the first half of the 1980s; and 2) learning by developing nations and American importers, who figured out how to circumvent the MFA in the US in ways that EEC administration of the MFA made far more difficult.

These divergent developments in the US and West Europe can be partly explained by the high dollar. The most forceful proponent of this view is William Cline of the Institute for International Economics, who argues that had the dollar remained at its 1980 level, when the trade balance in textiles was about even, the import surge in textiles and apparel would have been significantly reduced in the US. Cline notes that the rise of the dollar in real terms relative to the currencies of major developing-country suppliers of textile and apparel was as follows for the years 1980-1985: Taiwan, 22 percent; Hong Kong, 11 percent; Korea, 28 percent; China, 90 percent; Mexico, 24 percent; India, 27 percent; and Bangladesh, 19 percent. Only against the currencies of Singapore and the Philippines, among important suppliers, did the dollar fail to rise during this period. [47] This change in relative currency values prompted many supplier nations to look to the US rather than European markets.

Differences in US and Europe administration of bilateral agreements between developed and developing countries under the MFA have also played an important role in the divergence between US and European import penetration rates in the 1980s. It seems that two components of the US system have made it a less effective system of barriers against imports than the European: first, the heavier role of foreign policy considerations (and foreign policy bureaucrats) in the administration of the MFA and quotas, and secondly, the use in the US of a set of quota categories that are multiple and highly specific in contrast to the broader European categories.

The advantage of the narrower categories of the US system is that when an exporter begins to concentrate heavily on one good, then a quota can be placed upon it, without affecting that country's exports of other kinds of fabrics and products within the same broad family. The disadvantage is that an adaptive and dynamic exporting country can quickly shift its product mix away from the narrow lines with tight quotas into new lines that may not even have a quota. Thus, for example, the Hong Kong apparel industry, confronted with quota barriers for its conventional product lines, "discovered" ramie, a linen-like fiber not much used because of its roughness and hence not covered by quotas. As a result, increasing numbers of imported garments were made of ramie-blend. Given the slowness with which the US usually moves on calls and negotiates bilateral agreements, the exporting countries derive major advantages in the period before new arrangements are settled. The European system, in contrast, allows broad, fairly blanket coverage and makes it easier to prevent such shifting around to evade quotas. Such differences have undoubtedly aided the Europeans to protect themselves, at least in certain categories.

In 1986, bilateral agreements and administrative changes were introduced in the US to reduce the flexibility that had enabled developing countries to exploit the loopholes in US protection during a period of overvaluation of the dollar. It remains to be seen whether these changes will result in an effective tightening of protection for textiles and apparel in the US.

In Japan, the protection of the domestic textile industry depends not on the bilateral agreements reached under the MFA, but rather on the tightly structured connections among all segments of the industry. Japan has lower import duties than the US, particularly for apparel (about 14 percent nominal rate for apparel, in contrast to 22.5 percent in the US).[48] It has no import quotas, except on raw silk and silk thread, nor does it have origin-label legislation. [49] Rather, old and tight informal networks that link different segments of the industry together are what make penetration of the Japanese market extremely difficult for foreigners. Ronald Dore has analyzed the connections that form the structure of the Japanese textile industry and concludes that these patterns of interdependence are the most significant obstacle to foreign penetration of Japanese markets. He cites, for example, an estimate of only 20 percent of cotton cloth woven by weavers whose relations with other firms leave them sufficiently autonomous to be able to buy yarn freely on the market. Another 20 percent are tied to trading companies which might conceivably change to foreign yarns. Even fewer of the producers dealing with synthetic yarns are free to consider buying yarn from abroad. [50] Added to the more or less informal barriers that derive from the interconnectedness of the components of the industry are restraints that the bureaucrats counterpose to imports. One US apparel manufacturer, for example, told us of sending 30,000 dozen sweatshirts to Japan, only to have them remain on the docks when zealous customs inspectors discovered the count was short by seven shirts. When the seven missing shirts were dispatched by air, the original invoices were somehow found to be missing. By the time the unfortunate shipment reached the stores, a summer heatwave ensured the failure of the operation.

While these restraints on imports are highly effective in Japan, they are used more to slow transition than to stop it. Thus despite these barriers, the tide of imports has been rising rapidly. Imports from Korea, for example, increased over 50 percent from 1985 to 1986; almost 40 percent of all sweaters are imported; and imports of yarn from China have been mounting since the early 1980s. [51]

It is clear that protection, whether through tariffs, quotas, the MFA structure, or tight trading networks, has had an impact on trade flows into the US and other developed nations. But can we conclude that more effective European and Japanese protection explains superior performance by their textile firms? Our answer is: No. William Cline argues that the divergence in import penetration rates in the early 1980s may have been an exception, rather than a trend. Moreover, among the best performers in textiles and apparel today are countries that are least concerned about erecting high trade barriers. Furthermore, in the product lines in which the Japanese and Europeans do best, competition from lower-wage, lower-quality rivals is not a significant factor.

Within Europe, countries with the most protection (i.e. United Kingdom) have been least successful in remaining competitive. West Germany provides the most striking case for the limited role of protectionism in explaining competitive success, since the West Germans have been the most resistant of the European states to implement the MFA restrictions. [52] The evidence of openness of the West German system to imports is clear: The FRG is the second largest importer of textiles and apparel, after the United States; on a per capita basis, it is the largest, importing about twice as much as Britain and France and four times as much as the US. [53] In 1981, West Germany imported twice as much from developing countries as did the US. [54] And yet, at the same time, West Germany has successfully modernized and transformed its own textile sector, with productivity increases of 24 percent between 1980 and 1986. In 1960, the West Germans exported 11 percent of total output; in 1970, 21 percent; and by 1984, exports amounted to 48 percent of production. The Federal Republic is now the third largest world textile exporter (after Italy and Hong Kong). [55]

More broadly, there is wide-ranging evidence that the kinds of firms that are responsible for the export successes of European and Japanese textile firms are operating in market niches in which they experience relatively little competition from low-cost producers and in which, therefore, the protections afforded by the MFA are hardly relevant. These market niches are, typically, higher value-added categories, in which considerations of design, quality, responsiveness to fashion, and sensitivity and rapid adjustment to trends play major roles, and costs a lesser role.

In sum, while European administration of the MFA was more successful than the US in stemming the import of low-cost imports from dominant suppliers in developing countries through most of the 1980s, this explains little about the success and failure of European textiles. The fact that Italy can restrict imports from Hong Kong and Korea (but not from low wage EEC-associated countries like Portugal, Greece, and Turkey) does not explain why Italy is so successful in exporting knit wear, woolens, and apparel. Nor does it explain West German successes. Rather, with respect to trade patterns within the developed world--the markets of the US, Europe, and Japan--the most that can be claimed for MFA-based protection is that it leaves open competitive possibilities for firms within these markets that would have been closed under a more open international trade regime. Whether such opportunities have been pursued or missed by firms in these countries depends on factors other than protection from low cost imports.

Do Backwardness and Exploitation Explain Success Abroad?
The other major self-exculpating explanation of why textile companies in other advanced industrial countries have often done better than US firms is the claim that the former benefit from various forms of exploitation and social regressiveness that are no longer acceptable or legal in the United States. The items included under this rubric range from conditions that affect workers in particular (low wages, dangerous and stressful working conditions, job insecurity, subjection to arbitrary authority in the workplace) to conditions with negative impact on society at large (absence of environmental regulation, hence more pollution, consumer risk, and a transfer of costs that industry incurs onto society's books; failure to pay taxes and social security payments). With respect to the record of the developing countries and the NICs, the evidence of profits based on very low wages and bad working conditions is overwhelming. With respect to

the textile companies in advanced countries, however, the picture is more complex.

To consider only the two outstanding European textile successes--the West German and the Italian--there is no correlation between backwardness and profitability in the sector today. Wages in both countries are close to US wages in textiles (somewhat higher in West Germany, somewhat lower in Italy). Environmental regulation may impose heavier costs on US textile firms than on their European counterparts, though this conclusion can only be speculative, in the absence of solid research on the subject.[56] On the other hand, the inflexibilities that higher levels of unionization and more restrictive labor legislation impose on European firms are more constraining than any comparable US practices. In Italy and France, for example, lay-offs and plant closings over the past 15 years have been highly regulated and require bargaining with unions and bureaucratic authorizations. Similarly, the organization of shift work and weekend operations, the working conditions on the shop floor, subcontracting, and training are items that abroad frequently require negotiation with unions and/or state bureaucracies, whereas in US textile firms they are usually within the realm of managerial discretion.

There is a kernel of truth in the allegations that textiles in other advanced industrial societies have profited from low wages and unregulated environments but such competitive advantages, however significant in the past, have now largely disappeared. The general conclusion that emerges from the European and Japanese cases is that textile firms abroad used the advantages of backwardness to obtain the capital and time necessary for modernization. Today the prosperity of the textile industry in those countries no longer depends critically on exploitation of human or natural resources. Rather the advantages of the most profitable firms in advanced industrial countries derive from a successful adaptation and modernization of market strategy, technology, and labor policies.

The outstanding example of evolution from a textile sector that grew on the basis of low wages, insecure employment, and political protection is the Italian industry. The districts of Italy today in which the prosperity of the regional economy derives from dynamic, innovative, and export-oriented textile firms are areas that in the first three postwar decades had bad working conditions, low wages, uncertain employment, weak unions, and massive tax evasion. Studies carried out in the 1960s and 1970s on spinning and weaving in the Prato or Biella zones, knitting in Carpi, and ladies wear in Modena showed heavy reliance on subcontracting to homeworkers who made the same products at home on old machines they owned or rented. The homeworkers and workers in tiny shops in garages and spare rooms had, however, wages much lower than those in factories and little social security coverage. Their working conditions escaped all inspection. Subcontracting and work at home allowed the entrepreneurs to tune labor supply to market conditions.[57]

Today in the mid-1980s the same districts present a very different picture. As a result of major union mobilization and organizing campaigns at the end of the 1960s and through the 1970s, most workers in these areas have been unionized; the wage level has risen; and the differential between those employed in small shops and big plants has narrowed. The Italian textile firms in Carpi or Biella or Prato which in the 1960s produced cheap, undifferentiated goods for a mass market and succeeded because of low labor costs, low taxes, low cost recycled materials, and low capital costs, today prosper on entirely a different basis.

At the beginning of the 1970s a major crisis drastically reduced the number of firms in the industry. The firms that survived--big or small--were those with new market strategies that identified particular niches for higher quality and higher price goods and gave up mass production of low cost items. The second striking characteristic of the survivors was that they were firms that adapted their technological and production strategies to the new labor market conditions. However reluctantly, they accepted as irreversible the new strength of the unions with all that this implied for working conditions, for wages, and for employment security. While employers resisted particular demands or kinds of union intervention in management of the firm, the opposition to unions as such and the reliance on low cost production essentially disappeared. Instead of seeking to escape new labor market constraints by moving production to southern Italy or to underdeveloped countries, the textile owners and managers chose to modernize their plants and strategies in ways that accommodated the new facts. In fact, according to interviews with business association leaders, those firms which tried the "Southern strategy" experienced failure since competition based on exploitation could not guarantee the quality and service standards necessary to compete in the ever-more demanding international market.

Indeed many of the managers came to regard the labor agitations of the 1960s and 1970s as a kind of providential event with high short-term costs that had forced them to rationalize production in ways that would prove very profitable. A manager of a successful high fashion denim mill in the Bergamo area illustrated his conclusion that the labor situation resulting from strong union pressures had had overall positive effects on his company by commenting on a visit in the 1970s to a denim manufacturer in

Texas. In the Texas plant the workers' faces were so blue from denim dust that they could not even be identified. "I have no blue workers!" the Italian manager exclaimed. "The union wouldn't let me get away with it. I have had to invest in air cleaning systems that remove all that dust. And it's far better for us that we've done this. We operate better in a cleaner plant. Most important, you can't hope to get real cooperation from 'blue men'. We're at a point now with the unions that when we decided we needed to move to seven-day-a-week operations and the bishop attacked us publicly for Sunday shifts, it was the unions that came to our defense."

Similar patterns of shift away from labor-exploitative strategies can be found in West Germany and Japan. In West Germany in the 1970s, a rise in textile imports provoked a major crisis in the domestic industry in the course of which many firms closed--a one-third fall over ten years [58]--and employment in textiles and apparel was cut by about half. The first response of many German textile firms was indeed to search abroad for cheaper labor.[59] German firms bought finished goods in low-wage countries and sold them under German labels; they invested directly in foreign firms; and, in outward processing arrangements similar to the US 807 procedure, they contracted out to low-wage producers the most labor-intensive parts of production while retaining the more capital- and design-intensive parts of the operation in Germany. By 1981, about 25 percent of all textile and apparel imports to West Germany were goods that had been produced abroad and imported by German industry; half of them were partially manufactured abroad under outward processing contracts. [60]

At the same time, however, far from disinvesting in the domestic industry or from switching to strategies dependent on cheap foreign labor, German textile firms invested heavily in new technologies, in labor-saving machinery, and in new plants and turned to new market strategies based on higher quality and higher priced goods. Investment per employee more than doubled between 1970 and 1986.[61] The extent of rationalization in the industry is reflected in the average capital cost of creating a new job: 330,000 DM in textiles, compared to 230,000 in automobiles and 170,000 in machine tools.[62] One study concludes: [63]

> Internationalization should thus be viewed less as a permanent
> industrial relocation from North to South, than a temporary
> movement permitting adjustment in West Germany. On the one hand,
> outward processing allowed the old labor-intensive structures of
> the industry to die out, leaving the skilled and capital-intensive
> structures more concentrated and productive than before. On the
> other hand, it allowed firms to remain temporarily competitive in
> "exile" until more fundamental adjustments could be made at home.
> By thus buying time, firms could continue to invest in new tech-

nologies while accommodating their production strategies to the new market realities.

In Japan, too, the pattern of growth in the modern textile industry was one in which there were abundant possibilities for profitability via labor exploitation. The proportion of small-scale family enterprises in this sector is very high, and, as Dore describes, "proprietor families are prepared to exploit themselves to a greater degree than the law or convention or trade unions now permit employers to exploit paid employees. In particular they can sit out recessions by tightening their belts and eschewing some luxuries in a way that firms with large fixed wage bills cannot." [64]

But even for the small family firms in Japan, keeping labor costs down has been only one component among others in the strategies that have kept the sector viable. Linkages among small producers in cooperatives; linkages to big firms and to trading companies that provide not only orders but also information on new technologies and financial help in acquiring new machines; [65] government programs to foster cooperation among small owners and to shrink numbers in the industry by buying up surplus looms; government research institutes focused on issues important for small industry [66]--all of these plus continuing high rates of investment have contributed in major ways to the survival of small family-owned Japanese textile firms. However important low labor costs may have been in the past to small and big Japanese firms, today the productivity and profitability of the sector depend far more heavily on other factors. In sum, in Japan as in West Germany and Italy and other advanced European economies, success in textiles can no longer be attributed to social backwardness. While historically low wages or weak governmental regulation of environmental impacts may explain capital accumulation in earlier periods, today the success stories have to be explained by other factors.

Competitive Strategies: Market Niches

One common element in the strategies of the successful firms in high wage economies is identifying a segment of the market in which firms compete on the basis of factors other than or in addition to costs. Such factors include quality, style, originality, and prestige ("designer" labels). Certainly in the United States all textile manufacturers cannot survive by concentrating on the high quality, high price end. Within medium value-added categories, however, greater diversity of product can be achieved through smaller batches or shorter production runs, and this creates special quality in the product. In this section we examine this market niche or differentiated product strategy. We review foreign and domestic experiences with a shift away from long run production of standard goods for a mass market to shorter run production of more specialized and diverse products for limited market segments.

Foreign Applications. Successful European textile producers in Italy and West Germany have pursued a differentiated product strategy. The initial response of German textile producers to increased competition in the early 1960s was an increased emphasis on production of standardized fabric and clothing--the undifferentiated strategy. Realizing the limits to this approach, the big textile companies switched from an undifferentiated to a differentiated strategy in the late 1970s. Smaller production units, more flexible manufacturing, and modern technology were components of this change. [67]

The success of small Italian firms operating in specialized markets has been widely publicized in the US in popular and scholarly writings. [68] What is less well understood is that this phenomenon reflects not only small firms operating in traditional specialties, but the shift in strategy of large firms that in the first three postwar decades operated much as large-scale US firms did, mass producing relatively undifferentiated goods for large markets. Two cases out of many that were identified in the research in Italy illustrate these shifts.

GFT (Gruppo Finaziario Tessile) is a large garment manufacturer in Turin that modelled its operations after similar US firms. In the years of the postwar economic miracle and consumer boom, GFT was very successful, but after the 1960s began to suffer serious losses. The firm switched out of lower-middle price range and quality range product and moved up to higher quality, higher price garments. They developed close collaborations with well-known designers, who produced "collections" with their names for ready-made production by GFT. They developed product strategies for different market segments, and they gave up long runs. To implement such a strategy requires a large and highly skilled design capability within the firm and a skilled workforce.

Much of the GFT production (80 percent) is subcontracted out to small shops. These small firms are independently owned (unlike the Benetton system). GFT advises its subcontractors on a wide range of technical, financial, and organizational issues. In effect, GFT agrees with the subcontractor on costs and mark-ups, then it sends in its own technicians to advise on reorganizing production in order to lower costs and maintain quality. GFT also has close working ties with its suppliers, and with Marzotto--the largest integrated textile mill in Europe--is carrying out research on reducing production times.

Operating in a different segment of the industry, Lanificio Ferla, a woolen mill in the Biella area, went through a series of internal transformations in the 1970s that mirrored the changes at GFT. There was a major crisis in the 1960s in the area, and by the 1970s a process of industrial restructuration was in full swing. Those firms that moved away from more integrated forms of production and moved to specialize in the those parts of the productive process in which they had special strengths were more likely to survive the crisis and emerge as strong, competitive, profitable enterprises. Lanificio Ferla reduced its workforce from 150 in the 1960s to 75 today. At the same time it reduced the number of operations it performed within its own plant and entered into closer collaboration with others to provide needed services (e.g., finishing, dyeing). In order to deal with peaks and troughs of demand, it deals with a number of independent subcontractors, with whom it has long-term, stable relations.

Most important, Ferla changed its product line, moving to produce higher quality fabrics. The firm produces a large number of different articles. In the past the firm employed seven sales agents who traveled abroad; today it is the owner/manager who himself travels to Paris, Rome, and New York and maintains close contact with designers and his principal clients. He frequently attends fashion fairs. The textile manufacturers in the region organize one such fair; national trade associations, others. This is only one of many forms of collaboration among local textile manufacturers who also have set up a training program for managers and workers, have established a research facility, built an airport, and carry out a wide range of lobbying activities in Rome. Even more indicative of the extent of collaboration among competitors, Ferla told of visiting other firms to see new machinery in operation and of trying out his samples on the equipment.

The Japanese have traditionally endorsed a differentiated product market strategy. This is partially related to the structure of the Japanese textile industry. In the US a single firm tends to handle the entire weaving process. In Japan, however, the weaving stage is broken into a number of discrete activities, each carried out by a very small-scale firms. These firms are connected through a system of contractual relations and jointly share the risk of production. This system originally grew out of a relationship between landlords and tenants in which the former provided weaving machines to their farmers in slack season. After land reform these tenant farmers set up shop for themselves, but still depended on their former landlords to provide machinery and capital. These very small-scale weavers are able to manufacture in short production runs. For example, the weavers in the Nishiwaki industrial district which produces yarn-dyed cotton fabric typically produce in lot sizes of about 3000 yards for export, 1000 yards for domestic. [69] Weavers specialize in single product types and diversity is obtained by aggregating a number of small producers. Each weaver becomes an expert at what he does. One dobie weaver told us that it had taken him 15 years to learn his trade. The coordination and aggregation functions are performed by converters and trading companies.

The ability to manufacture small batches extends to parts of the Japanese textile complex with larger firm size as well. The Melbo Apparel Company is one of the major men's clothing manufacturing companies in Japan. Melbo has a unique production approach which combines state-of-the-art high technology with individual lot production. They do not manufacture in batches, but rather produce one suit at a time with unit production system technology.[70] Melbo switched to an individualized production system about ten years ago, after the oil crisis inventory began to accumulate in stores. In the US retailers take the risk for selling items; however, Japanese retailers sell on consignment. Thus during the slow-down after the oil crisis, inventory accumulation hurt the apparel manufacturers the most. Melbo management decided that since mass production items were not selling, a switch should be made to manufacturing to order. At the same time they began exploring new technology which would automate the process and give them increased flexibility in manufacturing.

One Melbo manager hopes that in the future suits can be ordered the way one choses in a sushi restaurant. One should have the feeling of being an individual and having an influence on outcome. In such a system, the customer could put in an order specifying style, fabric, size, and day of completion. The production schedule would be recorded in the computer, so that the customer could be told immediately when the order could be filled. The entire process should take no more than one week.

US Experience. US textiles have focused on long-run production of standard goods for mass markets. To capture higher levels of productivity textile mills installed ever faster looms, used inexpensive high production yarns, and emphasized their comparative advantage in synthetics.

The mass-production strategy was strengthened in the late 1940s when large corporations began to buy up existing small mills. This trend in corporate concentration gradually led to the abandonment of many of the specialty lines once carried by small manufacturers. Top management decided that long-run, standard products were more profitable.

This process was consolidated in the late 1960s with the double-knit fad. Between 1967 and 1972 most of the major textile mills rushed to buy double-knit machines which paid for themselves in three to four months. New weaving ground to a halt. One spokesman for the industry pronounced, "the loom is dead". Another former employee of a major textile mill recalls that his company abandoned a wide range of product lines in order to shift to double-knit production. Since his company was a latecomer to the knitting business, it began production just as the market was saturated. In 1971 the price for the product dropped from $3.75 - $4.25 a yard to $.95. Profit margins collapsed as a result of overproduction, lack of product variation, and price gouging by firms seeking to drive out competition. In the end, the company was left with useless equipment and a loss of capacity in traditional product lines.

This logic of mass production constrains the availability of high quality goods. The interviews in the US found many who said that imports were necessary in order to get fine yarn sizes, small weaving and dying batches, and a wide choice of shades and finishes. In cotton wovens, until recently the finest yarn available from US mills was 40/1. Japanese men's shirting fabric uses yarn sizes of 50/1 and above. Yarn-dyed fabric is readily available in Asia and Europe in batches of 1000 yards; in this country batches as low as 3000 yards have only recently become available.

The apparel industry has faulted the lack of domestically produced, quality fabrics as a major reason for growth in imports. For example, one designer dress manufacturer, well-known for whimsical print patterns, competes using a niche strategy. It makes no more than 300 of any one dress design in a given color, this using about 1000 yards of fabric per product. This highly successful manufacturer sews domestically (about 70 percent is sewn domestically), but must buy most textile fabrics abroad. A manager explained that he would like to buy from domestic mills, but cannot get the small batch sizes and quality necessary for the kind of garment the firm produces.

There is evidence that US manufacturers are beginning to change. Many of the more successful firms we visited have shifted to a more differentiated product strategy. Textile firms report that they have recently tried to respond to changes in the market which indicate demand for a greater diversity of product. This diversity demands a change in manufacturing strategy from mass to smaller batch production. The industry jargon stipulates that manufacturing should become "market driven" rather than "manufacturing driven." Accompanying this movement toward diversity has been a shift into higher value-added categories.

Milliken, perhaps the most successful US textile mill and industry leader, is rapidly moving toward shorter production runs in order to satisfy customer demand. A few years ago the average lot size at Milliken was 20,000 yards, now it is 4000 yards. Milliken has installed a variety of new equipment to implement this strategy. Jet dying now permits dye lots of 1000 to 2000 yards. The Millitron color wheel enables the company to match paint tabs and thus offer specialized production to customers.

The Dan River Textile Company has also made major changes in product line in order to offer higher quality and more diversified products. Before, the company produced mainly low- to middle-priced apparel fabrics geared to chains and discount stores. These categories of products were the most at risk from imports. Starting three to four years ago and accelerating one-and-a-half years ago, the company switched to the production of higher priced goods. They cut back their yarn dye capacity by 20 percent, stopped manufacturing goods for an open line, and built up the manufacturing of fancy goods to order.

Today Dan River offers 2000 different styles of fabric (including color, style, and fabric). Production runs used to be 10,000 to 12,000 yards per pattern; today they are 3,000 to 4,000 yards. Under special circumstances the company will manufacture runs as low as 1,800 yards of yarn-dyed fabric. In the last six months they have also begun using finer yarn sizes: up to 80/1. About five to seven percent of their shirting is woven with yarns as fine as 50/1. Dying is also done in smaller lots. Now one-half of their lots (less than 20 percent of total yardage) is done in batches of under 1000 yards. The big shift into the higher quality strategy was facilitated when Dan River bought J.P. Steven's fine apparel fabric division. Management at Dan River felt that they had an established base in fine fabrics, and could therefore profit from such a move. The business has since doubled and is profitable.

Dan River has also altered its marketing strategy. Now, rather than producing for an open line, production is begun when the order is in hand. All products are made for a closed line. The company has also opened a pilot weaving room where sample fabrics (between 23 and 200 yards and woven on 30 yard warps) can be created. Sample yardage can be worked out with customers. This sample operation costs $1 million a year in labor costs; however, Dan River feels that the increased flexibility offsets the costs.

At Dan River, as at Ferla, quality is a major dimension of the market niche strategy. The full weight of the decision to shift to high quality fabrics becomes apparent when one considers all of the changes necessary to implement the strategy. First, the company had to switch to ring spinning to make finer quality men's shirting. Dan River has also tried to alter the management structure to be more in keeping with the new product strategy. The entire top two tiers of marketing managers are new employees, hired because they seem to have a clearer sense of trends in the market, and because their capabilities match the new managerial requirements of more flexible operation.

One consequence of this emerging differentiated product orientation is *specialization* within firms. In part as a result of corporate disaggregation and decisions by large firms to sell off divisions, new firms emerge which focus on a single type of product. Forstmann Fabrics, for example, had been the woolen and worsted division of J.P. Stevens, but was sold to three of its executives when Stevens decided to shift into household applications. The average runs of Forstmann's woolen products are quite small, about 2500 yards; they have the capability to do batches as small as 1000 yards. The company now has about 35 percent of the market share, and 60 percent of the share in better quality woolens.

Since the former division was established as an independent company, several important changes have occurred. Under the old regime all changes in the division had to be approved with the long-term policy of the entire company in mind. Now decisions can be targeted to the needs of their product line. Communication lines are much shorter; misinterpretation of policy, less likely. One top executive reported that decision making is now "light years faster."

In response partly to the greater flexibility achieved through autonomy from the larger company and partly to changes in consumer tastes, this company now provides a product line characterized by higher fashion, more variety, and shorter lead times. Five or six years ago basic merchandise predominated; now styling and diversification of fabric has become important. The number of different fabrics offered for sale has increased 30 percent over 1981 levels: "We've gone about as complicated as you can get."

Specialization is also occurring in the older mills which formerly had a number of divisions or product lines. One respondent explained that the industry is currently undergoing a division of labor. Each company is narrowing the variety of kinds of products but increasing the variety of options within their product line. Thus both concentration and specialization proceed at the same time. West Point is, for example, moving out of apparel fabrics. J. P. Stevens has begun to concentrate on household applications. Springs has become the major piece-dyed broadcloth producer. Greenwood has focused on denim production and bought the denim divisions from both Dan River and Pepperell. Dan River now specializes in fancy yarn-dyed goods and controls half of the domestic Oxford market.

Competitive Strategies: Technology/Productivity

An alternative route to higher productivity runs through automation and capital investment. An automation strategy involves an emphasis on technological innovation, high rates of capital investment, and high levels of technological dissemination or rapid introduction of state-of-the-art machines, and a commitment to research and development.

Most of the largest companies in which we interviewed had a substantial commitment to research and development. The Milliken Corporation has been a frontrunner in research on performance fabrics. Milliken channels about two percent of sales into R&D, developing both product and process innovations and backing it up with a strong patent acquisition policy. A research manager explained that the company concentrates on products in which they will have first entry and proprietary rights. The average development takes three to five years from inception to prototype. The new products usually require hardware which does not yet exist. In order to protect the proprietary ownership of an innovation, Milliken builds many of its own machines. Sometimes it jointly works on projects with foreign textile machine manufacturers.

Milliken's commitment to the research process is demonstrated by some of the projects it has worked on for decades. An example is its work on the soil release process, begun in the late 1950s and resulting in a polyester fiber called VISA. The research and development laboratory has a special soil release division, with four chemists and several other PhDs. The first breakthrough on VISA came in 1971-2. At this point the company began to campaign to get people to see soil release as a problem and VISA as a solution. Milliken, in effect, had to create its own demand. Although VISA was of less commercial success than had been hoped, Milliken remained committed to the concept.

Successful large foreign firms are also committed to research and development. For example the large spinning and fiber company Toyobo spends over three percent of sales each year on research and development. Basic research is about 60 percent; development, 40 percent. Much of their polymer research at this time is not, however, textile-related. Rather they are looking for new applications for the fibers produced. Research decisions are based on long-term business plans. The firm makes a seven-year investment plan which specifies the direction of the company and identifies stages of product development.

Toyobo management system elicits process innovations through feedback from the production process and from customers. The line workers make many of the suggestions which lead to major process innovations. To identify new customer needs, the company investigates changes in sales patterns. Customers are even more directly involved in product innovations, frequently recommending new products which the company tries to develop.

The large Japanese apparel firm Melbo has committed major research efforts to developing better fabric. They worked with Kyoto University Professor Kawabata for the last 15 years to develop a system for evaluating the touch (the "hand") of a fabric. Melbo now uses the Kawabata system in making purchasing decisions and in determining which sewing or pressing machine to use. In contrast, US firms were uninterested in the Kawabata research until recently. Despite publications in English as well as Japanese, they largely ignored its potential.

Another common theme in those firms whose success is linked to use of capital-intensive advanced technology was commitment to high levels of investment. The Milliken Corporation, for example, claims to reinvest 96-98 percent of its cash flow back into the business. Although many in the business hope to write off new plant and equipment in less than a year, Milliken often expects a three-year payoff period. One manager explained that they "look much farther down the road." "Roger Milliken doesn't do anything for today's gain because he doesn't need today's gain." This person felt that quality should be a measure of return on investment.

Russell Corporation spends over ten percent of sales on capital equipment and reports that they do not even calculate a payback period. Rather, they just know that "they have to invest in equipment in order to reduce drudgery and increase quality." "By the time you think payback, you've already made the decision." An example was the $25 million worth of automatic ring-spinning machinery to spin high quality combed cotton yarn. The decision was market driven: their marketing department told top management that the investment would give them a jump on the competition. It is generally acknowledged that the payback period will be a long time; however, they are content with the decision.

Winning firms abroad also seemed to invest heavily in capital plant and equipment. In Japan the large corporations interviewed anticipated payback periods of three to five years. A small blanket manufacturer in Japan calculated a seven- to eight-year payback on capital expenditures.

We noted one interesting difference in the capital investment strategies of American and Japanese firms. In the United States new technology was often incorporated into a large lot, mass production model. The Japanese, by comparison, have tried whenever possible to use technology to maximize flexibility and produce small lots. Thus, Russell and Model Garment use unit production systems and computerized marking and grading systems in a mass production context. The Japanese firm Melbo applies CAD/CAM, unit production system technology, and automatic marking and cutting to individualized production. The Melbo application captures the full benefits of these flexible manufacturing technologies. Jaikumar found a similar divergence in technology in his comparative study of the application of numerically controlled machine tools. [71]

A major difference we observed between firms in the United States and elsewhere was the degree to which small textile firms also had access to advanced technology. In Japan for example a major effort has been made to disseminate technology to the smallest producers. Several institutions facilitate this dissemination: Here we consider the prefectural research institutions and industry cooperatives.

Japan has a system of state-operated research institutes, designed to assist small businesses which cannot support their own research and development operations. There are 46 textile research institutes in the 47 prefectures. The

Osaka Textile Research Institute, for example, is funded with a budget of about 200,000,000 yen. The institute is located in an area comprised of predominantly textile firms (82 percent of the local economy). The biggest textile manufacturer in the area has 300 employees; the average firm size is quite small.

The research institute carries out experiments or research and development, provides advice to business, and collects and provides data. The institute library offers books and a variety of magazine and trade journal subscriptions. The computer system has an on-line connection to the Scientific Research Center in Tokyo. Data about licenses and patents and a variety of industry statitics are available. The institute also provides information about fashion trends and distributes seasonal fashion colors.

The experiment service of the institute is designed to solve specific problems and therefore has a practical orientation. For example, if color is fading or bleaching out, the experiment section conducts an analysis. In some cases the experiments are a direct response to client's needs. The work is done on a fee-for-service basis: the charges reflect time and effort for the analysis and the materials used. Clientele also have the option of renting equipment and doing their own experiments.

The research institutes have no formal connections with universities, although staff often have private ties. Usually when universities get involved with a project, the subject must be very large and fall within the domain of basic research. The research institutes, by comparison, take small applied research projects. The institute tries to support firms in their current levels of technology.

Researchers may set about to develop research projects which would benefit the firms in their area. At the Osaka Research Institute staff were working on a computer program to make punch cards for jacquard looms. The current punching system takes about two to three weeks. The computer system could devise patterns much faster.

A second institution that accelerates the dissemination of technology is the industry cooperative. Cooperatives were set up in selected industries in order to strengthen small and medium sized firms. They are tied to geographical location. The function of the cooperative is to provide technical guidance, financial help, information, and advice about rationalization.

For example, the Nishiwaki Weaver's Cooperative has 716 member companies. The cooperative has been instrumental in upgrading the loom quality in the area. If a weaver wants a new loom, he may ask for financial help. The cooperative may then buy the loom and lease it to the weaver. Or if the weaver wants capital, the cooperative may function as a guarantor of the loan. About 2000 of the 11,348 looms (almost one-fifth) held by the membership are owned and leased by the cooperative. Usually the cooperative pays two-thirds of the costs, the weaver pays one-third and leases the remainder. A major task currently facing the association is to cut back capacity. Thus, the cooperative helps weavers who want to sell their loom share and move out of the business.

An Industrial Structure Strategy--Interfirm Linkages

The Interfirm Linkage Strategy. Industrial structure can contribute to a firm's competitiveness. Large firm size and industrial concentration offer various benefits: economy of scale, easier access to capital, and in the case of vertical integration, better coordination between stages of production. Corporate decentralization has its proponents as well. Smaller sized firms are often thought to be more innovative, flexible, and focused. A focused factory can concentrate all corporate resources on the marketing and production strategies best suited for its special product line.

One way to achieve the benefits of both concentration and decentralization --coordination and focus--is to develop linkages between autonomous firms. Contractual or informal relations between firms at different points in the textile complex enhance competitiveness by rationalizing the process, eliminating bottlenecks in the system, and encouraging domestic purchasing. Linkages between suppliers and customers can reduce inventory, cut down on order time, provide feedback about consumer preferences, and lead to new process and product innovations. Ronald Dore's writings on Japan illustrate the many advantages of this system.[72]

One major benefit of the linkage strategy is rationalization of the production process. Interfirm linkages permit partners to cut down on inventory and waste, pass along product information so that duplicate processes can be eliminated, and speed up production time. The Milliken Company, for example, has developed a Partners for Profits program to help their customers lower costs and remain more competitive. Milliken offers recommendations for waste reduction, inventory management, and investment in new technology. Benefits extend beyond providing advice: Milliken flags defects and provides its quality specifications so that inspection need not be repeated in the apparel firm. Rolls are loaded in a pre-arranged order to save customers time. Follow-up services are also provided.

Greenwood Mills has also moved to closer relations with partners. In order to develop stronger ties with its suppliers, Greenwood Mills recently halved the number of fiber producers with whom it does business. Until recently, they dealt with four fiber suppliers in order to reduce the risks of dependence. Today the company has opted for long-term, trusting relationships with two partners. In its choice of suppliers, price was the last factor considered; quality, service, product breadth, innovation, and push-pull market capability were the drawing features of the fiber producers chosen. A top manager recounted, "We all remember the days of adversarial relationships. Thank goodness they are gone. Selfishly, if our partners aren't profitable, how long will we be profitable?" In turn, Greenwood helped its major customer, Levi Strauss, cut inventory from four weeks to three days by pre-sorting shade for consistency, and loading trucks in sequences. With another customer, Lee, Greenwood brings up loaded trucks and Lee works directly out of them, eliminating warehousing.

The most ambitious project to rationalize production is the Quick Response Program. The idea behind Quick Response was that waste and inventory costs greatly reduce profit rates. Tighter links between segments of the textile pipeline would improve information flow, lower inventory levels, and improve turnaround time throughout the system. In the spirit of "just-in-time," participating groups attempted to eliminate waste and pare down inventory costs. With lower waste and faster turnaround, the industry could take more advantage of its location in the US market and thus offset the lower wage rates of Asian competitors. In the process of reorganizing for Quick Response, segments of the industry are coming to approximate the structure of contractual relations found in other countries.

In the absence of Quick Response, goods take 66 weeks to move through the pipeline: 19 weeks at retail, 24 weeks at apparel, 23 weeks in the textile and fiber stages. The product is being worked on for only 11 weeks of this period. The other 55 weeks, or 83 percent of the total time, is spent in inventory. Quick Response can shorten this 66 week cycle to 46 weeks or even to 21 weeks--by bypassing warehouses and producing directly to retail orders.[73] See table below:

Table 4. Present US apparel forced markdowns, stock-outs and inventory carrying costs, (percent of net retail sales) [74]

Problem	Fiber & Tex.	Apparel	Retail	Total
Forced Markdowns	0.6%	4.0%	10.0%	14.6%
Stock-Outs (Lost Contribution)	0.1%	0.4%	3.5%	4.0%
Inventory 15 percent Carrying Cost	1.0%	2.5%	2.9%	6.4%
Total	1.7%	6.9%	16.4%	25.0%

The first quick response pilot program was commissioned by the Crafted with Pride in USA Council and developed by Kurt Salmon Associates. It linked a textile firm, an apparel manufacturer, and a retailer: Milliken of Spartanburg, South Carolina; Seminole Manufacturing of Columbus, Mississippi; and Wal-Mart Stores. Two task forces were set up. The Seminole/Wal-Mart task force devised new packaging and carton-marking procedures to speed handling in the retail center. Replenishment orders were increased from once to twice a month in order to identify stock-outs early and reduce size of reorder shipments. The reorder cycle time was also cut 33 percent by sending the order electronically instead of counting inventory, and cutting down on the time between packing and shipping.[75]

Apparel manufacturers point out one shortcoming of Quick Response. It has most potential for high fashion, quick turnaround products; however, many textile manufacturers make long-run, low cost textiles. Until domestically manufactured short-run speciality fabric is readily available, apparel manufacturers may continue to purchase from foreign suppliers.

The Information Economy. Rationalization of production is only one benefit of the interfirm linkage strategy. The coordination achieved through these linkages permits much higher levels of information to be transmitted between stages of the textile pipeline. Information can be passed back regarding market demands and consumer tastes. Customers may be important sources for suggestions about product and process innovations. Cooperation is a way of keeping in tune with the pulse of the market.

Managers we interviewed reported efforts to improve internal information flows between departments. For example, Greenwood Mills has made major improvements in inventory management by improving internal information. The firm now turns over inventory 11 times per year; as recently as 1986, total inventory turned over only 3.87 times a year. They saved $40 million in inventory costs in the past two years and have used it to buy three new companies.

The system of contractual relations in Japan has been especially efficient in conveying information to different parties in the textile pipeline. The information experts in this system are the big trading companies. These firms specialize in following the trends in customer tastes at home and abroad, providing management expertise, and generally taking the larger view. They explained that they are generalists and can bring to the process all the benefits of this role.

A representative of the Japanese trading company Itochu recounted recent experience with developing a new product. Wool futons have recently become popular. However, there is no good way of washing wool futons. The trading company decided to find a solution and is working on a washing process. They brought together a machinery company and a futon maker to work on the technology. At a later date the trading company hopes to set up a franchise system to provide this service.

Obstacles to Diffusion of Factors Associated with Higher Productivity in Textiles
Given the existence within the United States and in other advanced societies of profitable textile firms with high rates of productivity growth in all sectors of the textile complex, how can we explain why the factors and patterns of success are not more broadly generalized and imitated within the American industry? Our research has focused on behavior at the firm level, and so we cannot properly evaluate the various claims that have been made for the significance of such macroeconomic factors as high capital costs or the level of the dollar. With respect to firm-level factors, however, we have concluded that the principal problems lie in five areas: the strength of the old mass production model; the human resources strategy; particular relations to the market; conflictual or distant interfirm relations; and short time horizons. These clusters of variables are highly complex and interrelated and can be separated into distinct areas only by virtue of considerable simplification of very messy realities.

The Tyranny of Old Ideas: Survival of the Mass Production Model

As described above, many of the most productive textile firms in high wage economies succeed by focusing on particular market niches. In so doing they renounce the potential gains from long runs of standard goods and bank on reaping the rewards of higher price, higher quality goods targeted at specific, hence more limited, groups of consumers. Such shifts from mass production of largely undifferentiated commodity goods to market niches with higher value-added goods are responsible for the turnaround of much of the Italian and German textile industries, while many of the firms in those countries who tried to continue in the mass production mode went out of business.[76]

How can we understand why this new pattern has made so little headway in the US? Our interviews found a number of companies (e.g., Cherokee-Spindale, Cascade Mills) in which managers are pushing to abandon shorter runs and more specialized products for longer runs, as well as companies in which the two models of production continue to co-exist in a rather unstable equilibrium (See the Fieldcrest/Cannon experience, or J.W. Packard Woolen Mills). It is as true in apparel as in textiles: when new technologies are introduced in the US, as, for example, with unit production system and computerized marking and grading, they are usually incorporated into mass production of large lots. The (TC)² new development projects are focusing on long-run garments; the MITI automated sewing project on more flexible machinery.

To these examples one might object that, on one hand, there are some American firms like Dan River, Fieldcrest, and Greenwood Mills, which have narrowed their product lines, moved to produce shorter runs of higher quality and higher priced goods, and are experimenting with ways of responding more rapidly to market changes. Even the industry giants, Du Pont and Milliken, for example, are moving away from a sole strategy of production of commodity goods. These firms show the various possibilities of adapting a niche strategy in the US. On the other hand, there are some US firms, like Russell, whose product lines, market situation, technological choices, and high levels of investment permit them to make major productivity gains while continuing in mass production of fairly standard products. But even allowing for the significant cases of shift away from mass production and for the cases in which it is profitable to continue in this way, we are struck by the slow pace at which the US textile industry has changed its production and market strategies, relative to the rather radical breaks with old patterns in other countries.

Why? In part at least, past American successes in mass production technologies and markets were so overwhelming that alternative modes of production and alternative ways of thinking about markets and production were effectively wiped out. In no other country in the world was the triumph of mass production so complete as in the US. In West Germany and Italy, for example, alongside big companies producing standard goods for low and middle value-added segments of the market there always co-existed other smaller firms in which elements of style, design, market sensitivities, and craft skills remained vital. In the transformation of the Italian and Germany textile industries over the past 15 years, the living examples of these alternative forms of production played a key role, as they served as models for the new market strategies. In the American case, we have had few domestic models to draw on in imagining new strategies for the industry.

Relations with Markets

The persistence of old mass production perspectives derives not only from the absence of alternative ideas and models in the US, but also from the particularities of the ways in which information flows from the market to textile producers. The US textile industry is a multilayered entity with major barriers to information flow between the layers. Often news about changes in markets arrives distorted and muffled by the many layers through which it has had to penetrate before reaching the manufacturer. It arrives so fragmented that there is little chance that manufacturers could reconstruct a reasonably coherent view of changes in their market on which to base major changes in production strategies.

Our interviews, for example, showed that many of the textile mill managers had had few or no contacts--ever--with the apparel firms that purchase their fabrics. (Cascade Mills, J.W. Packard). In these cases, it is sales agents who intermediate between the mills and the apparel manufacturers, sales agents who relay news about changes in the volume and composition of demand, changes in fashion; sales agents who hear from clients about product defects and about products that customers wish they could buy but cannot find on the market. These sales agents are independent entrepreneurs whose interests often differ from those of the companies they represent. Thus a manager from one of the textile mills described to us a rare and accidental meeting with a manager from Hartmarx, a major apparel firm, in which the Hartmarx man expressed astonishment over how low the textile prices were and described willingness to pay more to obtain certain special features. None of the vital information had ever been communicated by the sales agent, who believed he could sell most by pushing the mill prices down.[77] Similar issues arise when convertors are the intermediaries between the producers and their clients.

The argument here is not that intermediaries between producers and their customers are always obstacles to the flow of information about changing market conditions, to the transmission of the news that other market strategies need to be considered. The example of the Japanese trading companies, which perform a vital role in linking different sectors of the industry, in spreading market information, in providing credit to small firms, and in diffusing new technologies would obviously contradict any such generalization (as would the role of non-manufacturing intermediaries in some of the European subcontracting arrangments).[78] Rather the problem with these intermediary strata in the US case derives from the stakes they often have in maintaining distance between producers and the market, rather than in bridging the distance. Precisely because many of the sales agents and convertors are seen as valuable and are used in order to reduce and spread risk, they have an interest in controlling information flows in ways that do not allow direct access to market facts to their clients. Given the implausibility of inventing functional equivalents of Japanese trading companies in the US, the most likely route to removing distance is to circumvent the intermediaries and to enter into direct contact with customers. In the most successful firms we visited, such shifts seem well underway.

The second major specificity of the relations between US textile producers and markets is of course that they, far more than their counterparts in other major countries, have produced for domestic and not for export markets. There are great difficulties in developing sensitivities to foreign demand for those who have no experience with any markets other than US mass product markets.

Human Resources Strategy

In accounting for the persistence of old production and marketing models in the US textile industry and for their role in blocking the generalization of new patterns, ideas about labor are especially important. In the 1970s, when European textile manufacturers were coming to understand the need for major shifts in their modes of operation and were focusing their energies on the modernization of plant and reorganization of workforce to support the new strategies, US textile manufacturers continued to focus on one issue above all in their analysis of their difficulties --labor costs. From this perspective, two objectives assumed paramount importance: obtaining protection against imports from low wage economies and getting lower wages at home, by moving production into low wage regions and getting out of the reach of unions.

We have already discussed how an emphasis on protection obscures essential lessons of European and Japanese textile experience. Here we underscore, if only briefly, the costs of an almost obsessive focus on obtaining low wages and a more compliant workforce within the US labor market and the willingness to devote enormous resources to that objective: closing plants in some regions and cities; moving elsewhere; switching product lines, all in pursuit of a lower wage, non-unionized work force. All other concerns aside, taking into consideration only a comparison between the strategic choices and modernization undertaken abroad by managers who became reconciled, however reluctantly, to high wages and unions and the changes introduced, or not introduced, in US firms in the same critical period of the past 20 years, we see a largely negative score on the US side. US managers focused on the wrong set of issues, and this effort obscured the real choices that had to be made about markets, firm reorganization, technologies, and investment.

US human resource strategies seem to have entailed heavy costs in yet another sense over this period. In contrast to the perceptions of European and Japanese managers, the US managers we interviewed seemed largely to underestimate the importance of education and professional training for the quality of their workforce. Not one of the industry representatives we interviewed in the US mentioned the educational qualifications of their workers as a significant factor in firm productivity. When directly quizzed about this, they frequently explained that the native American talent for tinkering and skills acquired informally on the job were more than adequate for the tasks at hand.[79]   In contrast, in the interviews in Europe and Japan, we were frequently told of process and product innovations that would not have been possible without a high level of skill and initiative on the part of workers. At Melbo, a major men's clothing firm in Japan, the company gets between six and seven thousand suggestions a year for improvements in manufacturing processes from workers.[80] In France and Italy, managers described the interaction between designers and weavers, in which only a worker with a fairly abstract understanding of his machine, as well as long experience with it, could conceptualize the kind of modifications that might create a new fabric with the properties desired by a designer. The case for the contribution of skills and general literacy to productivity in the textile industry rests largely on anecdotal evidence and inference, and so our conclusions can only be tentative. There is, nonetheless, reason to believe that US perspectives and choices about human resources have contributed to the slowness of adaptation in this country.

Interfirm Relations

Among the factors that slow change in US textiles, the pattern of relations among firms located in different segments of the industry stands out as a significant barrier. We have already signaled two aspects of this. First, industrial segmentation reinforced by regional and ethnic differences has made it difficult to develop a forum in which the various parts of the industry might consider common problems. The mutual suspiciousness of managers located in different segments blocks cooperation and hinders the flow of information about markets and technologies. Second, the intermediary agents between textile producers and their markets--converters, sales agents--perform mainly the function of distributing risk. In contrast to equivalent economic agents in other countries, the Americans in this role only rarely provide such services as diffusing technology, offering credit, extending design, fashion, or other creative services.[81] Put simply, paid to deal with risk, the American intermediaries have little interest in reducing it or in permitting firms to acquire by themselves the kind of information about market trends that would allow them to plan.

But there are other dimensions of interfirm relations that are as important for explaining why new understandings of markets do not diffuse more rapidly and why new strategies are not more generally adopted in the US. One deserves particular mention: the behavior of dominant firms with respect to smaller, more subordinate firms. Our interviews turned up many examples of firms using positions of strength to force their suppliers into choices that were damaging to their interests. One denim manufacturer, for example, recounted how, in the past, a very large apparel manufacturer had operated. It would approach the weakest fabric producer, force his prices down, and then use that price to work down the prices of the others. The apparel company guarded as a vital secret its predictions of its annual requirements, lest its suppliers use this information to plan and stabilize their own operations. In this case, there has been a happy ending; today the apparel company has entered into longer-term plans with denim manufacturers, and in exchange for the security of these arrangments, the fabric suppliers load up their trucks by cut and shade so that the apparelmaker can work right out of them, thus greatly reducing the need for inventories and warehousing. This implementation of Quick Response is to the advantage of all the parties, but it involved a transformation of the previous pattern of relations.

Too often, however, the cases recounted to us were ones in which powerful firms continue to use their resources in ways injurious to the interests of firms dependent on them. One of the largest fiber producers, for example, recently developed a special treatment to make carpets more stain-resistant. Unable to produce enough of it to satisfy an enormous demand, the company rationed the product. Due to the rationing, this producer created havoc among carpetmakers with whom it had had previous dealings, causing upheaval in carpet markets in the process. The fiber producer practiced no advance planning and provided no advance notice to carpetmakers. In a world of competing firms, it would be naive to imagine companies entirely renouncing the possibilities that superior market position or technological advance provide in favor of collaboration with suppliers and clients. Nonetheless, when we compare the behavior of US firms with those we studied in Japan and West Europe, we were struck by the greater willingness to sacrifice the advantages of long-term relationships for the benefit of a short-term gain. We noted how little the Americans could appreciate the linkages between their own prosperity and that of other players in the textile arena.

Time Horizons

The choice of short-term gains over longer-term arises as an issue not only in the relations among firms but also and critically in attitudes about investment and research. Among the firms in which we carried out interviews, there were outstanding examples of long-term perspectives. Du Pont and Milliken, to mention the industry leaders, have vast research laboratories and engage projects with terminal points so distant from their initiation that no real calculation about payback or rates of return can be made. The development of nylon and Kevlar at Du Pont involved research and development efforts over more than 20 years in each case, and the company's new focus on composites is expected to have as long a lead time before commercialization. The decision to invest in new technologies at

Russell Corporation apparently precedes calculation about payback periods: the company looks all over the world for the best new equipment, with a great sense of self-confidence among the officers about their own objectives and about how their operations work and might be improved. What the new machinery costs is simply one factor among others, rarely the decisive one. The far horizon of Russell's calculations is illustrated by its policy of identifying bright high school students in Alexander City, Alabama, the site of its main operations, and financing their college and graduate education in the hope of increasing the stock of researchers the company could attract to work in its labs. But Dupont and Russell are exceptional cases.

Far more common in our interviews and in the industry in general are modes of reasoning that focus on short-term gains. The apparel manufacturers rarely envisage any capital investment with a payback period longer than six months to a year. Consider even an industry leader, Milliken, a firm with a major commitment to investment. (Milliken controls between three and five percent of the US textile market but accounts for between ten and 15 percent of its capital expenditures; it reinvests between 96 and 98 percent of its cash flow in contrast to an industry average of 85 percent.) At Milliken, investments are ordinarily expected to pay for themselves in two years.

Most of the textile mills operate on a much shorter leash. One company we visited invests three percent of sales per year. They do not envisage any purchase that does not "pay-out" in under a year and a half, since the backlog of machines they need, and that would pay for themselves within that period, is so great. Even more revealing of this firm's perspectives was its recent decision to buy a virtually bankrupt mill that also weaves woolen fabric for coats. Why had they acquired this firm? Did it fit into some long-term strategic plan? On the contrary: The company president, judging the state of the US garment industry fragile, had previously decided to shift production away from apparel fabrics and to move towards fabrics for office furniture. Buying the failing woolen mill, two hundred miles distant from their own company, was a step backwards, deploying resources for objectives the company had already decided were secondary. As the vice-president recounted, "We bought the mill because it was too cheap to pass by. Now we're in a quandary what to do with it. It's becoming a stone that may pull us all down."

The issue of investment decisions involves factors that have been deliberately excluded from the purview of the study: the cost of capital, alternative uses for capital, business environment, and so forth. One at least ought to be signaled as potentially significant in this industry: public versus private ownership. It may well be that our respondents focused on this issue because our study was conducted during the highly publicized attempted takeover of Burlington Mills. (Shortly after this period, the Central Research and Development Laboratory at Burlington was disbanded.) Comments in interviews, and our own observations of the rather longer perspectives of privately held companies, suggest that this issue may be significant.

Overcoming Obstacles to Change: The Future of Textiles
In this report we have identified four strategic shifts in textile firms in advanced industrial countries that appear to be associated with superior economic performance. The firms that are doing best appear to have adopted one or several of these responses to changed market conditions.

(1) The most striking break with best past practice is the shift to market and production strategies that identify particular market segments and organize production in order to satisfy the specific needs of these limited niches, rather than organizing production of commodity goods for mass markets. This switch is associated with the production of higher quality, higher priced goods and, in general, a reduction in the importance of cost relative to other factors that make a product desirable; with closer relations with customers, thus permitting better identification of customer needs and more rapid response to changes in these needs; with closer relations with suppliers and retailers, permitting more rapid response to market shifts as well as reduction in inventories and stock-outs; and with a reduction in the size of production runs.

(2) Yet another approach to the new market situation has been taken by firms who have invested heavily in new technologies, particularly in labor-saving technologies that reduce the wage bill and thus offer some chance of preserving American advantage in competition with foreign producers. Perhaps the most effective use of new technologies occur in conjunction with shifts in market strategy toward more flexible specialization. Japan, Italy, and West Germany provide outstanding examples of the success in combining the two. The American firms that have gone the farthest in the introduction of new technologies remain, in contrast, relatively closer to the old mass production model.

(3) Accompanying these changes in market, product and technology strategy, there have been shifts in the structure of companies. The dominant trend seems to be toward decentralization and away from vertical integration. This trend is more pronounced in West Europe and Japan than in the US. Indeed some of the most successful textile firms in the US (Milliken, Russell) are vertically integrated, though in other respects (e.g. average length of runs; relations with customers; relations with other firms in sector) they have changed substantially.

(4) Finally the most striking change in the US textile/apparel industry in the past three years lies in the area of relations among firms. Whether under the aegis of the Quick Response program or in the Crafted with Pride Council, the industry has exhibited a capacity for collective action that previously was possible only in its lobbying efforts for protection. The new forms of collective action involve the construction of linkages among sectors of the industry, and in many ways we discuss above, they are beginning to resolve serious problems. These linkages are still too new and fragile to permit much prediction about their resilience in a changed economic climate. But the degree of optimism about them in the industry and the fact that they could be created at all in a sector so divided and diverse are facts that militate in favor of a certain optimism.

After identifying these trends in the best firms here and abroad we tried to analyze why these patterns do not spread more rapidly than they have in the US. Here we found five principal obstacles to the diffusion of change, and they are discussed in section III. In large measure, we believe, the future of the industry as a whole depends on whether these obstacles can be overcome. There are no conceivable set of changes that could maintain US textiles at its current level of employment, nor any that could bring back the days when only an insignificant fraction of the textile goods purchased in the US came from abroad. There are, moreover, segments of the industry that are in all likelihood gone forever. For instance, should recent attempts by the textile machinery industry to modernize fail, the quality and dynamism of most of the US textile machinery sector will remain too low to make recovery realistic. [82] Likewise, the lowest price and quality apparel goods with high labor inputs are almost certainly lost to the developing countries. The open questions are what the dimensions of the textile sector will be, what US market share in world textile markets will be, and what standard of living those who work in the industry will be able to enjoy. The bottom line of our argument is that if we overcome the obstacles to adoption of the four new patterns, textiles/apparel can be a highly productive and profitable industry, with a stable share of world markets.

This optimistic conclusion depends, however, on a diffusion of those trends and practices that we saw exemplified in the best firms. Many of these trends are new and fragile: as, for example, the new interfirm linkages like Quick Response, Crafted with Pride, and the informal arrangements that have emerged in the last three or four years. Others--like the adoption of new technologies--seem to confer only a temporary advantage on the innovating firm which may soon face competition from unexpected quarters. In the past, newly industrializing countries relied heavily on the asset of cheap labor and did not threaten US production in areas dominated by capital intensive technologies. Today, however, there are reasons to believe that these societies are able to move more rapidly to adopt some of these technologies. China, in particular, with its extensive textile experience and many research and training institutes for textiles, may be preparing to leapfrog into areas requiring highly sophisticated technologies and may cease to rely exclusively on its vast cheap labor supply. In that case, US textile manufacturers may face competition in areas in which they previously felt relatively invulnerable.

Finally, and most important, the scope and depth of changes in the US textile industry depend on changes in the larger industrial environment. If textile manufacturers held out disastrously long against the tide of new ideas about mass production, labor, and the importance of education; if their horizons were on average short and their ability to forge stable, fruitful connections with customers and suppliers limited; it was because they shared the ideas and ways of operating of much of America. What is most hopeful in the changes we have observed is the textile industry's discovery of another set of models and practices, from which they are beginning to draw other lessons.

Appendix 1. List of interviewees

United States

Frederick Abernathy, (TC)², Cambridge, Massachusetts
Subash Batra, School of Textiles, North Carolina State University
Ron Blackwell, Amalgamated Clothing and Textile Workers Union, New York
American Association of Apparel Manufacturers, Washington, D.C.
American Textile Manufacturers Association, Washington, D.C.
Thomas Bailey, Conservation of Human Resources, Columbia University, New York
Cascade Woolen Mills, Oakland, Maine
Daniel Chenok, Office of Technology Assessment, Washington, D.C.
Cherokee-Spindale, New York
Crafted With Pride in America, New York
Wayne Current, Singer Sewing Machine Company, Edison, New Jersey
Dan River Corporation, Danville, Virginia
Ali El-Shiekh, School of Textiles, North Carolina State University
Forstmann Fabric, New York
Fieldcrest Corporation, New York
Milton Freedberg, Arthur J. Freedberg Co., Boston
Gordon Textiles International, New York
Greenwood Mills, New York
Head Sportswear, New York
Jerie Sales Company, New York
Henry Kelly, Office of Technology Assessment, Washington, D.C.
Kurt Salmon Associates, New York
James Lardner, *The New Yorker*, New York
John Lawson, Lawson-Hemphill, Central Falls, Rhode Island
Ron Levin, US Department of Commerce Office of Textiles and Apparel,
    Washington, D.C.
Liz Claiborne, Inc., New York
Frank Looney, Textile Fibers Department, Du Pont Chemical Company, Delaware
Milliken Corporation, Spartanburg, South Carolina
Model Garment Company, Pennsylvania
National Retail Merchants Association, Washington, D.C.
Nicole Miller Corporation, New York
Non-Stop Showroom, New York
J.W. Packard Woolen Mill, Ashland, New Hampshire
James Parrott, International Ladies Garment Workers Union, New York
Private Brand Company, Brooklyn, New York
Ludwig Rebenfeld, Textile Research Institute, Princeton, New Jersey
Russell Corporation, Alexander City, Alabama
Susan Salem, US State Department Office of Textiles, Washington, D.C.
Sandy Erhman Lace Company, New York
Frank Simon, Converter, New York
Tandler Textiles
Giuliana C. Tesoro, Polytechnic Institute of New York
Roger Waldinger, New York University
Frank Werber, Agricultural Research Service, US Dept. of Agriculture, Washington,D.C.
Sam Winchester, Textile Fibers Department, Du Pont Chemical Company, Delaware
Paul Zindwer, American Arbitration Association, New York

Italy

Textile Machinery

Dr. Neri, Sales Manager, Vamatex, Colzate (Bergamo)
Oliviero Godi, Sales Manager, Marzoli, Pallazolo Sull'Oglio(Br)
Giorgio Mambretti, Sales Manager, Marzoli
Peter Marzoli, Communications Manager, Marzoli
C.G. Lovera, General Manager, Somet, Colzate (Bergamo)
Masimo Masera, Sant'Andrea Novara, Novara
Luciano Locatelli, Plant Manager, Somet
Francesco Cecchinato Nuovo Pignone, External Relations, Schio (VC)
Dr. Bigagli(owner), Bigagli S.p.A., Prato

Business Associations

Dr. Ciampini, Secretary General, Federtessile
Valerio Astolfi, Secretary General, Associazione Cottoniero
Stefano Miccoli, Economics Section, Associazione Magliecalze
Paolo Lombardi, Director, Associazione Magliecalze
Alberto Brocca, Director, Unione Industriale Biellese
Stefano Cofini, Unione Industriale di Begamo
Arnaldo Cartott, Centro Studi, Unione Industriale Biellese
Pierpaolo Pollari, Ass. Italiana Ind. Tintori, Stampatori,
    Finitori Tess.
Brono Alcaro, Assoc. Dell'Industria Laniera Italiana
Dr. Parenti, Unione Industriale Pratese
Dr. Monti, President, ACIMIT (Textile Machinery Assoc.)
Dr. Brovia, Associazione Abbigliamento (Quick Response)

Apparel Firms

Marco Rivetti, President, Owner GFT
Giancarlo Sivornino, Women's Division, GFT
Giugliano Barucci, Plants Manager, GFT
Marina Mira, Strategic Planning Director, GFT
Lorenzo Trossarelli, Marketing Director, GFT
Ferruccio Tinghi, Director, GFT USA
Andrea Pinto, General Director, Krizia

Textile Firms

Paolo Ferla, Lanificio Egidio Ferla, Biella
Mario Coda, Gen. Dir., Tessiana, Biella
Franco Perazio, Owner, President, Tessiana
Pier Giorgio Colombo, Gen. Dir., Lanificio E. Zegna, Biella
Pier Luigi, Loro Piana, and Sergio Loro Piana
    Presidents of Lanificio Loro Piana, Biella
Paolo Botto, President, Owner, Guiseppe Botto e Figli, Biella
Sergio Gambarella, Gen. Dir., Leglertex, Bergamo
Signor Ongaro, Plant Manager, Leglertex
Alberto Archetti, President, Gruppo Tessile Niggeler and Kupfer, Brescia

Signor Raccanella, Raccanella Spinning
Stamperia Larianella High Tech Dyeing, Printing, Como
IRSA, High Tech Reprocessed Wool Plant, Prato

Schools and Textile Centers

Cleto Benucci, Director, Tessile di Como
Enrico Ottolini, Director, Centro Tessile Cottoniero Busto Arsizio
Loredana Legabue, Director, CITER, Carpi
Sergio Carpini, Promotrade, Prato
Istituto Tecnotex, itta degli Studi, Biella
Isti. Tecnico Industriale Statale di Busto-Arsizio
Instituto Tecnico Industriale Statale di Setificio, Como

Labor

Mario Agostinelli, Secr. General CGIL Lombard Region
Bruno Ravazio, Secr. FILTEA, Region of Lambardy
Gianni Amoretti, National Secretary, FILTEA, Rome
Dino Greco, Provincial Secretary, FILTEA, Brescia
Salvatore Barone, Provincial Secretary FILTEA, Como
Parodini, Provincial Secretary FILTEA, Busto-Arsizio

Japan

Arita Dying and Finishing Company
C. Itohchu Trading Company, Osaka
Kawashima Textile Company, Kyoto
Melbo Apparel Company, Osaka
Imai Michitaku, Carpet Manufacturer, Osaka
MITI Automated Sewing Project, Tokyo
Nishiwaki Dying and Finishing Cooperative, Nishiwaki
Nishiwaki Weaving Cooperative, Mr. Murakami, Nishiwaki
Osaka Textile Research Institute, Osaka
Kuniyuki Shoya, Momoyama University Professor, Osaka
Toyobo Spinning Company, Osaka
Hideyoshi Yoshioka, former weaving mill owner, Nishiwaki

France

Lectra, Cestas, Bordeaux
Thierry Concollombet, Paris

Greece

Chris Argyros, Argyros Yarn Company
Stelios Argyros, President, Federation of Greek Industries

West Germany

Erwin Baier, Business Director, Forschungskuratorium, Gesamttextil, Frankfurt
Klaus Berzel, Gesamttextil, Stuttgart
Herbert Blessing, Production supervisor, Hudson-Textilwerke GmbH, Stuttgart
Christian Dierig, Jr., Christian Dierig GmbH, Augsburg
Gerhard Egbers, Professor of Textile Engineering, University of Stuttgart;
Director of the Institute of Textile Research and Chemical Engineering,
    Denkendorf
Ernst Helmstaedter, Professor of Economics at the University of
    Muenster, Director of the Research Center for General and
    Textile Market-Economics, and member of the West German Council
    of Economic Advisors (Sachverstaendigenrat), Muenster
Hans J. Koslowski, Editor, Chemiefasern, Textilindustrie, Frankfurt
Rainer Schlatmann, Editor, Markt Intern: Textil, Bekleidung, Duesseldorf
Thomas Seile, Personnel Director, Gerhard Roesch GmbH, Tuebingen
Ulrich Urban, Assistant Editor, Textilpraxis International,
    Leinfelden/Echterdingen

Appendix II. Selected Textile Definitions

Braiding, Plaiting
The process of interlacing three or more threads in such a way that they cross one another and are laid together in diagonal formation. Flat, tubular, or solid constructions may be formed in this way.

Carding
The disentanglement of fibres by working them between two closely spaced, relatively moving surfaces clothed with pointed wire, pins, spikes, or saw teeth.

Combing
Straightening and parallelizing fibres and removing short fibres and impurities by using a comb or combs assisted by brushes and rollers, and sometimes by knives.

Drafting
The process of attenuating laps, slivers, slubbings, and rovings to decrease the masss per unit length (see "drawing").

Drawing (Staple Fiber)
Operations by which slivers are blended (or doubled), levelled, and by "drafting", reduced to the stage of roving. In the cotton section of the textile industry, the term is applied exclusively to processing at one machine, namely, the drawframe.

Drawing (Synthetic Polymers)
The stretching to near the limit of plastic flow of synthetic fibres of low molecular orientation. This process orients the crystallites in the direction of fibre length. The ways of carrying out this process have been described as "cold drawing" or "hot drawing".

Open-End Spinning
The production of spun yarns by a process in which the sliver or roving is opened or separated to its individual fibres or tufts and is subsequently reassembled in the spinning element into a yarn.

Opening
The action of separating closely packed fibres from each other at an early stage in the processing of raw material into yarn.

Spinning
Processes used in the production of yarns or filaments. This term may apply to the drafting and twisting of natural or manmade fibres, to the extrusion of filaments, to the production of silk-worms, or to the production of filaments from glass, metals, or fibre-forming polymers. In the spinning of manmade filaments, fibre-forming substances in the plastic or molten state, or in solution, are forced through the holes of a spinneret or die at a controlled rate (extrusion).

Textured Yarns
Yarns that have been processed to introduce durable crimps, coils, loops, or other fine distortions along the length of the fibres or filaments.

Texturing (False-Twist)
A process in which coninuous filament thermoplastic yarns are highly twisted, heat set, and untwisted in a continuous process to produce textured yarns.

Tufted Carpet
A carpet made on a machine in which the pile yarns are inserted in a primary backing, then fixed by an adhesive coating.

Warp Knitting
A method of making a fabric by normal knitting means in which the loops made from each warp thread are formed substantially along the length of the fabric. It is characterized by the fact that each warp thread is fed more or less in line with the direction in which the fabric is produced.

Winder
The machine used for transferring yarn from one package to another.

Bibliography

Abernathy, Frederick and Don Pippins. "Apparel, Textile and Education at its Best," *Bobbin*, September 1986.

Aggarwal, Vinod. "The Unraveling of the Multi-Fiber Arrangement, 1981: An Examination of International Regime Change." *International Organization*, Vol. 37, No. 4, Autumn 1983.

"Apparel," *1987 US Industrial Outlook*. Washington, D.C.: US Department of Commerce, US Government Printing Office, 1987.

Apparel Manufacturing Strategies. Washington DC: American Apparel Manufacturers Association, 1984.

"Apparel Profile for 1985." *The KSA Perspective*, June 1986.

"Apparel Profile for 1986." *The KSA 'Perspective*, June 1987.

Arpan, Jeffrey, Jose de la Torre, and Brian Toyne. *The US Apparel Industry: International Challenge, Domestic Response*. Atlanta: College of Business Administration Business Publishing Division, 1982.

----- and Brian Toyne. "The US Textile Industry: International Challenges and Strategies," in *Revitalizing American Industry*.

Backer, Stanley. "Textiles: Structures and Processes". in *Encyclopedia of Materials Science and Engineering*. New York: Pergamon Press, 1986.

Baier, Erwin. "Der Beitrag der Forschung fuer die Wettberbsfaehigkeit der deutschen Textilindustrie". Paper presented to the Gemeinsamen Tagung der Aachener Textilforschungsinstitute, Aachen, October 1986.

Bailey, Thomas. *Education and the Transformation of Markets and Technology in the Textile Industry*. New York: National Center on Education and Employment, Columbia University, October 1987.

Baily, Martin, and A.K. Chakrabarti., Innovation and the Productivity Crisis. draft manuscript, January 1987.

Barnhardt, Robert A. "Wettbewerb zwischen Industrie- und Entwicklungslaendern auf den Maerkten fuer Stapelfaserwaren". *Melliand Textilberichte* 67, June 1986. pp. 401-404.

Bayerische Hypotheken- und Wechsel-Bank. *Branchenanalysen: hohe Rationalisierungsanstrengungen fuehrten zu einer Ertragsverbesserung im Bekleidungsgewerbe*. Munich: Bayerische Hypotheken- und Wechsel-Bank, August 1985.

Benvignati, Anita Marie. *International Technology Lags: The Case of Textile Machinery*. PhD dissertation, University of Pennsylvania, 1978.

Berger, Suzanne. "Uso politico e sopravvivenza dei ceti in declino". in F.L. Cavazza and S. Graubard. *Il Caso Italiano*. Milan: Garzanti, 1974.

----- and Michael Piore. *Dualism and Discontinuity in Industrial Societies*, Cambridge: Cambridge University Press, 1980.

Bray, Frank, and Vince Vento. "Chapter Two Begins with Singer". *Bobbin,* September 1986.

Breitenacher, Michael. Die Textilindustrie in der Bundesrepublik Deutschland, *Wirtschafts- und Gesellschaftspolitische Grundinformationen*, Number 54. Cologne: Deutscher Instituts-Verlag, 1983.

-----, "Die Zukunft der Textil- und Bekleidungsindustrie". *Melliand Textilberichte* 65, March 1984. pp. 210-13.

-----, *Textilindustrie: Strukturwandlungen und Entwicklungs-perspektiven fuer die achtziger Jahre*, IFO-Institut fuer Wirtschafts-forschung, Berlin: Ducker & Humblot, 1981.

Carl Byoir & Associates, Inc. "Three-Part Quick Response Program Achieves Results," August 22, 198?.

"Changes in Our Textile Customers and Their Future Technological Needs". *Southern Textile News*, April 7, 1986.

Cline, William R. *The Future of World Trade in Textiles and Apparel*. Washington DC: Institute for International Economics, 1987.

Commissariat General du Plan. Commission Perspective des Echanges Internationaux. "L'Enjeu de textile francais". October 1986, p.29. [Rapporteur: Lynn Mytelka].

"The Cutting Edge". *Bobbin*, March 1987.

Destler, I.M. et al. *Managing an Alliance: The Politics of US-Japanese Relations*. Washington DC: The Brookings Institution, 1976.

Deutsche Institute fuer Textil- und Faserforschung Stuttgart, Informational leaflet. "Institut fuer Textil- und Verfahrenstechnik". Denkendorf: Deutsche Institute fuer Textil- und Faserforschung Stuttgart, November 1986.

"Die groessten Textilunternehmen der Welt: 1985." *Chemiefasern/Textilindustrie,* 37/39, February 1987. p. 76.

"Die Untersuchung des Friktionsspinnens unter besonderer Beruecksichtigung der Garngleichmaessigkeit und des Energiebedarfs". *Textilepraxis International*, 41, November 1986, p. 1166.

Dolan, Michael. "European restructuring and import policies for a textile industry in crisis". *International Organization*, Vol 37, No. 4, Autumn 1983.

Dore, Ronald. *Flexible Rigidities: Industrial Policy and Structural Adjustment in the Japanese Economy, 1970-80.* Stanford: Stanford University Press, 1986.

-----. *Taking Japan Seriously.* London: Athalone Press, 1987.

Edinger, Lewis J. *Politics in West Germany.* Second edition. Boston: Little, Brown & Company, 1977.

Emerging Textile-Exporting Countries, 1984. Washington DC: US International Trade Commission, July 1985.

Farrands, Chris. "Textile Diplomacy: The Making and Implementation of European Textile Policy 1974-1978". *Journal of Common Market Studies,* Vol. 18, No. 1, September 1979.

Flynn, Barry. "High Tech May Be Textile Industry's Stitch in Time". *Boston Business Journal*, July 6, 1987. p. 4.

Focus. Washington DC: American Apparel Manufacturers Association, 1986.

Frey, Luigi, ed. *Lavoro a domicilio e decentramento dell'attivita produttiva.* Milan: Franco Angeli, 1975.

Froebel, Folker, Juergen Heinrichs and Otto Kreye. *The New International Division of Labor: Structural Unemployment in Industrialisation in Developing Countries.* New York: Cambridge University Press, 1980.

Gesamttextil. *Der Unternehmerischen Initiative Raum Geben.* 3rd edition. Frankfurt, a.M.: Gesamttextil, 1986.

-----. *Die Sache mit dem Welttextilabkommen.* Frankfurt a.M.: Gesamttextil, 1985.

-----. *Einstieg fuer Aufsteiger: qualifizierende Fortbildung in der Textilindustrie*, 3rd edition. Frankfurt a.M.: Gesamttextil, 1986.

-----. *Ermittlung des Bedarfes an Ingenieuren/Ingenieurinnen in der Textilindustrie fuer die Jahre 1986-1988.* Frankfurt a.M.: Gesamttextil, 1986.

-----. *Textilforschung*, 34th edition, Frankfurt a.M.: Gesamttextil, 1986.

-----. *Zahlen zur Textilindustrie*, 1987 edition, Frankfurt a.M.: Gesamttextil, 1987.

Hallisey, Bill and Susan Sanabria. *(TC)² and the Apparel Industry.* Boston: Harvard Business School, 1987.

Harding, Peter. "The Balance of the Decade: The US View", Speech given at the Knitted Textile Association Annual Convention, Miami, March 22, 1985.

-----. "Vertical Restructuring in Consumer Products". Speech delivered at Kurt Salmon Associates' 13th Annual Financial Breakfast, New York, June 2, 1987.

Hartmann, Udo. "Erfahrungen mit der Umstrukturierung der Textilindustrie in der Bundesrepublik Deutschland und anderen Industrielaendern". Melliand Textilberichte 67, January 1, 1986. pp. 61-69.

Hays, Laurie. "DuPont's Difficulties in Selling Kevlar Show Hurdles of Innovation." *Wall Street Journal*, September 29,1987.

Helmstaedter, Ernst. "Zur langfristigen Sicherung der Wettbewerbsfaehigkeit der deutschen Textilindustrie". *Melliand Textilberichte* 67, May 1986. pp. 295-298.

Hergeth, Helmut H.A. *Investitionsstrategien fuer stagnierende Branchen--dargestellt am Beispiel der Textilindustrie der Bundesrepublik Deutschland.* Muenster: Lit Verlag, 1986.

Hoffman, Kurt. "Clothing, Chips and Competitive Advantage: The Impact of Microelectronics on Trade and Production in the Garment Industry". *World Development*, Vol 13, No. 3, 1985. pp. 371-392.

----- and Howard Rush. *Microelectronics and Clothing: The Impact of Technical Change on a Global Industry.* Sussex: University of Sussex Science Policy Research Unit, 1985.

Howell, Thomas R. and William Noellert. *The EEC and the Third Multifiber Arrangement.* Washington DC: The Fiber, Fabric and Apparel Coalition for Trade, 1986.

----- et al. *The Textile and Apparel Trade Crisis.* Washington DC: The Fiber, Fabric and Apparel Coalition for Trade, 1985.

Hufbauer, Gary Clyde et al. *Trade Protection in the United States: 31 Case Studies-* Washington DC: Institute for International Economics, 1986.

Ingersoll, Robert. "Germany's new alternative to Franco-Italian menswear". *International Management*, No. 41, May 1986.

Isaacs, McAllister III. "Spinning systems battle for world market share". *Textile World*, October 1986. pp. 81-84.

ITMA '87 Review. Raleigh: School of Textiles, North Carolina State University, 1987.

ITS Textile Leader. Special Edition. International Textile Bulletin, September 1987.

Jaikumar, Ramchandran. "Postindustrial Manufacturing". *Harvard Business Review*, November-December 1986.

Kruse, Wolf Dieter. "Wer fuer die Zukunft plant, bilde Menschen aus". *Jahrbuch der Textilindustrie 1987*. Frankfurt a.M.: Gesamttextil, forthcoming.

Lardner, James. "Annals of Business: The Sweater Trade," *The New Yorker*, January11 and January 18, 1988.

Lee, Andrea. "Being Everywhere: Luciano Benetton." *The New Yorker*. November 10, 1986.

Lennox-Kerr, Peter. "German Spinner Cuts Cost, Meets Competition". *Textile World*, No. 136, November 1986. p. 57.

Limprecht, Joseph A., and Hayes, Robert H. "Germany's world-class manufacturers". *Harvard Business Review*, No. 60, November-December 1982.

"Little steps, if you please". *The Economist*, December 6, 1986.

Looney, Franklin S. "A Look at the Future of Spinning Technologies". Paper delivered at Technical Advisory Committee, Institute of Textile Technology, Charlottesville, October 1984.

Lord, Peter. "Air Jet and Friction Spinning". *Textile Horizons*, Vol 7, 1987.

Lubove, Seth H. "In the Computer Age, Certain Workers are Still Vital to Success". *Wall Street Journal*. August 3, 1987.

Mahon, Rianne, and Lynn Krieger Mytelka. "Industry, the state, and the new protectionism: textiles in Canada and France". *International Organization*, Vol 37, No. 4, Autumn 1983.

Moore, George. "An Analysis of Textile Patents". *Textile International Outlook*.

The Multifiber Arrangement, 1980-84. Washington DC: US International Trade Commission, May 1985.

Nabseth, L., and G.F. Ray. *The Diffusion of New Industrial Processes.* Cambridge, England: Cambridge University Press, 1974.

National Research Council. *The Competitive Status of the US Fibers, Textiles, and Apparel Complex: A Study of the Influences of Technology in Determining International Industrial Competitive Advantage.* Washington, D.C.: National Academy Press, 1983.

Nehmer, Stanley, and Mark Love. "Textiles and Apparel: A Negotiated Approach to International Competition". in Bruce Scott and George Lodge, eds. *US Competitiveness in the World Economy.* Boston: Harvard Business School Press, 1985.

Nelson, Wayne Brooke. *Improving Competitiveness in Mature Industries: Lessons from the West German Textile Industry.* M.S. thesis, MIT Dept. of Political Science, 1987.

Office of Technology Asessment. *The US Textile and Apparel Industry: A Revolution in Progress--Special Report.* Washington DC: US Congress, Office of Technology Assessment, 1987.

Organization for Economic Cooperation and Development. *Textile and Clothing Industries*. Paris: OECD Publications, 1983.

Parsons, Carol. *The Employment Effects of International Trade in the Apparel Industry*. Washington DC: US Congress Office of Technology Assessment, 1985.

Pelzman, Joseph. "The Textile Industry". *The Annals of the American Academy*, Vol. 460, March 1982.

Perlow, Gary H. "The Multilateral Supervision of International Trade: Has the Textiles Experiment Worked?" *American Journal of International Law*, January, 1981.

Piore, Michael J., and Sabel, Charles F. *The Second Industrial Divide*. New York: Basic Books, 1984.

Planning & Implementing an Apparel Sourcing Strategy. Washington DC: American Apparel Manufacturers Association, 1986.

Plutte, Ernst-Guenter. "Der Anpassungsprozess braucht eine Flankensicherung". *Textilveredlung*, No. 21, January 1986. pp. 7-11.

Pomfret, Richard. "Trade Effects of European Community Preferences to Mediterranean Countries: The Case of Textile and Clothing Imports". *World Development*, Vol. 10, No. 10, 1982.

-----, "Strategies for a Fair Competition," *The Future of World Trade in Textiles*. Frankfurt: Gesamttextil, 1985.

"Quick Response for Retailing". *The KSA Perspective*, January 1986.

Raasch, Sibylle, and Wahnschaffe, Philipp. "Die Integration der Bundesrepublikanischen Textil- und Bekleidungsindustrie in die neue international Arbeitsteilung". *Mehrwert*, No. 26, September 1, 1985)

Ricks, David A. et al. *The United States Man-Made Fibers Industry: Global Challenges and Strategies for the Future*. Columbia SC: College of Business Administration, University of South Carolina, 1983.

Rosen, Stuart M. et al. *The Renewal of the Multi-Fiber Agreement: An Assessment of the Policy Alternatives for Future Global Trade in Textiles and Apparel*. New York: National Retail Merchants Association, June 1985.

Rothwell, Roy. "Innovation in Textile Machinery". in Keith Pavitt, ed. *Technical Innovation and British Economic Performance*. Sussex, G.B.: Macmillan Press, 1980.

Sabel, Charles F., Gary Herrigel, Richard Kazis and Richard Deeg. "How to Keep Mature Industries Innovative". *Technology Review*, No. 90, April 1987.

Shonfield, Andrew. *Modern Capitalism*. London: Oxford University Press, 1965.

Smith, Eric Owen. *The West German Economy*. London: Croom Helm, 1983.

"Sourcing: The Caribbean Option." *Bobbin*, January 1986.

"Sourcing: 807". *Bobbin*, October 1986.

"Special Issue on the Multifiber Arrangement IV". *Law and Policy in International Business*, Vol. 19, No. 1, 1987.

"Still hooked on exports". *The Economist*, December 6, 1986. pp. 20-23.

Stahr, Ernst-Heinrich. "Textilindustrie: eine Branche Behauptet sich im Strukturwandel". *Der Arbeitgeber*, May 1983.

Stufenausbildung Spinnerei-Industrie. Bielefeld: W. Bertelsmann Verlag, nd.

"Textiles". *1987 US Industrial Outlook*. Washington, D.C.: US Department of Commerce, US Government Printing Office, 1987.

Textile Terms and Definitions. Seventh Edition. Princeton N.J.: The Textile Institute, 1975.

Thurow, Lester. *Zero-Sum Solution: Building a World-Class American Economy*. New York: Simon and Schuster, 1985.

Toyne, Brian. *The US Textile Mill Products Industry: Strategies for the 1980's and Beyond*. Columbia, South Carolina: University of South Carolina Press, 1983.

----- , Jeffrey S. Arpan, Andy H. Barnett, David A. Ricks, Terence A. Shimp. *The Global Textile Industry*. London: George Allen & Unwin, 1984.

Triglia, Carlo. *Grandi partiti e piccole imprese*. Bologna: Il Molino, 1986.

US Imports of Textiles and Apparel Under the Multifiber Arrangement. Washington DC: US International Trade Commission, May 1987.

"US Retail Distribution Channels". Kurt Salmon Associates/NPD Purchase Panel.

Vogl, Frank. *German Business After the Economic Miracle*. New York: John Wiley & Sons, 1973.

Waldinger, Roger. *Through the Eye of the Needle: Immigrants and Enterprise in New York's Garment Trades*. New York: New York University Press, 1986.

Werner International Management Consultants. "Commentary on Hourly Labour Costs in the Primary Textile Industry Winter 85-86."

White, Robert. "Quick Response: What Is It?" *Apparel Industry Magazine*, December 1985.

Wohlfart, Hans. "Serviceleistungen der Textilforschung fuer die Unternehmen". *Jahrbuch der Textilindustrie 1987*. Frankfurt a.M.: Gesamttextil, forthcoming.

World Textiles: Investment, Innovation, Invention. Manchester: The Textile Institute, 1985.

Yamazawa, Ippei. "Renewal of the Textile Industry in Developed Countries and World Textile Trade". *Hitotsubashi Journal of Economics*, No. 24, June 1983.

Notes

1. Werner Associates, Inc. Labour Cost Comparison, Spring 1987. in Federtessile, *L'Industria Tessile Abbigliamento.* Internal document, 1987.

2. Stanley Nehmer and Mark W. Love. "Textiles and Apparel: A Negotiated Approach to International Competition". in Bruce R. Scott and George C. Lodge, eds. *Competitiveness in the World Economy.* Boston: Harvard Business School Press, 1985. p.244.

3. The German case is contrasted with the American in Charles F. Sabel, Gary Herrigel, Richard Kazis, and Richard Deeg. "How to Keep Mature Industries Innovative". *Technology Review*, April 1987.

4. Office of Technology Asessment. *The U.S. Textile and Apparel Industry: A Revolution in Progress--Special Report.* Washington DC; U.S. Congress, Office of Technology Assessment, 1987.

5. Ibid.

6. Commissariat General du Plan. Commission Perspective des Echanges Internationaux. *L'Enjeu de textile francais.* October 1986. p. 29.

7. Ibid.

8. U.S. Office of Technology Assessment, op. cit. pp.38-39.

9. Ibid.

10. Associazione Cotoniera Italiana. *Statistiche Cotoniere Italiane & Internazionali.* table 86. Supplement to *Industria Cotoniera*, No. 78, August, 1986.

11. U.S. OTA. op. cit. p. 46.

12. Thomas Bailey. *Education and the Transformation of Markets and Technology in the Textile Industry.* New York: National Center on Education and Employment, Teachers College, Columbia University, October 1987.

13. U.S. OTA. op. cit. p.49.

14. Ibid. pp.59-61.

15. *Textile Hilights*, December 1986. p. 30.

16. Ibid. p.31.

17. Ibid. pp.24.

18. U.S. OTA. op. cit. p.61.

19. "Apparel". *Industrial Outlook 1986*. pp.43-1--43-3.

20. Kurt Salmon Associates/NPD Purchase Panel. *U.S. Retail Distribution Channels*.

21. U.S. OTA. op. cit. p.4.

22. Ibid.

23. Ibid.

24. Ibid. p.60.

25. U.S. Department of Commerce, International Trade Administration. *A Competitive Assessment of the U.S. Textile Machinery Industry*. Washington DC: U.S. Government Printing Office, 1987.

26. U.S. OTA. op. cit. p.5.

27. Ibid.

28. Ibid. p.98.

29. Ibid. p.7.

30. American Apparel Manufacturers Association. Focus 1986. p.21.

31. Ibid. p. 7.

32. J.S. Fryer, A.H. Barnett, A.S. DeNisi, B.M. Meglino, C.G. Williams, and S.A. Youngblood. *The Textile Labor Force in the 1980s*. Columbia, SC: Division of Research, College of Business Administration, University of South Carolina, April 1981.

33. Werner International Management Consultants. *Commentary on Hourly Labor Costs in the Primary Textile Industry*. Winter 1985-86. p.2

34. American Textile Manufacturers Institute. *Textile Hilights*, March 1987. p.21.

35. Martin Bailey and A.K. Chakrabarti. Innovation and the Productivity Crisis. Draft Manuscript. January 1987. p. 14.

36. "US Textile Industries Turn Around". *New York Times*, Feb. 15, 1988.

37. U.S. OTA. p.3.

38. National Research Council. *The Competitive Status of the U.S. Fibers, Textiles, and Apparel Complex: A Study of the Influences of Technology in Determining International Industrial Competitive Advantage*. Washington, D.C.: National Academy Press, 1983. p. 33.

39. OECD, *Textile and Clothing Industries*. Paris: OECD, 1983.

40. American Apparel Manufacturers Association. *Planning and Implementing an Apparel Sourcing Strategy*. New York: AAMA, 1986. p.1.

41. OECD. op. cit.

42. Office of Technology Assessment. op. cit. See also Subhash Batra, *Research Needs in Fiber Textile and Related Industries*, Final Report of the National Science Foundation Planning Workshop (1987), which summarizes recent advances in textile mechanical processes. For details on the most recent machinery and process equipment offered at the 1987 Paris Machinery Exhibition see the *ITMA '87 Review* prepared by the School of Textiles of North Carolina State University. This report is the source of many of the machinery capacities cited in this section. Another valuable source of process production rates and improvements is to be found in the ITMA '87 special edition of the *International Textile Bulletin, ITS Textile Leader*, September 1987, Zurich.

43. Kurt Hoffman and Howard Rush. *Microelectronics and Clothing: The Impact of Technical Change on a Global Industry*. New York: Praeger Publishers, 1988.

44. The following section draws on interviews in spring and summer 1987 with Professor Frederick Abernathy, with the Director for Research and Vice-President for Marketing at Milliken, with representatives of Singer Sewing Machine Company, with the President of Russell Corporation as well as on Richard Kazis, *The Tailored Clothing Technology: A Case Study in Collaborative Research and Development*, January 1985.

45. The section is based on the research and interviews with the staff of the MITI Automated Sewing Project, 14 August 1987, carried out by Cathie Jo Martin.

46. For a full analysis of past experiments and a survey of the industry, see Hoffman and Rush, op. cit. Note that their optimism about reducing labor costs and regaining the domestic market is barely supported by their own evidence.

47. William R. Cline. *The Future of World Trade in Textiles and Apparel*. Washington DC: Institute for International Economics, 1987. pp. 60-61.

48. Cline, op. cit. p. 163.

49. Ronald Dore, *Flexible Rigidities: Industrial Policy and Structural Adjustment in the Japanese Economy, 1970-80*. Stanford: Stanford University Press, 1986, pp.153, 195.

50. Dore, op.cit., p.194.

51. Interview with consultant to MITI, August, 14, 1988; Dore, op. cit., p.204.

52. Brian Toyne et al. *The Global Textile Industry*. London: George Allen & Unwin, 1984. pp.128, 600.

53. Wayne Nelson. *Improving Competitiveness in Mature Industries: Lessons from the West German Textile Industry*. Master's Thesis, Department of Political Science, MIT, 1987, pp.46-9.

54. Ibid. p.48.

55. Ibid. pp.14-5.

56. We should note that our factory visits to plants of similar dimensions and product lines outside the U.S. also raised doubts about this conclusion. While pollution of the external environment could not be directly observed, the levels of noise and dust within some of the U.S. plants were greater than those we observed abroad. Our visits being far from random, we note only that this issue remains.

57. Suzanne Berger. "Uso politico e sopravvivenza dei ceti in declino". in F.L. Cavazza and S. Graubard. *Il Caso Italiano*. Milan: Garzanti, 1974; Luigi Frey, ed. *Lavoro a domicilio e decentramento dell'attivita produttiva*. Milan: Franco Angeli, 1975; Carlo Triglia. *Grandi partiti e piccole imprese*. Bologna: Il Molino, 1975.

58. Gesamttextile. *Zahlen zur Textilindustrie*. 1987 Frankfurt, A.M: Gesamttextile, 1987. Table 4. On this period see Nelson. op. cit.

59. The following account is based on Nelson's account, chapter 3.

60. Sibylle Raasch and Philipp Wahnschaffe. Die integration der bundesrepublikanischen Textil-und Bekleidungsindustrie in die neue international Arbeitsteilung. *Mehrwert* 26, September 1, 1985. p.120.

61. Gesamttextile. *Zahlen,* 1987. Table 12.

62. Gesamttextile. *Zahlen*, 1986. Table 13.

63. Nelson, op.cit., pp.23-4.

64. Dore. op.cit. p.191.

65. An interview with representatives of the C. Itohchu Trading Company provided many examples of the functions the trading companies perform for small firms, not only in absorbing some part of risk, but also in promoting innovation. For example, in order to develop a wool futon, the trading company brought together companies that could experiment with new processes and machines for preparing wool; eventually they will franchise the new technology to small producers. They also assist small producers to obtain loans.

66. See Dore. op.cit. Chapter 9.

67. Jeffrey Arpan and Brian Toyne. "The U.S. Textile Industry: International Challenges and Strategies." in *Revitalizing American Industry*. p.271. See also Nelson.

68. See Berger and Piore (1979), Sabel and Piore (1984).

69. Domestic runs are shorter, it was explained, because the tastes in Japan vary more.

70. They offer three kinds of orders: ready-made, special order (also called easy order), and order-made. Ready-made suits are simply made to standardized sizes. Special order suits are made up in standardized sizes and then adjusted to fit the customer. An order-made suit is custom made to a customer's measurements.

71. Ramchandran Jaikumar. "Postindustrial Manufacturing." *Harvard Business Review*, November-December 1986. pp. 69-76.

72. Ronald Dore. *Flexible Rigidities*; Dore. *Taking Japan Seriously*.

73. Kurt Salmon Associates. *The KSA Perspective*, March 1986. pp. 1-2.

74. Kurt Salmon Associates. *The KSA Perspective*, January 1986. p. 2.

75. Carl Byoir & Associates, Inc. Memo to Crafted with Pride in U.S.A. Council. *Three-Part Quick Response Program Achieves Results*. August 22, 198?.

76. The cases of the Biella textile mills and the Carpi knitting firms illustrate this point particularly well for Italy; for West Germany, see the Nelson thesis.

77. Consider also the question of fabric defects. A sales agent who wishes a customer to return next year has every reason to accept all claims for reimbursement--especially since it is the mill owner who pays the price of the returned fabric. Even when the sales agents were part of the same company, the disparity between their interests and those of the manufacturing branch cause problems, e.g., Burlington, which eventually moved quality control and rejects out of the New York sales office and relocated them in offices proximate to manufacturing.

78. Account based on Dore. *Flexible Rigidities*; also, interview at the C. Itohchu Trading Company, August 1987.

79. For a different reading of the industry perspective, see Thomas Bailey. *Education and the Transformation of Markets and Technology in the Textile Industry*. New York: National Center on Education and Employment, Columbia University, 1987.

80. Interview with Masatsugu Tsukigi, Melbo Apparel Company, August 1987.

81. There is of course a large economic literature on this issue, to which the main contributor has been Oliver Williamson. Ronald Dore compares patterns of interfirm relations in Japan, Britain, and the United States and identifies strengths of interfirm coordination in Japan in contrast to vertical integration in Britain and the U.S. in *Taking Japan Seriously*, Chapter 9.

82. See the description of the newly organized Textile and Apparel Machinery Modernization Foundation in *ATMA Executive Report*, Vol. 14, No. 1, January-February 1988.

MIT   Commission on Industrial Productivity
Working Paper

Education and Training in the United States:
Developing the Human Resources We Need
for Technological Advance and Competitiveness

Prepared by
Richard Kazis

for the
Commission Working Group on Education and Training

Suzanne Berger, Chair
Hans Betz
Laura Hastings
Richard Kazis
Richard Lester
Cathie Jo Martin

Table of Contents

List of Tables

List of Figures

Acknowledgments

In the course of carrying out the research for this project, the Working Group on Education and Training visited governmental and educational institutions in the United States, Italy, West Germany, Britain, Japan, and Sweden and interviewed more than a hundred individuals. We are grateful to them all for the time they devoted to explaining their efforts to us. Several institutions and people deserve special mention for their help in organizing our interviewed and their willingness to provide assistance on a continuing basis. Out MIT colleague, Paul Osterman, guided our understanding of the problems in vocational training and in youth unemployment. Professor Eleanor Westney, at the MIT School of Management, helped us think through the relevance of the Japanese experience. In Japan, Genya Chiba, at the ERATO Project, provided intellectual guidance and practical help in our visits to 20-odd plants and research laboratories. At Tokyo University, Professor Ishii was an invaluable interlocutor on the issues of concern to the Commission. In Germany, the Federal Office of Labor was especially helpful, as was the Manpower Services Commission in Britain.

Introduction and Summary

The Growing Centrality of Education and Training to Strategies for U.S. Industrial Competitiveness
In the 1980s, Americans were faced with signs of two crises: one educational and one economic. On the economic front, declining industrial competitiveness, as evidenced by a slowing rate of productivity growth, dramatic import penetration and the collapse of domestic capacity in many industries sparked a debate about how to revive the U.S. manufacturing base. In the area of education, declining performance on standardized tests, significant levels of illiteracy among youths and adults, and high and increasing dropout rates in urban high schools triggered a similar reevaluation of American schooling.

These two crises quickly became linked in the popular press and imagination. *Fortune* raised the possibility that "the schools were the main cause of the decline of America's industrial might." Cover stories in *Time* and *Newsweek* in the early 1980s also focused on the connection between education and economic growth. And a host of blue-ribbon panels and commissions convened by government, industry, and the education establishment made the connection explicit.

According to *A Nation at Risk,* the report of the National Commission on Excellence in Education appointed in 1981 by Secretary of Education Terrel H. Bell, easy grading and too little homework, inadequate attention to the basics of reading and writing, and a "rising tide of mediocrity" in teaching, administration, and learning were to blame for the "steady 15-year decline in industrial productivity." *Action for Excellence*, the report of the Education Commission of the States Task Force on Education for Economic Growth, chaired by North Carolina Governor James B. Hunt, concluded:

> There are few national efforts that can be legitimately called crucial to our national survival. Improving education in America—improving it sufficiently and improving it now—is such an effort....The stakes are high. If we fail, our children will experience a growing sense of loss and failure: a sense of falling behind that will reflect the reality of falling behind.

This country has a long history of seeing inadequate educational attainment as a root cause of social and economic problems and an equally long history of proposing educational reform as the solution to those problems. Just before World War I, with Germany ascendant militarily and economically, the chair of the National Manufacturers' Association Education Committee complained that "we are not in the race" and argued for improved vocational education, along the lines of the German apprenticeship and technical training system. In 1958, after the launch of Sputnik, education again commanded national attention. *Life* ran a cover story on American education, concluding that "(t)he schools are in terrible shape. What has long been an ignored national problem, Sputnik has made a recognized crisis."

Today, the claim is again made that our educational system is failing to produce a work force with the necessary skills, aptitudes, and motivations. Moreover, it is argued that, for two reasons, this failure is of greater import today than in the past: 1) technological breakthroughs and changes in the balance of international economic power are increasing the economic and social importance of education and training; and 2) independent of economic and technological developments, demographic shifts in the American population and work force will require that increased attention and resources be devoted to education and training in the coming years. This report examines these claims concerning the relationship between education and productivity in the United States today. The report is based on research by staff of the Commission on Industrial Productivity on education systems and economic performance in a number of industrial countries, including the U.S., West Germany, Japan, England, and Sweden. The report also makes use of an analysis by Commission staff of current and projected changes in the demand for work force skills and in the quality of labor supply in the United States. In addition, the report incorporates the findings of interviews conducted by Commission staff with eleven leading American manufacturing firms about their changing education and training needs and strategies. The conclusions can be summarized briefly.

The State of Education and Training in the U.S. The current American system of education and training has both strengths and weaknesses when examined in comparative perspective. American primary and secondary schooling prepares its elite students relatively well. However, the system fails many who pass through it. Average levels of proficiency and accomplishment are lower than in many industrial countries. Dropout rates are higher. The variance between the quality of education provided those at the top and the rest is far greater than in countries such as Japan and West Germany.

There is a serious gap in pre-employment training for the non-college bound—the approximately 20 million 16- to 24-year-olds often referred to as the "Forgotten Half." For the most part, these youths are left to make it in the world of work without the credentials, connections, and assistance that benefit college graduates. West Germany and Sweden have dealt with the transition from school to work for these youth more successfully.

America's colleges and universities compare quite favorably with university systems of other industrial countries. Diverse and decentralized, the system provides post-secondary education to a broad segment of the population. American research universities and graduate programs attract students from all over the world. Our more than 1200 community colleges are playing an increasingly important role in the training of certain groups of American workers, including technicians. While weaknesses in and new challenges to the system of higher education can be identified, college and university education does not appear to be a serious impediment to American economic performance.

Formal schooling is only one part of a nation's education and training structure. With over three-quarters of the American work force for the year 2000 already out of school and working, it is clear that firm-level training and a variety of continuing education opportunities are critical to the creation and maintenance of a quality work force. These efforts must incorporate remedial education—reading, writing, basic math and communications skills—as well as training for new technologies and forms of work organization. Yet, U.S. firms tend to underinvest in training, particularly of production workers. And training that takes place within U.S. firms is often of a narrow "follow Joe around" character. In contrast, German workers go through a firm-based apprenticeship program before entering employment and Japanese workers receive training and extensive and continual retraining through elaborate formal in-plant programs. In those countries, unlike the U.S., training and retraining are seen as routine, continuing, and essential to firm-level and national productivity.

The Relationship between Education and Training and Productivity. These relative and absolute strengths and weaknesses of the American education and training system affect industrial performance. The economic and sociological literatures, while limited in their ability to explain the mechanisms by which educational attainment and productivity are linked, show that the positive correlation indeed exists. Moreover, there is a growing body of cross-national empirical evidence which indicates that a better educated and trained work force contributes to productivity growth, particularly through the creation of value by involved employees and through labor cost savings from reduced layers of supervision made possible by higher levels of skill and initiative from the shop floor up.

Changing Corporate Strategy and the Demand for Skill, Education and Training. Changes in technology, particularly microcomputer-based technologies, together with the globalization of competition and changes in the nature of product markets, have altered the environment within which American manufacturing firms do business. This new competitive environment is driving a variety of strategic responses that affect decisions about product lines, technology, the organization of production and innovation systems, relations with both suppliers and customers, and relations with government and educational institutions.

In some firms and industries, the strategic response focuses on further reductions in production costs through automation, labor shedding, and overhead reduction. In others, the response is to move away from price-based competition in standardized, commodity-type products toward greater specialization, improved product quality, and the provision of unique products or services. In some cases, both strategies are being pursued as firms have either decided to hedge their bets or are not sure which strategy will be most profitable in the long-run.

As firms move toward strategies based on quality and service, as many of the nation's most successful firms are doing, there is a direct and significant impact on the distribution of work force skills and the demand for new skills from existing workers and from new work force entrants. The emphasis on quality, service, and specialization demands that all employees—from production workers to technicians, sales representatives, engineers, scientists, and managers—work in new ways, with new processes, materials and equipment, and in new and different interpersonal settings. In many cases, these changes require a higher basic level of education and new kinds of technical, interpersonal, and analytic skills.

Demographic Trends and the Demand for Education and Training. The demographic trends of the next decade will place increased pressure on firms, educational institutions, and government to ensure that new entrants to the work force are prepared for the jobs of the future. The pool of new entrants will shrink. The proportion of the work force comprised of members of minority or immigrant groups—groups that on average have lower levels of schooling, less on-the-job experience, and more extensive labor market problems—will increase. These demographic factors alone will make pre-employment and on-the-job education and training increasingly important. Combined with the technological and organizational factors that are making American managers think more coherently and strategically about education and training, these factors make the revaluation of education and training imperative—so that American industry can compete globally and so that American society and its work force are not in a two-tier structure of opportunity based not only on class and race but also on education.

The Structure of U.S. Education and Training

The Education System

The U.S. educational system is characterized by extreme organizational decentralization. The federal government has almost no authority over public education and provides less than seven percent of the funding for public schooling. Regulations and controls that exist at the federal level are addressed primarily to discrimination in education against minorities and the handicapped. Only during the Reagan administration was a cabinet-level Department of Education created. Despite the creation of various national-level blue-ribbon commissions on the future of education, there is no general mandate for federal action on education. In fact, the United States is one of the few nations in the world without a national rule of compulsory education.[1]

In the United States, educational policy is legally the province of the individual states. State government supervises the educational system and shapes its general contours. Issues such as the length of the school year and compulsory schooling are decided in state legislatures. State government provides almost half of total funding for public education.[2]

Although states have primary legal responsibility for educational policy, the locus of control and authority over education in the United States is actually at the local level. In all states except Hawaii, local school boards control the financing, administration, and content of public primary and secondary education. Local property taxes finance more than 40 percent of the cost of public education.

Historically, Americans have fought hard to keep decisionmaking authority concerning public education at the local level: as educational sociologist John Meyer of Stanford has written, in the United States, education is considered everybody's business.[3] In recent years, though, largely as a result of concern over the quality of U.S. education and the importance of education for economic performance, state legislatures, boards and departments of education have begun to use their legal authority to assert more control over education. States are exerting greater influence over curriculum standards, textbook selection requirements, graduation requirements, and school exit examinations. Roughly 40 states have raised high school graduation requirements; 46 have mandated competency tests for new teachers; 23 have created alternative routes to teacher certification; and six state legislatures have given the state education authorities the power to "take over" educationally deficient schools (though none have done so to date).[4] While resistance to federal control over education is deeply ingrained in American political life, the power tilt away from the local to the state level of decisionmaking in education is likely to continue.

This decentralized, multi-tier structure of educational organization is uniquely American. In no other industrial county are there anywhere near the more than 15,000 public school districts that exist in the United States. In most industrial nations, educational decisionmaking is more centralized. In Japan, the central government establishes national curricula for both public and private primary and secondary schools. In Germany, while the states have primary authority over educational policy, the Federal Ministry of Education and Science plays a central role in the direction and shaping of the Dual System of vocational education. In Great Britain, the national government has always played a fairly active role in financing, curriculum planning, examination standards, and other educational policy issues. Moreover, recent educational reforms have strengthened and expanded the role of the national government *vis a vis* the 104 Local Education Authorities.

Decentralization has both advantages and disadvantages. Experimentation and innovation are easier; but coherent national action to change educational priorities or policies is next to impossible. Decisions about education are made at the level closest to those affected; but in an era when education is seen as a critical national resource, such a structure can result in dangerous and costly parochialism. Education may be everybody's business; but the lack of organizational uniformity makes it difficult for educational reform efforts to build a constituency for specific, easily implemented recommendations.

Figure 1 provides a cross-sectional view of the structure of education in the United States. (For West German and Japanese comparisons, see Figures 2 and 3.) As is evident, different ways of organizing primary and secondary education exist: most school systems go from an eight-year elementary school to a four-year high school; others break the first eight years into elementary and middle schools; many systems provide six years of elementary school, three years of junior high, and three years of senior high school; and some have created a combined six-year junior and senior high school after the first six years of elementary education.

Figure 1 does not provide any sense of the flows through the system, but the numbers are readily available. Ninety-nine percent of children age six through thirteen are enrolled in school. Among children 14 through 17, the figure drops to 93.7 percent. Just under 75 percent of American youths graduate high school by age 17. However, many who do not complete high school with their cohort go back to school in their twenties and later. By age 24, 86 percent of Americans have earned high school diplomas.

Figure 1   Structure of Education in the U.S., 1987

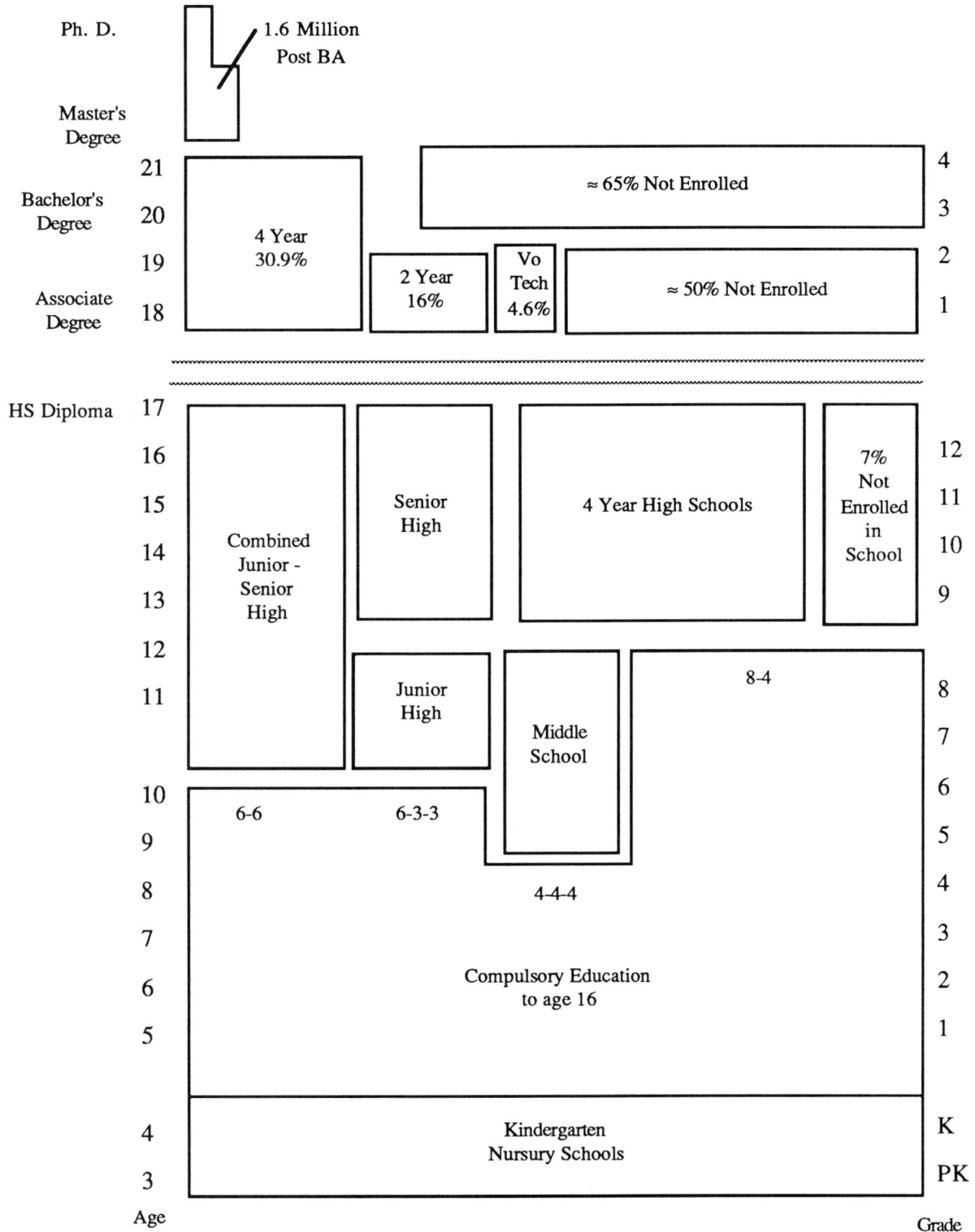

Source: *1987 Digest of Educational Statistics*

Figure 2 Progression Rates in the Japanese Educational System, 1985

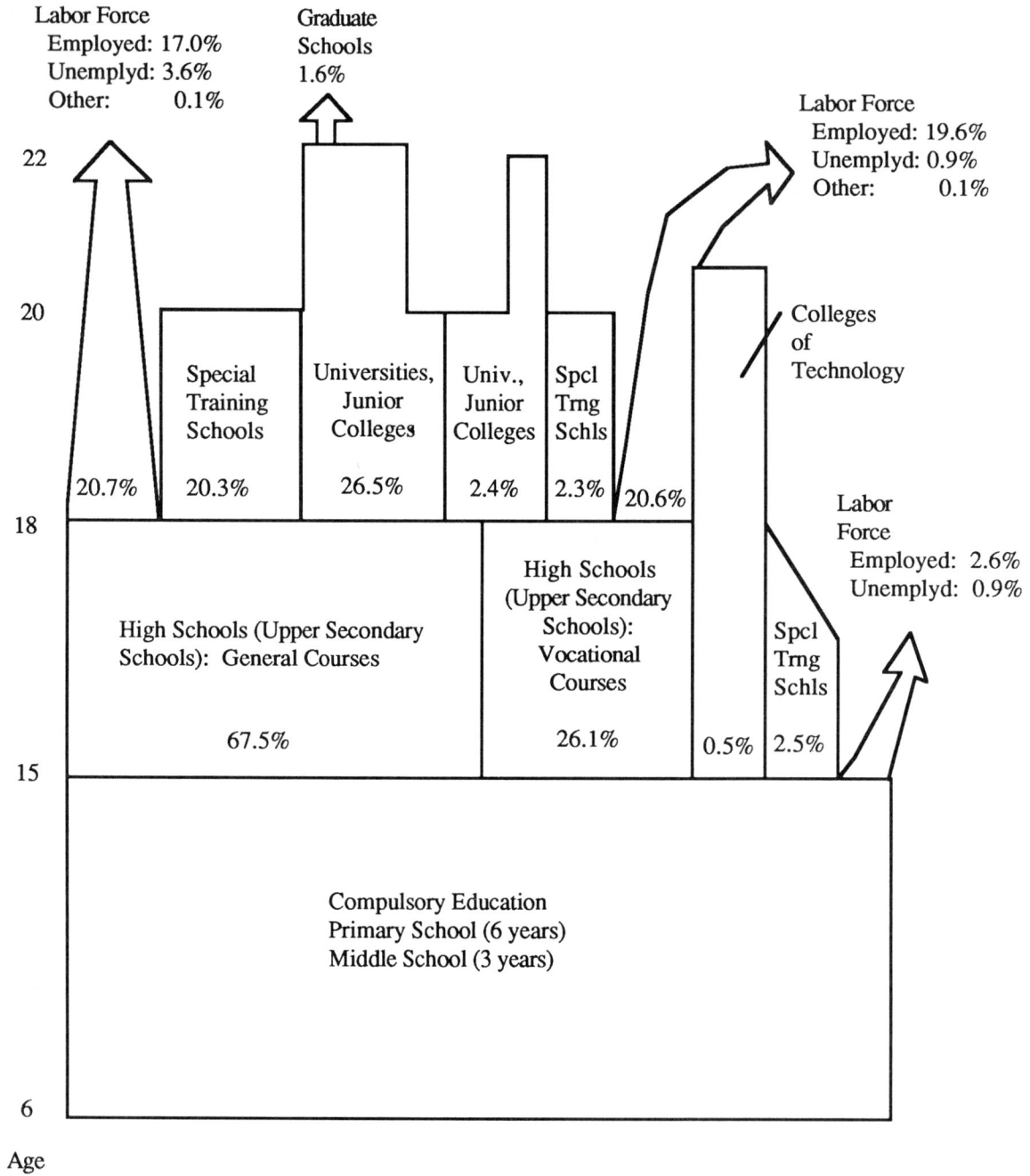

Labor Force
  Employed: 17.0%
  Unemplyd: 3.6%
  Other: 0.1%

Graduate
Schools
1.6%

Labor Force
  Employed: 19.6%
  Unemplyd: 0.9%
  Other: 0.1%

22

20

Special
Training
Schools

Universities,
Junior
Colleges

Univ.,
Junior
Colleges

Spcl
Trng
Schls

Colleges
of
Technology

20.7%   20.3%   26.5%   2.4%   2.3%   20.6%

Labor
Force
  Employed: 2.6%
  Unemplyd: 0.9%

18

High Schools (Upper Secondary
Schools): General Courses

High Schools
(Upper Secondary
Schools):
Vocational
Courses

Spcl
Trng
Schls

67.5%   26.1%   0.5%   2.5%

15

Compulsory Education
Primary School (6 years)
Middle School (3 years)

6

Age

Source: Ministry of Education, Science and Culture, *Mombu Tokei Yoran*, 1986.

Figure 3   Basic Structure of the Education System in Germany *

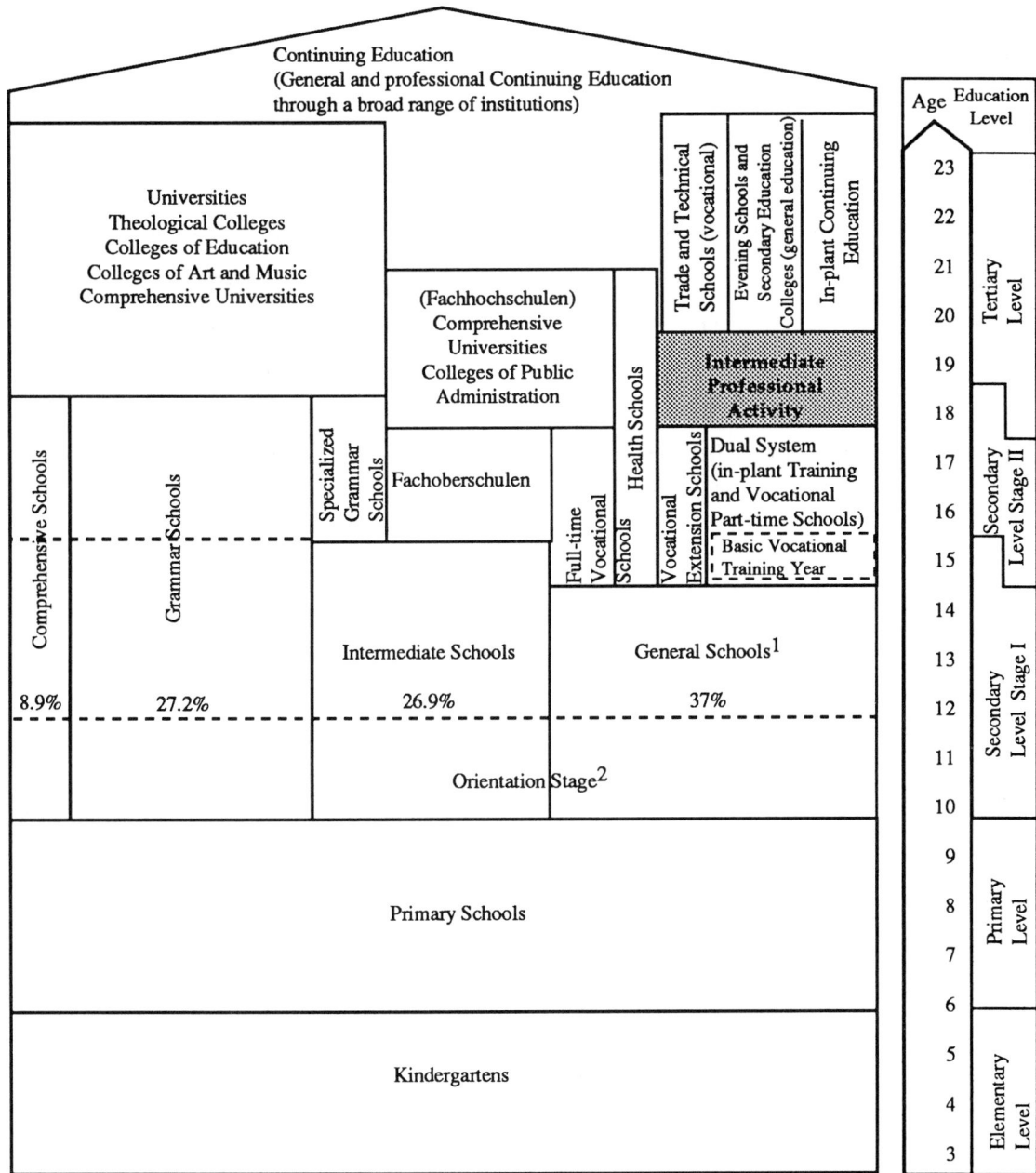

Continuing Education
(General and professional Continuing Education
through a broad range of institutions)

Age	Education Level

Universities
Theological Colleges
Colleges of Education
Colleges of Art and Music
Comprehensive Universities

(Fachhochschulen)
Comprehensive
Universities
Colleges of Public
Administration

Trade and Technical Schools (vocational)

Evening Schools and Secondary Education Colleges (general education)

In-plant Continuing Education

23
22
21
20
19
18

Tertiary Level

Intermediate Professional Activity

Comprehensive Schools

Grammar Schools

Specialized Grammar Schools

Fachoberschulen

Full-time Vocational Schools

Health Schools

Vocational Extension Schools

Dual System
(in-plant Training
and Vocational
Part-time Schools)

Basic Vocational
Training Year

17
16
15

Secondary Level Stage II

8.9%   27.2%

Intermediate Schools
26.9%

General Schools[1]
37%

14
13
12

Secondary Level Stage I

Orientation Stage[2]

11
10

Primary Schools

9
8
7

Primary Level

6
5

Kindergartens

4
3

Elementary Level

[1] About 20 percent of pupils in General Schools in addition
attended an additional tenth school year.
[2] About 64 percent of pupils in fifth and sixth school years
attended the Orientation Stage.
* There are slight differences within the individual Länder.

Figures in the right-hand column show the earliest possible age
of entry in an uninterrupted progress through the education
system.
The size of the rectangle is not proportional to the numbers
attending.

Source: *Grund- und Struktur Daten 1983/84*: Der Bundesminister für Bildung und Wissenschaft

These aggregate statistics hide racial variations. In central city areas where 56 percent of black Americans live, the dropout rate is closer to 20 percent annually—almost four times the national average. In 1984, a survey of blacks between the ages of 24 and 29 found that 78.8 percent had completed high school, lower than for whites, but an almost seven-fold increase from the 11.6 percent of 1940. For Hispanic Americans, completing high school seems to be even more difficult. Only 51 percent of all Hispanic adults over 25 in 1987 were high school graduates, compared to three out of four adults in the national population. Similarly, among those aged 18-24, 70 percent of Hispanic youths had completed high school, compared to 86 percent of all Americans.

Like its secondary education system, American higher education is decentralized and diverse. There are about 3400 colleges and universities in the United States. These include: major research universities; an extensive network of state colleges and universities; a wide range of liberal arts colleges, many with church affiliations; and a system of almost 1300 two-year community and technical colleges. About 78 percent of students are enrolled in public institutions. Just over half of the new entrants into American colleges and universities each year are enrolled in two-year colleges. In addition to these colleges and universities, there is a growing network of proprietary post- secondary institutions that offer vocational and technical training.

Post- secondary education in the United States differs greatly from the college systems of other industrial nations. First, access to higher education is unusually broad in the U.S. Over five percent of the nation's population (more than 12 million people) enroll annually in colleges and universities. In 1985, about 58 percent of all high school graduates went on to two- or four-year colleges. In Japan, where post-secondary enrollment is also high, only 29 percent of high school graduates enrolled in two- or four-year undergraduate programs (although another 12 percent entered vocationally-oriented privately-run special training schools similar in many ways to U.S. proprietary training schools). In the U.S., the range of post-secondary programs open to students is also great compared to other industrial nations where fewer youth go on to college and the choice of institutions of higher learning is more limited. In addition, the intertwining of schooling and work is more common in the U.S. More Americans drop in and out of college than their counterparts in other countries. It is not unusual for college students to begin a course of study, work for a while, then return to complete their degree or take another degree. Over two-fifths of American college students are enrolled part-time; more than half are 22 years or older, and more than one-third are 25 or older.[5]

Unlike most European university systems, which are still based on principles of elite education, there are no common national university curricula or performance standards in the U.S. In England, France, and Germany, for example, courses of study are fairly standardized, since students in the same fields are expected to have achieved the same levels of proficiency. In the United States, such centralized coordination does not exist and would be impossible to engineer, given the diversity of institutions and their administrative autonomy. There are advantages to high, common standards, foremost among them comparability of credentials and a clear sense of what it means to have completed a particular course of study. There are disadvantages as well: university curricula get crusty; change is slow; responsiveness to new trends and developments is limited. A 1985 report by the National Economic Development Council in Britain comparing the British education and training system to those of Japan, West Germany, and the United States, explained somewhat enviously that the U.S. system was able to "meet multiple and often conflicting goals" because of the diversity, complexity and autonomy, of its post-secondary educational system.[6]

The Training System

It is difficult to make a clean analytical distinction between education and training, since much of what is learned in formal education—and much of the informal learning people do in their families and communities—is in effect training for employment. For many workers, vocational courses in secondary school are all the pre-employment training they receive. And post-secondary education, particularly at the community college level, is increasingly vocational in orientation.

For our purposes, though, the intuitive distinction that sees employee training as picking up where formal schooling leaves off is helpful. In this framework, employee training refers to three different kinds of learning that take place once one has entered the labor force: 1) upgrading of existing skills, which includes remedial education provided to employees; 2) facilitating adaptation to new technologies or new problems at work; and 3) retraining of workers whose skills have become obsolete.

In this section, we examine the extent of employee training in the United States and the distribution of training opportunities within the manufacturing sector. Although the available estimates of training expenditures are notoriously inexact, they provide some sense of the structure of training in the U.S. and they make it possible to compare U.S. training efforts with those of other nations.

Like its education system, the training system in the United States is fragmented and uncoordinated. In fact, it is often referred to as a "non-system." A very large percentage of American workers are hired with no formal training beyond compulsory schooling. In a 1983 study conducted by the Bureau of Labor Statistics, 45 percent of all workers surveyed needed no specific training to qualify for their current jobs. In the occupational category of machine operators, assemblers, and inspectors, only 37 percent needed specific training.[7]

Formal apprenticeships, with curriculum certified by the government and agreed to by union and employer association, constitute a minor—and declining—training route for American skilled workers. The number of youths entering apprenticeships each year is negligible compared to the number of entrants into the work force: fewer than 150,000 new registrants compared to close to two million new work force entrants. And the number of available apprenticeships is shrinking. For example, the Machinists Union reports that its apprenticeship slots have dropped 45 percent to 12,000 since 1982. Since 1979, pipefitter apprenticeship slots have fallen to 11,200, a drop of 30 percent.[8]

The military, while a source of training for only two percent of the American work force, is an important training institution for some jobs. For example, about 45 percent of aircraft engine mechanics were trained in the service. About five percent of precision production, craft and repair workers were trained in the military and about one in five electronic repairers of commercial and industrial equipment.[9] Of course, quantity does not necessarily mean quality: there is currently a vigorous debate about the breadth and relevance of military training for post-service employment.

Government plays a limited role in the provision of training in the United States. Federal training programs are targeted to helping hard-to-employ populations enter the labor force. Direct and indirect costs of governmental training efforts are estimated to be roughly five billion dollars a year.

The single most common source of training for both obtaining jobs and for improving skills is on-the-job training. About 28 percent of U.S. workers have received their qualifying training on the job. For precision production, craft, and repair workers, the proportion is much higher: 40 percent of these workers learned their skills on the job. Occupations for which schooling plays a more important role include: managers, professionals, technical and sales employees, and people working in publicly-regulated jobs.[10]

On-the-job training can be formal or informal. In the United States and particularly on the manufacturing shop floor, informal training dominates. One learns primarily by "following Joe around." Thus, for many American workers, pre-employment training is non-existent or inadequate and work place employee training is informal and narrow.

The American Society of Training and Development, the trade association for the training industry, is perhaps the best source of estimates on the size of training efforts by U.S. employers. ASTD's chief economist, Anthony Carnevale, estimates that one in eight American workers receive some kind of formal training each year in 17.6 million employer-provided formal courses. He estimates that the direct and indirect costs to private firms for providing this formal training (not including wages and salaries paid during training time) are about $30 billion a year. While others have estimated that the figure is closer to $40 or $50 billion, it is widely acknowledged that there is little hope of developing an accurate accounting of training expenditures.[11]

In addition to the costs of formal training, there are costs associated with the informal training that characterizes so much of American workers' learning on the job. The Office of Technology Assessment uses a rough rule of thumb to arrive at a ball park figure. Since employee compensation in 1985 was roughly $3.5 trillion and there are estimates that between two and four percent of work time is devoted to informal training, then informal training costs firms between $50 and 100 billion a year. Carnevale believes that informal on-the-job training may cost as much as $180 billion a year.

Training efforts in the United States are unevenly distributed. Firms with fewer than 10,000 employees do very little formal training. A firm with 500 employees may have a personnel director; a firm with over 1000 workers may have an in-house trainer. Only at the level of more than 10,000 workers is training considered a routine cost of doing business and are elaborate formal training procedures put into place. For the small firms that make up the majority of American manufacturing firms, formal training more complex than having a vendor show workers how to operate new machinery is rare. Little training is provided to anyone under 25 or over 44. At both ends of the age spectrum, firms are afraid of not recouping the cost of their investment.

Training of non-supervisory workers is limited. Much of the $30 billion in formal training is spent on managerial training. In a 1977 Conference Board study, 60 percent of the companies surveyed—all of which had 500 or more employees—provided in-house management retraining while only 35 percent provided in-house courses for professional-technical workers and only 11 percent provided such courses for other hourly workers.[12] In 1981, white collar workers constituted around 75 percent of those receiving training while blue collar workers constituted less than 20 percent. The emphasis on training for managerial and professional workers creates an ironic imbalance. Better educated workers receive a disproportionately large share of the training. Workers with four or more years of college, while only 18 percent of the work force, constitute 35 percent of trainees. Workers with less than a high school degree, 23 percent of the labor force, constitute only five percent of the trainees.[13]

The Education and Training System as a Whole

Increasingly, it is difficult to examine either the education or training system in the United States without looking at the two together. For one reason, as noted above, the educational system provides significant employment-related skill and attitude training. In addition, as the demographics of the U.S. work force and the economic demands on U.S. employers change, education and training are becoming inseparable. The number of adult learners in post-secondary education has increased dramatically in recent years, postponing a predicted retrenchment in college enrollments as the smaller post-baby boom generation reached college age. And the rapidly changing technological and strategic developments in American manufacturing are giving rise to greater firm reliance on educational institutions for employee training.

Even prior to the changes of the past decade, the American model of education and training differed dramatically from that of other industrial nations, primarily in terms of the relationship between firms and educational institutions. In the United States, even though informal on-the-job training is the most prevalent form of training for workers, educational institutions are relied on more regularly and extensively for training than in either West Germany or Japan. This can be attributed to both the relative strength of post-secondary institutions in the U.S. and the relative weakness of in-house formal training in American industry.

Our colleges, technical schools, universities, and private proprietary schools are an important and valuable resource and firms make use of the expertise residing in those institutions to help train and retrain employees. According to one estimate, 43 percent of all courses given in employee training in the U.S. are provided by outside institutions.[14] Both two- and four-year post-secondary schools have expanded their offerings significantly in the past two decades. Community colleges, once simply a funnel into four-year state colleges, have become increasingly important providers of vocational training: today 66 percent of community college enrollments are in vocational programs compared to only 13 percent in 1965. In addition, many schools are aggressively reaching out to firms with offers to provide customized training for their employees. In Boston, Northeastern University has convinced some Route 128 firms to provide a classroom on-site for Northeastern-run seminars and courses.

There is, however, another reason why the U.S. education and training system provides a larger role to educational institutions than do most of our major competitors. The reason has to do not with the strength of the educational institutions, but the lack of a well-developed company-based post-secondary skill training system in the U.S. Although they are quite different systems, both Japan and West Germany have such company-based training systems.

The German system is built upon universal apprenticeships for those not going on to college after compulsory schooling ends at age 16. These apprenticeships are available in over 400 occupations, each certified by the state and having a common national curriculum developed primarily by employer associations and agreed to by officials from relevant employer associations, unions, and government agencies. This "dual system" is primarily an on-the-job training program with a one-day-a-week classroom component. Apprentices spend two- to three-and-a-half years working under the supervision of a specially qualified instructor (*Meister*). Classes are taught by university-trained vocational instructors and include basic theory, specialized fundamentals of the particular occupation, and some general education. At the completion of the apprenticeship, workers who successfully pass the qualifying examinations are certified as journeymen (*Facharbeiter*) . Further promotion within the firm requires experience and training beyond the apprenticeship and successful performance on additional examinations.[15]

In Japan, private companies organize and pay for their employees' skill training. There is no national curriculum to guide the training. Rather, each company works out its own carefully-planned program of "training and molding" its work force through experience, on-the-job training, and in-house educational programs.[16] Rather than rely on outside institutions, Japanese firms often have their own educational institutions. The goal is to train workers in specific tasks, but also in the company's general orientation to production and to the market.

At Sanyo, for example, which is fairly representative of large Japanese firms, employee training, which continues throughout the employee's work life, involves three components: 1) on-the-job training; 2) company-run off-site educational programs; and 3) correspondence courses offered by the firm and by industry associations.[17] On-the-job training is supervised by division managers for whom aptitude and success as a teacher is one of the factors considered most important for promotion. General skills are acquired on-the-job, primarily through a conscious policy of job rotation within the department and the company. For example, all Sanyo engineers—including PhDs—spend some time in sales, typically as clerks in small appliance stores. (This is typical: college graduates who take a job with Hotel Okura serve as apprentices for five years, beginning with bedmaking and rotating through the laundry or room service before being given management responsibilities).[18]

Sanyo's Corporate Educational Training Center provides courses attended by one-third of the firm's 30,000 employees annually. Each student spends at least three days at the center. Most of the out-of-plant training that Sanyo employees receive takes place within the company's own institutions.

Finally, employees take a variety of correspondence courses to develop specific skills. The costs of these courses are often reimbursed by the company (which is in turn partly subsidized by the government).[19]

The differences between the company-based but extensive formal employee training systems of West Germany and Japan and the U.S. system of education and training with its reliance on formal education and informal, skill-specific, on-the-job training are clear. In the U.S., production workers move typically from high school to work; technicians are likely to move into jobs from community colleges, proprietary training schools, or the military; engineers and managers spend four to six years in colleges and universities acquiring bachelor and master degrees before seeking employment. Once on the job, American workers—especially blue collar workers and workers in smaller firms—do not receive extensive training. And training is not generally incorporated into firms' strategic planning.

The American system of education and training is structured differently than the systems of many of its competitors. But do differences in the structure of national education and training systems make any difference to the competitiveness of manufacturing firms in each nation? This critical question is addressed in the next two sections of this report. The first identifies the strengths and weaknesses of different elements of the jumbled network of institutions and initiatives that constitute education and training in the United States. The second asks whether variations in economic performance can be linked to variations in the structure and characteristics of education and training systems.

The State of Education and Training in the U.S.

Primary and Secondary Education

In comparison with almost any other industrial country, American elementary and secondary scholastic performance is surprisingly weak. In math and science, which are the foundation for further scientific and engineering study, American students appear to be less well-prepared and less successful. And below the level of the student elite, the performance of American students, while improving in some measures in recent years, has for good reason become a focus of national concern.

Math and Science. National assessments of educational quality, making use of achievement test scores, indicate some decline in math and science preparation since the 1960s. The National Assessment of Educational Progress, a Congressionally-mandated study of student achievement in a number of areas, revealed continuous declines in science achievement scores of 9-, 13- and 17-year olds since 1969, with some improvement since the late 1970s in the scores of the younger age groups. Math scores declined through the 1970s, but for the 9- and 13-year olds, the declines were reversed by 1982.[20]

Perhaps more telling than whether test scores have been declining or rising are some other facts about math and science preparation in the United States. Over half of all high school students take no math or science course after tenth grade. Only one percent of American high school students study calculus, compared to twelve percent of Japanese high school students. According to one estimate, three-quarters of American high school graduates lack the preparation to take a college engineering course.[21] Fewer than one-third of American 17- year-olds can solve a math problem requiring several steps, such as "George had 3/4 of a pie. He ate 3/5 of that. How much pie did he eat?"[22]

International comparisons show U.S. student performance in math and science lagging behind— although methodological problems make these efforts to compare test scores across cultures less definitive than one would hope. One of the most frequently cited indicators is a set of achievement tests conducted under the auspices of the International Association for the Evaluation of Educational Achievement (IEA). In the most recent study comparing science achievement, American ten-year-olds placed eighth out of fifteen countries surveyed. American fourteen- and seventeen-year-olds placed even lower (Table 1). Japanese students scored near or at the top; students in Korea, Hungary, Finland, Sweden and the Netherlands all scored consistently higher than their American counterparts. Most troubling to many observers was the drop in U.S. students' relative test scores from the fifth to the ninth grade.

The variation begins early, according to recent research by a group led by Harold Stevenson at the University of Michigan. Comparing mathematics achievement of Taiwanese, Japanese, and American students at different ages, the researchers found that "American children appear to lag behind children in other countries in reading and mathematics as early as kindergarten and continue to perform less effectively during the years of elementary school."[23] Only 15 Americans scored in the top 100 in the first grade math tests and only one in the fifth grade exams. Of the 100 lowest scorers in each grade, 58 in the first grade group and 67 in the fifth grade group were American. (Of course, the fact that the differences appear by kindergarten point to influences other than formal schooling practices that must be taken into consideration, such as parental attitudes and involvement in education.)

Table 1. **Results of Science Achievement Tests Sponsored by International Association for the Evaluation of Educational Achievement (IEA), 1988.**

Rank Order of Countries for Achievement at Each Level

	10 year olds Grade 4/5	14 year olds Grade 8/9	Grade 12/13 Science Students		
			Biology	Chemistry	Physics
Australia	9	10	9	6	8
Canada (Eng)	6	4	11	12	11
England	12	11	2	2	2
Finland	3	5	7	13	12
Hong Kong	13	16	5	1	1
Hungary	5	1	3	5	3
Italy	7	11	12	10	13
Japan	1	2	10	4	4
Korea	1	7	-	-	-
Netherlands	-	3	-	-	-
Norway	10	9	6	8	6
Philippines	15	17	-	-	-
Poland	11	7	4	7	7
Singapore	13	14	1	3	5
Sweden	4	6	8	9	10
Thailand	-	14	-	-	-
U.S.A.	8	14	13	11	9
Total no. of countries	15	17	13	13	13

Source: *Science Achievement in Seventeen Countries: A Preliminary Report*, New York: Pergamon Press, 1988.

By high school, the differences are deeply ingrained. Preliminary results from the Second International Mathematics Study that tested arithmetic, algebra, geometry, statistics, and measurement among eighth graders in 20 countries yielded average scores for American students that ranged from eighth through eighteenth.[24] An indication of the inability of American high schools to prepare most of its students adequately in math is the fact that one out of four math courses taught in public four-year colleges today are remedial courses designed to teach students what they should already have learned in high school.[25]

General Education. In addition to deficiencies in math and science preparation, the general educational preparation of many American youth is poor. The American system of education has been described by some as more like that of a developing than an industrial nation: the elite is relatively well-served and educated, but education for the average student is less than adequate and for many at the bottom school is little better than marking time.[26]

For the average student, obstacles include: a "cafeteria" assortment of high school course offerings which, combined with a lack of articulation of expected standards by colleges and universities, results in course choices that leave significant gaps in general knowledge and education; inadequate financing that necessitates the use of antiquated and inappropriate textbooks and that results in unmanageable class size, unreasonable course load and inadequate professional training and development for teachers; unnecessarily low expectations of student abilities and capacities that translates into little opportunity for students to ask questions about what they are learning (five percent of instructional time, according to a national survey by UCLA's John Goodlad) or engage in open questioning that demands more of students than memory skills (one percent of instructional time, according to Goodlad). From recent survey, statistical, and case study data about American schools, there is reason to believe that "mediocrity" characterizes the education of the majority of American primary and secondary students.

If the inadequacy of education for the bulk of the student distribution in the U.S. is chronic, the failure of the education system to retain and teach those at the bottom—particularly in urban areas—is acute. In some New York City schools, such as Brooklyn's Thomas Jefferson High School, the dropout rate is so high that fewer than one in five entering freshmen leave school with a diploma four years later.[27] Although national annual dropout rates began to decrease in 1980, falling from 6.3 percent in 1978 to 5.2 percent in 1983 for 14- to 24-year-olds (primarily due to improvements among black males), urban schools still lose a staggering number of their students before graduation.[28] In Cleveland, for example, the high school dropout rate hovers around 40 percent.

Moreover, regardless of the dropout rate, schools are failing to transmit a basic level of proficiency in skills needed for daily life to a significant proportion of students. About eight percent of New York City's youth between the ages of 14 and 21 cannot read at a fifth grade level. The figure is not very different in most large cities, according to the National Center for Education Statistics.[29] In one test of reading proficiency, 16 percent of tested 17-year-olds could not read at an intermediate level—a level which requires "an ability to search for specific information, interrelate ideas, and make generalizations."[30] In a recent international survey sponsored by the National Geographic magazine, 45 percent of Americans did not know where Central America is located, only one-third identified Vietnam, and fewer than half the Americans tested could identify the United Kingdom, France, South Africa, and Japan on a map. American youths between the ages of 18 and 24 scored lower than their counterparts in the eight other countries surveyed.[31]

This educational deficiency is often revealed when young men and women try to enter the labor force. In 1981, half the people who took the exam to become telephone operators in New York City flunked. Estimates of functional illiteracy in the work force—i.e., the lack of reading, writing, and communication skills necessary to achieve self-defined objectives at work and at home—range as high as 20 percent. Even acknowledging the Census Bureau estimate that two-thirds of the illiterate in America are either over 65 or speak English as a second language, illiteracy is still a far more serious and widespread problem than in Japan, for example, where estimates of functional illiteracy are in the one percent range. According to one firm that conducts an annual survey of training by industry, about one in four of the 2600 firms surveyed were offering programs in basic and remedial education in 1985.[32]

A comparison between Japanese and American primary and high school educational systems is instructive. The most striking contrasts are between the average educational attainments of Japanese and American students. In both national and international achievement tests, Japanese students show high average attainment. There is relatively low dispersion of test scores around the mean; few Japanese receive very low scores.[33] This reflects the priority the Japanese school system places on bringing all students up to a common level of competence, so that new entrants to the work force are highly literate and numerate, better prepared to learn than their American counterparts.

Pre-Employment Training for the Non-College Bound

The lack of a systematic pre-employment training system is one of the glaring differences between the United States and a number of its European competitors, particularly West Germany and Sweden. Comparisons between U.S. vocational education at the high school level and the German and Swedish vocational education systems underscore the lack of provision made in this country for the non-college bound. High school vocational education in the U.S., though it has been supported by the federal government for over 70 years and enrolls about five million students annually, has an extremely disappointing performance record. And because the transition from school-to-work is so unstructured in the U.S., many youths who would find other avenues to training and employment in Germany or Sweden—as many as half of those who enroll in U.S. college programs—enroll in college only to drop out before completing their course of study.

The transition from school to work in the United States is chaotic, unstructured and quite idiosyncratic. While there is no evidence of any serious misallocation of human resources when compared to more structured systems, the lack of structured transition means that those who find employment tend to be less well prepared in their specific field and also in general skills than their European counterparts. This would be less of an impediment if, as in Japan where vocational education is also weak, employers were to take responsibility for elaborate in-house training. However, the limited and uneven nature of company-based formal training in the United States means that this pre-employment lack of preparation goes largely unredressed.

The U.S. high school vocational education system does not perform well. Over the years, vocational education has been much studied—and the evaluation literature has not been kind. As one report concluded, "Generally, benefits to vocational graduates in the labor market are variously reported as small, unreliable or nonexistent."[34] There is an exception: 35 percent of American secretaries acquire their skills in high school programs.

Studies have found that earnings of students who go through vocational tracks are no higher than those of comparable general track students. Another study concluded that more than half of U.S. vocational education students do not use the skills acquired during vocational courses in later jobs. A vocational student who specializes in machining or another field has no greater likelihood of finding a job as a machinist than any student in the general education track of the same high school. In addition, vocational schools often have trouble keeping up with changes in the labor market and in technology and equipment, partly because of the inertia of tenured instructors and partly because of limited resources for new purchases.[35]

For these and other reasons, employers generally do not consider vocational high school programs to be a prime source of skilled or even trainable workers. In fact, enrollment in high school vocational programs can be so stigmatizing in the eyes of employers that it more than cancels out skill and confidence gains made by participants. Because of the poor performance and the political entrenchment of the vocational high school system, some analysts have suggested creating a new form of pre-employment training structure akin to the British Youth Training Scheme post-secondary apprenticeship year. Others see the community colleges as an institution capable of bridging the gap; but that strategy abandons the possibility that young people can be trained for good jobs without having to continue their education past

There is another option for the non-college bound: cooperative education. Unlike vocational education which teaches job skills in classroom settings, co-op education mixes periods of classroom instruction with paid or unpaid work experience. Cooperative education has the advantage of taking students into real work settings where they learn skills but also important lessons about appearance, reliability, and appropriate behavior on the job—what are often called work maturity skills. Unfortunately, cooperative education places most of its students in retail and wholesale commercial establishments, not in manufacturing.

Moreover, only a small percentage of American high school students ever participate in cooperative education—only 2.5 percent, according to one estimate.[36]

College and University

In general, the American system of higher education is the envy of industrialized and developing nations. The many different institutions for both mass and elite, the high quality of research and instruction, the flexibility in adding new degree programs and altering curricula are all seen by foreign observers as worthy of emulation. And indeed, there is consensus that the American system of higher education is the finest in the world.

At the mass education end of the spectrum, the vibrant community and technical college system is seen as particularly flexible and responsive to the needs of working people, minorities, and learners with families. In many communities, community colleges have taken over where vocational schools have failed, providing pre-employment training for a variety of technical and professional specialties. Usually, community colleges have a good understanding of the dynamics of the local labor market, since their success depends upon placing graduates in jobs or enabling them to qualify for promotions.

Community colleges play an important role in improving the reading, writing, and communications skills that so many high school graduates still lack. And they are accessible to the poor. Partly because they do not conduct research, community colleges are comparatively inexpensive to operate, costing half what a public four-year college costs per pupil per year. Almost half the community college student population—compared to only 23 percent in four year institutions—is drawn from the lowest socio-economic quarter.[37]

The community college system is not without problems. Quality varies greatly. Uninspired and mediocre teaching staff and administrative vision are not uncommon. However, the evaluation literature on community colleges, while scanty, does allow for some optimism. Results of one relatively careful evaluation study indicate that for lower-skill occupations, such as dental technician, employment prospects of community college graduates are significantly improved. Evaluation studies aside, the combination of an older student body, a relatively tight linkage between community colleges and local employers, and flexible decisionmaking on program cost, content, and delivery increases the likelihood that community colleges will have greater success than secondary level vocational education in preparing people for work.

The community college model is viewed with interest by foreign observers. At a recent conference at Harvard that brought together Swedish and American labor market and training policy analysts, while the Americans wanted to know about Swedish retraining policies, the Swedes were especially interested in learning more about American community colleges.

At the highest levels of the university system—graduate education—U.S. universities are clearly superior. The best indication is the number of foreign students who come to the U.S. for advanced training. According to recent studies by both the Carnegie Foundation for the Advancement of Teaching and the

Office of Technology Assessment, the U.S. system of research-oriented universities remains the most effective in the world, particularly in training for basic research.[38] Four-year undergraduate education is also highly rated.

This does not mean that American colleges and universities do not face serious problems in the years ahead. These include: resource constraints caused by federal budget deficits; and continued shrinkage of the college-age pool which may accelerate the exodus of good young professors out of academia and force difficult choices about consolidation on many public systems. Concern has also been expressed about the education of scientists and engineers in the U.S.[39] Some think that American universities are not turning out adequate numbers of scientists and engineers: for example, six percent of U.S. baccalaureate degrees are in engineering compared to 20 percent in Japan and 37 percent in West Germany. The proportion of each Japanese age cohort that completes four years of college in a science or engineering field is twice the U.S. percentage (six percent versus three percent). There is concern that the percentage of foreign-born science and engineering graduates from American universities is too high and that the proportion on U.S. nationals in graduate science and engineering programs is declining. Studies have also emphasized the difficulty universities have competing with industry for top quality engineers scientists and the inability of many universities to provide state-of-the-art laboratory facilities for student and faculty researchers.[40] In addition, many argue that American engineers are educated with too great an emphasis on theory and insufficient attention to practical problem-solving and design, leaving them less well prepared for careers in industry than some of their foreign counterparts.[41] Management education has also been criticized for placing too little emphasis on technology and production. These debates about engineering and management education are addressed more fully elsewhere in the Commission report.

Like all our social institutions, our colleges and universities will have to struggle to maintain and improve their ability to educate and train the American citizenry. It is likely that the coming years will witness a variety of new institutional arrangements linking industry, the universities, and government and linking different levels of the educational system. More rather than less will be expected of higher educational institutions, even though they are not as flush as they once were. However, while complacency would be foolish, it is fair to say that higher education is not at the heart of America's educational woes. Nor does the system of higher education appear to be a significant obstacle to national adjustment to changing economic conditions.

Training for the Existing Workforce

American firms tend to undervalue and underinvest in training. Among small firms, as noted above, there is very little training beyond very narrow, task-related instruction. Even in many of the nation's large firms, there tends to be underprovision of training and unevenness in the allocation of training opportunities. This inadequacy of attention to human resource and skill development can be seen both in relation to training for employed workers and retraining of dislocated workers. It has an adverse impact on the ability of American workers to work to their capacity.

The most commonly given reason for underinvestment in training is the concern of employers that they will not be able to recoup training investments before workers move on to other jobs. This fear is based on the relatively high mobility rate of American workers—eleven different employers over the course of the average American's work life, compared to only five jobs for the average Japanese worker, according to Masanori Hashimoto of Ohio State University.[42]

There are reasons to believe that this calculus is not as rational as it may at first seem. For one thing, mobility drops off after the first few years of a person's work life and the first few years in a particular job. Training investments could be structured so as to take this statistical pattern into account. Moreover, if training is seen as a way not only to impart specific skills but also to create a shared corporate identity or to integrate "learning how to learn" into the daily routines of the organization, the narrow calculation of training benefits might change significantly.

There are, of course, American firms that have made a serious commitment to training their work force and have made work force skill development central to their competitive strategy. One of the most impressive examples is IBM, which divides its training into seven different functional groups (marketing, service, technical, information systems, finance and planning, management development, and employee development), each with its own educational campus. The computer giant is just completing a five-year effort to identify the company's 75 to 100 primary jobs, specify the educational requirements for each job, and develop a learning curriculum and education delivery strategy for workers in each job. According to one IBM executive, "We have now built education and training of people into the fabric of the company...We see this as a competitive edge. We are doing this education work for business purposes—to have our people know more and do more than the average in our industry."[43]

Other firms have made a similar commitment. However, they are the exceptions rather than the rule. For the most part, training in U.S. firms remains primarily "short, informal, and often inadequate instruction from a co-worker in lieu of more advanced training."[44]

The contrast with Japanese and German training is striking. In both countries, training and skill development have high priority. Ronald Dore recounts the following story about Japan which is impossible to imagine in the U.S. context. In the 1930s, the Japanese railway launched a campaign to improve worker skills that was structured around skill competitions. In the "smooth stop" section of the drivers' competition, judges sat impassively in the restaurant car with a row of different size metal bars standing on end on the table in front of them. The drivers' skill was measured by the longest bar that remained standing when the train came to a halt.[45] In both Japan and West Germany, continual learning is valued, encouraged and promoted. Wolfgang Streeck notes that in West Germany both employers and trade union officials have begun to refer to the firm of the future as a *Lernstatt*—a learning shop.[46] In Japan, too, there is the sense that the firm must be "as much an educational institution as it is a place of work," as Ykumatsu Takeda of Nippon Electric Company (NEC) has put it.[47] Few but the most forward thinking American firms see their training responsibilities and opportunities in this way.

Japanese and American on-the-job training efforts are very different in structure and function. Japanese firms often have engineers or experienced production workers employed full-time on the shop floor with the specific assignment of helping newly-hired team members or providing instruction during machine failures or other problems. Moreover, Japanese firms use extensive rotation of workers within a department and transfer through a number of departments in order to create a multiskilled, flexible work force that is prepared for change, new tasks, and further learning. Like the Japanese system of on-the-job training, training in West Germany is also more carefully conceived and more thorough than in the U.S. The worker in charge of training apprentices (known as the *Ausbilder*) must obtain a training license, which requires special instruction both in his or her occupation and in training methods.[48] While these workers do not work full-time as trainers and participate in daily production with the rest of the work force , neither are they trying to teach what they know on the fly, without the benefit of time, authority, or pedagogical experience, as is too often the case in the U.S.

In these and other nations, training of new and existing workers and retraining of workers whose jobs are being or have been eliminated are more central to strategies for competitiveness than in the U.S. Consider how different nations have responded to the restructuring, layoffs, and worker dislocation that have accompanied the past decade's dramatic changes in occupational and industrial mix. In Sweden, retraining of dislocated workers is a centerpiece of a national employment and training system focused on providing some protection for workers in the core of the economy. The innovative effort to relocate, retrain, and reemploy shipyard workers who lost their jobs in the planned phase-out of Sweden's shipbuilding industry enabled the Uddevalla region and its work force to make a smooth transition.[49] In Japan, the initiative is at the firm level. For example, as Nippon Steel has moved away from basic steelmaking into new electronics and communications ventures, it has retrained several thousand employees for new jobs. Blue-collar production workers are being hired as programmers, after several months of training. (These workers were able to make the transition because of their prior experience with computer technologies in highly automated steel mills and because of the high level of general education of Japanese high school graduates.) Engineers have been able to make the transition out of steelmaking and into new materials work and biotechnology.[50]

In the U.S., except for some interesting initiatives at the state level in states such as Massachusetts, New York, Michigan and California, retraining of dislocated workers has been minimally successful. This is in large part because federal employment and training programs are marginal to the operations of the labor market and are primarily targeted to low-income workers. It is also a result of the lack of a culture of learning and a priority on learning in American firms. In retraining, as in initial training and on-the-job skills upgrading, American industry—and American society in general—takes a narrow view and exhibits only a modest commitment.

The Relationship Between Education and Training and Productivity

The American system—or non-system—of education and training is obviously different in many respects from the structure of laws and institutions in other industrial nations. As detailed above, the strengths and weaknesses of the American system are fairly apparent. However, a catalogue of strengths and weaknesses begs the question: Do these variations make a difference in the competitiveness of American manufacturing?

What is the relationship between education and training and productivity? If the relationship is loose, then it may be difficult to justify major initiatives in the areas of pre-employment education or on-the-job training. If, however, it is true that higher levels of education and training make possible or make easier productivity-enhancing changes in technology, firm organization, and the organization of work, then the case can be made for greater attention to the ways we teach and train our current and future work force.

Beginning in the 1950s, economists have paid increasing attention to the role of education and the quality of human resources in economic development and productivity. One body of work that was highly influential in the late 1950s and early 1960s is growth accounting analysis, which attempts to quantify the relationship between aggregate levels of output in a society and aggregate levels of education. Epitomized by Edward Denison's detailed analysis of economic growth in the U.S. between 1929 and 1957, this literature tends to attribute a sizeable percentage of output growth (Denison's conclusion was about 23 percent for the U.S. in that period) to increased educational attainment of the work force. An important offshoot of the growth accounting literature looked at the role of education in modernization and posited increased education levels as one of the critical elements in the modernization process.

In the early 1960s, growth accounting studies were eclipsed by the "human capital" model as the dominant way of thinking about education and productivity. Led by Gary Becker and Theodore Schultz, this approach to the study of the economics of labor and education views individual decisions about education and training as investment decisions. The model equates decisions about obtaining higher levels of education—i.e., adding increments to one's human capital—with decisions about investments in physical capital. Because of their adherence to the neoclassical theory of marginal productivity, human capital theorists assume a direct relationship between increases in education, productivity, and income: increased education is assumed to raise a workers' productivity on the job, for which he or she is paid more.

Since the mid-1960s, human capital theory has come under intense attack. Economists and sociologists have challenged the assumptions and findings of human capital research concerning the relationships between education and earnings, productivity and earnings, and education and productivity. Because of the persuasiveness of many of the criticisms, human capital theory no longer holds a position of unchallenged preeminence.

For our purposes in trying to understand how education and training relate to productivity, both human capital theory and the growth accounting literature are of limited use. Both literatures consider increments of education as homogenous, continuous, and unidimensional. That is, they fail to differentiate among schools, programs, and education systems. Any year of schooling is like any other year and a year spent in any school or any track within a school is equivalent to any other. There is no room in either theory—both of which are primarily interested in quantifying the relationship between education and economic well-being—for a nuanced and context-specific appreciation of education and training. Whatever their strengths in accounting for aggregate levels of investment in education by individuals or firms or in identifying and explaining trends across whole societies, these theories are unable to offer concrete understandings of the links between different kinds of education and training on the one hand and the generation or regeneration of particular skills, aptitudes, and attitudes on the other. Nor can they specify the ways in which work force qualities and skills actually contribute to firm productivity. This is because both leave the two "black boxes" of education and productivity unexplored and unexplained. The question of how education and training translate into productivity gains at the firm level is outside the scope of these inquiries.

There is, however, another more recent body of research that has attempted to move toward greater specificity in analyzing the role of human resources and skill in productivity growth. The most interesting and useful of these studies involve comparative case studies of the organization of work in comparable production facilities in different countries and link the evolution of variations in work organization or industrial relations to the historical development of national patterns of education and training. Such studies include research comparing: matched pairs of French and German factories in the same industries;[51] matched pairs of British and Japanese firms;[52] British and German experiences with the use of computer numerically controlled machine tools;[53] British and German workers' educational experiences and their productive performance across a wide spectrum of industries;[54] the training and performance of Japanese and U.S. engineers in large computer companies;[55] and experiences across a number of countries with flexible manufacturing systems [56]. In addition to this body of explicitly comparative cases, there are numerous single country studies conducted by researchers with significant knowledge of other societies. The popular literature is also instructive: an excellent article by a Westinghouse engineer describing his experiences during a year at Mitsubishi and comparing those experiences with his work life in the U.S. is a fine example of the strengths of comparative studies of work, work organization, training, and productivity at the firm level.[57]

One group of comparative case studies has been conducted in the past decade by S. J. Prais and his associates at London's National Institute of Economic and Social Research. In a study of productivity growth in ten different industries in West Germany and Britain, Prais emphasizes the advantages that German firms derive from the three-year apprenticeship program and the network of technical schools that support the apprenticeship system, particularly when compared to the voluntary and limited apprenticeship system in Great Britain, the shallower pool of skilled workers, and the lower general education and work force skill levels that results. As Prais notes, "...(T)he median English youngster finishing his full-time schooling joins the labour market as an unskilled worker; whereas, as noted above, only a tenth of the corresponding age-group does so in Germany."[58]

In the conclusion to the report, Prais argues that inadequacies in training and the supply of skilled manpower appear to be a predominant source of British weakness in products in which engineering and technical skills play an important role. In West Germany, engineers are better trained, production workers are far better prepared with industrial skills, and there are clear incentives and opportunities to pursue advanced technical qualifications and promotions to intermediate jobs. While Prais does not quantify the relationship between skills acquisition through vocational education and training and productivity gains and competitiveness, the thrust of his findings is that such a relationship exists.

A second cluster of studies of crossnational variation in the interaction between national systems of education and training and both organizational structure and industrial relations have been conducted by researchers at the Laboratoire d'Economie et de Sociologie du Travail (LEST) in Aix-en-Provence, the International Institute of Management in Berlin, and Brunel University in England. These studies have attempted to illustrate how national variations in institutions for educating, training, recruiting, and promoting manpower contribute to the development of very different organizational structures, which in turn affect productivity growth.

In a study of the application of computer-numerically-controlled machine tools in Great Britain and West Germany, Arndt Sorge and his co-authors concluded that "performance is strongly influenced by education and vocational training: this makes not only for higher labour productivity in Germany, but also for higher capital or investment productivity, and for better adaptation to market requirements."[59]

In another study focused on Germany and Britain, Sorge and Malcolm Warner analyzed case study evidence from three matched pairs of manufacturing plants, one pair using continuous process technology, another mass production, and a third unit production.[60] The authors compared the relative size of different skill-groups in the work force in each plant, the number of levels of hierarchy, and other indications of the interaction between education and training and organizational structure. In all three types of facilities, the proportion of production workers in Germany was higher and the proportion of technical and managerial workers lower. The authors concluded that these differences were due primarily to the added responsibility of German production workers for technical decisions, a structure made possible by their high level of technical skill. In addition, the researchers found that in Germany, there was one less level of hierarchy between the shop floor and the plant manager. The *Meister* has far broader responsibilities than the British foreman, incorporating into daily work such tasks as inspection, production planning, and personnel decisions that in British factories are the responsibility of the superintendent. Sorge and Warner attribute this difference to the greater technical skill base of the German workers and the extra training required to become a *Meister*. Finally, managerial and technical staff are separated in Britain while technical functions and line authority are combined in German management positions. This structural difference can also be attributed to differences in skill levels: unlike most British managers, German managers tend to be technically trained and to have shop floor experience.

What are the implications of these organizational differences, shaped by national education and training systems, for understanding variations in productivity rates? The authors argue that "[g]reater variety of training increases the flexibility, satisfaction, and dedication of employees of all kinds, eliminates problems of coordination, and results in a more economical use of manpower because of greater labor productivity."[61]

A three year study of the introduction and use of flexible manufacturing systems, conducted by Ramchandran Jaikumar of the Harvard Business School, draws similar conclusions. Jaikumar compared U.S. with Japanese use of FMS technology and found that Japanese firms were better able to maximize the potential productivity gains of the new machines. U.S. companies produced about one-tenth the number of parts with the same system as did Japanese firms. Japanese firms were more innovative, producing 22 new parts for every new one produced in a U.S. system. Utilization rates and reliability were also higher in Japan.

One of the principal factors accounting for these performance differences among firms with similar technologies, according to Jaikumar, is the skill level and preparation of the work force: "Because software development lies at the heart of this increasingly information-intensive manufacturing process, the technological literacy of a company's workers is critical."[62] In the U.S. firms that were studied, only eight percent of the FMS workers were engineers and only 25 percent had been trained on CNC machines; in the Japanese firms, more than 40 percent of the work force were college-educated engineers and all had been trained on CNC machines. In addition, training to upgrade skills was three time longer in Japan than in the U.S. Jaikumar concludes that although success in FMS use is ultimately a management responsibility, the ability to draw on the expertise of a skilled work force that can reprogram on the shop floor, solve problems as they arise, and carry out experimental tests on performance provides a solid foundation for technological leadership and productivity gains.

Rainer Schultz-Wild and Cristoph Koehler have drawn similar conclusions from an analysis of FMS use among firms in West Germany and France. They argue that firms with a higher-skill work force are best able to make optimal use of the new technology. They point to the high degree of utilization possible in plants in which workers do not need to rely on personnel outside the unit for repairs, tool setting, and programming. In addition, higher skilled workers have a greater ability to assume the risks associated with small-batch production. Moreover, problems of coordination seem to be less significant in firms where the work force is more homogeneously high-skill rather than characterized by a strict and elaborate division of labor. Like Jaikumar, the authors conclude that there is a strong connection between breadth of skills, flexibility, and productivity in the case of FMS use.[63]

These studies of the relationship between education, training, skill, and productivity in particular industries are a significant step toward opening up the "black boxes" that aggregate economic analysis leaves unexplored. Although they fall short of quantifying the relationship (a challenge which may be impossible to meet), they show that: 1) differently structured systems of education and training can encourage or constrain the range of productivity-enhancing choices available to firms; and 2) that different systems of transition to work and of work organization can enhance or limit optimal deployment of workers within a firm, an industry, and across a national economy.

Of course, this line of argument is focused on the supply side: how do variations in the quality of the work force affect how technology is used and work is organized and how do these variations affect productivity? To fully understand the relationship between education and training and productivity at the firm level, it is also necessary to look at the demand side: i.e., how are available jobs defined and structured and how do these management choices affect the demand for workers with different types of skills and experiences? The key to sustained, long-term productivity growth is an efficient matching of workers with appropriate skills with jobs that have the potential for high productivity. The following section examines the demand side of the equation, with special attention to how changes in corporate strategy resulting from intensified global competition are affecting the demand for skill, education, and training in the United States.

Changing Corporate Strategy and the Implications for Skill, Education, and Training
In order to survive during the chaotic last two decades, American firms in most manufacturing industries have been forced to make dramatic changes in the way they think about and conduct business. Three powerful forces—competition, technology, and demographics—have altered the economic environment, shattering forever the post-war international order dominated for more than thirty years by the United States and making volatility and change a fact of economic life for American firms. These forces have driven managers to rethink almost all aspects of their business, including their approach to education, training, and skill development. As the business environment has become less forgiving, firms have had little choice but to adapt—or fail. Moreover, these forces are unlikely to weaken or be reversed in the coming years. As a recent Office of Technology Assessment report argues, "During the next two decades, new technologies, rapid increases in foreign trade, and the tastes and values of a new generation of Americans are likely to reshape virtually every product, every service and every job in the United States."[64]

Once unchallenged leaders in markets at home and abroad, American firms have been attacked head on by aggressive international competition. In part, this new competition is a natural evolution as nations that suffered mightily during World War II rebuilt their productive capacity. In part, it has been made possible by changes in technology that have weakened transportation, communication, and resource constraints and have made global production and distribution possible at previously inconceivable speeds and costs. During the 1970s, the extent of this competitive challenge became apparent as industries such as automobile, machine tools, steel, and apparel lost domestic market share to Japanese, Korean, West German, Italian, and other manufacturers. Today, foreign trade is so widespread and the integration of world markets so developed that few manufacturers in the U.S., even those who have never felt the pressure of international competition, can afford to assume their markets are secure.

The past two decades have also witnessed the beginning of a revolution in technology, as microelectronics-based information technologies are diffusing through manufacturing and other industries, changing product and process technologies and forcing a range of organizational, employment, and other changes. Of course, diffusion is not as rapid and widespread as many have claimed or predicted: in 1980, despite two decades of availability, computer-numerically- controlled machine tools accounted for only 26 percent of the value of machine tools shipped.[65] It always takes longer for new technologies to work right, get integrated into existing manufacturing systems, and reach acceptable levels of reliability.

However, diffusion is accelerating. Many observers see these new technologies as having reached the steeply-sloped segment of the "S"-shaped diffusion curve. Use of CNC machine tools is now increasing more rapidly. The uses of computers are multiplying in products; in manufacturing design and production processes; in office systems; for communication between and among offices, firms, and industries; and for accelerated scanning of information intelligence sources. The design of computer-based systems for use by those with limited computer literacy is improving. And firms are becoming more confident about operating in an environment where computers are used in production, distribution, planning, finance, and marketing. The result is an impressive burst of technological change: 40 percent of all new investments in plant and equipment are now in the category "information technology," double the share for that category ten years ago.[66]

In addition, demographic changes have also contributed to the volatility of the business environment. The role of women in the economy and in society has changed dramatically. The baby boom has entered the life cycle stage where major consumption decisions are made. The American population is aging and the elderly population is growing rapidly. The impact of these shifts can be seen in the changing structure of the work force (see the following section) and of household composition.

In and of themselves, these demographic changes have altered the structure of consumer preferences facing American producers. When combined with the changed patterns of global competition and the capabilities of new technologies to accelerate the introduction of new and varied products, the impact on product markets has been broad—and destabilizing. For firms in certain industries, such as machine tools, synthetic fibers, and steel, the competitive decline of their domestic industrial customers has altered traditional market patterns. Across many industries, global production has accelerated the saturation of mass markets, forcing the increase in strategies of market segmentation. More flexible technology, changing consumer tastes and competitive pressures have combined to drive a perceptible shortening of product cycles. According to a Kodak vice-president, the speed of new product introduction is now one the most significant challenges facing the photographic giant: while in the 1960s a camera might go three or four years without even the slightest change, today no camera lasts more than six months before it is redesigned and new features are added.[67] With consumers no longer exhibiting the same kind of loyalty to products or companies that they did twenty or thirty years ago, uncertainty and instability have become the norm.

American firms that have more or less successfully adapted to these new conditions have pursued one of the following two strategies—or some combination of the two. Many firms have tried to reduce the labor content of their products through automation and organizational restructuring targeted at reducing overhead. This is particularly true of firms pursuing a mass market or commodity strategy where they must compete to some extent on cost. As the president of Smith-Corona explained his company's strategy for producing typewriters: "Direct labor is now less than two hours per machine. At that rate, you can afford to build it in the United States."[68]

The second competitive strategy involves moving away from standardized commodity products and competition on price to competition based on quality and service, emphasizing the enhancement of value through quality improvements, customization, innovation, rapid delivery, and strong service support. This strategy is designed to take advantage of more sophisticated and varied tastes of consumers with higher levels of disposable income, as well as the capability of advanced manufacturing systems to reduce economies of scale and capitalize on economies of scope.

In either model—or in hybrid combinations of cost-cutting and quality-enhancement—successful firms are being forced to rethink organizational structure, human resource policies, and education and training strategies. The stability of employment is shaken by labor-shedding, technology-intensive strategies. The stability of existing employment patterns is also threatened by changing demands on the work force from the shop floor up through the managerial ranks as quality, speed of new product introduction, service, and flexibility become the bases of competitive advantage. Across the board, the likely outcome will be increased volatility of employment and shifting demands on the industrial work force—changes that will have to be accommodated and facilitated by the in-house training programs of employers, by the network of institutions that provide training to existing workers, and by the educational institutions that prepare new workers for the jobs of the future.

The volatility of employment caused by the introduction of labor-saving technology will require that workers be able to move more frequently from job to job, either within a firm or between firms. Thus, mastery of skills specific to a narrow job, such as operation of a particular machine, will no longer be sufficient to guarantee steady income.

Moreover, the kinds of jobs that will exist in more highly automated plants are likely to require workers to perform new tasks. These computer-mediated tasks require what Shoshana Zuboff of the Harvard Business School has called "intellective" as opposed to "action-centered" skills: workers perform more monitoring and maintenance functions and the work day is characterized by periods of inaction punctuated by periods of non-repetitive problem-solving. Increasingly, production workers will have to make sense of what is happening on the shop floor based on abstract rather than physical cues. This does not mean that workers will necessarily find the work more stimulating than simple machine tending: it does mean, however, that the more efficient workers in computer-mediated production will have to be comfortable with procedural and systemic thinking and be able to understand the production process as a whole, not just their specific task.[69]

Changes in the structure of employment and the nature of jobs triggered by the introduction of computer-based equipment in production will put new pressure on individual workers, manufacturing employers, and education and training providers to rethink skill needs, develop retraining programs, and reconceptualize pre-employment training.[70] Consider the case of Easco Hand Tools in Springfield, Massachusetts. In 1986, Easco managers decided to reorganize production to reduce costs and improve quality. The company brought in extensive new automated equipment. One result was a massive reduction in employment: more than 700 of the 1000 employees were let go. The other result was a new set of expectations of workers. The company determined that to make optimum use of the new machines, workers would have to be able to read blueprints, read and write English at a high school level, and understand basic mathematical and mechanical processes. Before the reorganization, the company had considered 20 percent of its work force functionally illiterate. Given the responsibilities workers would have in the automated factory, management estimated that seven out of ten workers (average age 52, average seniority 24 years) would be unable to make the transition. Today, the firm only employs around 350 workers; but all have the skills management sought and all are involved in a program of educational and training upgrading.[71]

It is possible to imagine a shift to a more capital-intensive production strategy that results in little upgrading in the skills required of workers. In fact, as the Commission's study of the textile industry has shown, this has been the trend in the restructuring of the American textile industry. There are powerful forces that argue against a reorganization of work that would require greater general skill and knowledge from the work force, including: managerial concerns about shifting the locus of control and decisionmaking; the fear that upgrading would result in a shortage of qualified workers at wages management wanted to pay; resistance to upsetting established industrial relations; and managerial traditionalism.

However, even if individual firms and whole industries work to reduce the skill level of jobs at the same time that they reduce the number of jobs required to produce a given output, the increased instability of employment will require workers to have more general skills if they are to find new employment. And in their attempts to cut costs further through labor shedding, firms are likely to broaden job definitions, reduce the number of narrow classifications and expect more flexibility from remaining employees. Moreover, it is an open question whether firms can survive if they do not make changes in the organization of work that extend worker capabilities in an effort to increase flexibility and the capacity of the production system to respond to rapid, and often unpredictable, technological and market changes.[72] Wolfgang Streeck, now of the University of Wisconsin, is one of many who now argue that, in the present period of industrial restructuring, "new competitive conditions in world markets place a premium on high skills, favoring firms that can build a skilled work force over those that cannot." [73]

Certainly, firms that adopt a strategy based on quality and service rather than price alone will demand greater involvement of employees at all levels and will tend to reorganize production in ways that demand new technical, communication and organizational skills from all segments of the work force. This tendency can be seen already in Japanese auto firms operating in the United States and in many of the nation's leading firms, as Commission interviews with eleven companies have revealed.[74] In the search for maximum flexibility to cope with the constantly changing external environment, firms are turning to broader job classifications. To enhance productivity through improved motivation and better utilization of the knowledge and skill of existing workers, many firms are increasing the opportunities for worker involvement and participation. To help managers stay abreast of impediments to production efficiency and quality, firms are instituting smoother and more rapid two-way information flow in the work force . To improve quality and make it central to corporate performance, firms are expecting more basic literacy, numeracy, and communications skills from workers. To increase the speed of product development, firms are building teams across functional lines and demanding more cooperation and less disciplinary narrowness. And to enable the firm to move toward shorter runs with more variation and greater responsiveness to customers, companies are demanding and providing broader knowledge of the production process.

In short, firms that are responding to competitive and other pressures by adopting a strategy based on quality and service are finding that such a strategy requires the organization of the production system—from design through distribution—in ways that demand new skills from employees on the shop floor and above. These skill requirements include the following:

Basic literacy. As responsibility for quality and productivity are pushed further down the hierarchy and closer to the point of production and distribution, more will be demanded of lower-level workers. They will have to be able to read more complicated manuals and memos and also keep better records of their own.

Electronics and computer literacy. As computers diffuse through the firm, familiarity with and working knowledge of electronics and computer logic will have to increase.

Math proficiency. As statistical process controls and other quality control techniques spread through American firms, the basic math proficiency of the typical production worker is proving inadequate.

Teamwork. As job classifications broaden, as efforts are made to break down functional specialization, and as teams become more widespread, the oral and written communications skills and the level of interpersonal confidence and interaction required by workers at all levels of the firm will increase.

Attitudinal and behavioral skills. Increasingly, workers at all levels of the firm will have to see the success of the firm as dependent upon their participation, initiative, diligence, and reliability.

Process technology skills. Among engineers, perhaps the most significant skill changes demanded will be among manufacturing process engineers. While in the past these engineers have often moved up off the shop floor and have not been trained as graduate engineers, this is likely to change. As process technologies become more complex, process engineers will need more knowledge of mechanical, chemical and electronic principles and processes. The skills of many existing process engineers will be insufficient. Some may be retrained, but the skill levels required of new entrants into process engineering are likely to rise.

Technological and managerial skills. Engineers and managers are likely to see their job requirements change. Foreign language skills and professional time spent in other countries will be important to career development. Technologists will have to be able to understand and communicate with individuals in other parts of the firm, as will non-technical managers.

It may well be, as Wolfgang Streeck argues, that what firms will find most valuable in workers as they make the transition and adapt to the new reality in manufacturing is not just functional skills—narrow skills that can be created by a "refresher course" or by a curricular change—but rather "skills as a generalized, polyvalent resource that can be put to many different and, most importantly, as yet unknown future uses." Streeck concludes, "Practitioners everywhere agree that the crucial work qualification today is the capacity to acquire more and new work qualifications."[75]

What are the implications of these new skill demands for the education and training system in the United States? The most obvious answer is that the demands on firms, schools, and other training institutions will increase. But how will they be met?

Already, many of the nation's most successful firms have increased the value they place on education and training and have made work force preparation more central to firm strategy. In the past, training departments of large companies had been the place to move managers who were no longer productive. Often, training department staff were burned out and the programs were largely ineffective. Since the late 1970s, there has been a change. In many firms, training department staff and expenditures have grown—and education and training have become more directly linked to corporate strategy. Tuition rebate programs, which had generally been viewed by management as a fringe benefit, are now being more carefully targeted to help improve performance. Work place literacy programs are being given greater attention and resources. Strategies for computer literacy, ranging from exposing workers to computers to subsidizing worker purchases of computers for the home, are spreading. In some large firms such as Ford and Xerox, training programs are being required of suppliers, so that the capacity for quality can be pushed further down the production chain.

Of course, as has been noted earlier in this paper, in-plant training in the United States is far less developed and evenly distributed than in several other industrial nations. In the United States, we tend to rely more on educational institutions for training. And there are indications that, in the future, U.S. firms—while likely to rethink their internal training efforts—will also put more pressure on the nation's educational institutions to provide workers for the new economy.

This argument is forcefully made by Columbia University's Thierry Noyelle. According to this view, technological change, combined with the expansion of formal education in the past two decades, has made it possible for firms to look to outside training institutions for workers with skills that previously had to be taught on-the-job. As more workers receive more advanced schooling, firms are able to hire technicians and lower level managers out of school rather than through internal promotion. In addition, the expansion of information technologies is creating a homogenization of skills across a wide range of industries, both within manufacturing and services, enabling firms to recruit more middle managers outside. The result: "a shift in the demand for training away from on-the-job training mechanisms within the firm to the vocational education institutions, the community colleges or even the four-year colleges."[76] Rather than rely on internal job ladders, firms can more easily externalize the costs of training and hire in at various rungs on the ladder.

This view that educational institution will be asked to play a larger role in preparing tomorrow's workers is seconded by the Department of Labor's *Workforce 2000* study. According to this study, of all the new jobs that will be created between now and the year 2000, more than half will require some education beyond high school and almost a third will be filled by college graduates. This compares to only 22 percent of today's jobs that require a college degree. While much of this aggregate change is the result of shrinkage in occupations that require less education and lower skills and rapid growth in occupations that require higher levels of education and skill, it is also apparent that workers in lower skilled manufacturing and service jobs of the future will be expected to read and understand directions, add and subtract, and be able to speak and think clearly.[77]

Clearly, it is too early to tell exactly how the firms and extra-firm institutions that make up the U.S. education and training system will evolve in the coming years in order to adjust to the pressures for increased and more complex education and training at all levels of the work force. While some, such as

Noyelle, argue that the pressure on educational institutions will be great and that our education-biased training system will tilt further in that direction, others, such as Wolfgang Streeck, contend that the proper place for training—and for learning broadly conceived—is the firm and that the firm must become a learning institution. Perhaps it is safest to conclude that the functional boundaries between school and work are likely to blur or break down in the future as demands multiply on both public and private, educational and productive enterprises in industrial nations. Just as nations have created different education and training systems and structures in the past, there will continue to be be variation in the future. Which mix will provide a competitive advantage may not yet be apparent—and it is likely that no national system will be useable as a full blueprint for any other society. However, it is clear that the societies that fail to make the full development of human resources central to their national strategy for competitiveness will ultimately be the poorer—culturally and economically.

Demographic Change and the Implications for Skill, Education, and Training

One final factor must be considered in an analysis of the strengths and weaknesses of American education today and for the future: demography. In the coming decade, great changes will occur in the nature of the American work force. The entrance of the baby boom generation into the work force has already ended. Today's and tomorrow's labor market entrants have a very different profile than those of the past twenty years—a profile that constitutes a serious challenge to the effectiveness of American education and training institutions.

For one thing, the growth of the work force will slow significantly. Between 1980 and 1996, the population between the ages of 15 and 24 is expected to fall 21 percent, from about 43 to 34 million.[78] As a percentage of the nation's population, youths between 15 and 24 will shrink from 18.8 to 13 percent.

With fewer young entrants, the work force as a whole will be aging. According to the Department of Labor's *Workforce 2000* report, the median age of those in the work force will rise from 35 in 1984 to about 39 in 2000. While the nation's population will increase about 15 percent between 1986 and 2000, the number of people between the ages of 48 and 53 will jump by 67 percent and the number between 35 and 47 will increase by 38 percent.[79]

According to *Workforce 2000*, white men will constitute only 15 percent of the new members of the American work force during the next decade. The new work force will have a larger proportion of working women: three-fifths of new entrants will be female. Minority and immigrant workers will also constitute a larger proportion of the work force. Minority workers will account for 29 percent of the new entrants to the work force. While it is impossible to predict immigration flows (legal and illegal), the proportion of Hispanic and Asian workers in the labor force will continue to increase. According to Census Bureau projections, the black and Hispanic youth populations will continue to rise through the early years of the next century, while the white youth population will fall. The number of black youth will rise slightly by

2000 to 6.4 million from its 1980 level of 5.8 million. The number of Hispanic youths is projected to double from 3.1 to 6.2 million. Nearly one in five youths born in the 1980s will grow up in a house where English is not spoken. More than one in four will come from a family that lives in poverty.

These shifts in the composition of the work force pose both an opportunity and a challenge to the nation. On the one hand, the tightening of the labor market will force employers to reach further down the labor queue to find workers and will force them to hire and train workers they might otherwise have ignored. On the other hand, though, minority and immigrant groups enter the labor force with lower average levels of schooling, higher levels of unemployment and less on-the-job experience, and a range of labor market disadvantages. Given the demand by employers for a better educated, more highly skilled work force, the educational disadvantages that face many minority youths may keep them out of jobs—even as their numbers in the work force increase.

According to a recent National Assessment of Educational Progress conducted by the U.S. Department of Education, black and Hispanic youths between the ages of 21 and 25 had more difficulty performing tasks reflecting basic literacy than did their white counterparts (though results for the white cohort were also troubling). Only about three-fifths of whites, two-fifths of Hispanics and one quarter of blacks tested could locate information in a news article or almanac. Only a quarter of whites, seven percent of Hispanics and three percent of blacks could read a bus schedule correctly. And only 44 percent of whites, 20 percent of Hispanics and eight percent of blacks could correctly determine the change they were due from a two-item restaurant meal purchase. The risk is real that, even though the competition for entry level jobs will decrease in the next decade, only a concerted effort to raise the basic skill levels of millions of black and Hispanic youths will avoid the generation of a large cohort of youths who will be able to find only unstable, dead-end, entry-level jobs if they are able to find work at all.[80]

This supply-side prospect for the American labor force—tighter labor markets and a large segment of the work force that is inadequately prepared for employment—is a major factor behind the current increase in corporate and governmental support for innovative public education programs, particularly in the nation's largest cities. When coupled with changes on the demand side—i.e., the likelihood that tomorrow's jobs, from entry level on up, will require higher and different technical and general skills—the education and training challenge becomes that much more compelling. And the weaknesses identified in this report in the American system of preparing its residents for work and for citizenship become much more of a national liability.

Notes

1 John W. Meyer. "The Politics of Educational Crises in the United States." in Cummings, William K. et al. *Educational Policies in Crisis*. New York: Praeger 1986. pp. 47-8.

2 U.S. Department of Education. Office of Educational Research and Improvement. Center for Education Statistics. *Digest of Education Statistics, 1987*. Washington DC: U.S. Government Printing Office, 1987. p. 107

3 Meyer. *op.cit.* p 50.

4 Melinda Beck *et al.* "A Nation Still at Risk." *Newsweek*, May 2, 1988. p 54.

5 Arthur M. Hauptman with Charles J. Andersen. *Background Paper on American Higher Education*. Washington DC: Commission on National Challenges in Higher Education, American Council on Education, 1988.

6 NEDC. *Competence and Competition: Training and Education in the Federal Republic of Germany, the United States and Japan*. London: NEDO, 1984. p. 2.

7 U.S. Department of Labor *How Workers Get their Training*. Washington DC: Government Printing Office, 1985. p 2.

8 Constance Mitchell. "A Growing Shortage of Skilled Craftsmen Troubles Some Firms." *Wall Street Journal*, September 14, 1987. p 1.

9 U.S. Department of Labor. *op. cit.*

10 Stephen Hills. *How Craftsmen Learn Their Skills; A Longitudinal Analysis.* unpublished paper. August 1981.

11 Anthony P. Carnevale and Harold Goldstein. *Employee Training: Its Changing Role and an Analysis of New Data*. Alexandria VA: American Society for Training and Development, 1983.

12 Seymour Lusterman. *Education in Industry*. New York: The Conference Board, 1977.

13 Anthony P. Carnevale and Harold Goldstein. *op. cit.* p 55.

14 *ibid.* p 65.

15 Hans Betz. "Meeting the Challenge: Vocational Education and Training in the Federal Republic of Germany." M.I.T. Commission on Industrial Productivity Working Paper, March 1988.

16 Rosalie L. Tung. *Key to Japan's Economic Strength: Human Power*. Lexington MA: Lexington Books, 1984. p 30.

17 Description is drawn from an interview with Hiroyasu Kawai, Managing Director, Sanyo Corporate Educational Training Center, Kobe, 2 February 1988. Interviews at Nippon Steel, Seiko Instruments, Kyocera, NEC, and Tokyo Electric Power showed very similar patterns. On the job training of blue-collar workers in analyzed in Ronald Dore: *Taking Japan Seriously*. London: Athlone Press, 1987. Chapter 2; and Ronald Dore and Mari Sako. *Vocational Education and Training in Japan*. London: Center for Japanese and Comparative Industrial Research, Imperial College, n.d.

18 Rosalie Tung. *op. cit.*

19 Dore and Sako. *Vocational Education.* pp 69-81.

20 National Science Board. *Science Indicators: The 1985 Report.* Washington DC: U.S. Government Printing Office, 1985. p 125-6.

21 Electronic Industries Association. *Engineering: Education Supply/Demand and Job Opportunities.* Washington DC: Electronics Industries Association, 1982.

22 Lawrence C. Stedman and Marshall S. Smith. "Weak Arguments, Poor Data, Simplistic Recommendations: Putting the Reports under the Microscope." in Beatrice and Ronald Gross. *The Great School Debate.* New York: Touchstone Books, 1985.

23 Harold W. Stevenson, Shin-Yin Lee, and James W Stigler. "Mathematics Achievement of Chinese, Japanese and American Children." *Science*, February 14, 1986. pp 693-699.

24 "Preliminary Report: Second International Mathematics Study." Urbana: University of Illinois, 1984.

25 National Commission on Excellence in Education. *A Nation at Risk.* Washington DC: US Government Printing Office, 1983.

26 *Science Achievement in Seventeen Countries: A Preliminary Report.* New York: Pergammon Press, 1988.

27 Jane Perlez. "Memo to Schools Chief: System in Turmoil." *New York Times*, January 11, 1988. p. B1.

28 *The Forgotten Half: Non-College Youth in America.* Washington DC: The William T Grant Foundation Commission on Work, Family, and Citizenship, 1988. p 10.

29 cf. Lester Thurow. *The Zero-Sum Solution.* New York: Simon and Schuster, 1985. Chapter 7.

30 Carol Jusenius Romero. "Past is Prologue: Educational Deficiencies and the Youth Labor Market Problem." Washington DC: National Commission on Employment Policy, April 1987.

31 Crispin Campbell. "What in the World Do We Know?" *Boston Globe*, July 28, 1988. p. 2.

32 Anne Skagen. *Workplace Literacy.* New York: American Management Association, 1986. p 5.

33 William K. Cummings. "International Comparison of Science and Engineering Workforce Policies: Japan." Draft report for the Office of Technology Assessment, 1988. p. 27.

34 *The Forgotten Half.* p 50.

35 Paul Osterman. "The Place of Vocational Education in a National Employment Policy." Cambridge: Sloan School of Management, 1987.

36 *The Forgotten Half.* p 42.

37 Karen Baehler. *Lifelong Learning Part II: Training for a Competitive Work Force.* Washington DC: Roosevelt Center for American Policy Studies, 1987.

38 Frank Newman. *Higher Education and the American Resurgence.* Princeton: The Carnegie Foundation for the Advancement of Teaching, 1985; Office of Technology Assessment, *Educating Scientists and Engineers: Grade School to Grad School.* Washington DC: Government Printing Office, 1988.

39 Office of Technology Assessment. *Educating Scientists and Engineers: Grade School to Grad School.* Washington DC: U.S. Government Printing Office, 1988.

40 Bruce L.R. Smith (editor). *The State of Graduate Education.* Washington DC: The Brookings Institution, 1985.

41 Arnold D. Kerr and R. Byron Pipes. "Why We Need Hands-On Engineering Education." *Technology Review*, October 1987. pp. 36-42.

42 Masanori Hashimoto and John Raisian. "Employment Tenure and Earnings Profiles in Japan and the United States". *American Economic Review*, September 1985. pp 721-735.

43 Interview with several training and curriculum managers at IBM, Armonk NY, 9 May 1988.

44 Haruo Shimada and John Paul Macduffie. *Industrial Relations and Humanware: Japanese Investments in Automobile Manufacturing in the United States.* Cambridge: Sloan School of Management, December 1986.

45 Ronald Dore. *Taking Japan Seriously.* Chapter 2.

46 Wolfgang Streeck. "Skills and the Limits of Neo-Liberalism: The Enterprise of the Future as a Place of Learing." mimeo, 1987 p 34.

47 "The Great Educational Gap." *Far Eastern Economic Review*, December 22, 1983. p. 74.

48 Wolfgang Streeck. *op. cit.*

49 Presentation by B. Ekman of Sweden Works at Conference on Training and Education in Sweden and the United States. Harvard University, Kennedy School of Government. 20 January 1988.

50 Interview with Takama Makamura, President, Nippon Steel Human Resources Development Company and Hideo Hamada, Group Manager, Personnel Division, Nippon Steel. 3 February 1988; also, interview with Dr. Hara, President Seiko Industrial Instruments. 5 February 1988.

51 Marc Maurice, Francois Sellier, Jean-Jacques Sivestre. *The Social Foundations of Industrial Power.* Cambridge: MIT Press, 1986.

52 Ronald Dore. *British Factory--Japanese Factory.* Berkeley: University of California Press, 1973.

53 Arndt Sorge and Malcolm Warner. "Manpower Training, Manufacturing Organization, and Workplace Relations in Great Britain and West Germany." *British Journal of Industrial Relations*, November

1980. 18(3); and Sorge, et al. *Microelectronics and Manpower in Manufacturing*. Aldershot: Gower, 1985.

54 S.J. Prais. *Productivity and Industrial Structure*. Cambridge: Cambridge University Press, 1981.

55 D. Eleanor Westney and Kiyonori Sakakibara. *Comparative Study of the Training, Careers, and Organization of Engineers in the Computer Industry in Japan and the United States*. Cambridge: MIT-Japan Science and Technology Program, September 1985.

56 Rainer Schultz-Wild and Christoph Koehler. "Introducing New Manufacturing Technology: Manpower Problems and Policies." *Human Systems Management* No. 5, 1985. Also, Ramchandran Jaikumar. "Post-Industrial Manufacturing." *Harvard Business Review*, November-December 1986.

57 Daun Bhasavanich. "An American in Tokyo: Jumping to the Japanese Beat. *IEEE Spectrum*, September 1985. see also Dore. *op. cit.* and Gary Werskey. "Training for Innovation: How Japanese Electronics Companies Develop their Elite Engineers." London: General Electric Company, 1987.

58 Prais. *op. cit.* p 31.

59 Sorge *et al. op. cit.* p 5.

60 Sorge and Warner. *op. cit.*

61 *ibid.* p 330.

62 Ramchandran Jaikumar. *op. cit.* p 70.

63 Schultz-Wild and Koehler. *op. cit.*

64 Office of Technology Assessment. *Technology and the American Economic Transition: Choices for the Future*. Washington: US Government Printing Office, 1988. p 3.

65 Wassily Leontief and Faye Duchin. *The Future Impact of Automation on Workers*. New York: Oxford University Press, 1986. p. 31.

66 Office of Technology Assessment. *op. cit.* p 16.

67 Interview with several vice-presidents for manufacturing at Kodak. Rochester NY, 5 May 1988

68 *Business Week*, June 9, 1986. p 70.

69 Shoshana Zuboff. *In the Age of the Smart Machine: The Future of Work and Power*. New York: Basic Books, 1988.

70 Paul Osterman, *Employment Futures*. New York: Oxford University Press, 1988. Also Thierry Noyelle, *Beyond Industrial Dualism: Market and Job Segmentation in the New Economy*. Boulder: Westview Press, 1987.

71 Mark McLaughlin. "If You Can Read This, You've Got a Jump on Many Workers." *New England Business*, February 2, 1987. pp. 21-24.

72   Harvey Brooks and Leslie Schneider, with Keichi Oshima. *Potential Impact of New Manufacturing Technology on Employment and Work in Industrial and Developing Countries*. mimeo, 1986.

73   Wolfgang Streeck, *op. cit.*

74   Haruo Shimada and John Paul Macduffie. *op. cit.* The firms are: Analogic, Boeing, Bytex, Chaparral Steel, Digital Equipment, Ford Motor Co., General Electric, IBM, Kingsbury Machine Tool, Kodak, and Polaroid.

75   Streeck. *op. cit.* p. 21.

76   Thierry Noyelle. *op. cit.* pp. 15-16.

77   William B Johnston. *Workforce 2000*. Indianapolis: Hudson Institute, 1987.

78   *The Forgotten Half.* p 9.

79   Johnston, *op. cit.* p 78-9.

80   *ibid.* pp 89-90.